The Best of Cooking

Arne Krüger & Annette Wolter
Photography by Christian Teubner

HAMLYN
London New York Sydney Toronto

Introduction

English edition published by
The Hamlyn Publishing Group
Limited, part of Reed
International Books
Michelin House,
81 Fulham Road,
London SW3 6RB

ISBN 0 600 31979 2

First published under the title
Koch vergnügen wie noch nie
© Copyright by Gräfe und Unzer
GmbH, München

Phototypeset by Tradespools Ltd.,
Frome, Somerset

Produced by Mandarin Offset
Printed and bound in Hong Kong

52045 / 15

In *The Best of Cooking*, the magnificent all-colour cookery
book containing recipes for every occasion, we have
created a comprehensive guide to good cooking and eating.
In it every recipe is illustrated, to help you in deciding
what to cook. The measurements are given in metric and
Imperial measures and the recipes are clearly set out,
From the vast selection of carefully chosen and tested
recipes you'll never run out of ideas for what to serve –
whatever the occasion. If you are having guests, special
demands are made on your cooking skills and imagination
and this demand has been catered for in the first section
which covers recipes for entertaining at home. Whether
you're cooking country style and want to serve a delicious
homely peasant meal, or entertaining on a grander scale,
the recipes are here.

The second section contains a selection of classic gourmet
recipes for special occasions, which when prepared and
served at home are certainly much less expensive than
eating such dishes in a restaurant.

We have to eat every day, so why not serve dishes which
the family will really enjoy? In the section on cooking for
every day you'll find a host of recipes which will bring
variety, flavour and imagination to your daily fare.

At some time in our lives most of us have to consider our
waistlines so a section has been included on recipes for
healthy eating. Here we have proved that you can consider
the calories and still enjoy food. To guide you, the calorie
counts have been given alongside each recipe so that you
can pursue your gastronomic inclinations with a degree of
moderation!

Every cook wants to be able to produce delicious cakes
and biscuits. Whether you are looking for something sweet
or savoury, simple or more elaborate the section on home
baking is your guide to baking for all occasions.

The final recipe section is devoted to drinks, and it caters
for those who have the odd bottle in the cupboard as well
as those whose shelves are more abundantly stocked. In
this section recipes are given for well known drinks as well
as some for more unusual and adventurous concoctions.
There are punches for cold winter evenings, cups for
summer parties, aperitifs and long drinks.

In order to ensure that *The Best of Cooking* is as complete
as possible we have given hints on the uses of herbs and
spices in cooking, on the home freezing of dishes, which is
fast becoming an accepted part of every cook's life, and
on entertaining.

We hope that this cookery book will bring you success
and enjoyment in cooking and be one which you will use
for many years to come.

Acknowledgements
The Publishers would like to
thank the following for their
co-operation in supplying two
photographs for pages 4 and 5
of this book:
Mazola Pure Corn Oil – top
photograph
Colman's Mustard – centre
photograph

Arne Krüger
Annette Wolter
Christian Teubner

The Best of Cooking

Useful facts and figures

Notes on metrication
In this book quantities are given in metric and Imperial measures. Exact conversion from Imperial to metric measures does not usually give very convenient working quantities and so the metric measures have been rounded off into units of 25 grams. Over 16 oz the approximate kilo conversions are given. The table below shows the recommended equivalents.

Ounces	Approx. g to nearest whole figure	Recommended conversion to nearest unit of 25
1	28	25
2	57	50
3	85	75
4	113	100
5	142	150
6	170	175
7	198	200
8	227	225
9	255	250
10	283	275
11	312	300
12	340	350
13	368	375
14	397	400
15	425	425
16 (1 lb)	454	450
1 lb		0·5 kg
1¼ lb		
1½ lb		0·75 kg
1¾ lb		
2 lb		1 kg
2¼ lb		

Note: When converting quantities over 16 oz first add the appropriate figures in the centre column, then adjust to the nearest unit of 25. As a general guide, 1 kg (1000 g) equals 2·2 lb or about 2 lb 3 oz. This method of conversion gives good results in nearly all cases but in certain pastry and cake recipes a more accurate conversion is necessary to produce a balanced recipe. On the other hand, quantities of such ingredients as vegetables, fruit, meat and fish which are not critical are rounded off to the nearest quarter of a kg as this is how they are likely to be purchased.

Liquid measures The millilitre has been used in this book and the following table gives a few examples:

Imperial	Approx. ml to nearest whole figure	Recommended ml
¼ pint	142	150 ml
½ pint	283	300 ml
¾ pint	425	450 ml
1 pint	567	600 ml
1½ pints	851	900 ml
1¾ pints	992	1000 ml (1 litre)

Note: For quantities of 1¾ pints and over we have used litres and fractions of a litre.
Spoon measures All spoon measures given in this book are level.
Can sizes At present, cans are marked with the exact (usually to the nearest whole number) metric equivalent of the Imperial weight of the contents, so we have followed this practice when giving can sizes.
Herbs The herbs used in the recipes are fresh unless stated otherwise.

Oven temperatures
The table below gives recommended equivalents.

	°F	°C	Gas Mark
Very cool	225	110	¼
	250	120	½
Cool	275	140	1
	300	150	2
Moderate	325	160	3
	350	180	4
Moderately hot	375	190	5
	400	200	6
Hot	425	220	7
	450	230	8
Very hot	475	240	9

Note: When making any of the recipes in this book, only follow one set of measures as they are not interchangeable.

Notes for Australian users
Ingredients in this book are given in metric and Imperial measures. In Australia, the American 8-oz measuring cup is used in conjunction with the Imperial pint of 20 fluid ounces. It is most important to remember that the Australian tablespoon differs from both the British and American tablespoons; the table below gives a comparison between the standard tablespoons used in the three countries. The British standard tablespoon holds 17·7 millilitres, the American 14·2 millilitres, and the Australian 20 millilitres. A teaspoon holds approximately 5 millilitres in all three countries.

British	American	Australian
1 teaspoon	1 teaspoon	1 teaspoon
1 tablespoon	1 tablespoon	1 tablespoon
2 tablespoons	3 tablespoons	2 tablespoons
3½ tablespoons	4 tablespoons	3 tablespoons
4 tablespoons	5 tablespoons	3½ tablespoons

Contents

Hawaiian Toasts

METRIC/IMPERIAL
4 slices toast
25 g/1 oz butter
4 slices lean cooked ham
4 canned pineapple rings
4 thin slices cheese
½ teaspoon curry powder
pinch cinnamon
pinch allspice

Spread the slices of toast with butter. Place a slice of ham, a pineapple ring and a cheese slice on each piece of toast, making sure the cheese slices are large enough to cover the pineapple. Cut each in four with a sharp knife. Place on a greased baking tray, sprinkle with the curry powder, cinnamon and allspice and cook in a moderate oven (180° C, 350° F, Gas Mark 4) for 20 minutes. Serve warm. *Serves 4*

Variation
Use fresh pineapple in place of the canned. It is less sweet and gives the Hawaiian toasts a delicious flavour.

Cucumber Rings

METRIC/IMPERIAL
1 cucumber
3 eggs
2 tablespoons cream
½ teaspoon salt
½ teaspoon white pepper
½ teaspoon paprika pepper
25 g/1 oz butter
50 g/2 oz ham, chopped
1 tablespoon chopped parsley
Garnish
parsley
tomato wedges

Remove the end from the cucumber and cut into 1-cm (½-inch) slices and scoop out some of the cucumber with a teaspoon, leaving the shells intact. Drain the slices on kitchen paper and chop 2 tablespoons of the scooped-out cucumber; drain on paper.
Lightly beat the eggs with the chopped cucumber, cream, salt, pepper and paprika. Heat the butter in a saucepan and cook the egg mixture until set, stirring all the time. Stir in the ham and parsley. With a teaspoon, spoon the egg mixture into the cucumber slices. Arrange on a serving plate and garnish with parsley and tomato wedges. *Serves 4*

Canapés

*1 large white thinly sliced
    loaf
butter
toppings (see method)*

Canapés make ideal
savouries to serve with pre-
lunch or pre-dinner drinks.
Remove the crusts from the
bread, spread with butter
and cut each slice into three.
Use any of these toppings:
1 A slice of cheese and
hard-boiled egg garnished
with a walnut.
2 Slices of salami topped
with hard-boiled egg.
3 Slices of cooked lean
meat, garnished with
mayonnaise and chopped
pistachio nuts.
4 A slice of pâté topped
with chopped green and
red peppers and cocktail
onions.
5 Cream cheese mixed with
soured cream and topped
with a lemon slice and
parsley.
6 A slice of cooked pork,
topped with sliced canned
mushrooms and capers and
garnished with red pepper.
7 Slices of salami, formed
into cornets; garnished with
hard-boiled egg and parsley.
8 Slices of smoked salmon,
formed into rolls, and
garnished with mayonnaise,
lump fish roe and olives.
9 Shelled prawns and
drained canned pineapple
cubes, garnished with a
wedge of hard-boiled egg
and chopped chives.
10 A slice of cooked ham,
topped with half a canned
pineapple ring drained and
garnished with soured
cream and a glacé cherry.
11 A slice of cheese,
tomato and hard-boiled egg
garnished with a slice of
canned truffle.
12 A slice of cooked beef,
topped with two slices of
hard-boiled egg and
garnished with soured
cream and olives.

Appetisers

Victorian Rolls

METRIC/IMPERIAL
4 rolls
100 g/4 oz liver sausage
1 gherkin
2 eggs, hard-boiled
1 tablespoon chopped parsley
few drops anchovy essence
1 tablespoon tomato purée

Cut the rolls in half and take out the soft centres. Spread with liver sausage. Chop the gherkin and hard-boiled eggs and mix with the parsley, anchovy essence and tomato purée. Spoon into each half roll, put the halves back together and place on a greased baking tray. Cook in a moderately hot oven (200° C, 400° F, Gas Mark 4) for about 10 minutes. To serve, cut each roll in half.
Serves 4

Variation
The filling in these rolls may be varied. In place of the liver sausage use sausagemeat blended with a pinch of mixed herbs, or a smooth-textured pâté.

Cook's Tip
A speedy way of preparing chopped parsley is to cut the sprigs with a pair of scissors.

Veal Toasts

METRIC/IMPERIAL
4 veal escalopes
juice of 1½ lemons
1 teaspoon salt
1 teaspoon white pepper
3 tablespoons oil
4 slices white bread
3 tablespoons mango chutney
2 large tomatoes
4 slices cheese
2 teaspoons paprika pepper
3 tablespoons chopped
    parsley

Flatten the veal and sprinkle on both sides with lemon juice and salt and pepper. Heat the oil in a pan and fry the escalopes on each side for 4 minutes. Keep warm.

Toast the bread and spread with mango chutney. Arrange a veal escalope on each slice, then top with the tomato slices. Finally, place a slice of cheese over the tomatoes. Place under a moderate grill, until the cheese melts. Garnish with paprika and chopped parsley.
Serves 4

Cook's Tip
To flatten the veal escalopes, place them between two sheets of greaseproof paper and beat with a steak bat or wooden rolling pin.

Egg and Prawn Toasts

METRIC/IMPERIAL
4 eggs
pinch salt
40 g/1½ oz butter
4 slices bread
2 teaspoons made mustard
225 g/8 oz shelled prawns
Garnish
4 teaspoons tomato ketchup
capers

Whisk the eggs with 1 tablespoon water and pinch of salt. Heat 25 g (1 oz) of the butter in a pan and lightly brown the bread on one side. Place on a serving dish with the browned side uppermost. Keep warm. In the same pan heat the remaining butter and cook the egg mixture, stirring, until lightly set. Spread the fried bread with mustard then spoon on the egg mixture. Lastly top with the prawns and serve garnished with tomato ketchup and a few capers. Serve with a celery salad.
Serves 4

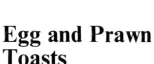

Cook's Tip
Do not overcook the egg mixture as it will separate. Remove the pan from the heat just as the mixture sets – it will continue cooking in the heat from the pan.

Dutch Toasts

METRIC/IMPERIAL
225 g/8 oz cooked chicken
1 small gherkin
2 small tomatoes
1 tablespoon chopped parsley
1 tablespoon oil
2 teaspoons capers
6 tablespoons mayonnaise
4 slices bread
½ cucumber
4 slices Gouda cheese

Cut the chicken into small pieces and chop the gherkin finely. Put the tomatoes into boiling water for 2-3 minutes; peel and cut into thick slices. Mix the chicken with the gherkin, parsley, oil, capers and mayonnaise. Toast the slices of bread.

Cover with tomato slices and then spoon on the chicken mixture. Slice the cucumber very thinly and arrange on the chicken mixture. Cover with a slice of cheese and place under a moderate grill until the cheese melts.
Serves 4

Variation
In place of the cooked chicken use either flaked canned salmon or tuna. Use the oil from the can to moisten the mixture. Season the salmon or tuna with black pepper.

Smoked Eel Savouries

METRIC/IMPERIAL
225 g/8 oz smoked eel
2 dessert apples
juice of 1 lemon
75 g/3 oz liver sausage
8 canned pineapple slices
pinch cayenne pepper
Garnish
parsley sprigs

Cut the smoked eel into cubes. Peel, core and slice the apples; sprinkle with lemon juice. Spread each apple slice with some liver sausage, then place a ring of pineapple on each. Sprinkle with a pinch of cayenne pepper and top with a cube of smoked eel. Cut in half and secure each savoury with a wooden cocktail stick. Serve garnished with parsley sprigs.
Serves 4

Variation
Smoked mackerel fillets may be used in place of the eel. Other fresh or canned fruits may be used in place of the apples and pineapple, but choose fruits which complement each other – try a combination of pears and apricots, or bananas and peaches. If using fresh fruits sprinkle the cut surfaces with lemon juice to prevent them from discolouring.

Cheese Puffs

METRIC/IMPERIAL
250 ml/scant ½ pint water
75 g/3 oz butter
pinch salt
175 g/6 oz plain flour
4 eggs
Filling
100 g/4 oz cream cheese
½ teaspoon paprika pepper
pinch celery salt
1 tablespoon chopped chives
3–4 tablespoons milk
Garnish
stuffed olives, gherkins,
  walnut halves, glacé
  cherries and red pepper
  strips

Put the water in a small pan with the butter and a pinch of salt and bring to the boil. Remove the pan from the heat and add the flour. Mix with a wooden spoon to form a paste. Return to the heat and beat until the mixture forms a smooth ball. Cool, then beat in the eggs, one at a time. Pipe or spoon the mixture in small balls on to greased baking trays. Cook in a hot oven (230° C, 425° F, Gas Mark 7) for about 20 minutes, until well risen and golden brown.
Remove, cut in half and leave to cool on a wire tray. Mix the ingredients together for the filling and pipe some into half the cheese puffs. Top with the remaining puffs and pipe with the rest of the filling. Garnish as shown in the picture.
Serves 4

Cheese and Pepper Toasts

METRIC/IMPERIAL
50 g/2 oz butter
½ teaspoon made mustard
juice of 1 lemon
4 slices bread
4 slices Gouda cheese
1 green pepper
1 red pepper
*4 tablespoons thick
    mayonnaise*
paprika pepper

Cream the butter with the mustard and lemon juice. Spread on the bread slices. Lay a slice of cheese on each piece of bread. Cut the peppers with a sharp knife into slices, discarding the core and seeds. Arrange on the cheese. Garnish with a piping of mayonnaise and sprinkle with paprika.
Serves 4

Note Do not prepare these more than 1 hour in advance of serving as the cheese will become dry.

Cook's Tip
To make these savouries look more attractive, try to buy a pepper which is both green and red, so that when it is sliced the two colours will show.

Open Sandwiches

METRIC/IMPERIAL
225 g/8 oz cottage cheese
6 tablespoons milk
1 teaspoon salt
1 onion
2 tablespoons chopped chives
*2 tablespoons chopped
    parsley*
2 canned peach halves
40 g/1½ oz butter
2 slices rye bread
2 slices brown bread
Garnish
tomato slices
cucumber slices
dill sprigs
maraschino cherries

Mix the cheese with the milk and salt, until it is smooth, then divide the mixture into three equal parts. To one-third mix in the finely chopped onion; to the second third, the chopped herbs; to the final third, the cubed peach halves. Spread on the buttered bread slices, cut into halves and garnish as shown in the picture with tomato and cucumber slices, dill sprigs and cherries.
Serves 4

Variation
Instead of using bread as a base for these open sandwiches try crispbread for a change. Do not prepare them too far in advance of serving as the crispbread will soften.

Sardines on Toast

METRIC/IMPERIAL
2 cans sardines in oil
2 tablespoons mayonnaise
2 sprigs parsley
2 sprigs tarragon
2 sprigs dill
2 egg yolks
4 slices bread
3 tablespoons grated cheese
50 g/2 oz butter
Garnish
parsley sprig

Mash the sardines and oil with the mayonnaise and mix until smooth. Chop the herbs finely and mix into the sardine mixture. Beat in the egg yolks. Toast the bread. Spread the sardine mixture on to the toast.

Sprinkle with cheese and dot with butter. Place under a moderate grill until heated through and the cheese melts. Serve garnished with parsley.
Serves 4

Cook's Tip
The egg whites left from this recipe can be used to make meringues or a meringue topping for a pudding. Whisk with 100 g (4 oz) castor sugar.

Sausage and Cheese Kebabs

METRIC/IMPERIAL
1 (226-g/8-oz) can pimientos
1 green pepper
0·5 kg/1 lb continental
    sausage
½ teaspoon white pepper
pinch dry mustard
100 g/4 oz Edam cheese
3 tablespoons oil
25 g/1 oz butter

Drain and slice the pimientos. Halve the green pepper and discard the core and seeds. Cut the flesh into cubes. Cut the sausage into 2-cm (5-inch) cubes and sprinkle with the seasonings.
Cut the cheese into cubes the same size as the sausage.

On each piece of sausage place a cube of cheese, then a slice of pimiento and a slice of green pepper. Spear with a cocktail stick. Heat the oil and butter in a frying pan and fry the kebabs until lightly browned on all sides. Drain on absorbent paper and serve hot.
Serves 4

Variation
These sausage and cheese kebabs may be served cold and without being fried in the oil and butter. Arrange on a serving plate and serve garnished with parsley sprigs.

Turkish Liver Toasts

METRIC/IMPERIAL
350 g/12 oz calves' liver
1 tablespoon flour
1 tablespoon oil
25 g/1 oz butter
1 teaspoon salt
¾ teaspoon pepper
2 teaspoons meat extract
2 tablespoons sultanas
6 tablespoons Madeira
1 clove garlic, crushed
3 tablespoons chopped
almonds
4 slices toast
Garnish
chopped parsley

Cut the liver into strips and toss in the flour.
Heat the oil in a pan and fry the liver quickly for 2 minutes, then remove from the pan. Place the butter, salt, pepper, meat extract, sultanas, Madeira and garlic in the pan, bring to the boil, stirring, and simmer for 3–4 minutes. Lower the heat, replace the liver and cook for a further 2 minutes. Add the chopped almonds. Spoon on to the slices of toast and serve garnished with chopped parsley.
Serves 4

Cook's Tip
When cooking liver, never overcook it, otherwise it becomes tough.

Beef and Anchovy Savouries

METRIC/IMPERIAL
8 slices bread
50 g/2 oz butter
225 g/8 oz lean minced beef
2 egg yolks
1 teaspoon dry mustard
pinch cayenne pepper
½ teaspoon salt
½ teaspoon celery salt
3 tablespoons grated
horseradish
2 tablespoons brandy
1 small can anchovy fillets
in oil
Garnish
tomato quarters
gherkins

Spread the bread with butter. Mix the beef with the egg yolks, mustard, cayenne pepper, salt, celery salt, horseradish and brandy. Spread the meat mixture on the bread, forming a slight dome in the centre of each slice. Form a diagonal cross with 2 anchovy fillets on each savoury and spoon over a little oil from the can.
Place on a baking tray and cook in a moderately hot oven (200° C, 400° F, Gas Mark 6) for 20 minutes. Cut into small squares and serve garnished with tomato quarters and gherkins.
Serves 6–8

Danish Open Sandwiches

METRIC/IMPERIAL
2 onions
4 slices brown bread
25 g/1 oz butter
3 tablespoons chopped dill
8 canned sardines
2 tomatoes
100 g/4 oz cucumber
6 tablespoons mayonnaise
   or soured cream
½ teaspoon sugar

Peel the onions and cut into thin slices. Pour over boiling water, and leave to cool. Spread the bread thinly with the butter and sprinkle over half the dill. Drain the sardines and arrange two on each piece of bread. Cut the tomatoes into thick slices and chop the cucumber coarsely. Place the drained onion and tomato slices on the sardines, and top with the cucumber mixed with the mayonnaise, sugar and remaining dill.
Serves 4

Variation
The cucumber topping on these sandwiches may be replaced with a potato salad topping. Omit the sugar and replace the dill with chopped chives.

Roast Beef Sandwiches

METRIC/IMPERIAL
1 tablespoon mayonnaise
juice of 1 lemon
1 tablespoon chopped mixed
   pickles
½ teaspoon sugar
4 slices wholewheat bread
4 slices roast beef
1 orange
pinch celery salt

Mix the mayonnaise with the lemon juice, chopped mixed pickles and sugar. Spread over the pieces of bread and place the roast beef on top. Peel and slice the orange and use to garnish each sandwich. Sprinkle with celery salt.
Serves 4

Variation
In place of the mixed pickles blend 1 teaspoon made mustard with the mayonnaise and lemon juice.
The recipe is equally good with slices of lamb or pork.

> **Cook's Tip**
> This is an excellent way of using up any leftover meat from a Sunday roast.

Beef and Cheese Toasties

METRIC/IMPERIAL

1 medium onion
2 egg yolks
1 tablespoon oil
1–2 tablespoons grated
  horseradish
1½ teaspoons dry mustard
1–2 teaspoons paprika
  pepper
1 teaspoon celery salt
½ teaspoon pepper
225 g/8 oz cooked minced
  beef
1 tablespoon cream cheese
1 tablespoon tomato ketchup
1 tablespoon mayonnaise
4 slices white bread
Garnish
parsley

Peel and chop the onion
and mix with the egg yolks,
oil, horseradish, mustard,
paprika, celery salt, pepper
and minced beef.
Beat the cheese with 3
tablespoons hot water, the
ketchup and mayonnaise
until frothy.
Lightly toast both sides of
the white bread and spread
evenly with the meat
mixture. Place on a baking
tray and cook in a
moderately hot oven
(200° C, 400° F, Gas
Mark 6) for 20 minutes.
Spoon over the cheese
mixture and return to the
oven for a further 5
minutes. Serve garnished
with parsley.
Serves 4

Minced Beef Squares

METRIC/IMPERIAL

8 slices bread
50 g/2 oz butter
225 g/8 oz minced beef
2 egg yolks
1 teaspoon dry mustard
pinch cayenne pepper
½ teaspoon salt
½ teaspoon celery salt
2 tablespoons brandy
2 tablespoons grated
  horseradish
1 can anchovy fillets
4 teaspoons capers

Spread the bread with
butter, and quarter each
slice. Mix the meat with the
egg yolks, mustard,
seasonings and brandy.
Spread the mixture on the
bread, making a dome in
the middle. Place a spoonful
of horseradish on the top
of each and then garnish
with a piece of anchovy
fillet and a few capers.
Serves 6–8

Cook's Tip
This is a version of
the famous steak
tartare recipe. The
beef should be
freshly minced rump
or fillet steak.

Horseradish Dip

METRIC/IMPERIAL
2 dessert apples
juice of 1 lemon
2 teaspoons grated horse-
  radish
1 teaspoon made mustard
1 tablespoon cream cheese
1 teaspoon sugar
7 tablespoons double cream

Peel and quarter the apples, removing the cores, and chop very finely, or blend in the liquidiser with the lemon juice. Add the horseradish, mustard, cheese, sugar and blend for a further 2–3 minutes. Lightly whip the cream and fold into the apple mixture. Either serve this as a dip,

or spread thickly on small savoury biscuits.
Serves 4

Variation
Soured cream may be used in place of the double cream. If fresh horseradish is not available, use the bottled horseradish sauce.

Cook's Tip
If serving the horse-radish mixture on biscuits, do not prepare them far in advance of serving as the biscuits will become soft.

Philadelphia Truffles

METRIC/IMPERIAL
2 teaspoons caraway seeds
225 g/8 oz Philadelphia
  cream cheese
4 tablespoons chopped
  parsley
1 teaspoon paprika pepper
½ teaspoon white pepper
2 slices pumpernickel bread
Garnish
parsley

Mix the caraway seeds with the cheese, chopped parsley, paprika and pepper. Leave to chill for 30 minutes. Crumble the pumpernickel bread. Form the cheese mixture into small balls and coat in the pumpernickel crumbs. Chill for a further

30 minutes. Arrange in a dish and serve garnished with parsley.
Serves 4

Variation
Finely chopped walnuts may be used in place of the pumpernickel crumbs to coat the cheese balls. The caraway seeds may be replaced by 1 teaspoon curry paste.

Cook's Tip
These cheese balls may be frozen. Open freeze until solid, then pack in layers with dividers, in a rigid container. Allow to defrost at room temperature.

Miniature Cheese Savouries

METRIC/IMPERIAL
*1 packet pumpernickel
    bread
50 g/2 oz butter
275 g/10 oz cheese
225 g/8 oz cream cheese
½ teaspoon paprika pepper
pinch each salt, pepper and
    celery salt
3 tablespoons port
3 tablespoons milk
100 g/4 oz cooked ham
small savoury biscuits*
Garnish
*strips red pepper
strips cheese
stuffed olives
chopped pistachio nuts*

Cut the pumpernickel
slices into rectangles
measuring 3 cm by 6 cm
(1½ inches by 3 inches).
Cut the cheese into slices
the same size. Spread two
pieces of pumpernickel
with butter on one side,
and spread two pieces on
both sides. Put the cheese
slices between the pumpernickel, as shown in the
picture.
Mix together the cream
cheese, seasonings, port and
milk. Chop the ham and
fold into the cheese mixture.
Use to sandwich the
biscuits together in threes.
Pipe or spoon some of the
cheese mixture on the top
biscuit and garnish with
red pepper strips, strips of
cheese, sliced stuffed olives
and a few chopped pistachio
nuts.
Serves 6–8

Hungarian Rolls

METRIC/IMPERIAL
1 Vienna loaf
50 g/2 oz butter
100 g/4 oz salami slices
4 tablespoons mayonnaise
½ teaspoon dry mustard
Garnish
lemon slices
paprika pepper
chopped parsley

Cut the loaf in half lengthways and cut each half in two, making four portions in all. Spread with the butter. Form each slice of salami into a cone by cutting each one from the centre to the outside. Arrange some salami cones on each half of bread. Mix the mayonnaise with the mustard and use to fill the salami cones.
Serve garnished with lemon slices, paprika and chopped parsley.
Serves 4

Variation
The salami may be replaced by slices of any continental sausage.

> **Cook's Tip**
> The easiest way to fill the salami cones is to place the mayonnaise in a piping bag fitted with a large star tube and to pipe a star of mayonnaise into each cone.

Cheese-Stuffed Potatoes

METRIC/IMPERIAL
8 even-sized potatoes
2 teaspoons salt
100 g/4 oz cottage cheese
2 tablespoons chopped chives
1 teaspoon white pepper
50 g/2 oz butter
2 teaspoons coarse salt
1 teaspoon paprika pepper

Wash the potatoes and cook in their skins in boiling, salted water, until tender. Drain and cut each one in half.
Using a spoon, scoop out the insides carefully and mix with the cottage cheese, chives, pepper and butter to form a smooth mixture.

Fill the jackets with this mixture and place the two halves back together. Place on a baking tray, sprinkle with the coarse salt and paprika. Cook in a moderate oven (180° C, 350° F, Gas Mark 4) for 10 minutes.
Serves 8

Variation
In place of the cottage cheese use crumbled blue cheese and omit the chopped chives.
If preferred the potatoes may be wrapped in foil and cooked in the oven instead of being cooked in boiling water.

Cornish Toasts

METRIC/IMPERIAL
1 orange
2 tablespoons mayonnaise
6 tablespoons double cream
*1 tablespoon grated horse-
  radish*
2 cooking apples
1 onion
50 g/2 oz butter
4 slices roast beef
½ teaspoon pepper
½ teaspoon salt
4 large slices white bread

Squeeze the juice from the
orange. Whisk together the
orange juice, mayonnaise,
cream and horseradish.
Peel and quarter the apples,
remove the cores and cut
into very thin slices. Peel
and slice the onion. Heat
the butter in a pan and
cook the slices of apple and
onion together for 10–15
minutes, making sure they
do not brown. Remove
and keep warm. Sprinkle
the meat with pepper and
cook in the pan for 2–3
minutes on each side.
Season with salt. Arrange
a slice of beef on each
piece of bread and spoon
over the apple and onion
slices. Top with the orange
mayonnaise and serve at
once.
Serves 4

Flemish Cabbage Rolls

METRIC/IMPERIAL
1 small head white cabbage
2 teaspoons salt
1 tablespoon oil
1 onion, diced
50 g/2 oz breadcrumbs
1 small can tuna
1 teaspoon white pepper
2 eggs
2 cartons natural yogurt
*1–2 teaspoons paprika
  pepper*
1 teaspoon sugar

Separate the cabbage leaves
and cook for 5 minutes in
boiling, salted water. Drain
and keep the cooking
liquor. Cut away the larger
stalks from the leaves.
Heat the oil in a pan and
fry the diced onion until
softened. Stir in the
breadcrumbs, tuna, pepper
and eggs. Form the mixture
into rolls and around each
one wrap a cabbage leaf,
making a secure parcel.
Place in a pan and pour
over the reserved cooking
liquor. Simmer in the
liquor for 5 minutes.
Meanwhile, mix the yogurt
with the paprika and sugar.
Drain the rolls and place in
a serving dish. Spoon over
the yogurt sauce.
Serves 4

Variation
Soured cream may be used
in place of the natural
yogurt. The tuna may be
replaced by a small can of
sardines.

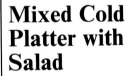

Mixed Cold Platter with Salad

METRIC/IMPERIAL
225 g/8 oz sliced roast veal
225 g/8 oz sliced roast pork
225 g/8 oz sliced roast beef
1 (226-g/8-oz) can mixed
   vegetables
4 gherkins
6 tablespoons soured cream
2 tablespoons mayonnaise
1 teaspoon dry mustard
1 teaspoon sugar
2 tablespoons chopped chives
Garnish
parsley sprigs
tomato wedges
mixed pickles

Arrange the slices of meat attractively on a large dish, leaving the centre empty. Mix the drained vegetables with the chopped gherkins. Mix the soured cream with the mayonnaise, mustard, sugar and chives. Mix with the vegetable mixture and spoon into two small dishes. Place in the centre of the serving dish. Serve garnished with parsley, tomato and pickles.
Serves 6

> **Cook's Tip**
> This dish may be prepared in advance of serving, but cover the platter with cling film or foil so that the edges of the meat do not dry. Store in the refrigerator.

Charleston Balls

METRIC/IMPERIAL
2 slices white bread
100 g/4 oz minced beef
1 can sardines
1 teaspoon salt
½ teaspoon celery salt
1 teaspoon paprika pepper
pinch cayenne pepper
pinch curry powder
4 tablespoons chopped
   parsley
2 eggs
6 tablespoons oil
4 tablespoons chopped fresh
   herbs
6 tablespoons double cream

Soften the bread slices in water and then squeeze dry. Mix with the minced beef, drained sardines, seasonings, parsley and eggs. Form the mixture into small balls and fry in the heated oil until browned on all sides. Drain on absorbent paper. Cool and spear with a cocktail stick.
Mix together the herbs and cream and serve with the meatballs.
Serves 4

> **Cook's Tip**
> The meat mixture may be prepared in advance and stored in the refrigerator. Fry and cool just before serving.

Quick Veal Rolls

METRIC/IMPERIAL
50 g/2 oz liver sausage
4 tablespoons chopped
    parsley
6 pickled onions, chopped
25 g/1 oz walnuts, chopped
2 tablespoons sultanas
4 gherkins, chopped
4 tablespoons port
100 g/4 oz sliced roast veal
Garnish
parsley sprigs

Mix the liver sausage with the parsley, chopped onions, walnuts, sultanas and chopped gherkins. Mix in the port. Divide the mixture between the slices of veal, form into rolls and secure with a cocktail stick. Arrange on a serving dish and garnish with parsley sprigs.
Serves 4

Variation
If liver sausage is not available, cooked chopped chicken may be used instead. Other cooked sliced meat may be used in place of the veal.

Tasty Fish Flan

METRIC/IMPERIAL
1 can anchovy fillets
½ teaspoon salt
0·5 kg/1 lb fish fillets,
    skinned and cubed
2 teaspoons Worcestershire
    sauce
½ teaspoon white pepper
1 teaspoon made mustard
2 tablespoons oil
1 small onion, diced
225 g/8 oz shortcrust pastry
1 green pepper, seeded and
    chopped
2 tomatoes, peeled and
    chopped
4 tablespoons chopped
    parsley
4 slices Edam cheese
75 g/3 oz butter

Drain the anchovy fillets, chop and mix with the salt, fish, Worcestershire sauce, pepper, mustard, oil and diced onion; leave for 30 minutes.
Roll out the pastry thinly and use to line a 20-cm (8-inch) flan tin. Drain the fish cubes from the marinade and place in the base of the flan. Sprinkle over the pepper, tomatoes and parsley; pour over the marinade and top with the cheese slices. Dot with butter and bake in a moderately hot oven (200° C, 400° F, Gas Mark 6) for 30 minutes. Serve warm.
Serves 4–6

Sausage and Orange Salad

METRIC/IMPERIAL
1 lettuce
2 oranges
225 g/8 oz ready-made vegetable salad
1 gherkin
225 g/8 oz liver sausage
100 g/4 oz continental sausage, sliced
4 tablespoons mayonnaise
4 tablespoons chopped parsley
100 g/4 oz sliced cooked ham
Garnish
lemon slices
parsley
gherkin fans

Arrange the lettuce leaves on a serving platter. Cut the oranges across one end so that a flat base is formed, then slice one-third from the other end. Scoop out the flesh, chop roughly and mix with the prepared salad. Fill the oranges with this mixture and replace the lids. Stand the oranges in the centre of the platter. Chop the gherkin finely and mix with the liver sausage. Chill until firm, then form into oval balls and arrange around the oranges. Arrange slices of continental sausage between the liver sausage balls.
Mix the mayonnaise with the parsley and spread over the ham slices. Arrange on the dish. Serve garnished with lemon slices, parsley and gherkin fans.
Serves 6

Pickled Herring Rolls with Salad

METRIC/IMPERIAL
20 pickled herring fillets
3 tablespoons milk
5 tablespoons vinegar
3 tablespoons dry white wine
100 g/4 oz mixed pickles
225 g/8 oz gherkins
2 tomatoes
2 pears
2 apples
1 canned pimiento, chopped
little sugar
Garnish
parsley

Separate the fish from the bones and cover with cold water. Leave for 4 hours, changing the water after 2 hours.
Drain the fish, add the milk, 6 tablespoons water, the vinegar and wine. Leave to marinate. Chop the mixed pickles and gherkins. Peel and chop the tomatoes, pears and apples. Mix with the pimiento, a little sugar to taste, and a little of the fish marinade.
Remove the fish from the marinade and drain. Roll each fillet into a large ring, place on a serving dish and fill the centre with the salad mixture. Serve garnished with parsley.
Any extra salad mixture can be blended with a little mayonnaise and served separately.
Serves 6

Tasty Sausage Sticks

METRIC/IMPERIAL
0·75 kg/1½ lb sausagemeat
2 teaspoons paprika pepper
1 teaspoon flour
1 teaspoon pepper
½ teaspoon cayenne pepper
½ teaspoon caraway seeds
1 clove garlic, crushed
1 tablespoon cottage cheese
1 carton natural yogurt
2 teaspoons celery salt
½ teaspoon sugar
150 ml/¼ pint oil
Garnish
parsley

Mix the sausagemeat with the paprika, flour, pepper, cayenne pepper, caraway seeds and garlic. Chill for 15 minutes, then cut into even-sized sticks.
Mix together the cottage cheese, yogurt, celery salt and sugar. Chill for 10 minutes.
Heat the oil in a pan and lightly brown the sausage strips all over. Remove and drain on absorbent paper. Arrange on a dish and garnish with parsley. To serve, dip the warm sausage sticks into the chilled yogurt sauce.
Serves 4

Cook's Tip
If a smooth sauce is preferred, press the cottage cheese through a nylon sieve or blend it in the liquidizer.

Puff Pastry Pizzas

METRIC/IMPERIAL
450 g/1 lb frozen puff pastry
12 slices salami
50 g/2 oz cooked ham, chopped
2 onions, sliced
2 slices cheese, cubed
2 tomatoes, peeled and sliced
1 teaspoon paprika pepper
1 teaspoon black pepper
150 ml/¼ pint oil
4 tablespoons chopped parsley

Defrost the pastry. On a floured board, roll it out thinly and use to line four 10-cm (4-inch) flan tins.
On the pastry arrange the salami, ham, onion, cheese and tomatoes. Sprinkle with the seasonings and over each pizza spoon 2 tablespoons oil. Cook in a hot oven (220° C, 420° F, Gas Mark 7) for 20–25 minutes. Sprinkle with chopped parsley and serve hot.
Serves 4

Cook's Tip
These puff pastry pizzas may be prepared and cooked in advance and then frozen. To freeze, wrap each one in freezer foil or film and pack together in a rigid container. Reheat from frozen.

Raclette

METRIC/IMPERIAL
3 kg/6 lb potatoes
½ a whole semi-soft cheese
100 g/4 oz butter
2–3 tablespoons coarse salt

Raclette is a Swiss cheese dish, a speciality from Valais. It is made by holding a large piece of the local cheese over the open fire and scraping off the softened part as it melts. The melted cheese is put on a plate and eaten with potatoes cooked in their jackets and a selection of salads.

Traditionally, the white wine from Valais is served with raclette.

It is an ideal dish to serve at an informal party and with the potatoes and salads is surprisingly filling.

Scrub the potatoes and cook in their skins in boiling water for 25–30 minutes. Drain, split, add a knob of butter and sprinkling of coarse salt. Serve with the raclette.

To make the raclette, cut the cheese into serving portions and place under a moderate grill to melt the cheese.

Each guest has a portion of cheese which is beginning to melt and eats it with the potatoes and a selection of salads.

Serves 8–10

Cook's Tip
Choose a semi-soft cheese with a high fat content for this recipe so that it will melt readily – use Bagnes or Conches.

Curried Chicken Drumsticks

METRIC/IMPERIAL
12 chicken drumsticks
1 tablespoon flour
4 tablespoons oil
2 onions, sliced
4 tablespoons dry white wine
1–2 tablespoons curry powder
1 teaspoon black pepper
1–2 tablespoons mango chutney
2 tablespoons chopped parsley
6 tablespoons milk
Garnish
parsley
tomato wedges

Toss the chicken drumsticks in the flour. Heat the oil in a pan and fry the onions until softened. Add the wine and cook for 3 minutes. Remove from the heat and add the curry powder, pepper, chutney and parsley. Spread over the chicken drumsticks and leave to marinate for 30 minutes.
Remove the chicken from the marinade, pat dry and cook under a moderate grill, turning, for 15–20 minutes.
Meanwhile, put the marinade in the liquidiser with the milk and blend. Serve the joints hot or cold with the marinade as a dip. Garnish with parsley and tomato wedges.
Serves 6

Bean Salad

METRIC/IMPERIAL
150 ml/¼ pint oil
2 tablespoons wine vinegar
1½ teaspoons salt
½ teaspoon ground black pepper
pinch tarragon
1 teaspoon mustard
1 (650-g/1¾-lb) can haricot beans
1 onion
350 g/12 oz minced beef
1 egg
2 tablespoons breadcrumbs
3 tablespoons tomato ketchup
1 teaspoon paprika pepper
Garnish
lettuce leaves

Mix half the oil, the vinegar, 1 teaspoon of the salt, the pepper, tarragon and mustard together. Mix with the drained beans. Peel and grate onion and mix with the minced beef, egg, breadcrumbs, tomato ketchup, paprika and remaining salt. Form into small balls and fry in the remaining oil, until browned on all sides. Drain on absorbent paper and allow to cool.
Arrange the lettuce leaves on a serving plate and around the edge of the dish place the meat balls. Pile the bean salad in the centre.
Serves 4–6

Party Snacks

Tomato Jellies

METRIC/IMPERIAL
0·75 kg/1½ lb tomatoes
20 g/¾ oz gelatine
2–3 tablespoons water
1 teaspoon salt
¼ teaspoon celery salt
¼ teaspoon pepper
pinch sugar
2 tablespoons tomato purée
2 cartons natural yogurt
1 teaspoon sugar
3–4 tablespoons chopped
parsley

Pour boiling water over the tomatoes, leave for 2–3 minutes, then remove and peel. Chop the tomatoes and blend in the liquidiser. Cover the gelatine with cold water and soak for 10 minutes, then heat to dissolve. Measure the tomato juice and dissolved gelatine and make up to 750 ml (1¼ pints) with water. Pour into a saucepan, add half the salt, the celery salt, pepper and a little sugar. Whisk in the tomato purée and heat gently. Rinse four to six small moulds with cold water and fill with the tomato mixture. Allow to set in the refrigerator.
Mix the yogurt, sugar, remaining salt and the parsley together. Serve with the unmoulded jellies.
Serves 4–6

Scampi Kebabs

METRIC/IMPERIAL
350 g/12 oz frozen scampi
½ cucumber
1 onion
8 pimiento-stuffed olives
4 bay leaves
2 tablespoons oil
6 tablespoons tomato
   ketchup
2 teaspoons paprika pepper

Defrost the scampi. Cut the cucumber into thick slices; peel and quarter the onion. Place the scampi alternately with onion quarters, olives, bay leaves and slices of cucumber on skewers.
Heat the oil in a pan and fry the scampi kebabs for 8–10 minutes over a moderate heat, turning them to cook on all sides. Drain on absorbent paper. Heat the ketchup with the same quantity of water, and the paprika, stirring well. Serve as a sauce with the kebabs.
Serves 4

Cook's Tip
If preferred, the kebabs can be brushed with oil and cooked under a moderate grill.
The kebabs may be prepared in advance, covered with cling film and stored in the refrigerator. Fry just before serving.

Herring and Apple Salad

METRIC/IMPERIAL
8 pickled herrings
2 tablespoons wine vinegar
1 tablespoon sugar
2 red-skinned apples
juice of 1 lemon
2 onions
2 large gherkins
500 ml/generous ¾ pint
    soured cream

Lay the fish in a dish and cover with cold water to extract the salt. Leave in the refrigerator for 12 hours, changing the water three times.
Drain and skin the herrings then cut from the head along the backbone and open out both sides.

Remove the fins.
Place the fillets in a bowl and add the vinegar and sugar; marinate for 2 hours. Core and slice the apples and sprinkle with lemon juice. Slice the onions and gherkins. Mix the apple, onion and gherkins with the herring fillets. Spoon over the soured cream and chill for 30 minutes before serving.
Serves 4

Cook's Tip
Pickled herrings, preserved in spiced vinegar, are available from delicatessens.

Savoury Fish Cakes

METRIC/IMPERIAL
500 ml/generous ¾ pint milk
1½ teaspoons salt
25 g/1 oz butter
1 small packet instant
    potato
5 tablespoons flour
2 eggs
2 teaspoons anchovy essence
0·5 kg/1 lb white fish fillets
2 onions, quartered
2 leeks, sliced
2 tablespoons chopped
    parsley
100 g/4 oz fat for frying
Garnish
parsley

Bring the milk to the boil with ½ teaspoon of the salt and the butter. Lower the heat and mix in the potato powder. Turn into a bowl, add the flour, eggs and anchovy essence. Mix well. Lay the fillets in a fire-proof dish, cover with water, the remaining salt, the onions, and leeks. Cover and simmer for 20 minutes. Remove the fish with a draining spoon and flake the flesh. Then remove the onions and leeks and chop finely. Mix the fish and vegetables together with the potato mixture, and chopped parsley. Form into small cakes, flatten, and chill for 10 minutes.
Heat the fat and fry the fish cakes for 5 minutes on each side. Drain on absorbent paper and serve garnished with parsley.
Serves 4–6

Maryland Steaks

METRIC/IMPERIAL
50 g/2 oz Edam cheese
0·5 kg/1 lb minced lean pork
50 g/2 oz liver sausage
100 g/4 oz sausagemeat
3 tablespoons chopped parsley
2 eggs
5 tablespoons oil
1 (500-g/1-lb) can sweetcorn
25 g/1 oz butter
Garnish
parsley
tomato wedges

Dice the cheese and mix with the minced pork, liver sausage, sausagemeat, parsley and eggs. Form the mixture into eight cakes. Heat the oil in a pan and cook the steaks for 5 minutes on each side. Drain on absorbent paper. Meanwhile, heat the corn, drain and toss in butter. Spoon on to a heated serving dish and arrange the steaks on top. Serve garnished with parsley and tomato wedges.
Serves 4–6

Cook's Tip
These Maryland steaks freeze well. Prepare the mixture and freeze, in layers, in a rigid container. Fry, from frozen, but allow 8 minutes on each side and cook over a low heat.

Kipper Bake

METRIC/IMPERIAL
600 ml/1 pint milk
50 g/2 oz butter
1 teaspoon salt
1 large packet instant potato
2 large kippers
1 onion
1 tablespoon oil
1 tomato
100 g/4 oz breadcrumbs
50 g/2 oz cheese, grated

Heat the milk with 25 g (1 oz) of the butter and the salt. Remove from the heat and whisk in the instant potato. Skin the kippers and remove the bones, making sure that all small ones are removed. Peel and slice onion and fry in the heated oil until golden brown. Grease an ovenproof dish with some of the remaining butter and line the dish with half the potato. Layer the kippers, onion and sliced tomato in the dish. Top with the remaining potato, smooth over and sprinkle with breadcrumbs and grated cheese. Dot with the remaining butter and cook in a moderately hot oven (200° C, 400° F, Gas Mark 6) for 20 minutes
Serves 4

Party Snacks

Farmhouse Omelette

METRIC/IMPERIAL
4 onions
1 teaspoon salt
½ teaspoon each celery and
   garlic salt
100 g/4 oz bacon
100 g/4 oz ham
100 g/4 oz roast beef
1 kg/2 lb cooked potatoes
6 tablespoons oil
12 eggs
2 teaspoons paprika pepper
1 teaspoon black pepper
4 tablespoons chopped
   parsley
Garnish
parsley

Peel the onions and dice
them finely; mix with the
salt, celery and garlic
salts. Dice the bacon, ham
and roast beef. Dice the
potatoes.
Heat half the oil and fry
the sliced onion until
softened. Add the diced
bacon, ham and beef, stir
well, and cook for a further
5 minutes.
Brush a large baking tin
with the remaining oil.
Whisk the eggs with the rest
of the ingredients, pour half
into the tin, then add the
onion. Pour in the rest of
the egg mixture. Cook in a
moderately hot oven
(200° C, 400° F, Gas
Mark 6) for 25–30 minutes,
until set. Turn out, garnish
with parsley and serve
cut into portions.
Serves 6

Stuffed Peppers

METRIC/IMPERIAL
10 peppers, tops removed
   and seeded
4 onions, peeled
1 small can tuna
225 g/8 oz gherkins, diced
4 hard-boiled eggs, sliced
225 g/8 oz minced pork
225 g/8 oz minced beef
¼ teaspoon white pepper
5 tablespoons vinegar
200 ml/generous ¼ pint oil
6 tablespoons soured cream
2 teaspoons cornflour
225 g/8 oz sausagemeat
50 g/2 oz butter

Blanch the peppers in salted
water for 5 minutes, then
drain. Slice two of the
onions and chop the other
two. Flake the tuna and
mix with the gherkins and
eggs. Mix the minced meats
with chopped onions and
pepper. Heat the vinegar,
oil, cream and 6 table-
spoons water. Thicken
with blended cornflour.
Fill three of the peppers
with sausagemeat and
three with the tuna mixture.
Spoon over a little of the
soured cream mixture. Fill
four peppers with mixed
minced meats.
Place all the peppers in an
ovenproof dish and pour
over the rest of the soured
cream mixture. Top with
the sliced onion and dot
with butter. Cover with a
lid and cook in a moderate
oven (180° C, 350° F, Gas
Mark 4) for 20–25 minutes.
Serves 6

Spare Ribs with Pineapple

METRIC/IMPERIAL
1·5 kg/3 lb spare rib pork
  chops
pinch of salt
1 teaspoon allspice
pinch of black pepper
4 tablespoons oil
2 tablespoons malt vinegar
2 tablespoons soy sauce
4 teaspoons brown sugar
1 small can pineapple rings
pinch of grated nutmeg
pinch of cayenne pepper

Cut the ribs so that each
piece contains three ribs
in all. Rub with the salt,
allspice, pepper and 2
tablespoons of the oil.
Heat the remaining oil in a
large pan together with the
vinegar, soy sauce, brown
sugar, 5 tablespoons
pineapple juice from the
can, nutmeg and cayenne
pepper. Add the ribs and
cook for 6 minutes over a
moderate heat, turning the
ribs to brown them.
Cut the pineapple rings into
small pieces and add to the
ribs together with any
remaining juices. Cover the
pan and cook for a further
10 minutes. Arrange on a
serving dish and spoon
over the cooking liquor.
Serves 4

Sausages with Orange Dip

METRIC/IMPERIAL
1 orange
4 tablespoons horseradish
  sauce
2 teaspoons lemon juice
250 ml/scant ½ pint double
  cream
50 g/2 oz breadcrumbs
2 eggs
4 tablespoons chopped
  parsley
225 g/8 oz sausagemeat
1 teaspoon black pepper
1–2 teaspoons paprika
  pepper
2 teaspoons flour
50 g/2 oz fat

Mix the grated rind and
juice of the orange with the
horseradish sauce and
lemon juice. Whip the
cream until stiff and fold
in the orange mixture.
Place in refrigerator.
Mix the breadcrumbs with
the eggs, parsley and
sausagemeat. Season with
pepper and paprika. Form
the mixture into sausage
shapes; coat lightly in
flour and fry in the hot fat
until browned on all sides.
Drain on absorbent paper
and serve with the orange-
flavoured horseradish
cream.
Serves 4

Cheesy Meatballs

METRIC/IMPERIAL
125 g/5 oz butter
50 g/2 oz cream cheese
2 onions
0·5 kg/1 lb minced pork
225 g/8 oz minced beef
½ teaspoon celery salt
½ teaspoon black pepper
2 eggs
1½ tablespoons breadcrumbs
3 tablespoons chopped
*   parsley*
6 tablespoons oil

Beat 100 g (4 oz) of the butter with the cream cheese. Peel and slice the onions. Heat the remaining butter and fry the onion slices until softened and golden brown. Mix the meats with the onions, celery salt, pepper, eggs, breadcrumbs and chopped parsley.

Form the mixture into balls, placing a knob of the cream cheese mixture in the centre of each. Leave to chill for 15-20 minutes in the refrigerator.

Heat the oil and fry the balls for 8 minutes, turning to brown them on all sides. Drain on absorbent paper and serve with coleslaw.
Serves 4

Cook's Tip
When forming the mixture into balls, lightly coat your hands with flour.

Stuffed Cucumber

METRIC/IMPERIAL
1 large cucumber
225 g/8 oz ready-made
*   salad*
225 g/8 oz cooked peas
3 tablespoons chopped
*   parsley*
2 tablespoons wine vinegar
1 teaspoon sugar
½ teaspoon salt
100 g/4 oz sliced cooked ham
1 packet cheese slices
Garnish
onion rings

Cut away the top one-third of the cucumber lengthwise, peel and cut finely. On the underside of the remaining two-thirds, cut lengthways, so that a level base is formed, and then hollow out the middle, using a spoon. Mix the cucumber flesh with the finely cut one-third, the prepared salad, peas and parsley. Mix the vinegar with 1 tablespoon water, the sugar and salt. Pour into the hollow cucumber and leave for 5 minutes.

Cut the ham slices in halves and form each one into a small roll. Cut the cheese into triangles. Pour the vinegar mixture out of cucumber, and fill it with the salad. Top with the ham rolls and cheese triangles. Garnish with onion rings.
Serves 4

33

Savoury Rice Balls

METRIC/IMPERIAL
225 g/8 oz round-grain rice
1 teaspoon each salt and
    white pepper
50 g/2 oz cheese, grated
100 g/4 oz salami slices
100 g/4 oz cooked tongue,
    minced
2 tablespoons chopped
    parsley
50 g/2 oz fat
Garnish
parsley

Rinse the rice under cold
water, then cook in 1 litre
(1¾ pints) water in a saucepan. Drain well. Add the
salt and pepper and leave
over the heat for 2 minutes,
stirring to drive off the
excess moisture. Stir in the
cheese.
Chop the salami and mix
with the tongue and
parsley. Mix with the rice.
Form the mixture into balls
and chill for 20 minutes.
Fry in the heated fat for
10 minutes, turning until
browned on all sides. Drain
on absorbent paper and
serve garnished with
parsley.
Serves 4

Cook's Tip
Do not throw away
scraps of cheese.
Grate them finely and
store in a covered
container in the
refrigerator.

Grilled Cheesy Sausages

METRIC/IMPERIAL
4 large pork sausages
1 tablespoon oil
1 teaspoon paprika pepper
175 g/6 oz Gouda cheese
4 teaspoons each made
    mustard and tomato
    ketchup
8 rashers streaky bacon

Cut the sausages almost in
half lengthways and brush
with a mixture of oil and
paprika. Cut the cheese
into four large slices and
put in the sausages. Mix
the mustard with the
ketchup and spoon into the
split in each sausage. Wrap
two rashers of bacon
around each sausage.
Secure each one with a
wooden cocktail stick. Heat
the grill and cook the filled
sausages for 8 minutes,
turning to brown evenly on
all sides. Serve hot or cold.
Serves 4

Variation
Omit the cheese, mustard
and ketchup and spread the
inside of each sausage with
a spoonful of smooth pâté.

Cook's Tip
These cheesy sausages
make ideal picnic or
barbecue fare. Serve
them with a tomato
and onion salad.

Ham and Cheese Ring

METRIC/IMPERIAL
225 g/8 oz lean cooked ham
2 onions
3 tablespoons chopped
  parsley
2 tablespoons brandy
4 eggs
½ teaspoon salt
2 teaspoons paprika pepper
pinch dry mustard
100 g/4 oz cottage or cream
  cheese

Chop the ham finely. Peel
and chop the onions finely.
Mix both with the parsley
and brandy; cover and leave
for 20 minutes.
Whisk the eggs with the
salt, paprika, mustard and
cottage cheese. Mix the egg
mixture with the ham
mixture and ladle into a
buttered 900-ml (1½-pint)
fluted mould. Stand the
mould in a roasting tin
half-filled with water and
cook in a moderate oven
(180° C, 350° F, Gas Mark
4) for 40 minutes.
Allow to cool, then
carefully turn out on to a
serving plate. To serve,
cut in wedges like a cake.
Served with a selection of
salads, this ham and cheese
ring makes an ideal lunch
dish.
Serves 4–6

Party Loaf

METRIC/IMPERIAL
1 small uncut white loaf
50 g/2 oz butter
450 g/1 lb cottage or curd
  cheese
1 teaspoon each salt,
  paprika pepper and sugar
100 g/4 oz Cheshire cheese,
  grated
6 tablespoons tomato
  ketchup
100 g/4 oz cooked ham,
  chopped
3 tablespoons chopped
  parsley
3 tablespoons chopped chives
Garnish
wedges hard-boiled egg
tomato and radish slices
stuffed olives

Remove the crusts from all
sides of the loaf. Cut
lengthways in three thick
slices. Spread each slice, on
one side, with the butter.
Mix half the cottage cheese
with the salt, paprika, sugar
and grated cheese. Spread
one slice of bread with this
mixture and cover with a
second slice. Mix the
remaining cottage cheese
with the tomato ketchup
and ham. Spread the second
slice of bread with the
cheese and ham mixture and
cover with the third slice.
Press chopped herbs into
the sides of the loaf. Chill
for 30 minutes, then cut
into slices to serve. Garnish
with wedges of hard-boiled
egg, tomato and radish
slices and stuffed olives.
Serves 4

Quick Spanish Soup

METRIC/IMPERIAL
1 onion
1 large tomato
1 tablespoon olive oil
1 clove garlic, crushed
2 tablespoons chopped ham
1 bay leaf
50 g/2 oz long-grain rice
6 tablespoons dry white wine
pinch saffron powder
*   (optional)*
½ teaspoon lemon juice
750 ml/1¼ pints stock
100 g/4 oz frozen prawns
1 small can mussels
2 tablespoons chopped
*   parsley*
Garnish
1 hard-boiled egg, chopped

Peel and chop the onion. Peel and chop the tomato. Heat the oil in a pan and fry the onion and garlic for 5 minutes. Add the chopped tomato, ham and the bay leaf. Simmer for 5 minutes. In another pan, place the rice, wine, saffron powder (if used), lemon juice and stock. Bring to the boil and simmer until the rice is cooked. Add the contents from the frying pan, the prawns and mussels and simmer for a further 3 minutes. Check the seasoning, remove the bay leaf and stir in the parsley. Ladle the soup into bowls and serve garnished with chopped hard-boiled egg.
Serves 4

Bean Soup

METRIC/IMPERIAL
350 g/12 oz dried haricot
*   beans*
50 g/2 oz bacon rashers
2 onions
4 tomatoes
3 tablespoons chopped red
*   pepper*
½ teaspoon salt
¼ teaspoon celery salt
¼ teaspoon white pepper

Rinse the beans in cold water, and leave, covered with water, in a saucepan overnight.
The next day, add a further 500 ml (generous ¾ pint) to the beans, cover and cook until softened. Dice the bacon finely. Peel and chop the onions. Heat the diced bacon in a pan together with the onion and fry until golden brown. Add the peeled and chopped tomatoes, red pepper and seasonings. Simmer for 5 minutes. Then stir into the cooked beans and liquid. Check the seasoning.
Serves 4

Cook's Tip
If time is short, canned haricot beans may be used in place of the dried ones. Add them with the tomatoes and red pepper with sufficient liquid from the can to make a soup consistency.

Hungarian Goulash Soup

METRIC/IMPERIAL
150 g/5 oz lean pork
100 g/4 oz chuck steak
2 onions
1 small carrot
1 green pepper, seeded
1 small can tomatoes
25 g/1 oz butter or margarine
¼ teaspoon salt
1 teaspoon paprika pepper
pinch each pepper and
*   garlic salt*
6 tablespoons soured cream

Trim and cube the pork and beef. Peel the onions and cut into rings. Peel and slice the carrot; slice the pepper.
Heat the fat in a large pan and fry the onion until golden brown. Add the meats and fry for a further 5 minutes. Add the carrot, green pepper, tomatoes, paprika, salt, pepper and garlic salt. Stir well. Add 500 ml (generous ¾ pint) water, cover and simmer for 1 hour, adding more liquid if necessary. Before serving, add the cream.
Serves 2

Variation
This traditional Hungarian soup recipe may be varied by adding a pinch of cumin and some potatoes. Peel and cube 2 potatoes and add them to the soup for the last 30 minutes of cooking.
Croûtons of bread fried in butter may be sprinkled over the soup just before serving.

Cauliflower Salad

METRIC/IMPERIAL
1 cauliflower
2 teaspoons salt
1 small packet frozen peas
*1 small packet frozen mixed
  vegetables*
1 lettuce
1 cucumber, sliced
4 tomatoes, peeled
*1 small can pimientos,
  drained*
6 tablespoons mayonnaise
1 teaspoon made mustard
1 teaspoon paprika pepper
Garnish
chopped parsley
hard-boiled egg quarters

Prepare and cook the
cauliflower, whole, in
salted water until tender.

Remove. Cook the peas
and mixed vegetables
together in the same water.
Drain.
Arrange the lettuce leaves
on a serving plate and
place the cauliflower in the
centre. Around the cauli-
flower place a circle of
cucumber slices, the whole
tomatoes and the mixed
vegetables and pimientos.
Mix the mayonnaise with
mustard and paprika, and
spoon over the cauliflower.
Garnish with chopped
parsley and hard-boiled
egg quarters.
Serves 6

Shrimp and Fruit Salad

METRIC/IMPERIAL
12 frozen shrimps or prawns
2 ripe bananas
*1 small can mandarin
  oranges*
1 orange
1 pear
1 apple
12 walnut halves
*3 tablespoons mayonnaise
  or soured cream*
1 tablespoon orange juice
juice of 1 lemon
1 teaspoon sugar
1 tablespoon double cream

Defrost the shrimps. Peel
and slice the bananas.
Drain the mandarins. Peel
and cube the orange, pear
and apple. Mix the shrimps

with the prepared fruit and
walnuts. Mix the mayon-
naise with the orange and
lemon juice, the sugar and
cream and spoon over the
salad.
Serves 4

Variation
This salad looks most
attractive if served in a
glass bowl lined with
lettuce leaves. Add a sprig
of watercress to garnish.

Cook's Tip
When preparing
apples, bananas and
pears for a dish,
sprinkle the cut
surfaces with lemon
juice to prevent them
from discolouring.

Chicken and Rice Salad

METRIC/IMPERIAL
1 small packet frozen peas
1 small can bamboo shoots
3 oranges
225 g/8 oz cooked chicken
225 g/8 oz cooked long-grain rice
4 eggs, hard-boiled
2 cloves garlic, crushed
5 tablespoons olive oil
½ teaspoon salt
1 teaspoon paprika pepper
¼ teaspoon cayenne pepper
pinch each ground ginger and dry mustard
1 tablespoon wine vinegar
3 tablespoons dry white wine
1 small can artichoke hearts
Garnish
lemon wedges
parsley

Cook and drain the peas. Drain the bamboo shoots. Peel the oranges and cut the flesh into bite-sizes. Cut the chicken meat into small pieces. Mix the rice, peas, bamboo shoots and orange pieces together. Chop the eggs. Mix the chopped egg with the garlic, oil, salt, paprika, cayenne pepper, ginger and mustard. Add the vinegar and wine, and stir well. Fold into the rice mixture and add the chicken. Pile into a serving dish and arrange a ring of artichokes around the edge of the dish. Garnish with lemon wedges and parsley.
Serves 4–6

Fennel and Apple Salad

METRIC/IMPERIAL
4 heads fennel
3 tablespoons wine vinegar
½ teaspoon salt
pinch garlic salt
1 teaspoon pepper
6 tablespoons olive oil
100 g/4 oz ham, cut in strips
1 apple, sliced
1 orange, diced

Clean the fennel and cut into strips. Put in a large salad bowl, pour over the vinegar and sprinkle with the salts and pepper; finally add the oil. Mix well and then add the strips of ham and apple and lastly the diced orange. This dish should be served immediately.
Serves 4–6

Variation
The apple and orange may be replaced by 1 grapefruit. If available, Parma ham cut into strips goes well with fennel.

> **Cook's Tip**
> If it is more con-
> venient to prepare the
> salad in advance of
> serving, do not add
> the oil and vinegar,
> but toss the apple
> slices in lemon juice
> to prevent them
> discolouring.

Asparagus Salad

METRIC/IMPERIAL
375 g/12 oz cooked ham
1 small can mushrooms
2 bananas
450 g/1 lb canned asparagus
    tips
5 tablespoons dry red wine
1 tablespoon wine vinegar
1 teaspoon salt
pinch garlic salt
½ teaspoon ground black
    pepper
pinch cayenne pepper
1 teaspoon dried rosemary
250 ml/scant ½ pint double
    cream
3 tablespoons mayonnaise
lettuce leaves
4 rings canned pineapple

Cut the ham into strips. Drain and slice the mushrooms. Peel and slice the bananas. Drain and chop the asparagus tips. Mix together the bananas, asparagus, ham and mushrooms. Stir the wine, vinegar, salts, peppers and rosemary together. Lightly whip the cream, fold in the mayonnaise and the red wine mixture. Mix this sauce with the asparagus salad.
Arrange the lettuce leaves and pineapple rings on a serving plate and spoon on the asparagus salad.
Serves 4–6

Tuna Salad

METRIC/IMPERIAL
4 button onions
1 small can tuna
juice of 1 lemon
1 red pepper, seeded and
    chopped
1 green pepper, seeded and
    chopped
2 oranges
1 tablespoon orange liqueur
6 tablespoons mayonnaise
¼ teaspoon pepper
1 teaspoon salt
pinch paprika pepper
1 teaspoon Worcestershire
    sauce
4 lemons
Garnish
onion rings

Peel and chop the onions. Drain and flake the tuna and sprinkle with the lemon juice. Mix with the peppers and onion.
Peel the oranges, removing a thick layer of skin, and chop the flesh. Mix with the orange liqueur.
Mix the mayonnaise, seasonings and Worcestershire sauce. Halve the lemons and scoop out the centre. Mix the pepper and orange mixtures and spoon into the scooped-out lemons. Top with a spoonful of mayonnaise mixture and serve the remainder separately.
Garnish with onion rings.
Serves 4

Mussel Salad

METRIC/IMPERIAL
450 g/1 lb canned mussels
300 ml/½ pint dry white wine
8 stuffed olives
1 onion
6 tablespoons mayonnaise
1 tablespoon tomato purée
1 teaspoon paprika pepper
1 tablespoon chopped
   tarragon

Drain the mussels and pour over the wine. Leave in a cool place for 30 minutes. Slice the olives and onion. Drain the wine from the mussels and mix into the mayonnaise with the tomato purée and paprika. Mix the mussels, onion, olives and tarragon in a salad bowl. Either serve the mayonnaise separately, or spoon it over the salad.
Serves 4–6

Variation
If available, fresh mussels may be used in this recipe. Use 2·25 litres (4 pints) fresh mussels and after cleaning leave them in cold salted water for 30 minutes.

Cook's Tip
It's a good idea to make up a batch of mayonnaise and store it in a covered rigid container in the refrigerator. It will keep for up to a week.

Savoury Rice Salad

METRIC/IMPERIAL
225 g/8 oz long-grain rice
1 onion
1 tablespoon oil
100 g/4 oz cooked peas
½ teaspoon salt
½ teaspoon paprika pepper
4 eggs
½ cucumber
6 tablespoons mayonnaise
1 tablespoon tomato purée
½ teaspoon sugar
1 carton natural yogurt
1 lettuce

Cook the rice in boiling salted water until tender. Drain and rinse in cold water.
Dice the onion finely and fry in the oil, until softened. Add to the rice, with the peas, salt and paprika. Leave to cool.
Hard-boil and quarter the eggs; cut the cucumber into thin slices. Mix the mayonnaise with the tomato purée, sugar and yogurt. Spoon the rice mixture on to a serving dish and garnish with lettuce, cucumber slices and egg quarters.
Either spoon over the mayonnaise mixture, or serve it separately.
This savoury rice salad is a good accompaniment to a selection of cold meats.
Serves 4

Variation
The natural yogurt may be replaced by soured cream.

Dutch Cheese Salad

METRIC/IMPERIAL
225 g/8 oz Gouda cheese
225 g/8 oz cooked ham
½ green pepper
1 red pepper
1 gherkin
1 cucumber
1 apple
1 carton natural yogurt
1 tablespoon soured cream
1 tablespoon lemon juice
½ teaspoon grated
    horseradish
2 teaspoons chopped dill
1 teaspoon each salt, pepper
    and sugar

Cut the cheese into strips
and dice the ham. Seed and
dice the peppers; chop the
gherkin and dice the
cucumber, and chop the
apple. Mix together the
prepared cheese, ham,
peppers, gherkin and apple.
Blend together the yogurt,
soured cream, lemon juice
and horseradish. Add the
dill and season with the
salt, pepper and sugar.
Mix the salad ingredients
with the sauce and leave to
chill for 30 minutes.
Serves 4

Variation
Use 100 g (4 oz) cooked
ham and 100 g (4 oz)
continental sausage or
salami.

Bean Sprout Salad

METRIC/IMPERIAL
1 (510-g/1-lb 2-oz) can
    bean sprouts
3 tablespoons wine vinegar
juice of 2 lemons
1 teaspoon sugar
½ teaspoon salt
3 tablespoons oil
few lettuce leaves

Rinse the beans in cold
water, drain and put in a
bowl. Mix together the
wine vinegar, lemon juice,
sugar, salt and oil and toss
the bean sprouts in the
dressing.
Arrange the lettuce leaves
on a serving dish and spoon
on the salad.
Serves 4

Variation
Mix 350 g (12 oz) finely
chopped cooked chicken
or ham with the bean
sprouts before adding the
dressing.
Sprinkle the salad with 2–3
tablespoons chopped
parsley.

Cook's Tip
Once this salad
has been dressed it
should be served
immediately.

Stuffed Avocados

METRIC/IMPERIAL
4 avocados
juice of 1 lemon
100 g/4 oz shelled prawns
pinch each salt and pepper
1 small can celery hearts
2 eggs, hard-boiled
few drops Tabasco sauce

Avocado pears are available, imported, all the year round. They are not always ready for eating when purchased. To test for ripeness, press the flesh gently at the rounded end – it should yield slightly. Avoid pears with blackened skins as they will be too ripe to use.
Cut the avocados in half, remove the stones and immediately sprinkle the avocados with lemon juice to prevent them discolouring.
Mix together the prawns and seasoning and use to fill four of the avocado halves.
Drain and slice the celery hearts and mix with the chopped hard-boiled eggs and Tabasco sauce. Use this mixture to fill the other four halves.
Serve with mayonnaise or dressing.
Serves 8

Variation
Other fillings may be used – try canned or frozen lobster meat mixed with double cream, black pepper and a squeeze of lemon juice; or scoop out the flesh and mix it with soured cream and a few chopped almonds or walnuts. Return to the avocado shells and serve garnished with chopped parsley.

Salads

Piquant Cheese Salad

METRIC/IMPERIAL
100 g/4 oz Cheshire cheese
2 onions
175 g/6 oz salami
6 tomatoes
6 gherkins
3 tablespoons brown sugar
2 tablespoons pineapple juice
pinch cayenne pepper
3 drops Tabasco sauce
1 teaspoon ground black
    pepper
2 tablespoons dry white wine
4 tablespoons oil
3 tablespoons finely chopped
    pineapple
Garnish
chopped chives

Dice the cheese. Peel the onions and cut into rings. Dice the salami and the tomatoes; slice the gherkins. Mix together the cheese, onions, salami and gherkins. To make the dressing, mix together the sugar, pine-apple juice, cayenne pepper, Tabasco sauce, pepper, wine and oil and stir in the pineapple.
Just before serving, toss the salad in the dressing and serve garnished with chopped chives.
Serves 4–6

Variation
Other cheeses may be used in place of the Cheshire, but choose a mildly-flavoured crumbly cheese such as Double Gloucester.

Sausage Salad

METRIC/IMPERIAL
225 g/8 oz continental
    sausage
225 g/8 oz green grapes
12 stuffed olives
100 g/4 oz cooked tongue
1 onion
150 ml/$\frac{1}{4}$ pint vinegar
4 tablespoons oil
$\frac{1}{2}$ teaspoon salt
$\frac{1}{2}$ teaspoon dry mustard
$\frac{1}{2}$ teaspoon ground mace
1 teaspoon sugar

Cut the sausage into cubes; halve and seed the grapes. Slice the olives and cut the tongue into strips or cubes. Finely chop the onion. Mix these ingredients together and place in a serving bowl. Make a dressing with the vinegar, oil, seasonings and sugar and just before serving pour over the salad.
Serves 4

Variation
The cooked tongue may be replaced by cubes of cooked ham.

Cook's Tip
An easy way to make a dressing is to put all the ingredients into a screw-topped jar and shake until well mixed.

Gourmet's Salad

METRIC/IMPERIAL
6 heads chicory
350 g/12 oz cooked duck
100 g/4 oz cooked tongue
150 ml/¼ pint mayonnaise
1 teaspoon paprika pepper
few drops Tabasco sauce
2 teaspoons wine vinegar
pinch sugar
2 tablespoons chopped
    parsley
Garnish
lemon slices
parsley sprigs

Wash the chicory heads,
then cut into thin slices.
Place in a bowl. Cut the
duck and tongue into strips
and add to the chicory.
Mix the mayonnaise with 2
teaspoons of hot water, stir
in the paprika, Tabasco
sauce, vinegar, sugar and
chopped parsley.
Add to the chicory mixture
and stir round lightly.
Turn into a serving dish
and garnish with lemon
slices and parsley sprigs.
Serves 4–6

Variation
If chicory is not available,
a head of celery, chopped,
may be used instead. With
the celery add 50 g (2 oz)
chopped walnuts and 1
dessert apple, cored and
chopped.

Liver Sausage Salad

METRIC/IMPERIAL
350 g/12 oz liver sausage
1 red pepper
2 large gherkins
4 sticks celery
2 onions
225 g/8 oz cooked peas
3 tablespoons oil
1 tablespoon wine vinegar
½ teaspoon salt
1 teaspoon sugar
¼ teaspoon white pepper
pinch garlic salt

Cut the liver sausage into
slices. Seed and slice the
pepper and cut the gherkins
into strips. Chop the
celery; peel and slice the
onions. Mix together the
sliced sausage, pepper,
gherkins, celery, peas and
onions in a salad bowl.
Mix the remaining ingre-
dients together, to form a
dressing, and use to toss
the salad just before serving.
Serves 4

Variation
Before placing the salad
ingredients in the serving
bowl, rub the inside of the
bowl with a cut clove of
garlic to give the salad a
slight flavour of garlic.

Cook's Tip
Served with French
bread, this salad
makes a suitable
lunch dish.

Salads

Pasta Salad

METRIC/IMPERIAL
350 g/12 oz pork luncheon
    meat
100 g/4 oz stuffed olives
2 sticks celery
2 red-skinned apples
4 gherkins
225 g/8 oz cooked pasta
    (macaroni, pasta shells,
    spirals or bows)
2 anchovy fillets
6 tablespoons mayonnaise
1 teaspoon soy sauce
juice of 1 lemon
½ teaspoon salt
pinch cayenne pepper
1 teaspoon mixed spice

Slice the pork luncheon
meat; slice the olives and
celery. Core and slice the

apples and slice the
gherkins. Mix together the
pasta, luncheon meat,
olives, celery, apples and
gherkins.
Chop the anchovy fillets and
mix into the mayonnaise
together with the soy sauce,
lemon juice and seasonings.
Chill lightly in the refrigerator before serving with the
pasta salad.
Serves 4–6

Cook's Tip
Any cooked leftover
pasta may be used
for this salad.

Mixed Vegetable Salad

METRIC/IMPERIAL
1 (225-g/8-oz) packet frozen
    mixed vegetables
1 small cauliflower
100 g/4 oz French beans
6 tomatoes
225 g/8 oz cooked ham
6 tablespoons mayonnaise
3 tablespoons chopped
    parsley
2 tablespoons vinegar
1 teaspoon paprika pepper
½ teaspoon white pepper
pinch curry powder
pinch dry mustard
1 lettuce
Garnish
1 egg, hard-boiled
sprigs parsley

Cook the mixed vegetables,
cauliflower and French
beans in boiling salted
water until just tender.
Drain and cool, breaking
the cauliflower into florets.
Peel and chop the tomatoes.
Cut the ham into strips.
Mix together the prepared
vegetables and ham and
chill while preparing the
dressing.
Mix together the mayon-
naise, parsley, vinegar,
paprika, white pepper,
curry powder and mustard.
Line a salad bowl with the
lettuce leaves and spoon in
the salad. Spoon over the
mayonnaise mixture and
serve garnished with hard-
boiled egg quarters and
parsley sprigs.
Serves 4–6

Cheese and Fruit Salad

METRIC/IMPERIAL
4 canned pear halves
1 (226-g/8-oz) can cherries
*1 small can mandarin
    oranges*
225 g/8 oz blue cheese
2-3 cooked prunes
*250 ml/scant ½ pint soured
    cream*
juice of 1 lemon
1 teaspoon sugar
½ teaspoon salt
pinch pepper
*2–3 tablespoons chopped
    parsley*
4 lettuce leaves

Drain and chop the pear
halves; drain the cherries
and mandarin oranges,
reserving a little of the
juice. Dice the cheese and
mix with the pears, cherries,
mandarin oranges and
prunes.
Lightly beat the soured
cream and mix with the
lemon juice, 2 teaspoons
reserved mandarin juice,
the sugar, salt, pepper and
parsley.
Line a salad bowl with the
lettuce leaves and spoon in
the salad. Serve the soured
cream dressing separately.
Serves 4–6

Variation
Blue cheese is particularly
good in this salad, but
cubes of Cheddar,
Lancashire or Cheshire
cheese may be used instead.

Herring and Beetroot Salad

METRIC/IMPERIAL
10 pickled herring fillets
225 g/8 oz cooked ham
100 g/4 oz cooked beetroot
4 gherkins
2 onions
2 apples
1 egg, hard-boiled
1 tablespoon mayonnaise
2 tablespoons single cream
1 teaspoon white pepper
1 teaspoon sugar
Garnish
hard-boiled egg slices
tomato wedges

Chop the herring fillets
and ham. Chop the beetroot
coarsely and dice the
gherkins. Peel and chop the
onions. Peel, core and chop
the apples. Chop the hard-
boiled egg. Mix together
all these ingredients and
place in a salad bowl.
Mix the mayonnaise,
cream, pepper and sugar
together and fold into the
salad. Leave to chill for
1 hour.
Serve garnished with slices
of hard-boiled egg and
tomato wedges.
Serves 4

Cook's Tip
Buy Bismarck
herrings for this
recipe which are flat
fillets preserved in a
spiced vinegar.

Macaroni al Pesto

METRIC/IMPERIAL
1 tablespoon pine nuts or
  walnuts
1 clove garlic
few sprigs fresh basil
4 teaspoons salt
4 tablespoons grated
  Parmesan cheese
pinch cayenne pepper
5 tablespoons olive oil
450 g/1 lb macaroni

Finely chop the nuts; peel and crush the garlic and chop the basil with a little salt, to prevent it from discolouring. Place the nuts, garlic, basil, cheese and cayenne pepper in a mortar and crush until a fine mixture is formed. (If you do not have a pestle and mortar, the ingredients can be blended in the liquidiser.) Gradually beat 4 tablespoons of the oil into the cheese and basil mixture. The sauce should be of the same consistency as creamed butter.
Cook the macaroni in boiling salted water until *al dente* (just tender, but not soggy). Drain, toss in the remaining oil and spoon into a hot dish. Spoon over the *pesto* (the herb sauce) and serve at once.
Serves 4

Variation
This traditional Italian sauce may be served with any type of pasta.

Kidneys with Saffron Rice

METRIC/IMPERIAL
6 tablespoons oil
2 onions, chopped
225 g/8 oz long-grain rice
1 beef stock cube
2 strands saffron
½ teaspoon white pepper
0·75 kg/1½ lb calves' kidneys
1 tablespoon salt
1 tablespoon flour
2 teaspoons paprika pepper
1 teaspoon black pepper
2 tomatoes

Heat 3 tablespoons of the oil in a pan and fry the onions until softened. Add the rice and fry for a further 3 minutes.
Make 1 litre (1¾ pints) stock with the stock cube and pour over the rice. Add the saffron strands and white pepper. Cover and simmer for about 20 minutes, until the liquid has been absorbed.
Slice the kidneys, sprinkle with salt and leave for 20 minutes. Rinse under cold water and then drain. Dry. Mix the flour with the paprika and black pepper and toss the kidneys in the seasoned flour. Heat the remaining oil and fry the kidneys over a high heat. Halve tomatoes and cook under a moderate grill. Arrange the rice and the kidneys. Garnish with the grilled tomatoes. If liked, mayonnaise mixed with chopped fresh herbs may also be served.
Serves 4

Rustic Pork Jelly

METRIC/IMPERIAL
2 eggs
100 g/4 oz frozen peas
salt
1 jar pickled small corn cobs (optional)
1 small can button mushrooms
2 pickled red peppers
4 cooked carrots
2 dill pickles
50 g/2 oz gelatine
1 litre/1¾ pints stock
2 teaspoons vinegar
10 black peppercorns
600 g/1¼ lb sliced roast pork

Hard-boil the eggs for 10 minutes, drain and cool in cold water.
Cook the peas in boiling salted water for about 3–4 minutes according to the directions on the packet. Drain and refresh under cold water. Drain the corn cobs if used and the mushrooms. Slice the mushrooms and peppers thinly.
Slice the carrots and dill pickles with a fancy cutter if liked to give a fluted effect. Soften the gelatine in a little cold water. Heat the stock and add the softened gelatine. Allow to dissolve completely. Add the vinegar and peppercorns. Allow to cool until on the point of setting. Shell the eggs and slice. Arrange slices of the meat with the egg, corn if used, mushrooms, peppers, carrots, pickles and peas attractively in a serving dish. Pour over the cooked stock carefully and allow to set for 5–6 hours in a refrigerator.
Serve with French bread.
Serves 4

Artichoke Pizza

METRIC/IMPERIAL
225 g/8 oz frozen puff
   pastry, or pizza dough (see
   page 57)
4 tomatoes
3 tablespoons grated
   Parmesan cheese
225 g/8 oz canned artichoke
   hearts
10 black olives
1 clove garlic
1 tablespoon chopped parsley
2 tablespoons oil

Roll out the pastry or pizza
dough and use to line a
20-cm (8-inch) flan dish or
tin.
Skin and halve the tomatoes
and place in the flan dish.
Drain the artichokes and

place between the tomatoes.
Dot with the olives and
sprinkle over the Parmesan
cheese, crushed garlic and
parsley. Brush with oil.
Bake in a hot oven (220° C,
425° F, Gas Mark 7) for
20–25 minutes. Serve hot
with a salad.
Serves 4

Cook's Tip
This pizza may be
frozen either unbaked
or baked. If freezing
unbaked do not add
the garlic, parsley and
oil until the reheating
stage. Reheat (or
cook) from frozen in
a hot oven.

Swedish Meat Loaf

METRIC/IMPERIAL
350 g/12 oz shortcrust pastry
100 g/4 oz cooked tongue
100 g/4 oz cooked ham
450 g/1 lb minced pork
225 g/8 oz minced beef
4 tablespoons Madeira
100 g/4 oz liver sausage
3 egg yolks
3 tablespoons breadcrumbs
1 small pork fillet
1 tablespoon oil
1 teaspoon salt
1 teaspoon white pepper
6 prunes, stoned and
   chopped

Roll out the pastry thinly
to a rectangle and use to
line a 1-kg (2-lb) loaf tin.
Dice the tongue and ham

and mix with the minced
pork and beef, Madeira,
liver sausage, egg yolks and
breadcrumbs.
Fry the pork fillet in the
heated oil for 5 minutes,
until browned on all sides.
Season and leave to cool.
Bake the pastry blind in a
moderately hot oven
(200° C, 400° F, Gas
Mark 6) for 20 minutes.
Place half the meat mixture
in the pastry-lined tin, add
the pork fillet, then the
chopped prunes.
Cover with the remaining
meat mixture, pressing it
down well. Smooth the
surface and bake for a
further 45 minutes, covering
with foil after 20 minutes.
Leave to cool, turn out and
serve cut in slices.
Serves 6–8

Supper Dishes

Liver and Bacon Rolls

METRIC/IMPERIAL
0·75 kg/1½ lb calves' liver
225 g/8 oz pig's liver
1 tablespoon flour
½ teaspoon salt
½ teaspoon dried marjoram
  or oregano
½ teaspoon dried thyme
100 g/4 oz streaky bacon
3 tablespoons oil

Cut liver into pieces 2 cm
(about 1 inch) thick.
Sprinkle with flour, salt
and herbs. Wrap each
piece of liver in a piece of
streaky bacon and secure
with a wooden cocktail
stick. Place the liver and
bacon rolls in the grill
pan and brush with oil.

Cook under a moderate grill
for 3 minutes on each side.
Serve with grilled tomatoes
and baked jacket potatoes.
Serves 4

Variation
These liver and bacon rolls
may be placed on a baking
tray, brushed with oil, and
cooked in a moderately hot
oven (200° C, 400° F,
Gas Mark 6) for 10–15
minutes.

Cook's Tip
These liver and bacon
rolls may be served
with pre-lunch or pre-
dinner drinks. Make
them bite-sized for
this occasion.

Pork en Croûte

METRIC/IMPERIAL
225 g/8 oz frozen puff
  pastry
100 g/4 oz canned
  mushrooms
100 g/4 oz liver sausage
2 tablespoons chopped
  parsley
1 350-g/12-oz piece pork
  fillet
3 tablespoons oil
½ teaspoon each salt and
  white pepper
beaten egg to glaze
Garnish
parsley
tomato wedges

Defrost the pastry and roll
out thinly to a rectangle.
Cut off 2 or 3 small strips.

Drain and slice the mush-
rooms and mix with the
liver sausage and spread
over the pastry. Sprinkle
over the parsley.
Trim the pork fillet and
brown on all sides in the
heated oil. Season with salt
and pepper. Cool.
Place the cooked pork
fillet in the centre of the
pastry and bring up the
pastry to make a neat
parcel, sealing the joins
well. Decorate with the
pastry strips and brush
with beaten egg.
Cook in a moderately hot
oven (200° C, 400° F, Gas
Mark 6) for 20–25 minutes.
To serve, cut in slices.
Garnish with parsley, and
tomato wedges.
Serves 3–4

Beef with Noodles

METRIC/IMPERIAL
0·5 kg/1 lb beef fillet
2 teaspoons salt
1 tablespoon cornflour
2 tablespoons dry sherry
2 tablespoons soy sauce
2 teaspoons sugar
50 g/2 oz Chinese noodles
1 onion
6 tablespoons oil
100 g/4 oz frozen peas

Cut beef into strips 3 cm (about 1½ inches) by 1 cm (½ inch). Make a marinade with the salt, cornflour, sherry, soy sauce, sugar and 1 tablespoon water. Pour over the meat and leave to marinate for 2 hours. Cook the noodles in boiling salted water for 6 minutes. Drain and rinse in cold water.
Peel and slice the onion. Heat the oil in a pan and lightly fry the onions for 1 minute. Add the strips of meat, plus the marinade, and fry for a further 5 minutes, stirring continuously. Lastly, mix in the noodles and peas. Allow to heat through and serve at once.
Serves 4

Cook's Tip
Beef fillet should be used for this recipe. The other prime cuts are not sufficiently tender.

Chicken Breasts on Rice and Walnuts

METRIC/IMPERIAL
2 onions
2 tomatoes
1 leek
50 g/2 oz butter
2 tablespoons chopped parsley
4 chicken breasts
225 g/8 oz long-grain rice
3 tablespoons oil
50 g/2 oz walnuts, chopped
Garnish
parsley

Peel and finely dice the onions. Peel and chop the tomatoes. Wash and slice the leek. Heat the butter and sauté the vegetables for 5 minutes. Mix in the chopped parsley.
Slice each breast crossways, almost through and fill each pocket with some of the sautéed vegetables. Secure with wooden cocktail sticks.
Cook the rice in boiling salted water until tender. Drain, rinse and keep warm. Heat the oil in a pan and fry the chicken breasts over a moderate heat for 5 minutes on each side. Remove the cocktail sticks. Arrange the rice on a serving dish and top with the chicken breasts. Sprinkle with chopped walnuts and serve garnished with parsley.
Serves 4

Chinese Beef

METRIC/IMPERIAL
0·5 kg/1 lb beef fillet
4 tablespoons soy sauce
1 tablespoon dry sherry
1 teaspoon salt
2 onions
1 tablespoon flour
5 tablespoons oil
1 clove garlic, crushed
1 teaspoon white pepper
1 (510-g/1-lb 2-oz) can bean sprouts
4 teaspoons sugar
2 teaspoons cornflour

Cut meat into thin slices or strips. Mix with 1 tablespoon of the soy sauce, the sherry and salt and leave to marinate for 30 minutes.

Peel and chop the onions. Remove the meat from the marinade and toss in the flour. Heat the oil in a frying pan and fry the onions and meat for 4 minutes. Add the marinade, the remaining soy sauce, the garlic, pepper, drained bean sprouts and sugar. Mix together and cook for a further 3–4 minutes. Thicken with the blended cornflour, check the seasoning and serve.
Serves 4

Variation
Pork fillet may be used in place of the beef fillet. Other prime cuts of meat are not sufficiently tender for this recipe.

Stuffed Aubergines

METRIC/IMPERIAL
4 large aubergines
6 tablespoons oil
275 g/10 oz minced pork
275 g/10 oz minced beef
1 teaspoon garlic salt
¾ teaspoon black pepper
1 tablespoon breadcrumbs
4 tablespoons brandy
3 egg yolks
4 tablespoons grated cheese

Aubergines (or eggplant) have distinctive shiny purple skins and are available, imported, all the year round.
Cut the aubergines in half, lengthways. Place cut-sides upwards on a baking tray, brush with oil and cook in a moderately hot oven (200° C, 400° F, Gas Mark 6) for 30 minutes. Carefully remove the flesh from the aubergines. Chop finely and mix with the minced meats, garlic salt, pepper, breadcrumbs, brandy and egg yolks. Return the mixture to the aubergine shells. Sprinkle the tops with cheese and return to the oven for a further 30 minutes. Serve with baked tomatoes.
Serves 4

Variation
The minced meats may be replaced with flaked, canned tuna. Omit the brandy and use the oil from the tuna to moisten the mixture.

Lasagne

METRIC/IMPERIAL
1 onion
3 tablespoons olive oil
225 g/8 oz minced beef
1 teaspoon salt
½ teaspoon white pepper
4 tablespoons red wine
1 tablespoon tomato purée
5 tablespoons double cream
pinch dried oregano
600 g/1¼ lb lasagne
50 g/2 oz butter
pinch grated nutmeg
3 tablespoons grated
    Parmesan cheese

Peel and dice onion. Heat
the oil in a pan and fry
the meat and onions for
5 minutes, until browned.
Add the salt, pepper, wine
and tomato purée and cook
until thick. Stir in the
cream and oregano.
Cook the lasagne in boiling
salted water until just
tender (*al dente*). Drain
and rinse under cold water.
Dry with absorbent paper.
Arrange the lasagne and
meat sauce in layers in a
greased ovenproof dish,
ending with a layer of
lasagne. Dot with butter
and sprinkle with nutmeg
and grated cheese. Cook
in a moderate oven
(180° C, 350° F, Gas
Mark 4) for 10 minutes.
Serves 3–4

Veal Escalopes with Rice

METRIC/IMPERIAL
2 stock cubes
250 ml/scant ½ pint dry
    white wine
2 medium onions
100 g/4 oz butter
225 g/8 oz long-grain rice
½ teaspoon white pepper
0·5 kg/1 lb veal escalopes
1 teaspoon salt
1 tablespoon flour
2 eggs
5 tablespoons breadcrumbs
50 g/2 oz grated Parmesan
    cheese
Garnish
tomato wedge
sprig parsley

Dissolve the stock cubes in
750 ml (1¼ pints) hot
water. Add the wine.
Peel and chop the onions.
Heat 50 g (2 oz) of the butter
in a pan and fry the onions
for 3 minutes. Stir well, and
add the rice and pepper.
Pour in the stock mixture,
cover and simmer for 20
minutes, until the liquid is
absorbed.
Beat the veal out thinly,
then toss in the salt and
flour. Coat in beaten egg
and breadcrumbs. Heat the
remaining butter and fry
the veal until browned on
both sides.
Spoon the rice into a
serving dish and arrange the
veal on top. Pile the
Parmesan cheese in the
centre and serve garnished
with a tomato wedge and
parsley.
Serves 4

Pork with Pineapple

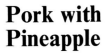

METRIC/IMPERIAL
0·5 kg/1 lb pork fillet
225 g/8 oz canned bamboo
shoots
4 slices canned pineapple
1 tablespoon soy sauce
1 teaspoon each salt and
black pepper
4 tablespoons vinegar
3 tablespoons sugar
1 tablespoon canned
pineapple juice
5 tablespoons oil
2 tablespoons cornflour

Trim the pork and cut into cubes. Drain the bamboo shoots; drain and chop the pineapple slices.
Mix together the soy sauce, salt, pepper, vinegar, sugar, pineapple juice and 1 tablespoon of the oil. Pour over the cubes of meat and turn until they are all moistened. Remove the meat from the marinade and sprinkle with 2 teaspoons of the cornflour. Heat the rest of the oil in a frying pan and fry the meat until browned on all sides. Remove and keep warm.
Pour the marinade into the frying fat and add the bamboo shoots and pineapple. Cook for 2–3 minutes. Blend the remaining cornflour with 1 tablespoon cold water and add to the pan. Stir until thickened. Check the seasoning, stir the meat back into the pan and serve.
Serves 4

Indonesian Rice

METRIC/IMPERIAL
2 onions
250 ml/scant ½ pint oil
1 chicken stock cube
225 g/8 oz long-grain rice
1 large apple
50 g/2 oz butter
25 g/1 oz curry powder
225 g/8 oz cooked chicken
225 g/8 oz cooked ham
To serve
fried eggs
grated coconut
mango chutney
gherkins

Peel and chop the onions. Heat the oil and fry the onions over a high heat for 3 minutes.
Dissolve the stock cube in 1 litre (1¾ pints) hot water. Pour over the onions; add the rice, cover and simmer for 20 minutes, until all the liquid is absorbed.
Peel, core and chop the apple. Heat the butter in a pan and sauté the curry powder and apple for 5 minutes. Add the chopped chicken and ham and the cooked rice and onions and cook for another 5 minutes, stirring continuously.
Serve the rice with fried eggs, grated coconut, mango chutney and gherkins.
Note Traditionally this dish is also served with prawn crackers. These are available in specialist stores. When fried in oil, they become puffy.
Serves 4

Nasi Goreng

METRIC/IMPERIAL
225 g/8 oz long-grain rice
100 g/4 oz canned prawns
100 g/4 oz canned crab
225 g/8 oz cooked chicken
3 small onions
1 clove garlic
1 small red pepper
250 ml/scant ½ pint oil
1 tablespoon curry powder
Garnish
chopped parsley

Cook the rice in boiling salted water for 15 minutes. Drain, return to pan and stir over a low heat until dry.
Drain the prawns and crab. Cut the chicken into thin strips. Peel and chop the onions; crush the garlic. Seed and chop the pepper. Heat the oil in a pan, and, over a medium heat, fry the onions, garlic and pepper for 3–4 minutes. Add the curry powder, and cook, stirring, for a further 2–3 minutes. Stir in the chicken and rice and cook for a further 5 minutes. Finally, stir in the prawns and crab and allow to heat through. Spoon the mixture on to a serving dish and sprinkle with chopped parsley. Serve with a selection of the following side dishes: chilli sauce, pickled gherkins, mango chutney, pineapple and banana slices, shredded coconut. *Serves 4*

Variation
The traditional Indonesian dish is sometimes garnished with an egg mixture. Lightly whisk 2 eggs with salt and pepper and cook as for an omelette in a little heated oil. Turn the cooked egg mixture out and cut into strips. Arrange the strips over the top of the rice dish.

Loin of Pork, Provençale Style

METRIC/IMPERIAL
1 (1·5-kg/3-lb) pork loin
1 teaspoon salt
1 teaspoon dried rosemary
2 tablespoons chopped parsley
2 tablespoons grated horse-radish
2 eggs
3 tablespoons breadcrumbs
3 tablespoons oil

Ask the butcher to bone and roll the loin of pork, removing the outer skin. Mix the salt with the rosemary, parsley and horse-radish. Rub into the meat so that a crust is formed around the meat. Whisk the eggs. Dip the meat into the beaten eggs, and then in the breadcrumbs, pressing them on well. Place the meat in a greased roasting tin, pour over the oil and cook in a moderately hot oven (200° C, 400° F, Gas Mark 6) for 1½–1¾ hours, covering the joint with foil if the breadcrumb mixture becomes too brown. Serve the pork with baked tomatoes and baked jacket potatoes which can be cooked in the oven with the meat.
Serves 4–6

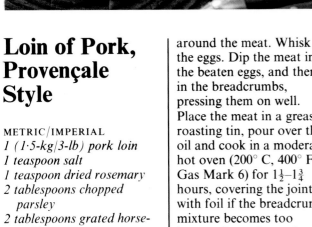

Traditional Pizza

METRIC/IMPERIAL
225 g/8 oz plain flour
15 g/½ oz fresh yeast
½ teaspoon sugar
150 ml/generous ¼ pint milk
5 tablespoons olive oil
1 teaspoon salt
4 tomatoes
1 teaspoon celery salt
1 teaspoon black pepper
2 teaspoons dried oregano
100 g/4 oz Mozarella cheese
2 onions, chopped
10 anchovy fillets
few capers

Sieve the flour and make a well in the centre. Cream the yeast with the sugar, 6 tablespoons of the luke-warm milk and 1 tablespoon of the flour. Leave covered, in a warm place for 10 minutes, until frothy. Pour into the well in the flour; leave for 30 minutes. Stir the yeast, flour, re-mainder of the warm milk, half the oil and the salt together, until a dough is formed. Roll out thinly to a large circle. Place on a greased baking tray and turn up the edges slightly. Peel and slice the tomatoes and place on the dough. Add the celery salt, pepper, oregano and slices of cheese. Scatter over the onions, anchovies, capers and the remaining oil. Bake in a moderately hot oven (200° C, 400° F, Gas Mark 6) for 30 minutes. Serve hot.
Serves 4

Fondues

Burgundy Meat Fondue

METRIC/IMPERIAL
Herb mayonnaise
4 tablespoons mayonnaise
1 tablespoon each chopped
*   tarragon, parsley and dill*
1 tablespoon cream
Pepper and tomato sauce
25 g/1 oz butter
2 green peppers, chopped
1 onion, chopped
4 tablespoons water
4 tomatoes, peeled
few drops Tabasco sauce
pinch each salt and pepper
1 kg/2 lb rump or fillet steak
oil for deep frying

Mix together the
mayonnaise, herbs and
cream and spoon into a
small dish.

To make the pepper sauce,
heat the butter in a frying
pan and sauté the peppers
and onion until softened.
Add chopped tomatoes and
the remaining ingredients
and simmer for 10–15
minutes. Cool, then spoon
into a second small dish.
Trim the beef and cut into
small cubes. Two-thirds fill
a metal fondue pan with the
oil and heat on the cooker.
Bring the heated oil to the
table and place on the spirit
burner.
The guests spear a cube of
meat on the fondue fork
and cook it in the heated
oil. The cooked meat is then
dipped in the chosen sauce.
With a burgundy meat
fondue serve baked potatoes,
salads and stuffed olives.
Serves 4

Mediterranean Fondue

METRIC/IMPERIAL
0·5 kg/1 lb frozen prawns
juice of 1 lemon
2 onions
225 g/8 oz Gruyère or
*   Emmenthal cheese*
1 litre/1¾ pints chicken stock
3 tablespoons chopped dill
pinch cayenne pepper
½ teaspoon pepper
½ teaspoon sugar

Defrost the prawns, sprinkle
with lemon juice and leave
for 10 minutes.
Peel and chop the onions.
Grate the cheese. Pour the
stock in a metal fondue pan
and heat on the cooker. Add
the grated cheese and stir
over a low heat until melted,
but do not allow the
mixture to boil. Remove
from heat and stir in the
onions, dill, cayenne pepper,
pepper and sugar.
Bring the fondue pan to the
table and place on the
spirit burner. Drain the
prawns and pat dry with
absorbent paper. Spear on
the fondue forks, dip in the
fondue for 1 minute, then
eat.
Serve with slices of crusty
hot French bread.
Serves 4–6

Paprika Fondue

METRIC/IMPERIAL
8 tomatoes
1 green pepper
50 g/2 oz butter
0·75 kg/1½ lb Emmenthal cheese, grated
½ teaspoon black pepper
½ teaspoon paprika pepper
pinch dried marjoram
½ teaspoon celery salt
3 tablespoons tomato purée
6 tablespoons double cream
1 teaspoon cornflour
4 tablespoons dry white wine
16 thick slices white bread

Place the tomatoes in boiling water for 2–3 minutes, then peel and halve. Seed and chop the pepper.

Melt the butter in a fondue pan or flameproof dish placed on the cooker and sauté the tomatoes for 5 minutes. Add the pepper and sauté for a further 5 minutes. Add the grated cheese and allow it to melt over a low heat, stirring all the time. Add the pepper, paprika, marjoram, celery salt, tomato purée and cream. Stir in the cornflour blended with a little of the wine. Stir in the remaining wine. Bring the fondue pan to the table, and place on the spirit burner. Serve cubes of bread to dip into the fondue.
Serves 4–6

Cheesy Herb Fondue

METRIC/IMPERIAL
100 g/4 oz button mushrooms
1 kg/2 lb Danish blue or Gorgonzola cheese
225 g/8 oz Brie cheese
50 g/2 oz butter
4 tablespoons dry white wine
3 tablespoons brandy
3 tablespoons chopped herbs
½ teaspoon ground nutmeg
2 French loaves

Slice the mushrooms; crumble the blue cheese and and dice the Brie.
Place the butter in a metal fondue pan and melt on the cooker. Add the wine and brandy and heat. Add the cheese and allow to melt over a gentle heat, stirring

all the time. Stir in the mushrooms, herbs and nutmeg. Bring the fondue pan to the table and place it on the spirit burner.
Serve cubes of bread to dip into the fondue. A selection of salads, olives and gherkins may also be served with this fondue.
Serves 6

Cook's Tip
When making cheese fondues, it is essential to allow the cheese to melt slowly over a gentle heat, stirring all the time with a wooden spoon.

Fondues

Beer Fondue

METRIC/IMPERIAL
500 ml/generous ¾ pint pale ale
250 ml/scant ½ pint brown ale
75 g/3 oz butter
0·75 kg/1½ lb Cheddar or Cheshire cheese, grated
few drops Tabasco sauce
1 teaspoon made mustard
2 teaspoons Worcestershire sauce
1 teaspoon cornflour

Place the pale and brown ales in a metal fondue pan and add 500 ml (generous ¾ pint) water, the butter and cheese. Heat gently on the cooker, until the cheese melts, stirring. Add the Tabasco sauce, mustard and Worcestershire sauce.
Mix the cornflour with a little cold water to form a smooth paste, and then pour into the hot fondue; stir well, until thickened.
Bring the fondue pan to the table and place it on the spirit burner.
Serve with French bread and a selection of chopped raw vegetables to dip into the fondue.
Serves 6

Cook's Tip
When giving a fondue party, make sure that the fondue pan and spirit burner are placed safely in the centre of the table.

Veal and Wine Fondue

METRIC/IMPERIAL
0.75 kg/1½ lb veal fillet
1·5 litres/2¾ pints dry white wine
pinch allspice
12 coriander seeds
1 cinnamon stick
5 black peppercorns
1 teaspoon sugar
1 teaspoon salt
½ teaspoon celery salt
¼ teaspoon garlic salt

Cut the meat into thin slices. Place the wine and allspice in a metal fondue pan and bring to the boil on the cooker.
Tie the coriander seeds, cinnamon stick and peppercorns in a square of muslin and suspend it in the wine. Add the sugar to the wine and allow to simmer for 5 minutes.
Discard the muslin bag.
Move the fondue pan to the spirit burner on the table.
Spear the veal on the fondue fork and cook in the simmering wine. Serve sprinkled with the mixed salts and accompany with French bread and sauces.
Serves 4

Cook's Tip
If your fondue set has an earthenware pan and not a metal one, heat the oil or stock in a saucepan on the cooker and then transfer it.

Breton Cheese Fondue

METRIC/IMPERIAL
100 g/4 oz butter
900 g/2 lb cottage cheese
2 teaspoons flour
500 ml/generous ¾ pint milk
¼ teaspoon salt
pinch celery salt
pinch cayenne pepper
1 teaspoon paprika pepper
4 egg yolks
100 g/4 oz cooked tongue

Place the butter in a metal fondue pan and heat on the cooker. Mix in the cottage cheese, flour and milk and, stirring all the time, bring just to the boil. Season with the salt, celery salt, cayenne pepper and paprika. Beat in the egg yolks, making sure the fondue does not boil. Cut the tongue into strips and stir into the fondue.
Bring the fondue pan to the table and place it on the spirit burner. Serve squares of bread and a selection of raw vegetables to dip into the fondue.
Serves 4

Cook's Tip
It is advisable to stand the spirit burner on a tray or mat to protect the table.

Oriental Fondue

METRIC/IMPERIAL
225 g/8 oz sweetbreads
pinch salt
few drops vinegar
225 g/8 oz calves' kidneys
225 g/8 oz veal fillet
225 g/8 oz rump steak
225 g/8 oz lean pork
225 g/8 oz calves' liver
1·5 litres/2¾ pints chicken stock
½ teaspoon dried mixed herbs
150 ml/¼ pint dry sherry

Put the sweetbreads in a pan, cover with water and add a pinch of salt and a few drops of vinegar. Bring to the boil and drain.
Cut the kidneys, veal, steak, pork, liver and sweetbreads into thin slices and place in separate containers.
Place the chicken stock, herbs and sherry in a metal fondue pan and bring to the boil on the cooker. Bring to the table and place on the spirit burner.
Spear the individual slices of meat and cook in the liquid.
Serve with crusty French bread and a selection of salads and sauces.
Serves 6

Cook's Tip
With the oriental fondue keep the flame on the spirit burner high, as the cooking liquor must be kept at boiling point.

Fondues

Turkish Meat Fondue

METRIC/IMPERIAL
0·5 kg/1 lb veal fillet
0·5 kg/1 lb pork fillet
Sauce
1 onion, chopped
2 green peppers, seeded and chopped
2 tablespoons chopped gherkins
25 g/1 oz butter
4 tablespoons water
salt and pepper
few drops chilli sauce
2 litres/3½ pints chicken stock

Cut the meats into thin slices and place in separate bowls.
Sauté the prepared onion, peppers and gherkins in the butter until softened. Add the remaining ingredients, bring to the boil, and simmer for 5 minutes, stirring occasionally. Pour into a small dish and leave to cool.
Pour the stock into a metal fondue pan and bring to the boil on the cooker, then place on the spirit burner. Spear the meat on fondue forks and dip into the stock for about 30 seconds. Dip into the sauce and eat.
Serve with French bread and a selection of salads.
Serves 4
Note Any of the sauces on pages 72–77 may also be served with this fondue.

Fish Fondue

METRIC/IMPERIAL
225 g/8 oz plaice fillets
0·5 kg/1 lb smoked haddock fillets
225 g/8 oz halibut fillets
1 tablespoon flour
2 egg whites
1 teaspoon paprika pepper
½ teaspoon salt
¼ teaspoon white pepper
Sauce
2 teaspoons Worcestershire sauce
2 tablespoons breadcrumbs
3 tablespoons tomato ketchup
5 tablespoons oil
2 tablespoons vinegar
1 teaspoon sugar
oil for deep frying

Skin and cut the fish into small pieces. Mix the flour with the egg whites, paprika, salt and pepper. Toss the fish in this mixture.
Mix together the ingredients for the sauce and place in a small dish.
Two-thirds fill a metal fondue pan with oil and heat on the cooker. Bring to the table and place on the spirit burner. Spear the pieces of fish and cook in the oil for 30 seconds, until they are golden brown; dip in the sauce before eating.
Serve with French bread and a green salad.
Serves 6–8

Chocolate Fondue

METRIC/IMPERIAL
2 oranges
2 bananas
2 pears
225 g/8 oz stoned cherries
juice of 1 lemon
450 g/1 lb plain chocolate
pinch ground cinnamon
150 ml/¼ pint double cream
100 g/4 oz icing sugar,
  sieved

Peel the oranges, bananas and pears. Cut the flesh into cubes and mix with the cherries. Sprinkle with lemon juice and place in a serving dish.
Grate the chocolate and place in the fondue pan with the cinnamon. Place on the spirit burner and allow to melt, stirring from time to time. Stir in the cream.
Spear the pieces of fruit, dip in the sieved icing sugar then into the chocolate fondue.
Serve with sponge finger biscuits.
Serves 4

Variation
For a mocha fondue, stir 2 teaspoons coffee essence into the melted chocolate, before adding the cream. Marshmallows and cubes of plain cake may be served, in addition to the fruits, to dip into the fondue.

Cheese Fondue

METRIC/IMPERIAL
225 g/8 oz Camembert
  cheese
0·75 kg/1½ lb Gruyère or
  Gouda cheese
250 ml/scant ½ pint milk
75 g/3 oz butter, melted
½ teaspoon white pepper
1 teaspoon paprika pepper
1 onion, finely chopped

Remove the Camembert from refrigerator before using and leave it at room temperature for 4 hours. Grate the Gruyère or Gouda cheese coarsely and dice the Camembert. Place the cheeses in a metal fondue pan, together with the milk, butter, seasonings and onion. Place on the cooker and heat gently, stirring, until the cheese melts. Do not allow the fondue to boil.
Bring the fondue pan to the table and place on the spirit burner. Serve cubes of bread to dip into the fondue, and accompany with bowls of olives, gherkins and potato crisps.
Note With a cheese fondue serve a lightly chilled dry white wine.
Serves 6

Cook's Tip
If a cheese fondue should curdle, due to overheating, stir in a little lemon juice to rectify it.

Veal Steaks with Garlic

METRIC/IMPERIAL
*225 g/8 oz frozen French
  beans*
2 tablespoons oil
½ teaspoon sugar
1 tablespoon wine vinegar
4 cloves garlic
1 teaspoon salt
½ teaspoon black pepper
4 thick veal escalopes
Garnish
chopped chives

Cook the beans in boiling
salted water until just
tender. Drain, cool and mix
with half the oil, the sugar
and vinegar.
Peel the garlic and leave
whole. Rub the salt and
pepper into both sides of the
veal and push a clove of
garlic into each steak; brush
both sides with the
remaining oil. Grill under a
moderate heat for 2–3
minutes on each side.
Serve sprinkled with
chopped chives and with the
bean salad.
Serves 4

Variation
In place of the veal
use boneless pork slices
cut from the leg. Cook for
5 minutes on each side.

> **Cook's Tip**
> For a less pronounced
> garlic flavour, halve
> the cloves and rub the
> cut sides over the
> veal before cooking.

Balkan Meat Rolls

METRIC/IMPERIAL
0·5 kg/1 lb minced beef
½ teaspoon salt
¼ teaspoon black pepper
4 onions
1 clove garlic
3 tablespoons oil
1 tablespoon flour
*4 tablespoons chopped
  parsley*
1 teaspoon paprika pepper
Garnish
parsley

Mix the meat with the salt
and pepper. Peel the onions
and garlic and chop
together finely, then add to
the meat. Mix in half the
oil, the flour, parsley, and
paprika.
Form the mixture into small
sausage shapes and cook
under a heated grill for 5–8
minutes, turning to brown
them on all sides.
Garnish with parsley and
serve with a cabbage salad
mixed with a few caraway
seeds, and French bread.
Serves 4

Variation
Minced pork may be used
in place of the minced beef.
Add a pinch of dried
rosemary.

Fruity Meat Kebabs

METRIC/IMPERIAL
225 g/8 oz beef fillet
225 g/8 oz pork fillet
225 g/8 oz veal fillet
1 large banana
juice of 1 lemon
8 canned apricot halves
½ teaspoon salt
pinch garlic salt
1 tablespoon oil

Kebabs are ideal to serve when entertaining as they can be prepared in advance and kept in the refrigerator. Cut the meat into fairly large cubes. Peel the banana and cut into 12 thick slices and sprinkle with lemon juice.
Arrange the meat, apricot halves and slices of banana alternately on four skewers. Season with salts, then brush with oil.
Cook under a moderate grill for 5–8 minutes, turning to brown the kebabs on all sides.
Serve with rice and a green salad.
Serves 4

Variation
In place of the apricots and bananas, use canned pineapple cubes and figs, or cooked prunes and cubes of apple.

Cook's Tip
If you choose a less expensive cut of meat for these kebabs, allow the cubes of meat to marinate in a mixture of oil and vinegar for 1 hour.

Grills and Barbecues

Grilled Fish with Herbs

METRIC/IMPERIAL
2 haddock fillets
1 teaspoon lemon juice
2 tablespoons chopped
parsley
2 tablespoons chopped
chives
salt
2 teaspoons oil

Sprinkle the haddock with lemon juice, herbs, salt and oil. Leave in the refrigerator to marinate for 30 minutes. Cook under a moderate grill for about 4 minutes on each side, brushing with more oil from time to time. Serve with a tomato and onion salad.
Serves 2

Variation
Other white fish fillets may be used in place of the haddock – try plaice, cod or turbot.

Cook's Tip
If there is any doubt about the freshness of the fish obtainable in your area it is preferable to purchase frozen fish. Allow it to defrost before using.

Cheesy Pork Chops

METRIC/IMPERIAL
3 heads chicory
1 bulb fennel
1 carton natural yogurt
juice of 1 orange
juice of 1 lemon
1 teaspoon sugar
pinch each salt and white
pepper
2 onions
25 g/1 oz butter
75 g/3 oz cheese
50 g/2 oz dried apricots
100 g/4 oz liver sausage
4 boneless pork chops
1 tablespoon flour
3 tablespoons oil

Trim and cut the chicory and fennel into strips. Mix the yogurt with the orange and lemon juices, sugar, salt and pepper and spoon over the mixed chicory and fennel. Chill.
Peel and chop the onions. Heat the butter in a pan and brown the onion. Dice the cheese; chop the apricots. Mix together the liver sausage, browned onions, diced cheese and apricots. Trim and flatten the chops. Spread with the liver sausage mixture and fold each chop in half. Secure with wooden cocktail sticks. Coat with flour, and brush both sides with oil. Cook under a moderate grill for about 8 minutes on each side.
Remove the cocktail sticks and serve with the chicory and fennel salad.
Serves 4

Ranch-Style Chicken

METRIC/IMPERIAL
50 g/2 oz breadcrumbs
2 tablespoons chopped
  parsley
1 red pepper, seeded and
  chopped
1 green pepper, seeded and
  chopped
1 onion, chopped
2 teaspoons chopped basil
1 egg
pinch each salt and black
  pepper
3 tablespoons grated cheese
2 poussins
2 tablespoons oil
2 teaspoons paprika pepper

Mix together the
breadcrumbs, parsley,
peppers, onions, basil, egg,
seasonings and cheese to
form a stuffing. Use to stuff
the chickens.
Place the chickens in a
roasting tin and brush with
oil. Cover with foil and
cook in a moderately hot
oven (200° C, 400° F, Gas
Mark 6) for about 30
minutes.
Remove the foil, brush
with a little more oil and
sprinkle with paprika.
Return to the oven for a
further 10 minutes to
brown.
Split each poussin in half
and serve with a tangy
barbecue sauce.
Serves 2–4

Spit-Roasted Lamb

METRIC/IMPERIAL
1 (2-kg/4½-lb) leg of lamb
150 ml/¼ pint oil
1 teaspoon paprika pepper
¼ teaspoon cayenne pepper
2 teaspoons salt
1 tablespoon Worcestershire
  sauce
4 tablespoons red wine
1 teaspoon black pepper
1 bay leaf
12 juniper berries
225 g/8 oz streaky bacon

Ask the butcher to bone and
tie the lamb.
Remove the skin from the
lamb and place the meat in
a large dish. Mix together
the oil, peppers, salt,
Worcestershire sauce, wine
and pepper. Pour over the
lamb, add the bay leaf and
leave to marinate in the
refrigerator for up to 6
hours.
Remove the meat from the
marinade, pat dry with
absorbent paper and push
the juniper berries into the
lamb. Cover with bacon and
secure with wooden cocktail
sticks.
Place the meat on the spit
so that the weight is evenly
distributed. Place the spit
on the rotisserie and cook
the joint for 1½–2 hours.
While the joint is cooking,
from time to time spoon
over a little of the marinade.
To serve, remove the bacon
rashers and cocktail sticks
and place the lamb on a
carving dish.
Serves 6

Grilled Salmon Steaks

METRIC/IMPERIAL
1 piece crystallised ginger
juice of 1 lemon
3 tablespoons soy sauce
2 tablespoons canned
*   crushed pineapple*
1 teaspoon curry powder
½ teaspoon salt
4 salmon steaks
4 leeks
1 tablespoon flour
½ teaspoon black pepper
25 g/1 oz butter

Chop the ginger finely.
Make a marinade with the
lemon juice, soy sauce,
pineapple, curry powder,
salt and chopped ginger.
Spoon over the salmon
steaks and leave to
marinate for 20 minutes.
Slice the leeks.
Remove the salmon from
the marinade, toss in flour
and place on the grill pan.
Cook under a moderate
grill for 6 minutes on each
side, brushing with the
marinade from time to time.
Meanwhile, cook the leeks
in boiling salted water until
just tender. Drain and toss
in black pepper and butter
and serve with the salmon
steaks.
Serves 4

Fish and Ham Rolls

METRIC/IMPERIAL
0·75 kg/1¾ lb haddock fillets
½ teaspoon salt
1 teaspoon paprika pepper
2 tablespoons grated cheese
2 teaspoons chopped parsley
2 teaspoons chopped dill
4 thin slices cooked ham
1 tablespoon oil
Garnish
parsley sprigs
dill sprigs

Cut the fish into four equal
pieces and sprinkle with the
salt, paprika, grated cheese
and herbs. Roll a slice of
ham around each piece of
fish and secure with a
wooden cocktail stick.
Brush the rolls with oil and
cook under a moderate
grill for about 15 minutes,
turning the rolls halfway
through the cooking time.
Before serving, remove the
cocktail sticks and garnish
with parsley and dill sprigs.
Serves 4

Variation
Use plaice instead of the
haddock and cook for a
total of about 12 minutes.
If liked, the slices of ham
may be lightly spread with
a little mild mustard.

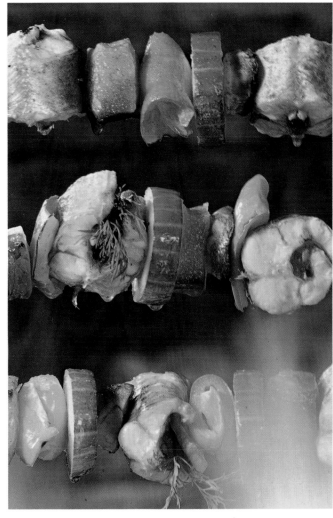

Grilled Halibut Steaks

METRIC/IMPERIAL
4 halibut steaks
½ teaspoon salt
1 tablespoon grated cheese
1 teaspoon paprika pepper
3 tablespoons oil
1 carrot
2 onions
1 leek
1 stick celery
50 g/2 oz butter
4 slices cooked ham

Sprinkle the halibut steaks with the salt, cheese, paprika and oil. Cook under a moderate grill for about 15 minutes, turning the steaks halfway through the cooking time.
Meanwhile, chop the vegetables finely and sauté in the butter until softened. Place a spoonful of sautéed vegetables on each slice of ham and form into a roll; secure the ham rolls with a wooden cocktail stick.
Place beside the halibut and grill for 5 minutes. Remove the cocktail sticks before serving.
Serve with fresh spinach.
Serves 4

Eel Kebabs

METRIC/IMPERIAL
0·75 kg/1½ lb fresh eel
½ teaspoon celery salt
½ cucumber
1 red or green pepper
100 g/4 oz streaky bacon
few dill sprigs
12 button mushrooms
juice of 1 lemon
3 tablespoons oil
½ teaspoon paprika pepper

Eel is always sold alive and should be cooked as soon as possible after killing.
Buy the eel already skinned and cut into small pieces.
Sprinkle the eel with the celery salt.
Cut the cucumber into 1·5-cm (½-inch) slices. Seed and cut the pepper into cubes. Rind, and make the bacon into rolls.
Thread pieces of eel, dill, cucumber, bacon rolls, mushrooms and pepper on to skewers. Sprinkle with lemon juice, oil, and paprika. Cook the kebabs under a moderate grill for 5 minutes, turning to brown them evenly.
Serves 4

Variation
If fresh eel is not available in your area smoked eel may be used instead.

Lobster with Garlic Toast

METRIC/IMPERIAL
2 cooked lobsters
225 g/8 oz mushrooms
100 g/4 oz butter
2 teaspoons dry mustard
4–6 slices bread
1 clove garlic
1 teaspoon lemon juice
pinch white pepper
pinch onion salt

Cut the lobsters in half lengthways. Remove the meat, chop roughly and mix with the chopped mushrooms, 50 g (2 oz) of the butter and the mustard. Fill the lobster shells with the mixture. Place under a moderate grill and cook for 5 minutes.

Toast the slices of bread. Crush the garlic and blend with the remaining butter, the lemon juice and seasonings. Spread on the toast, cut in halves or quarters, and serve with the lobster.
Serves 4

Cook's Tip
When purchasing lobster, choose one of medium size which feels heavy for its size. Avoid ones with white shells as this is a sure sign of an old lobster. Lobsters are available all the year round, but they are best between April and August. ·

Stuffed Veal Escalopes

METRIC/IMPERIAL
4 thick veal escalopes
½ teaspoon celery salt
½ teaspoon paprika pepper
pinch white pepper
2 onions
50 g/2 oz butter
100 g/4 oz liver sausage
3 tablespoon chopped parsley
3 tablespoons chopped chives
1 tablespoon breadcrumbs
1 tablespoon oil

Trim the veal and cut each escalope three-quarters of the way through, making a pocket. Mix the celery salt, paprika and pepper, and rub into the escalopes.

Peel and chop the onions. Heat the butter in a frying pan and cook the onions until softened. Remove from the heat and add the liver sausage, herbs and breadcrumbs, stirring well. Leave to cool.
Spread the stuffing in the pocket of each escalope and secure with wooden cocktail sticks. Brush the escalopes with oil and place in the grill pan. Cook under a moderate grill for 4 minutes on each side.
Remove the cocktail sticks and serve the veal escalopes with peas.
Serves 4

Grills and Barbecues

Stuffed Pork Chops

METRIC/IMPERIAL
4 thick boneless pork chops
2 slices white bread
6 tablespoons double cream
½ teaspoon salt
¼ teaspoon white pepper
*3 tablespoons chopped
  parsley*
*1 tablespoon chopped
  chives*
1 tablespoon chopped chervil
3 tablespoons oil
1 teaspoon paprika pepper

Slit each chop horizontally so that a small pocket is formed.
Dice the bread and mix with the cream, salt, pepper and herbs. Mix thoroughly and use to fill the pocket in each chop. Secure with wooden cocktail sticks. Brush the chops with oil and sprinkle with paprika, then cook under a moderate grill for 10–15 minutes on each side.
Remove the cocktail sticks and serve the chops on a bed of braised cabbage, or sauerkraut.
Serves 4

Variation
In place of the chopped chives and chervil use a pinch of dried rosemary, or grill the chops with a sprig of fresh rosemary.

Trout with Dill Butter

METRIC/IMPERIAL
4 trout
1 teaspoon salt
½ teaspoon mixed spice
juice of 2 lemons
1¼ teaspoons white pepper
3 tablespoons chopped dill
50 g/2 oz butter
4 tablespoons oil
0·5 kg/1 lb tomatoes
1 onion, finely chopped

Trout is available all the year round, fresh or frozen Allow frozen trout to defrost before using.
Rub the insides of the trout with salt and mixed spice, ¼ teaspoon of the pepper and half the lemon juice. Mix the dill with the butter and spread inside the trout. Lay the fish on the grill pan, brush with oil and cook under a moderate grill for about 5 minutes on each side.
Meanwhile, peel the tomatoes, halve or slice and sprinkle with the remaining lemon juice and pepper and chopped onion. Serve with the grilled trout.
Serves 4

Cook's Tip
If river trout is available, they are particularly delicious cooked this way. They are best between March and September.

Piquant Malaga Sauce

METRIC/IMPERIAL
2 eggs, hard-boiled
2 eggs
1 teaspoon ground black
    pepper
½ teaspoon cayenne pepper
150 ml/¼ pint olive oil
100 g/4 oz almonds
50 g/2 oz sultanas
1 tablespoon clear honey
3 tablespoons wine vinegar
3 tablespoons tomato
    ketchup

Chop the hard-boiled eggs
and mix with the raw eggs,
pepper, cayenne pepper and
oil.
Stir in the chopped almonds,
the sultanas and remaining
ingredients. Leave in a cool
place for 20 minutes to
allow the flavours to blend.
Serve this sauce with grilled
fish, kebabs or meat
fondues.
Serves 6

Variation
Red or white wine may be
used in place of the wine
vinegar. Instead of the
tomato ketchup use 2
tablespoons tomato purée
blended with 1 tablespoon
water.

> **Cook's Tip**
> Always check the
> seasoning of sauces
> just before serving
> and adjust if
> necessary.

Spanish Sauce

METRIC/IMPERIAL
1 red pepper
1 green pepper
250 ml/scant ½ pint soured
    cream
2 tablespoons wine vinegar
6 tablespoons olive oil
1 teaspoon white pepper
7 tablespoons dry white wine
1 teaspoon salt
1 teaspoon garlic salt
2 eggs, hard-boiled
2 tablespoons chopped
    chives
3 tablespoons breadcrumbs

Halve, seed and chop the
peppers.
Mix together the soured
cream, vinegar, oil, pepper,
wine, salt and garlic salt
with 6 tablespoons warm
water; blend until smooth.
Chop the eggs and add to
the sauce with the chopped
chives and breadcrumbs.
Serve this sauce with grilled
or fried meats or kebabs.
Serves 6

Variation
Fresh double cream may be
used in place of the soured
cream. Add 1 teaspoon
lemon juice.

Sauces for Fondues and Grills

Garibaldi Sauce

METRIC/IMPERIAL
2 egg yolks
2 teaspoons made mustard
½ teaspoon garlic salt
few drops anchovy essence
pinch cayenne pepper
300 ml/½ pint oil
2 tablespoons wine vinegar
1 tablespoon tomato ketchup
1 tablespoon capers

Place the egg yolks, mustard, salt, anchovy essence and cayenne pepper in a bowl. Whisk lightly, then drop by drop, whisk in the oil until the mixture is thick. Thin the mayonnaise with 1 tablespoon boiling water and the vinegar. Stir in the tomato ketchup and capers.

Serve this sauce with grilled or fried herrings or mackerel, and meat fondues.
Serves 6

Cook's Tip
This sauce may be made in advance and stored for 1–2 days in a covered polythene container in the refrigerator.

Provençale Sauce

METRIC/IMPERIAL
2 onions
250 ml/scant ½ pint tomato ketchup
5 tablespoons capers
2 tablespoons chopped chives
6 tablespoons double cream
2 teaspoons dried rosemary
1 teaspoon dried marjoram
2 eggs, hard-boiled
½ teaspoon garlic salt
2 tablespoons oil
1 tablespoon wine vinegar

Peel and finely chop the onions. Mix with the tomato ketchup, capers, chives, lightly whipped cream, rosemary and marjoram.

Chop the eggs and mix with the garlic salt, oil and wine vinegar.
Just before serving the sauce, blend the hard-boiled egg mixture into the tomato mixture.
Serve this sauce with meat fondues and grilled or fried lamp chops.
Serves 6

Variation
A clove of garlic may be used in place of the garlic salt. Peel and crush the garlic before using.

Cucumber Sauce

METRIC/IMPERIAL
2 eggs
½ cucumber
2 onions
4 dill sprigs
3 tarragon sprigs
1 tablespoon Pernod
(optional)
1 teaspoon Worcestershire
sauce
2 tablespoons oil
3 tablespoons wine vinegar

Hard-boil the eggs for 10 minutes, shell and chop finely. Peel the cucumber and cut the flesh into small pieces. Chop the onions. Place the cucumber, herbs and onions in the liquidiser and blend until smooth.

Pour the purée into a bowl and add the Pernod, Worcestershire sauce, oil and vinegar. Sprinkle the chopped hard-boiled egg on the top of the sauce. Serve this sauce with grilled turbot, halibut or salmon, or with grilled veal or lamb or with meat fondues.
Serves 6

Cook's Tip
If you do not have a liquidiser, grate the cucumber and onions and then mix with the other ingredients. Use a pinch each of dried dill and tarragon.

Garlic Mayonnaise

METRIC/IMPERIAL
4 large cloves garlic
¼ teaspoon salt
pinch celery salt
2 teaspoons lemon juice
2 egg yolks
250 ml/scant ½ pint olive oil

This is a speciality in Spain where it is served with grilled fish and meat.
Peel and crush the garlic, then mix with the salts and lemon juice.
Place the egg yolks in a bowl with the garlic mixture. Whisking all the time, add the oil, drop by drop, until a thick sauce is formed. Do not add the oil quickly as the sauce will separate. If

the mayonnaise is too thick, thin it down with a little wine vinegar, but do not make it a pouring consistency.
Garlic mayonnaise may be made successfully in the liquidiser. Place the garlic mixture and egg yolks in the goblet, switch on to high speed and, in a steady stream, pour in the oil to form a thick sauce.
Serves 4–6

Cook's Tip
When making mayonnaise, have all the ingredients at room temperature. Do not use eggs straight from the refrigerator.

Sauces for Fondues and Grills

Piquant Tomato Sauce

METRIC/IMPERIAL
2 onions
3 tablespoons oil
3 tablespoons dry white wine
4 tomatoes
50 g/2 oz cooked ham
½ teaspoon garlic salt
2 teaspoons sugar
2 teaspoons grated horseradish
½ teaspoon white pepper

Peel and chop or grate the onions. Mix with the oil and wine and stir thoroughly. Peel the chop the tomatoes; cut the ham into strips. Stir the tomatoes and ham into the sauce, together with the salt, sugar, horseradish and pepper.

Serve this sauce with grilled fish, pork or lamb or with meat fondues.
Serves 4

Variation
Ready-made horseradish sauce made be used in place of the fresh horseradish.

> **Cook's Tip**
> For this recipe use large, fully-ripe tomatoes. The sauce may be prepared in advance and stored in the refrigerator.

Rosehip Sauce

METRIC/IMPERIAL
150 g/5 oz rosehips
250 ml/scant ½ pint single cream
3 tablespoons oil
6 tablespoons port
grated rind and juice of 1 lemon
1 teaspoon salt
2 teaspoons paprika pepper
pinch cinnamon
pinch ground cloves
2 teaspoons sugar
1 teaspoon Worcestershire sauce

Wash and slit the rosehips, then crush them in the liquidiser, or with a fork. Mix with the cream, oil and port.

Put the lemon rind and juice, the salt, paprika, cinnamon, cloves and sugar in a small bowl and mix together. Mix into the rose-hip mixture. Finally, stir in the Worcestershire sauce. Leave for 20 minutes for the flavours to blend.
Serve this sauce with grilled pork or veal, and with meat fondues.
Serves 6

Variation
If preferred the sauce may be sieved to remove the pips.

Soured Cream Sauce

METRIC/IMPERIAL
2 onions
6 dates
3 tablespoons capers
3 tablespoons wine vinegar
1 teaspoon sugar
3 tablespoons oil
250 ml/scant ½ pint soured
    cream
2 tablespoons chopped
    parsley

Peel and chop the onions; stone and chop the dates. Mix together the onions, dates, capers, vinegar and sugar and blend in the liquidiser until smooth. Transfer to a bowl and whisk in the oil, soured cream and parsley.

Serve this sauce with baked jacket potatoes, grilled pork chops or steaks, or meat fondues.
Serves 4–6

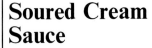

Cook's Tip
If you are unable to purchase soured cream in your area, add 3–4 drops of lemon juice to 150 ml (¼ pint) double cream and leave it at room temperature for 30 minutes.

Madeira Sauce

METRIC/IMPERIAL
50 g/2 oz smooth liver pâté
300 ml/½ pint stock
6 tablespoons Madeira
100 g/4 oz button mushrooms
3 tablespoons soured cream
1–2 tablespoons breadcrumbs
25 g/1 oz butter

Blend the liver pâté with the stock and bring to the boil. Stir in the Madeira and sliced mushrooms and simmer for 5 minutes. Add the soured cream, breadcrumbs and butter. Reheat, but do not boil. Serve this sauce with veal, venison, game, or kidney and bacon rolls.
Serves 4–6

Variation
If preferred the breadcrumbs and butter can be omitted and the sauce thickened with beurre manié. Knead together 25 g (1 oz) each of flour and butter to form a paste. Whisk small amounts of the flour and butter paste into the sauce and cook, stirring until thickened. Add the soured cream, but do not allow the sauce to boil.

Sauces for Fondues and Grills

Spicy Apple Sauce

METRIC/IMPERIAL
3 tablespoons raisins or
    sultanas
0·5 kg/1 lb cooking apples
1 teaspoon salt
½ teaspoon white pepper
pinch cayenne pepper
2 teaspoons cinnamon
1 tablespoon horseradish
    sauce (optional)
3 tablespoons cream

Soak the raisins or sultanas in hot water.
Peel, core and slice the apples and cook in a small amount of water until softened. Beat the cooked apple to a purée and mix with the drained raisins, the salt, peppers, cinnamon and horseradish sauce. Reheat and just before serving stir in the cream. Serve this sauce with grilled pork chops, gammon steaks or meat fondues.
Serves 4–6

Cook's Tip
Keep a few sultanas or raisins stored in a jar containing 2–3 tablespoons dry sherry. The dried fruit will be plump and impart a delicious flavour to dishes.

Blender Barbecue Sauce

METRIC/IMPERIAL
1 onion
4 tomatoes
1 clove garlic, crushed
300 ml/½ pint red wine
1 tablespoon wine vinegar
few drops Tabasco sauce
1 tablespoon brown sugar
1 teaspoon Worcestershire
    sauce
1 teaspoon black pepper
1 tablespoon redcurrant jelly
pinch salt

Chop the onion; peel and chop the tomatoes. Place in a pan with the remaining ingredients, bring to the boil and simmer for 10 minutes. Cool slightly, then blend in the liquidiser. Return to the pan, check the seasoning and reheat.
Serve this sauce with sausages, steaks or grilled chicken.
Serves 4

Cook's Tip
To crush a clove of garlic, sprinkle a little salt on to a board, add the peeled clove of garlic and crush it with the salt using the tip of a round-bladed knife.

77

Jellied Tomato Cocktail

METRIC/IMPERIAL
15 g/½ oz gelatine
2–3 tablespoons water
1 teaspoon celery salt
1 teaspoon white pepper
1 teaspoon Worcestershire
  sauce
pinch garlic salt
750 ml/1¼ pints tomato juice
Garnish
orange and lemon slices
2 tablespoons chopped chives

Soften the gelatine in cold water. Add the celery salt, pepper, Worcestershire sauce and garlic salt to the tomato juice and heat. Dissolve the gelatine in the heated tomato juice. Pour into a shallow container, cool and allow to set. Just before serving, cut the tomato jelly into cubes and arrange in chilled serving dishes. Garnish with orange and lemon slices and a sprinkling of chopped chives. Serve with the toast.
Serves 4

Cook's Tip
A speedy way of cutting chives is to snip them with a pair of scissors.

Cream Cheese Cup

METRIC/IMPERIAL
225 g/8 oz cream cheese
1 carton natural yogurt
little milk
few drops anchovy essence
½ teaspoon caraway seeds
1 teaspoon celery salt
½ teaspoon white pepper
2 eggs, hard-boiled
4 tomatoes
Garnish
2 tablespoons chopped herbs
2 teaspoons lump fish roe
  (mock caviar)
1 stick celery, chopped

Mix the cream cheese and yogurt together until smooth and creamy, adding a little milk if necessary to make a soft consistency. Add the anchovy essence, caraway seeds, celery salt and pepper. Shell the eggs and peel the tomatoes and cut into slices. Put the egg and tomato slices into four glasses. Spoon over the cream cheese mixture and garnish with the herbs, lump fish roe and chopped celery.
Serves 4

Cook's Tip
To peel tomatoes, nick the skins, plunge into boiling water and leave for 2–3 minutes. The skins will then easily peel off.

Lobster with Truffles

METRIC/IMPERIAL
*2 lobsters, each weighing
  about 0·5 kg/1–1¼ lb*
Garnish
*1 small can truffles
1 orange
parsley sprigs
1 egg, hard-boiled
1 tablespoon mayonnaise*

With a sharp knife cut each lobster in half down the middle joint mark, first towards the head, then towards the tail. Remove the claws from the body. Crack the claws with the flat side of the knife until they split, then shell them. Take the meat from the tail. From the inside of the lobster remove and discard the so-called gut – a dark-looking thread – with the tip of the knife. Cut the meat from the tail into slices.
Slice the truffles thinly and lay them on the top of the lobster alternately with the tail meat. Halve the orange and place the halves, cut side up, on a large dish. Arrange the body of the lobster on the dish with the claws beside it.
Halve the hard-boiled egg, remove the yolk and mix it with the mayonnaise. Pipe the mixture back into the egg whites and arrange on the dish with the lobster. Garnish with parsley. Serve with freshly made toast and butter.
Serves 6

Turbot Vols-au-Vent

METRIC/IMPERIAL
0·5 kg/1 lb turbot or other
    firm-fleshed white fish
150 g/5 oz butter
juice of 1 lemon or 2 table-
    spoons dry white wine
4 large or 8 small baked
    vol-au-vent cases
4 egg yolks
1 teaspoon paprika pepper
½ teaspoon salt

Skin the fish and cut into
pieces. Place in an oven-
proof dish with 25 g (1 oz)
of the butter and half the
lemon juice or wine. Cover
and cook in a cool oven
(150° C, 300° F, Gas
Mark 2) for 15 minutes.
Remove the bones and flake
the fish; keep warm. Heat
the vol-au-vent cases in the
oven.
In a bowl, whisk the egg
yolks with the remaining
lemon juice, the paprika,
salt and 4 tablespoons of
water; place the bowl over
a pan of hot water and
continue to whisk the
mixture until it begins to
thicken. Melt the remaining
butter and gradually add to
the whisked mixture.
Continue whisking until the
butter is completely
absorbed.
Fill the vol-au-vent cases
with the flaked fish and
pour over the sauce. Serve
any remaining sauce
separately.
Serves 4

Crab Salad

METRIC/IMPERIAL
225 g/8 oz canned or frozen
    crab meat, or prawns
juice of 1 lemon
1 teaspoon onion salt
2 eggs, hard-boiled
4 small tomatoes
1 small can pear halves,
    sliced
50 g/2 oz mustard pickles,
    chopped
50 g/2 oz canned button
    mushrooms, drained
2 tablespoons milk
4 tablespoons mayonnaise
3 tablespoons Drambuie
    (optional)
pinch chilli powder
150 ml/¼ pint double cream
1 tablespoon finely chopped
    gherkins
1 teaspoon paprika pepper
salt
2 heads chicory

Mix the crab meat with the
lemon juice and onion salt.
Shell and chop the eggs.
Peel and chop the tomatoes.
Mix the eggs, pears,
tomatoes, pickles and
mushrooms with the crab.
Mix the milk, mayonnaise,
liqueur and chilli powder
into the lightly whipped
cream. Add the gherkins
and season the mixture with
paprika and salt. Spoon
over the crab mixture.
Wash and halve the
chicory heads, removing
the coarse outer leaves.
Arrange the crab mixture
in the chicory leaves.
Serves 4–6

Celebration Starters

Spring Rolls

METRIC/IMPERIAL
3 tablespoons dried Chinese
mushrooms
275 g/10 oz lean pork, sliced
seasoned flour
225 g/8 oz canned bamboo
shoots, sliced
6 tablespoons oil
2–3 tablespoons soy sauce
2 teaspoons cornflour
275 g/10 oz flour
1 teaspoon salt
1 egg
1 egg white

Soak the mushrooms in hot
water then cut into thin
strips. Coat the meat in
seasoned flour.
Heat 2 tablespoons of the
oil in a frying pan and fry

the mushrooms and
bamboo shoots; add 1
teaspoon of the soy sauce,
cook for 3 minutes.
Fry the meat slices in 2
tablespoons of the oil, add
2 tablespoons water and the
remaining soy sauce and
stir in the vegetables.
Thicken with the blended
cornflour. Cool.
Sieve the flour and salt.
Mix with 7 tablespoons
boiling water. Add the egg
and knead to form a dough.
Roll out very thinly and cut
into eight squares. Put some
of the filling on each
square and make into
parcels; seal the edges with
egg white. Heat the
remaining oil and fry the
rolls until golden. Drain and
serve hot.
Serves 8

Danish Toasts

METRIC/IMPERIAL
1 apple
lemon juice
4 eggs, hard-boiled
125 ml/¼ pint double cream
2 teaspoons dry mustard
2 tablespoons mayonnaise
4 tablespoons chopped fresh
dill (optional)
4 slices toast
100 g/4 oz smoked salmon

Peel, core and slice the
apple; dip in lemon juice.
Shell and slice the hard-
boiled eggs. Lightly whip
the cream and mix with the
mustard, mayonnaise and
dill, if used.
Remove the crusts from the
slices of toast and arrange

the smoked salmon slices
on each piece. Top with an
apple slice and slices of
hard-boiled egg. Finally,
spoon over the mayonnaise
mixture.
Serves 4

Cook's Tip
If smoked salmon is
not available,
canned salmon mixed
with freshly ground
black pepper and a
squeeze of lemon
juice may be
substituted.

Palm Hearts with Salmon

METRIC/IMPERIAL
1 small can palm hearts
1 tablespoon wine vinegar
2 tablespoons oil
2 tablespoons white wine
8 thin slices smoked salmon
Sauce
4 tablespoons mayonnaise
1 teaspoon paprika pepper
½ teaspoon Tabasco sauce
1 tablespoon chopped green
  pepper
1 tablespoon chopped red
  pepper
1 tablespoon chopped chives
1 tablespoon chopped
  beetroot
2 tablespoons wine vinegar
2 tablespoons soured cream
½ teaspoon sugar
Garnish
1 tablespoon chopped truffles

Drain the palm hearts. Mix
the vinegar with the oil and
wine, pour over the palm
hearts and leave covered in
the refrigerator for 30
minutes to marinate.
Remove from the marinade
and wrap a slice of smoked
salmon around each palm
heart. Arrange on a dish
and sprinkle with the
chopped truffles.
Mix the ingredients for the
sauce together and serve
separately.
Serves 4

Cook's Tip
If canned palm hearts
are not available,
they may be substi-
tuted with canned or
fresh asparagus tips,
artichoke hearts or
celery.

Chilled Fish Salad

METRIC/IMPERIAL
4–6 soused herrings
2 apples
2 onions
1 canned pimiento, sliced
1 carton soured cream
1 carton natural yogurt
juice of ½ lemon
¼ teaspoon salt
pinch pepper
Garnish
onion rings

Soak the herrings in cold water for 1 hour. Drain and cut into strips. Peel and core the apples and slice thinly. Peel the onions and grate finely. Mix the herrings, apple slices, onions and pimiento together. Mix together the soured cream, yogurt, lemon juice and salt and pepper.
Arrange the fish salad in a serving bowl and chill in the refrigerator for 20 minutes. Spoon over the sauce and serve garnished with onion rings.
Serves 4–6

Special Stuffed Eggs

METRIC/IMPERIAL
8 eggs, hard-boiled
50 g/2 oz butter, melted
1 tablespoon mayonnaise
1 teaspoon curry powder
3 tablespoons cream cheese
1 tablespoon cream
4 stuffed olives
3–4 pieces canned or fresh peach
2 teaspoons lump fish roe (mock caviar)
8 glacé cherries

Halve the hard-boiled eggs. Melt half the butter. Remove the yolks from eight of the egg halves and mix with the melted butter, mayonnaise and curry powder. Chill for 30 minutes. Mix the yolks from the remaining halved eggs with the cream cheese and cream. Pipe into eight of the egg whites. Garnish with sliced olives, pieces of peach and the lump fish roe. Pipe the chilled curried mixture into the remaining egg halves and garnish with a glacé cherry.
Serves 4

Abalone Soup from China

METRIC/IMPERIAL
1 (150-g/5-oz) can abalones
1 teaspoon cornflour
1 teaspoon soy sauce
1 teaspoon dry sherry
500 ml/generous ¾ pint
  chicken stock
about 1 teaspoon salt
Garnish
chopped parsley

Abalones are large mussels available in dried, salted or canned form.
Drain and slice the abalones. Mix the cornflour with the soy sauce and sherry. Pour over the abalone slices and allow to marinate, for 30 minutes, turning from time to time.

Place the chicken stock and liquid from the can in a pan and bring to the boil. Add the abalone slices plus the marinade and simmer for 5 minutes. Season with salt. Serve sprinkled with chopped parsley.
Note If liked, pieces of cooked chicken may also be added to the soup.
Serves 4

Cook's Tip
If you have difficulty obtaining abalones use canned mussels. Do not allow the mussels to boil – they should just be allowed to heat through.

Spanish Tomato Broth

METRIC/IMPERIAL
4 small tomatoes
1 (425-g/15-oz) can
  consommé
2 tablespoons chopped
  chervil
4 tablespoons chopped
  parsley
salt and pepper
1–2 teaspoons paprika
  pepper
Garnish
tomato strips

Nick the tomato skins, plunge into boiling water, leave for 2–3 minutes, then peel off the skins and cut the tomatoes into quarters.
Put the consommé in a pan and bring almost to the boil, add the tomatoes, chervil and parsley. Simmer for 5 minutes. Add the seasoning and paprika. Serve garnished with tomato strips.
To make this soup more substantial serve it with rounds of brown bread, spread with pâté and sandwiched in pairs with lettuce. Top each sandwich with a slice of orange.
Serves 4

Cook's Tip
If fresh chervil is not available replace it with chopped fresh basil, which blends well with tomato dishes.

Rice Soup

METRIC/IMPERIAL
750 ml/1¼ pint beef stock
75 g/3 oz cooked rice
1 (425-g/15-oz) can turtle
    soup
100 g/4 oz cooked tongue
4 tablespoons flaked almonds
knob butter

Place the stock and rice in a pan, bring to the boil and simmer for 5 minutes. Rub through a fine sieve, or blend in a liquidiser. Return to the pan and reheat. Add the turtle soup and allow to heat. Cut the tongue into thin strips and divide between four soup bowls. Pour over the rice soup and sprinkle with flaked almonds. Add a knob of butter before serving.

Variation
Heat the cooked rice in 750 ml (1¼ pints) beef stock. Cut 150 g (5 oz) of cooked ham into thin strips and add to the soup and heat through. Peel and chop 4 small tomatoes. Divide between four bowls and pour over the hot soup. Sprinkle each serving with 1 tablespoon grated mild cheese.
Serves 4

Italian Tomato Soup

METRIC/IMPERIAL
2 stock cubes
6 tomatoes
25 g/1 oz butter
salt and pepper
1 tablespoon vinegar
4 eggs
Garnish
sieved hard-boiled egg yolk
4 tablespoons chopped
    parsley
2 tablespoons chopped chives

Dissolve the stock cubes in 1·5 litres (2¾ pints) water and bring to the boil. Nick the tomato skins, plunge into boiling water for 2–3 minutes and peel off the skins. Halve the tomatoes and squeeze out the pips. Add to the stock and leave on a low heat. Add the butter and allow it to melt. Season to taste.
In another pan bring 1 litre (1¾ pints) water to the boil with the vinegar. Break the eggs, one at a time, on to a wet saucer and let them slip into the water. When all 4 eggs are in the water lower the heat and simmer the eggs for 5 minutes, until they are firm.
Ladle the soup into deep soup plates. To each serving add some sieved hard-boiled egg yolk and a poached egg. Sprinkle with chopped parsley and chives.
Serves 4

Liver Dumpling Soup

METRIC/IMPERIAL
3 stale bread rolls
salt
6 tablespoons lukewarm milk
100 g/4 oz liver
1 onion
1½ tablespoons oil
2 tablespoons chopped
    parsley
1 egg
pinch white pepper
pinch dried marjoram
grated rind of ¼ lemon
1 litre/1¾ pints stock
Garnish
chopped chives

Cut the rolls into very thin slices. Sprinkle over ½ teaspoon of salt and pour over the lukewarm milk to

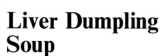

soften them.
Mince the liver finely. Peel the onion and chop finely. Heat the oil in a frying pan and fry the chopped onion until transparent; add the parsley. Mix together the onion, softened bread, liver, egg, pepper, marjoram, lemon rind and ½ teaspoon salt. With wet hands, form the mixture into balls about the size of a tomato. Bring the stock to the boil and simmer the liver dumplings, covered, for about 15 minutes. Spoon into soup bowls and serve garnished with chopped chives.
Serves 4

French Onion Soup

METRIC/IMPERIAL
6 large onions
100 g/4 oz butter
1 teaspoon pepper
1·5 litres/2¾ pints stock
2 slices bread, crusts
    removed
150 ml/¼ pint dry white wine
50 g/2 oz cheese, grated

Peel the onions and cut into thin rings. Heat 75 g (3 oz) of the butter in a pan. Add the onion rings and sauté until they are transparent. Add the pepper and stock, bring to the boil and simmer for 10 minutes. Meanwhile, heat the rest of the butter in a frying pan. Cut the bread into small

cubes and fry in the butter until brown. Drain on absorbent paper.
Stir the white wine into the soup, check the seasoning and reheat. Ladle into a tureen or individual soup bowls. Sprinkle the croûtons and the grated cheese over the top.
Serves 4

Cook's Tip
If you ladle the hot soup into ovenproof soup bowls you can sprinkle over the croûtons and grated cheese, dot with butter and heat under the grill until the cheese melts and turns golden brown.

Winter Soup

METRIC/IMPERIAL
900 ml/1½ pints milk
300 ml/½ pint chicken stock
1 bay leaf
6 peppercorns
3 cloves
1 small onion
100 g/4 oz pork sausagemeat
*2 tablespoons dry bread
    sauce mix*
½ teaspoon dried mixed herbs
2 teaspoons chopped parsley
salt and pepper
*40 g/1½ oz butter or
    margarine*
40 g/1½ oz plain flour
100 g/4 oz cooked peas

Place the milk and chicken stock in a saucepan with the bay leaf, peppercorns, cloves and peeled and quartered onion. Bring very slowly to the boil; remove from the heat and allow to infuse for 20 minutes. Meanwhile, make up the meat balls by mixing the sausagemeat, bread sauce mix, herbs, parsley, salt and pepper together. Make into eight even-sized balls. Strain the milk into a measuring jug. Melt the butter or margarine in a large pan, add the flour and cook for 1 minute then gradually blend in the strained milk. Bring to the boil stirring. Add the meatballs and simmer for 10–15 minutes. Stir in the cooked peas. Taste and adjust seasoning if necessary.
Serves 4

Gazpacho

METRIC/IMPERIAL
1 medium cucumber
350 g/12 oz tomatoes
1 red pepper
1 green pepper
2 large Spanish onions
*1 teaspoon finely chopped
    garlic*
*100 g/4 oz fresh white
    breadcrumbs*
*2 tablespoons red wine
    vinegar*
2 teaspoons salt
2 teaspoons olive oil
*½ teaspoon paprika pepper or
    chilli sauce*

Wash the cucumber, tomatoes and peppers. Chop the cucumber, peel and chop the tomatoes, seed and chop the peppers. Peel and chop the onions. In a basin mix the vegetables with the garlic, breadcrumbs, about 500 ml (generous ¾ pint) water, the vinegar and salt. Blend the mixture in a liquidiser. Whisk the oil and paprika or chilli sauce into the tomato mixture and leave, covered, in the refrigerator for 2 hours. Before serving, stir well and ladle into chilled soup bowls.
Serve with separate bowls of cubes of bread, finely chopped onion, chopped cucumber and chopped red and green peppers.
Serves 4

Chilled Cucumber Soup

METRIC/IMPERIAL
2 cartons natural yogurt
½ cucumber
½ teaspoon salt
¼ teaspoon black pepper
500 ml/generous ¾ pint buttermilk
500 ml/generous ¾ pint chicken stock
1 egg, hard-boiled
½ teaspoon paprika pepper

Place the yogurt in a basin. Peel and grate the cucumber. Mix the yogurt and grated cucumber, cover and leave in the refrigerator overnight.
The following day, add the salt and pepper, pour in the buttermilk and the stock and mix well. Shell the egg and chop finely. Ladle the soup into bowls and sprinkle with chopped egg and paprika.
Serves 4

Cook's Tip
If preferred, you may chop the cucumber, instead of grating it, and blend the soup in the liquidiser.

Princess Soup

METRIC/IMPERIAL
75 g/3 oz long-grain rice
450 g/1 lb cooked chicken
2 tomatoes
4 tablespoons chopped fresh herbs
salt and pepper
Garnish
chopped parsley

Cook the rice in boiling salted water until tender. Drain and rinse under cold running water. Mince or blend the chicken. Add 1 litre (1¾ pints) water to the minced chicken and simmer for 5 minutes. Meanwhile nick the skins of the tomatoes, plunge into boiling water for 2–3 minutes and peel; chop coarsely and stir into the chicken with the herbs. Season to taste and stir in the rice. Allow to heat through, then serve garnished with chopped parsley.
Serves 4

Variation
To the above soup, add 1 small can of asparagus tips, chopped, and 100 g (4 oz) frozen peas. Simmer for 5 minutes.

Cream of Vegetable Soup

METRIC/IMPERIAL
0·5–0·75 kg/1–1½ lb vege-
 tables as available
½ teaspoon salt
1 tablespoon butter
1–2 tablespoons flour
250 ml/scant ½ pint milk
2 egg yolks
6 tablespoons cream
salt and pepper
Garnish
chopped parsley

Suitable vegetables would
be cauliflower, white
asparagus stalks, or green
asparagus tips, peas,
tomatoes, carrots or
potatoes.
Prepare the vegetables
according to kind. Cook in
a small amount of salted
water until tender. Rub
through a sieve with the
vegetable water.
Melt the butter in a saucepan, add the flour and cook
for 2–3 minutes, stirring.
Gradually stir in the milk,
bring to the boil and add
the vegetable purée;
reheat.
Beat the egg yolks with the
cream. Put a few spoonfuls
of hot soup into the yolk
and cream mixture, remove
the soup from the heat and
stir the yolk and cream
mixture into the soup.
Season to taste and serve
sprinkled with chopped
parsley.
Serves 4

Cook's Tip
The flavour of this
vegetable soup may
be varied by stirring
in 2–3 tablespoons
chopped fresh herbs.
Grated cheese may be
sprinkled over, or the
soup may be topped
with a spoonful of
soured cream.

Devilled Prawns

METRIC/IMPERIAL
*about 0·75 kg/1½ lb frozen
    prawns, crab or scampi*
1 teaspoon garlic salt
1 teaspoon celery salt
100 g/4 oz long-grain rice
100 g/4 oz frozen peas
4 tablespoons oil
2 bay leaves
juice of 1 lemon
½ teaspoon cayenne pepper
Garnish
1 bay leaf

Defrost the shellfish, rinse
in cold water then drain
and pat dry with absorbent
paper. Sprinkle the garlic
and celery salts over the
shellfish. Cook the rice in
boiling salted water until
tender. Drain and keep
warm. Cook and drain the
peas; keep warm.
Heat the oil in a shallow
pan, place in the shellfish
very closely together in a
single layer and cook for 3
minutes. Turn over, place
the bay leaves on top and
sprinkle with the lemon
juice; dust evenly with the
cayenne pepper. Cook for
a further 3 minutes.
Mix the rice with the peas
and arrange around the
edge of a serving dish.
Remove the shellfish from
the pan, drain on absorbent
paper and spoon into the
centre of the rice. Serve
garnished with a bay leaf.
Serves 4

Danish Fishballs

METRIC/IMPERIAL
2 bread rolls
4 onions
*0·5 kg/1 lb white fish fillets,
    skinned*
2 tablespoons capers
few drops anchovy essence
4 tablespoons flour
2 eggs
150 ml/¼ pint single cream
*pinch each cayenne, nutmeg
    and curry powder*
1½ teaspoons salt
50 g/2 oz butter
750 ml/1¼ pints milk
¼ teaspoon white pepper
*1 tablespoon horseradish
    sauce*
*100 g/4 oz white bread-
    crumbs*
juice of ½ lemon

Soften the bread rolls in
water. Peel and quarter the
onions. Mince or blend the
fish, onions, capers,
anchovy essence and
softened bread. Place in a
bowl and mix with the
flour, eggs, cream and
seasonings.
Bring 1 litre (1¾ pints)
water and 1 teaspoon of the
salt to the boil. Form the
fish mixture into balls and
simmer for 5 minutes.
Remove and keep warm.
Melt the butter and add the
milk, the remaining salt
and pepper. Whisk in the
horseradish sauce, bread-
crumbs and lemon juice
until the mixture has
thickened. Serve with the
fishballs.
Serves 4

Stuffed Plaice

METRIC/IMPERIAL
4 whole small plaice
4 tablespoons chopped chives
50 g/2 oz butter
1 teaspoon salt
juice of 1 lemon
1 teaspoon Worcestershire
  sauce
1 teaspoon horseradish sauce
1 teaspoon dry mustard
1 teaspoon sugar
300 ml/½ pint dry white wine
4 tomatoes

Make a cut on the darker side of the plaice along the spine as far as the middle bone and make an incision to make a pocket.
Mix together the chives, butter, salt, lemon juice, Worcestershire sauce, horseradish sauce, mustard and sugar. Put the seasoned butter into the incisions in the plaice.
Place the fish in an oven-proof dish and pour in the wine. Nick the skins of the tomatoes and lay them on the plaice. Cover and cook in a moderately hot oven (200° C, 400° F, Gas Mark 6) for 15–20 minutes. Lift on to a heated serving dish and spoon over the cooking liquor.
Serves 4

Fishballs with Shrimps

METRIC/IMPERIAL
100 g/4 oz frozen shrimps
0·5 kg/1 lb white fish fillets,
  skinned
2 onions
salt
¼ teaspoon white pepper
2 teaspoons paprika pepper
2 eggs
150 ml/¼ pint single cream
300 ml/½ pint white sauce
150 ml/¼ pint dry white wine
4 tablespoons chopped dill

Defrost the shrimps and cut the fish fillets into small pieces. Peel and chop the onions. Place the fish pieces, salt, pepper, paprika, eggs, onions and cream in the liquidiser. Blend to a purée.
Bring a pan of salted water to the boil. Form the fish mixture into balls and drop into the boiling water, lower the heat and simmer for 5 minutes. Remove with a draining spoon and place in an ovenproof dish. Mix the shrimps with the white sauce, wine and dill and pour over the fishballs. Cover and cook in a moderately hot oven (200° C, 400° F, Gas Mark 6) for 20 minutes. Serve with boiled rice.
Serves 4

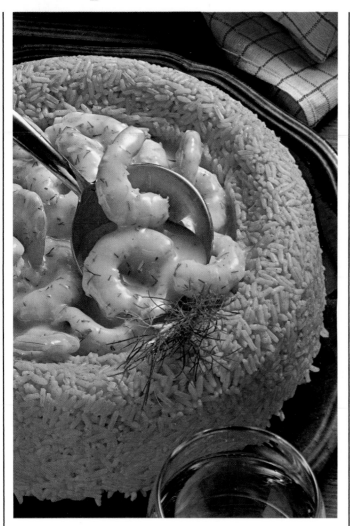

Prawns with Dill and Rice

METRIC/IMPERIAL

0·5 kg/1 lb frozen prawns
225 g/8 oz long-grain rice
6 tablespoons single cream
½ teaspoon salt
½ teaspoon sugar
½ teaspoon white pepper
25 g/1 oz butter
1 tablespoon flour
2 tablespoons chopped dill
6 tablespoons oil
1–2 teaspoons paprika
  pepper
Garnish
dill sprigs

Defrost the prawns. Cook
the rice in boiling salted
water until tender. Rinse in
cold water and drain.
Reheat in a colander,
placed over a pan of hot
water.
Heat the cream with 250 ml
(scant ½ pint) water, the
salt, sugar and pepper.
Work the butter into the
flour to form a paste and
whisk small amounts into
the sauce until it thickens.
Stir in the chopped dill and
prawns. Keep hot.
Mix the rice with the oil
and paprika and press into
an oiled ring mould. Turn
out on to a heated dish,
and spoon the prawn sauce
into the centre. Serve
garnished with dill sprigs.
Serves 4

Pike Balls

METRIC/IMPERIAL

1 kg/2 lb pike or carp
1 onion
150–300 ml/¼–½ pint dry
  white wine
1 bay leaf
4 eggs
pinch salt
pinch pepper
pinch grated nutmeg
150 g/5 oz butter
100 g/4 oz flour
250 ml/scant ½ pint milk

Skin and bone the fish.
Peel the onion. Place the
fish trimmings in a pan with
300 ml (½ pint) water, the
wine, onion and bay leaf.
Bring to the boil and
simmer for 15 minutes.
Strain and season the fish
stock.
Cut the fish into pieces and
purée in a liquidiser, or
chop finely. Separate the
yolks from the egg whites
and whisk the whites until
firm. Mix in the puréed
fish, season with salt,
pepper and nutmeg and
leave in refrigerator for
30 minutes. Make a thick
sauce with the butter, flour
and milk. Cool, then
gradually add the egg yolks
and fish purée. Shape the
mixture into balls and cook
in the fish stock for 15
minutes. Remove with a
draining spoon and serve
with spinach and buttered
potatoes.
Serves 4

Fish Specialities

Trout with Almonds

METRIC/IMPERIAL
4 trout
150 ml/¼ pint milk
1 teaspoon salt
3 tablespoons flour
100 g/4 oz butter
25 g/1 oz flaked almonds
Garnish
tomato wedges
lemon wedges
sprigs parsley

Marinate the trout in the milk and salt for 10 minutes. Remove and roll in the flour. Melt 75 g (3 oz) of the butter in a frying pan and cook the trout for 4–6 minutes over a medium heat. Place on a heated dish and keep warm. Add the remaining butter to the pan and fry the flaked almonds until they are golden brown. Scatter over the trout. Garnish with the tomato and lemon wedges and parsley.
Serves 4

Cook's Tip
An easy way to coat the fish in flour is to place the flour in a polythene bag with one trout and shake the bag until the fish is evenly coated.

Sweet and Sour Fish with Mushrooms

METRIC/IMPERIAL
2 tablespoons dried Chinese mushrooms
0·5 kg/1–1¼ lb cod fillets
1 tablespoon monosodium glutamate
2 tablespoons soy sauce
2 onions
2 tablespoons cornflour
1 tablespoon flour
1 litre/1¾ pints oil
6 tablespoons tomato ketchup
2 tablespoons wine vinegar
4 teaspoons sugar

Soak the mushrooms in hot water. Cut the fish into 3-cm (1½-inch) cubes. Sprinkle over the monosodium glutamate and soy sauce and leave for 10 minutes.
Peel and slice the onions; drain the mushrooms. Mix 1 tablespoon of the cornflour with the flour. Roll the fish cubes in the flour mixture. Heat the oil and fry the fish cubes in the oil until golden brown. Drain on absorbent paper and keep warm. Fry the onion slices in 2 tablespoons oil in a frying pan. Add the mushrooms, heat through and mix with the fish cubes. Mix the ketchup, vinegar, sugar and remaining cornflour together. Cook, stirring, over a moderate heat until the sauce thickens. Serve separately.
Serves 4

Fillets in Batter

METRIC/IMPERIAL
0·75 kg/1½ lb white fish
   fillets
1½ teaspoons salt
2 teaspoons paprika pepper
½ teaspoon white pepper
few drops Angostura bitters
2 tomatoes
100 g/4 oz cheese, sliced
4 tablespoons flour
2 eggs
100 g/4 oz butter

Cut each fillet into 3–4 pieces, making 6 or 8 portions. Dust each piece with salt, paprika pepper and white pepper and sprinkle over a few drops of Angostura bitters. Nick the tomato skins, plunge into boiling water for 1 minute; peel off the skins and cut into thick slices.
Place a slice of cheese and tomato on 3 or 4 of the fish pieces. Cover each with another piece of fish, making a sandwich. Press together and secure with a wooden cocktail stick. Sieve the flour into a bowl and make a thick batter with the eggs and a little water.
Melt the butter in a pan. Dip the prepared fish in the batter and cook in the butter until golden brown, turning at least twice during cooking. Do not turn the heat up too high otherwise the fish will not be cooked. Drain on absorbent paper and serve with potato salad.
Serves 4

Liver Sausage-Stuffed Plaice

METRIC/IMPERIAL
8 frozen plaice fillets
50 g/2 oz liver sausage
4 tablespoons chopped
   parsley
4 tablespoons grated cheese
75 g/3 oz butter

Defrost the plaice. Pound the liver sausage to a smooth paste. Place the fillets on a board and spread each one with some liver sausage, then sprinkle on the parsley and cheese. Sandwich two fillets with the sausage sides together, and secure with a wooden cocktail stick. Heat the butter in a frying pan and brown the fish on each side.

Drain on absorbent paper and serve at once.
Serves 4

Cook's Tip
Save scraps of cheese, grate them finely and store in an airtight container in the refrigerator. Different varieties of cheese may be mixed together to give a good flavour.

Prawns with Vegetables

METRIC/IMPERIAL
0·5 kg/1¼ lb frozen prawns
1 leek
4 tablespoons oil
100 g/4 oz frozen peas
½ teaspoon cayenne pepper
½ teaspoon celery salt
1 teaspoon ground ginger
1 teaspoon sugar

Defrost the prawns, then rinse in cold water and pat dry with absorbent paper. Clean, trim and finely slice the leek. Heat the oil in a pan and cook the prawns until they are pale brown. Add the leek and peas and cook for a further 5 minutes. Sprinkle with the cayenne pepper, celery salt, ginger and sugar. Turn into a heated dish and serve.
Serves 4

Variation
Frozen scampi may be used in place of the prawns.

Cook's Tip
This dish doesn't benefit by being kept hot and should be served immediately it is cooked.

Haddock in Mustard Sauce

METRIC/IMPERIAL
1 kg/2 lb haddock steaks
1 teaspoon paprika pepper
1 teaspoon salt
½ teaspoon white pepper
100 g/4 oz butter
4 tablespoons chopped parsley
2 ripe bananas
25 g/1 oz hazelnuts
25 g/1 oz currants
3 tablespoons flour
500 ml/generous ¾ pint milk
100 g/4 oz mild mustard
1 tablespoon sugar
juice of ½ lemon
few drops Tabasco sauce
4 tablespoons dry white wine
Garnish
parsley sprigs

Dust the haddock steaks with the paprika, salt and pepper and place in an ovenproof dish. Dot with half the butter and sprinkle over the parsley. Slice the bananas and place on top. Coarsely chop the hazelnuts; wash the currants. Melt the remaining butter in a saucepan, stir in the flour and lightly brown; add the milk and stir until thickened. Then stir in the mustard, sugar, lemon juice, Tabasco sauce, nuts and currants. Pour the sauce to cover the fish. Pour over the wine. Cook in a cool oven (150° C, 300° F, Gas Mark 2) for 25–30 minutes. Garnish with parsley and serve with buttered potatoes.
Serves 4

Ragoût of Carp

METRIC/IMPERIAL
*1 carp, weighing 0·75 kg/
    1¾ lb*
6 medium onions
1 clove garlic
salt
6 tablespoons oil
flour
2 tablespoons paprika pepper
1 teaspoon beef extract
100 g/4 oz cooked noodles
4 tablespoons soured cream

Ask the fishmonger to gut the carp.
Thoroughly clean the inside of the fish under running water. Cut thick slices across the body and then cut them in half on the middle bone. Peel the onions and slice thinly. Peel the garlic and crush with a little salt with the tip of a knife. Heat the oil in a flameproof casserole. Lightly brown the onions, stirring all the time. Add the crushed garlic. Roll the pieces of carp in a little flour, place on top of the onions and sprinkle over the paprika. Cover with a lid and cook for 25 minutes. Stir in the beef extract and check the seasoning. Arrange the noodles on four serving plates and spoon over the ragoût. Top with a spoonful of soured cream. Serve with creamed potatoes.
Serves 4

Stuffed Herrings

METRIC/IMPERIAL
4 herrings
4 slices bread
150 ml/¼ pint milk
2 eggs
½ teaspoon salt
½ stock cube
½ teaspoon black pepper
½ teaspoon cayenne pepper
*8 tablespoons chopped
    parsley*
25 g/1 oz butter, melted
150 ml/¼ pint oil
Garnish
parsley sprig

Score the herrings. Slit open on the under side, gut and wash thoroughly in cold water. Dry with absorbent paper.
Cut the bread into cubes and heat the milk. Put the bread in a bowl with the heated milk to soften it. Beat in the eggs and seasonings. Lastly add the parsley and melted butter. Use to stuff the herrings. Brush the grill pan and the herrings with oil and cook under a moderate heat for 12–15 minutes. Serve garnished with parsley, and a potato salad sprinkled with chopped chives.
Serves 4

Stuffed Fish Fillets

METRIC/IMPERIAL
*0·75 kg/1¼ lb white fish
    fillets*
juice of 1 lemon
½ teaspoon salt
1 onion
4 tomatoes
few sprigs rosemary
4 thin slices hard cheese
Garnish
rosemary sprigs
lemon wedges

Wash the fillets under cold running water and pat dry with absorbent paper. Squeeze the lemon juice over the fillets and rub in the salt. Peel the onion and slice into rings.
Nick the skins of the tomatoes, plunge into boiling water, leave for 2–3 minutes and then peel. Cut into thick slices.
Place half the fillets in an ovenproof dish. Then place the onion rings, sliced tomatoes, rosemary and cheese slices on top and cover with the remaining fillets. Cover and cook in a hot oven (220° C, 425° F, Gas Mark 7) for 15–20 minutes.
Arrange the cooked fish on a dish and garnish with rosemary and lemon wedges. Serve with cooked long-grain rice, and peppers and corn.
Serves 4

Cook's Tip
The best type of cheese to use for this recipe is either Gruyère or Gouda. They are both mildly flavoured cheeses and go particularly well with fish.

Kebabs

Fish Kebabs

METRIC/IMPERIAL
225 g/8 oz each of fresh eel,
perch and sole
1 small packet frozen plaice
2½ teaspoons salt
½ teaspoon white pepper
2 teaspoons dry mustard
1 teaspoon Worcestershire
sauce
few drops Tabasco sauce
½ teaspoon caraway seeds
100 g/4 oz shallots
¼ cucumber
225 g/8 oz long-grain rice
100 g/4 oz button mushrooms
100 g/4 oz bacon rashers
100 g/4 oz vegetable fat

Skin and bone the eel.
Defrost the plaice. Wash all
the fish, cut into cubes
(not too small) and put in a
bowl. Add the salt, pepper,
mustard, Worcestershire
sauce, Tabasco sauce and
caraway seeds; toss the
fish cubes in the seasoning.
Peel and halve the shallots.
Slice the unpeeled cucumber
thickly. Cook the rice in
boiling salted water until
tender, Rinse, drain and
keep warm.
Meanwhile, remove the
fish from the marinade and
arrange alternately with the
cucumber slices, shallots,
mushrooms and bacon
slices, made into rolls, on
skewers. Heat the fat in a
frying pan. Add the kebabs
and fry for 10 minutes on
each side. Drain on
absorbent paper and serve
with the rice.
Serves 4

Beef Kebabs

METRIC/IMPERIAL
2 teaspoons seasoned salt
1 teaspoon pepper
2 tablespoons chopped dill
16 very thin slices beef fillet
2 large leeks
1 red pepper
1 cucumber
100 g/4 oz streaky bacon
oil for deep frying

Mix together the seasoned
salt, pepper and dill and
rub over the beef and allow
the flavours to penetrate.
Meanwhile, wash the leeks
and seed the pepper. Cut the
leek, pepper, cucumber and
the bacon into 16 narrow
strips as long as the pieces
of meat and put one on
each slice. Roll up and
thread on to skewers.
Heat the oil in a deep pan
and cook the beef rolls for
5 minutes, turning occasionally. Drain on absorbent
paper and arrange on a
serving dish.
Serve with a green salad.
Serves 4

Cook's Tip
To test the tempera-
ture of the oil for
deep frying, drop in a
cube of white bread.
If the oil is the
correct temperature,
the bread will turn
golden brown in
1 minute.

Aubergines in Batter

METRIC/IMPERIAL
3 aubergines
1 teaspoon paprika pepper
100 g/4 oz flour
4 tablespoons cream cheese
2 eggs
2 tablespoons grated cheese
2 apples
1 teaspoon celery salt
1 litre/1¾ pints oil
*4 tablespoons chopped
   parsley*
Garnish
tomato wedge
parsley sprig

Peel the aubergines thickly
and cut into bite-sized
pieces.
Make a thick batter with the
paprika, flour, the cream
cheese, 4 tablespoons cold
water, the eggs and the
grated cheese. Peel, core
and slice the apples.
Sprinkle the celery salt
over the apple slices and
aubergine pieces.
Heat the oil in a deep pan.
Dip the aubergines and
apple slices in the batter;
thread several pieces
alternately on to skewers
and deep fry in the heated
oil. Remove the fried
kebabs with a draining
spoon, sprinkle immediately
with the chopped parsley
and keep warm until all the
kebabs are cooked.
Serve garnished with tomato
and parsley.
Serves 4

Serbian Kebabs

METRIC/IMPERIAL
0·5 kg/1 lb minced beef
2 pork chipolata sausages
1 egg
2 large onions
1 green pepper
1 teaspoon garlic salt
2 teaspoons salt
4 teaspoons paprika pepper
1 teaspoon black pepper
pinch cayenne pepper
2 tablespoons breadcrumbs
2 pickled cucumbers
3 tablespoons oil

Mix the minced beef and
sausages (squeezed out of
their skins) with the egg.
Peel and finely dice the
onions. Halve, seed and
chop the pepper.

Mix the onions and pepper
with the meat. Add the
garlic salt, salt, paprika
pepper and cayenne. With
floured hands, form the
mixture into small sausage
shapes and roll in the
breadcrumbs.
Slice the cucumbers thickly.
Push the sausages alter-
nately with the cucumber
slices on to skewers and
brush with the oil. Grill for
7 minutes, turning occa-
sionally.
Serve with tomato sauce
and potatoes baked in foil
and topped with herb
butter.
Serves 4

Kebabs

Chicken Kebabs

METRIC/IMPERIAL
0·5 kg/1 lb chicken breasts
1 teaspoon celery salt
½ teaspoon garlic salt
½ teaspoon allspice
2 tablespoons oil
1 orange
6 tablespoons mayonnaise
6 tablespoons soured cream
2 teaspoons dry mustard

Cut the chicken breasts into pieces about 5 cm (2 inches) wide. Mix together the celery salt, garlic salt and allspice and rub over the chicken pieces.
Push these slices on to skewers; place in an oven-proof dish and sprinkle over the oil. Cook the kebabs in a hot oven (220° C, 425° F, Gas Mark 7), or under a hot grill, for 8 minutes.
Meanwhile, peel the orange, cut into small pieces and remove the pips. Mix the mayonnaise with the soured cream and mustard. Stir in the orange slices.
Serve with the kebabs.
Serves 4

Cook's Tip
Chicken breasts are available from some supermarkets. If using frozen chicken breasts allow them to defrost completely before preparing the recipe.

Swiss Liver Kebabs

METRIC/IMPERIAL
0·5 kg/1 lb pig's liver
100 g/4 oz streaky bacon
2 small onions
4 tablespoons oil
1 teaspoon salt
2 teaspoons paprika pepper
4 button mushrooms
2 tomatoes
4 tablespoons tomato purée
150 ml/¼ pint stock
50 g/2 oz butter
1 tablespoon flour

Chop the liver into small pieces. Cut the bacon into pieces the same size as the liver and peel and quarter the onions. Heat the oil in a frying pan. Dust the liver with the salt and paprika and cook for 4 minutes, turning constantly. Remove. Fry the bacon until it looks transparent, the onions, mushrooms and halved tomatoes.
Thread the prepared pieces of food on to skewers, arranging them colourfully. Keep hot. In a bowl mix the tomato purée with the stock. Bring to the boil. Work the butter into the flour to form a paste and whisk into the stock until a thick, smooth sauce is formed. Season, and pour over the kebabs. Serve with rice.
Serves 4

Scampi Kebabs

METRIC/IMPERIAL
225 g/8 oz frozen scampi
¼ cucumber
100 g/4 oz smoked eel
100-g/4-oz piece streaky
 bacon
12 stuffed olives
100 g/4 oz canned button
 mushrooms
2 teaspoons paprika pepper
½ teaspoon salt
¼ teaspoon white pepper
pinch monosodium glutamate
1 teaspoon dill powder
6 tablespoons oil

Defrost the scampi, rinse quickly in cold water and drain. Slice the cucumber thickly. Skin the eel, remove the bones and cut into bite-sized pieces. Cube the bacon.
Thread the scampi on to skewers with the olives, cucumber slices, eel, bacon and mushrooms. Mix the paprika, salt, white pepper, monosodium glutamate and dill together and sprinkle over the kebabs, turning them all the time so that they are seasoned all over. Leave in the refrigerator for 30 minutes. Place the kebabs in a shallow oven-proof dish, pour over the oil and cook in a moderately hot oven (200° C, 400° F, Gas Mark 6) for 10–15 minutes.
Serves 4

Caucasian Kebabs

METRIC/IMPERIAL
0·5 kg/1 lb rump steak
½ teaspoon salt
½ teaspoon meat tenderising
 salt
4 onions
2 teaspoons paprika pepper
½ teaspoon black pepper
12 button mushrooms
150 ml/¼ pint oil
Garnish
strips red pepper
strips onion

Cut the meat into even bite-sized cubes. Mix the salt and the meat tenderiser together and rub all over the meat cubes. Leave for 15 minutes.
Meanwhile, peel and quarter onions. Rub the paprika into the onions and sprinkle the black pepper on the mushrooms. Thread the meat cubes, onions and mushrooms on to skewers. Brush the kebabs with oil and place on the grill pan. Grill under a moderate grill for 8 minutes, turning to cook them evenly. Serve on a bed of turmeric-flavoured rice and garnish with pepper and onion strips.
Serves 4

Steaks

Fillet Steak Cussy

METRIC/IMPERIAL
4 thick fillet steaks
2 tablespoons oil
1 teaspoon coarsely ground
  black pepper
1–2 teaspoons paprika
  pepper
1 can artichoke hearts
100 g/4 oz unsweetened
  chestnut purée
3–4 tablespoons oil
100 g/4 oz button mush-
  rooms
5 tablespoons Madeira
1 teaspoon salt
½ teaspoon garlic salt
Garnish
chopped parsley

Trim the steaks if necessary.
Spoon over the oil, sprinkle
with black pepper and
paprika. Leave to marinate
in the refrigerator for 2
hours.
Fill the centre of each
artichoke with some
chestnut purée and heat
gently in the liquid from the
can for 10 minutes.
Heat the oil in a frying pan
and fry the steaks for 3
minutes on each side.
Remove and keep warm.
Add the mushrooms and
fry for 1–2 minutes.
Sprinkle over the steaks.
Add the Madeira, the salt
and garlic salt to the pan
and cook for 30 seconds;
pour over the steaks.
Arrange a filled artichoke
on each steak and serve
garnished with chopped
parsley.
Serves 4

Wine-Merchant's Beefsteak

METRIC/IMPERIAL
225 g/8 oz butter
1 onion, cut into rings
325 ml/generous ½ pint red
  wine
½ bay leaf
¼ teaspoon dried thyme
4 sprigs parsley
2 teaspoons beef extract
4 rump steaks
2 tablespoons vegetable oil
1 teaspoon salt
freshly ground black pepper

Melt 25 g (1 oz) of the
butter, over a moderate
heat, in a frying pan. When
the butter stops bubbling
fry the onions for 2 minutes,
until they become trans-
parent. Pour on the red
wine and simmer for 15
minutes with the bay leaf,
thyme and parsley.
Dissolve the meat extract
in 2 tablespoons warm
water and stir into the
sauce. Soften 100 g (4 oz)
of the butter and stir into
the sauce.
Fry the steaks in the
remaining butter and the
oil for 1 minute on each
side to seal them, then
again for 1½ minutes on
each side. Place on a warm
dish and season with salt
and pepper. Pour the wine
sauce into the steak pan.
Stir round to mix in the
sediment, then serve with
the steaks. Serve with peas
and potatoes.
Serves 4

Entrecôte Westmorland

METRIC/IMPERIAL
1 small cauliflower
4 entrecôte steaks
1½ teaspoons seasoned salt
1 teaspoon black pepper
1 teaspoon dry mustard
450 ml/¾ pint oil
1 teaspoon salt
Sauce
300 ml/½ pint brown sauce
4 teaspoons mild mustard
4 tablespoons white wine
4 tablespoons brandy
Garnish
sprig parsley

Wash the cauliflower and break into sprigs.
Trim the steaks and rub with the salt, pepper and mustard.

Heat 4 tablespoons of the oil in a frying pan and fry the steaks for 3 minutes on each side. Remove and keep warm.
Heat the rest of the oil in a saucepan and cook the cauliflower sprigs for 6 minutes, until golden brown. Drain on absorbent paper and sprinkle with salt. Place the cauliflower with the steaks.
Heat the sauce, add the mustard, wine and the brandy and cook for 2 minutes. Pour over the steaks and serve with the cauliflower sprigs. Garnish with parsley.
Serves 4

Sirloin Steaks on Pastry

METRIC/IMPERIAL
350 g/12 oz frozen puff
  pastry
3 egg yolks
4 carrots, diced
2 sticks celery, chopped
225 g/8 oz asparagus
2 (0·5-kg/1-lb) sirloin
  steaks
6 tablespoons oil
1½ teaspoons salt
1 teaspoon black pepper
100 g/4 oz butter
4 tablespoons brandy
2 egg yolks
4 tablespoons double cream
Garnish
1 canned truffle (optional)

Defrost the pastry and roll out until 3 mm (⅛ inch)

thick. Use to line two tins, about the size of each steak. Brush with egg yolk and bake in a moderately hot oven (200° C, 400° F, Gas Mark 6) for 20 minutes.
Cook the prepared vegetables in a little salted water. Drain and keep hot.
Trim the steaks and fry in the heated oil for 5–8 minutes on each side. Remove, season and keep warm. Add the butter to the pan. Pour the brandy into the melted butter, mix the egg yolks with the cream and stir into the pan. Reheat (but do not boil). Arrange each steak on a pastry round. Top with the vegetables and garnish with grated truffle, if liked. Serve the sauce separately.
Serves 4

Rump Steak Melba

METRIC/IMPERIAL
4 medium tomatoes
8 tablespoons grated cheese
4 rump steaks
4 tablespoons oil
1 teaspoon salt
½ teaspoon black pepper
4 tablespoons port
Garnish
lettuce leaves

Cut the tomatoes in half, hollow out and fill with the grated cheese and brown under the grill.
Fry the steaks in the heated oil for 3 minutes on each side, lowering the heat after 1 minute. Season with salt and pepper and keep warm. Stir the port into the frying pan, scraping up all the sediment. Bring to the boil and pour into a sauce boat. Arrange the steaks on a serving dish and garnish with lettuce leaves and the tomatoes.
Serve the sauce separately.
Serves 4

Cook's Tip
When frying steaks, they should be sealed on each side over a high heat for 1 minute and the heat then lowered until the steaks are cooked to your liking.

Rump Steak Mirabeau

METRIC/IMPERIAL
4 rump steaks
75 g/3 oz butter
6 teaspoons anchovy paste or few drops anchovy essence
juice of 1 lemon
6 stuffed olives
4 tablespoons oil
1 teaspoon salt
½ teaspoon ground black pepper
8 anchovy fillets

Trim the steaks.
Beat 50 g (2 oz) butter (which should be at room temperature) with the anchovy paste and lemon juice. Chill.
Slice the olives. Heat the oil in a pan and fry the steaks for 3 minutes on each side. Place on a serving dish, season with salt and pepper and keep warm.
Melt the rest of the butter in the pan, scrape up the sediment and pour over the steaks. Arrange the anchovy fillets, crosswise, and olives on top. Serve slices of the anchovy butter separately. Serve with chipped potatoes.
Serves 4

Cook's Tip
Rump steaks are considered to be the best-flavoured steaks. Choose steaks with about 5 mm (¼ inch) of fat around the edge and no gristle.

Tournedos Helder

METRIC/IMPERIAL
1 teaspoon black pepper
1 teaspoon garlic salt
4 fillet steaks
4 tomatoes
75 g/3 oz butter
1 teaspoon salt
½ teaspoon white pepper
*2 tablespoons chopped
    parsley*
4 tablespoons oil

Press the black pepper and garlic salt on to each side of the steaks.
Nick the skins of the tomatoes, plunge them into boiling water for 2–3 minutes and peel off the skins. Cut into quarters and squeeze out the juice and the seeds. Chop the flesh and put in a saucepan with the butter, salt, white pepper and parsley; cook for 5 minutes, over a moderate heat, stirring occasionally.
Heat the oil in a frying pan and fry the steaks over a high heat for 2–3 minutes on each side. Arrange the steaks on a heated dish and spoon the tomato mixture on top.
As an accompanying vegetable, serve asparagus tips coated with a cheese sauce.
Serves 4

Entrecôte Meyerbeer

METRIC/IMPERIAL
1 lamb's kidney
4 entrecôte steaks
4 tablespoons oil
1 teaspoon garlic salt
1 teaspoon black pepper
1 teaspoon salt
6 tablespoons Madeira
1 beef stock cube
4 tablespoons cream
*2 tablespoons chopped
    canned truffles (optional)*
Garnish
parsley sprig

Soak the kidney in water for 1 hour. Trim the steaks.
Heat the oil in a frying pan and fry the steaks for 2 minutes on each side, remove and season with the garlic salt and pepper; keep warm.
Slice the kidney thinly, sprinkle with salt and fry for 1 minute in the frying pan. Arrange on the steaks.
Stir the Madeira into the sediment in the frying pan and dissolve the stock cube in it. Bring to the boil. Remove from the heat and stir in the cream and truffles, if used. Spoon over the steaks. Serve garnished with parsley.
Serves 4

Classic Steaks

METRIC/IMPERIAL
2 rump steaks
2 tablespoons oil
salt
ground black pepper
Garnish
few sliced mushrooms or onions
chopped parsley

Trim the steaks.
Heat the oil in a frying pan and fry the steaks for 1 minute on each side. Reduce the heat and fry for a further 3 minutes on each side. (If you prefer your steaks rare, cook them for a total of 2–3 minutes.) Season with salt and pepper. Remove and keep warm. Add the sliced mushrooms or onions and cook until softened. Spoon over the steaks and sprinkle with chopped parsley. Serve with a selection of vegetables in season, or a salad.
Serves 2

Variation
Tournedos are cut from the best part of the fillet. These steaks are very tender. Brush the steaks with melted butter or oil, season and grill under a moderate heat for about 3 minutes on each side. Serve with herb butter and corn-on-the-cob. *Porterhouse steaks* are cut from the chump end of the sirloin, containing part of the fillet. Brush the steaks with oil and grill for 9–12 minutes on each side.

Cook's Tip
The cooking times given for the steaks will give a medium steak. If you prefer a rare or well done steak adjust the times accordingly.

Grilled Steak with Herbs

METRIC/IMPERIAL
1–2 cloves garlic
4 thick rump steaks
1 tablespoon finely chopped
  onion
1 teaspoon each salt and
  pepper
6 tablespoons dry sherry
1 egg, hard-boiled
4 tablespoons chopped fresh
  herbs (chives, parsley,
  dill)
2 teaspoons dry mustard
100 g/4 oz butter

Peel and crush the cloves of garlic and press into the steaks. Place the steaks in a shallow dish, sprinkle over the onions, seasoning and sherry and leave to marinate in a cool place for up to 4 hours.
Chop the hard-boiled egg and mix with the herbs, mustard and butter. Remove the steaks from the marinade and cook under a pre-heated grill for 7–9 minutes, brushing with the marinade, until cooked to your liking. Spread each steak with the herb butter and serve with grilled tomatoes.
Serves 4

Cook's Tip
Before grilling whole tomatoes, make a cross in the skins to prevent the tomatoes bursting during cooking.

Fillet Steak Verdi

METRIC/IMPERIAL
3 large onions
5 tablespoons oil
1 tablespoon flour
1 stock cube
6 tablespoons cream
4 slices liver pâté
1 teaspoon salt
½ teaspoon white pepper
4 fillet steaks
Garnish
parsley

Slice the onions. Heat 3 tablespoons of the oil in a pan and fry the onions until softened. Stir in the flour and cook for 2–3 minutes. Dissolve the stock cube in 300 ml (½ pint) water.
Gradually add the stock to the pan, stirring until the mixture has thickened. Stir in the cream and leave on a low heat.
Heat the remaining oil in a separate pan and cook the pâté until browned on both sides. Remove and keep warm. Season the steaks and cook in the pan for about 3 minutes on each side. Arrange the steaks in a heatproof dish, top each one with a slice of pâté, then spoon over the sauce. Quickly brown under a hot grill and serve garnished with parsley.
Serves 4

Steaks

Steaks Flambé

METRIC/IMPERIAL
2 peppers
100 g/4 oz mushrooms
6 large tomatoes
4 tablespoons oil
4 fillet steaks
100 g/4 oz butter
1 teaspoon each salt, garlic salt and black pepper
4 tablespoons brandy

Cut the peppers in half and remove the stalk and the seeds; slice the mushrooms; peel and chop the tomatoes. Heat the oil in a pan and fry the steaks on a medium heat for 3 minutes on each side.
In a separate pan, heat the butter and sauté the tomatoes with ½ teaspoon each of salt, garlic salt and pepper. Add the peppers and mushrooms and cook until softened.
Add the remaining seasoning to the steaks. Pour over the brandy and ignite. Shake the pan backwards and forwards over the heat, until the flames die down. Arrange the steaks on a serving dish and pour over the cooking liquor. Arrange the vegetables around the steaks.
Serves 4

Variation
100 g (4 oz) cooked French beans may be sautéed with the other vegetables.

Tournedos Rossini

METRIC/IMPERIAL
1 teaspoon black pepper
4 fillet steaks
8 thin bacon rashers
4 tablespoons oil
1 teaspoon salt
½ teaspoon garlic salt
6 tablespoons Madeira
100 g/4 oz liver pâté

Rub the pepper into the fillet steaks. Put 2 bacon rashers around each steak and secure with thread. Heat the oil in a pan and fry the steaks on a medium heat for 3 minutes on each side; take out of the pan and remove the thread and bacon. Season the steaks with salt and garlic salt, place on a dish and keep warm. Pour off any excess oil from the pan and add the Madeira. Stir round and boil for 30 seconds, then pour over the steaks. Top the steaks with 1 or 2 slices of pâté.
Serve with peas and French fried potatoes.
Serves 4

Cook's Tip
When purchasing fillet steaks choose ones which have tiny flecks of fat running through the lean part. This is a good indication that the steaks will cook well.

Gammon Steaks with Mustard

METRIC/IMPERIAL
1 tablespoon wine vinegar
2 tablespoons oil
pinch salt
ground black pepper
1 teaspoon made mustard
2 gammon steaks
1 small can button mush-
  rooms
1 tablespoon finely chopped
  parsley

Mix the wine vinegar with 1 tablespoon of the oil, the salt, pepper and mustard. Trim the steaks and snip the fat around the edge to prevent the gammon curling during cooking. Spread this mixture on both sides of the gammon and leave for 1 hour.
Heat the rest of the oil in a frying pan. Remove the steaks from the marinade and, without letting them drain, cook in the hot oil for 5 minutes on each side, until browned and crisp. Remove and keep warm. Drain and slice the mush-rooms and add to the pan with the leftover marinade and the parsley. Stir round to absorb the sediment and heat the mushrooms. Arrange the gammon on a serving dish and spoon over the mushroom mixture. Serve with creamed potatoes and peas.
Serves 2

Balkan Chops

METRIC/IMPERIAL
3 medium-sized onions
3 red peppers
1 (226-g/8-oz) can sweetcorn
6 tablespoons olive oil
1 teaspoon salt
½ teaspoon cayenne pepper
¼ teaspoon garlic salt
¼ teaspoon paprika pepper
¼ teaspoon celery salt
4 lamb or veal chops

Peel and dice the onions. Seed the peppers and cut into strips. Drain the sweetcorn. Mix the prepared vegetables together.
Heat the oil in a pan and cook the chops for 3–5 minutes on each side, depending on the thickness.

Sprinkle with the seasonings and arrange on a serving dish. Spoon some of the salad mixture in the centre and serve the rest separately.
Serves 4

Variation
If preferred the chops may be brushed on each side with oil and cooked under a moderate grill for a total of 8–10 minutes.

Cook's Tip
When turning chops or steaks during cooking use a pair of tongs. A sharp-pointed knife will pierce the meat and lose natural juices.

French Veal Cutlets

METRIC/IMPERIAL
about 3 slices white bread
6 tablespoons milk
100 g/4 oz calves' liver
1 onion
100 g/4 oz mushrooms
225 g/8 oz minced pork
3 eggs
1 tablespoon olive oil
½ teaspoon salt
pinch white pepper
50 g/2 oz butter
6 small veal cutlets
100 g/4 oz Gruyère cheese, grated

Remove the crusts from the bread and soak the slices in the milk. Chop the liver finely. Peel and slice the onion; slice the mush-

rooms. Mix the minced pork with the soaked bread, chopped liver, onions and mushrooms. Beat the eggs with the oil, salt and pepper and add to the meat mixture.
Heat the butter in a frying pan and fry the cutlets for 2 minutes on each side, then place in a roasting tin and spread with the meat mixture. Sprinkle over the cheese and cook in a hot oven (220° C, 425° F, Gas Mark 7) for 10 minutes. Serve with new potatoes, tossed in melted butter and chopped parsley, and peas.
Serves 4–6

Paprika Pork Chops

METRIC/IMPERIAL
1 leek
1 carrot
1 stick celery
1 teaspoon flour
2 teaspoons paprika pepper
1 teaspoon garlic salt
1 teaspoon celery salt
1 teaspoon white pepper
4 loin pork chops
50 g/2 oz fat
4 tablespoons double cream
Garnish
parsley

Prepare the vegetables and cut into fine strips.
Mix the flour with the seasonings and coat each chop in the seasoned flour.
Heat the fat in a frying pan and fry the chops on a moderate heat for 5 minutes on each side, depending on the thickness. Remove and keep warm.
Add the cream to the fat in the pan, then the vegetable strips, pour on 6 table-spoons water and simmer for 5 minutes, but do not allow to boil.
Arrange the chops on a serving dish and spoon over the vegetables and cream sauce. Garnish with parsley and serve with a salad.
Serves 4

Variation
Gammon steaks may be used in place of the pork chops.

Veal Steaks Maryland

METRIC/IMPERIAL
225 g/8 oz long-grain rice
4 veal loin chops
1½ teaspoons salt
½ teaspoon white pepper
2 teaspoons paprika pepper
3 tablespoons flour
2 eggs
4 tablespoons breadcrumbs
6 tablespoons oil
4 rashers streaky bacon
2 bananas
Garnish
parsley

Cook the rice in boiling salted water until tender. Drain and keep warm.
Trim the chops to a neat shape. Mix together the salt, pepper, paprika and flour.

Lightly beat the eggs. Coat the chops in the flour, then in the beaten egg and finally in the crumbs, pressing them on well.
Heat the oil in a frying pan and cook the chops over a moderate heat for 5–7 minutes on each side, depending on the thickness. Remove and keep warm.
Fry the bacon and halved bananas in the same pan. Arrange the rice on a serving dish. Place on the veal chops, top with the bacon and bananas and garnish with parsley. Serve with sweetcorn.
Serves 4

Hungarian Pork

METRIC/IMPERIAL
1 green pepper
100 g/4 oz button onions
100 g/4 oz mushrooms
2 gherkins
1 tablespoon paprika pepper
4 slices pork fillet
6 tablespoons oil
1 teaspoon salt
6 tablespoons tomato
  ketchup
Garnish
chopped parsley

Wash the pepper, seed and dice finely; chop the onions and slice the mushrooms; slice the gherkins. Rub the paprika into the pork. Heat the oil in a frying pan and fry the pork for 5 minutes on each side. Remove, season with salt and keep hot.
Place the peppers, onion, mushrooms and gherkins in the frying pan and cook for 5 minutes. Add the ketchup and bring to the boil. Arrange the pork on a serving dish, spoon over the vegetables and sauce. Serve sprinkled with chopped parsley.
Serves 4

Veal Chops with Kidney

METRIC/IMPERIAL
1 calf's kidney
4 veal loin chops
½ teaspoon onion salt
1½ teaspoons salt
½ teaspoon white pepper
1 teaspoon made mustard
2 tablespoons oil
4 eggs
2 tablespoons chopped
  parsley
1 tablespoon chopped chervil
50 g/2 oz butter
4 tablespoons brandy

Soak the kidney for 1 hour in water. Trim and shape the chops. Season with the onion salt, ½ teaspoon of the salt and the pepper; spread on the mustard.
Heat the oil in a frying pan and fry the chops over a medium heat for 3–5 minutes on each side; remove and keep warm. Beat the eggs with ½ teaspoon salt, 4 tablespoons cold water and the herbs. In another saucepan, melt the butter and cook the eggs until lightly scrambled. Keep warm. Drain and slice the kidney and cook in the pan used for the chops for 30 seconds. Sprinkle with the remaining salt. Pour over the brandy and stir into the kidneys. Arrange the chops on a serving dish and spoon the scrambled eggs and kidneys on top.
Serves 4

Wiener Schnitzel

METRIC/IMPERIAL
4 veal escalopes
1 teaspoon salt
4 tablespoons flour
2 eggs
50 g/2 oz breadcrumbs
6 tablespoons oil
Garnish
lettuce leaves
lemon wedges

Beat the escalopes as thinly as possible, sprinkle with salt and coat in the flour. Beat the eggs with 2 tablespoons cold water. Dip the veal slices in the egg then coat in the breadcrumbs. Heat the oil in a frying pan and fry quickly, for 2 minutes on each side, to a golden brown colour. Drain on absorbent paper and serve garnished with lettuce leaves and lemon wedges.
Serves 4

> **Cook's Tip**
> Breadcrumbs for coating food are made by pressing white bread, with the crusts removed, through a sieve; or make them in the liquidiser. Breadcrumbs can be stored in the freezer in polythene bags.

Minute Steak with Vegetables

METRIC/IMPERIAL
225 g/8 oz beef fillet
225 g/8 oz lean pork
50 g/2 oz butter
1 tablespoon oil
1 teaspoon salt
$\frac{1}{4}$ teaspoon white pepper
$\frac{1}{2}$ teaspoon paprika pepper
1 gherkin
2 tablespoons capers
4 tablespoons chopped cooked beetroot
1 small can button mushrooms
4 tablespoons double cream

Trim the meats and cut into strips, or thin slices. Heat the butter and oil in a frying pan and fry the meat strips for 3–4 minutes. Sprinkle over the seasonings and add the gherkin, cut into strips, and the capers. Add the diced beetroot and drained mushrooms. Cook for a further 2–3 minutes. Finally, stir in the cream and spoon into a serving dish.
Serves 4

Variation
If liked, 4 tablespoons Madeira can be added with the mushrooms.

Quick Meat Dishes

Mixed Grill

METRIC/IMPERIAL
2 pork loin chops
2 rump steaks
½ teaspoon salt
¼ teaspoon celery salt
¼ teaspoon black pepper
1 teaspoon paprika pepper
2 teaspoons Worcestershire
  sauce
4 tablespoons oil
4 rashers streaky bacon
Garnish
parsley

Trim the chops and steaks and flatten the steaks. Mix together the salt, celery salt, pepper, paprika, Worcestershire sauce and oil. Add the meats and leave in a cool place to marinate for 20 minutes. Brush the grill pan with oil. Remove the meats from the marinade and dry on absorbent paper. Cook under a moderate grill for 5–8 minutes on each side. Grill the bacon rashers until crisp. Arrange the meats on a serving dish and serve garnished with parsley.
Serves 2

Variation
The ingredients for the mixed grill may be varied according to what is available. Mushrooms and tomatoes may be included. In place of the chops, lambs' liver may be used.

Veal Slices in Marsala

METRIC/IMPERIAL
225 g/8 oz button mushrooms
0·5 kg/1 lb veal escalopes
½ teaspoon salt
½ teaspoon white pepper
2 tablespoons flour
75 g/3 oz butter
4 tablespoons Marsala
pinch dried basil
pinch dried oregano
Garnish
chopped parsley

Slice the mushrooms. Beat the escalopes until they are thin. Mix the salt, pepper and flour and use to coat the veal.
Heat the butter in a frying pan and cook the veal slices quickly on both sides until they are pale brown, 2–3 minutes. Arrange on a serving dish and keep warm. Toss the mushrooms for 2 minutes in the fat remaining in the pan. Pour in the Marsala, add the herbs and cook for another 2 minutes. Pour the wine sauce and mushrooms over the meat and sprinkle with chopped parsley.
Serve with rice, peas and asparagus.
Serves 4

> ### Cook's Tip
> When purchasing veal, look for soft, moist flesh. Avoid veal which looks flabby and wet, or dry and brown.

Quick Meat Dishes

Pork Chops in Burgundy

METRIC/IMPERIAL
500 ml/generous ¾ pint red
   Burgundy
1 bay leaf
5 peppercorns
2 juniper berries
4 pork chops
2 tablespoons flour
½ teaspoon salt
½ teaspoon black pepper
4 tablespoons oil
6–8 button onions
50 g/2 oz streaky bacon,
   chopped
2 tablespoons double cream
Garnish
parsley

Bring to the boil the red wine with the bay leaf, peppercorns, and juniper berries; cover and simmer for 30 minutes, then strain. Trim the pork chops. Mix the flour with the salt and black pepper. Coat the chops in the seasoned flour.
Heat the oil in a deep frying pan and fry the chops on both sides with the onions and bacon, until lightly browned. Gradually stir in the red wine; cover and simmer for 15 minutes. Remove the chops and onions and keep warm. Cook the wine over a high heat until it has reduced by half. Stir in the cream, check the seasoning then spoon over the chops and onions. Garnish with parsley and serve a pepper and onion salad separately.
Serves 4

Cook's Tip
Serve the same wine with this dish as you use in the cooking.

Veal Cordon Bleu

METRIC/IMPERIAL
4 veal escalopes
4 slices cooked ham
4 slices Edam cheese
3 tablespoons flour
1 teaspoon paprika pepper
2 eggs
4 tablespoons oil
Garnish
parsley
tomato wedges

Beat the veal until it is 1 cm (½ inch) thick. On each veal escalope place a slice of ham and cheese. Fold over and secure with a wooden cocktail stick.
Mix the flour with the paprika. Add the eggs and about 2 tablespoons of water and beat to make a thick batter. Heat the oil in a frying pan. Dip the steaks in the batter and cook in the oil over a moderate heat for 5 minutes on each side. Drain on absorbent paper and remove the cocktail sticks. Serve garnished with parsley and tomato wedges. Serve a green salad separately.
Serves 4

Cook's Tip
Use a mildly flavoured cheese, such as Edam or Gouda, so that it does not overpower the delicate flavour of the veal.

Veal Rolls

METRIC/IMPERIAL
4 veal escalopes
½ teaspoon paprika pepper
2 teaspoons made mustard
1 gherkin
100 g/4 oz liver sausage
50 g/2 oz butter
1 carton natural yogurt
½ teaspoon salt
½ teaspoon white pepper

Beat the veal escalopes until they are very thin, dust with the paprika and spread with mustard. Cut the gherkin, lengthways, in four. Spread some liver sausage on each escalope then place a piece of gherkin on each. Roll the slices up and secure with thread or wooden cocktail sticks.
Heat the butter in a frying pan and brown the rolls on all sides. Then add the yogurt and season with salt and pepper. Cover and cook over a low heat for 20 minutes.
Remove the cocktail sticks; arrange on a serving dish, spoon over the sauce and serve with rice and a green salad.
Serves 4

Cook's Tip
The veal rolls may be prepared in advance and frozen. Wrap each closely in freezer film or foil. Defrost before frying.

Milanese Calves' Liver

METRIC/IMPERIAL
225 g/8 oz macaroni
75 g/3 oz butter
50 g/2 oz grated Parmesan
  cheese
6 tablespoons oil
1 teaspoon salt
¼ teaspoon white pepper
pinch dried marjoram
4 thick slices calves' liver
3 tablespoons flour

Cook the macaroni in plenty of boiling salted water for 20 minutes. Drain, and while hot mix in the butter and cheese. Place on a serving dish and keep warm.
Heat the oil in a frying pan. Rub a mixture of salt, pepper and marjoram into the liver and then coat in the flour. Fry the liver slices in the hot oil for a total of 5 minutes. Place the fried liver slices on the macaroni. Serve with a tomato sauce.
Serves 4

Cook's Tip
As liver is highly nutritious and relatively inexpensive, try to include it in your menus once a week.

Liver with Bacon

METRIC/IMPERIAL
2 slices calves' liver
1 teaspoon dried rosemary
1 rasher streaky bacon
2 bay leaves
25 g/1 oz butter
2 tablespoons oil
225 g/8 oz cooked green
  tagliatelli, or other pasta
Garnish
tomato slices

Sprinkle the liver with rosemary. Cut the bacon rasher in half and place one half on each piece of liver; top with a bay leaf and secure with a wooden cocktail stick.
Heat the butter and oil in a frying pan and fry the liver slices on both sides, for a total of 5 minutes. Remove the cocktail sticks and keep the liver warm.
Heat the pasta in the same fat in the frying pan, turning constantly. Arrange the liver slices and pasta on a serving dish. Garnish with tomato slices and serve with an asparagus and cress salad.
Serves 2

Cook's Tip
Calves' or lambs' liver are more suitable for grilling and frying. Use the coarser, tougher ox liver in a casserole.

117

Roast Veal

METRIC/IMPERIAL
1-kg/2-lb piece roasting veal
1 teaspoon salt
½ teaspoon white pepper
2 teaspoons paprika pepper
2 carrots
2 onions
2 tomatoes
4 tablespoons oil
6 tablespoons dry white
  wine
5 tablespoons double cream
Garnish
parsley

If necessary trim the meat, then rub all over with the salt, pepper and paprika. Place the meat in a roasting tin. Peel and chop the carrots, onions and tomatoes and place with the meat. Pour over the oil and wine and cook in a moderately hot oven (200° C, 400° F, Gas Mark 6) for 1–1½ hours. Remove the meat to a serving dish and keep warm while finishing the sauce. Either blend the vegetables and cooking liquor in the liquidiser, or rub through a sieve. Reheat, check the seasoning and stir in the cream. Pour around the meat and serve garnished with parsley.
Cooked spinach topped with grated cheese and browned under the grill would make a good accompanying vegetable to this roast veal dish.
Serves 4

Pot-Roast of Beef

METRIC/IMPERIAL
1 teaspoon salt
pinch black pepper
1 teaspoon paprika pepper
1-kg/2-lb piece beef topside
4 tablespoons oil
sprig rosemary
225 g/8 oz small potatoes
4 button onions
6 sticks celery
2 tomatoes
few sprigs parsley
50 g/2 oz butter
4 tablespoons red wine

Rub the salt, pepper and paprika into the meat and brush with oil. Place the meat and rosemary in an ovenproof dish.
Cube the potatoes, peel the onions and chop the celery. Halve the tomatoes. Place the vegetables around the meat and sprinkle over the coarsely chopped parsley. Dot the butter over the meat. Pour in the wine, cover and cook in a moderate oven (180° C, 350° F, Gas Mark 4) for 1½–1¾ hours. Serve with a salad.
Serves 4–6

> **Cook's Tip**
> This method of cooking is particularly suitable for the less prime joints, such as topside and brisket.

Loin of Lamb Provençale

METRIC/IMPERIAL
1 teaspoon salt
1 teaspoon garlic salt
1 teaspoon black pepper
1 loin of lamb, 6–8 chops
2 onions
150 ml/¼ pint oil
2 aubergines
1 teaspoon dried rosemary
4 tablespoons dry white wine
8 small tomatoes
4 tablespoons breadcrumbs
4 tablespoons grated cheese
50 g/2 oz butter

Rub seasoning into meat. Peel and quarter the onions. Heat the oil in a roasting tin, add the meat and onions; cook in a hot oven (220° C, 425° F, Gas Mark 7) for 15 minutes.
Slice the aubergines. Lower the oven temperature to moderate (180° C, 350° F, Gas Mark 4). Place the aubergines around the meat, sprinkle with rosemary and pour in the wine. Return to the oven for a further 30 minutes.
Cut the tops off the tomatoes. Mix 1 tablespoon of the breadcrumbs with 1 tablespoon of the cheese and spread on the tomatoes; dot with butter; replace tops. Lay the meat with the fatty side up on the grill pan and sprinkle thickly with the remaining cheese and breadcrumbs. Grill with tomatoes for 5 minutes. Serve with the vegetables and cooking liquor.
Serves 4–6

Beef with Prunes

METRIC/IMPERIAL
50 g/2 oz fat bacon
1-kg/2-lb piece beef fillet
1 teaspoon salt
1 teaspoon white pepper
little oil
1 onion
1 tomato
225 g/8 oz stoned prunes
piece thinly peeled lemon peel
1 cinnamon stick
4–6 tablespoons port
6 tablespoons double cream
2 teaspoons cornflour

Cut the bacon into thin strips. Trim the meat and lard with the bacon strips. Rub the meat with the salt and pepper, and place in a roasting tin. Brush the meat with oil and cook in a moderately hot oven (200° C, 400° F, Gas Mark 6) for 30 minutes. Meanwhile, chop the onion and peel and chop the tomato. Add to the roasting tin after 15 minutes cooking time. Cover the prunes with water, add the lemon peel, cinnamon and wine and simmer for 10 minutes. Lift the meat on to a serving dish and keep warm. Place the roasting tin over the heat and stir in the port. Bring to the boil, scraping up all the sediment. Mix the cream with the cornflour and pour into the sauce. Reheat, season and pour around the meat. Drain the prunes and use to garnish.
Serves 4–6

Glazed Gammon

METRIC/IMPERIAL
1·5-kg/3-lb piece gammon
12 cloves
4 tablespoons clear honey
1 tablespoon brown sugar

Gammon is cut from the hind leg of the cured pig. It is generally more expensive than bacon joints, but the flavour is considered superior.
Soak the gammon in cold water for at least 6 hours. Drain the gammon, wrap in foil and place in a roasting tin. Make a slit in the foil for the steam to escape. Cook in a moderate oven (180° C, 350° F, Gas Mark 4) for 1 hour.

Remove the foil. With a sharp knife, make incisions in the rind in a diagonal pattern. Insert a whole clove in each cross. Spoon the honey over the gammon and sprinkle over the brown sugar. Return the gammon to a hot oven (220° C, 425° F, Gas Mark 7) for a further 20 minutes, until glazed.
Serve hot or cold.
Serves 6–8

Cook's Tip
To make the glazed gammon look more festive, it can be studded with cloves and with glacé cherries secured with cocktail sticks.

Stuffed Breast of Veal

METRIC/IMPERIAL
1 onion
6 tablespoons oil
5 tablespoons long-grain rice
1 stock cube
1 teaspoon paprika pepper
175 g/6 oz calves' liver
25 g/1 oz butter
¼ teaspoon white pepper
½ teaspoon salt
1 egg
2 tablespoons chopped peanuts
0·5 kg/1 lb boned breast of veal
2 tablespoons flour

Peel and finely dice the onion and fry in 4 tablespoons of the oil until softened. Add the rice and

fry for a further 2 minutes. Dissolve the stock cube in 500 ml (generous ¾ pint) hot water, add to the rice and cook for 20 minutes, until the liquid is absorbed. Mix in the paprika. Cool.
Chop the liver and cook in the butter for 3–5 minutes. Mix into the rice with the seasoning, beaten egg and peanuts. Allow to cool.
Lay the veal flat, spread with the stuffing and form into a roll and secure. Sprinkle with flour.
Heat the remaining oil in a flameproof dish and brown the veal on all sides. Add 6 tablespoons water, cover and cook over a moderate heat for 40–50 minutes. adding more liquid if necessary.
Serves 4

Marinated Beef

METRIC/IMPERIAL
250 ml/scant ½ pint wine vinegar
few sprigs parsley
1 bay leaf
1 onion, sliced
2 cloves
3 peppercorns
1-kg/2-lb piece beef topside
50 g/2 oz streaky bacon
1 tablespoon cornflour
3 tablespoons cream

Place the wine vinegar, herbs, onion, cloves and peppercorns in a pan together with 300 ml (½ pint) water and bring to the boil. Allow to cool.
Place the beef in a bowl, pour over the cold marinade and leave in the refrigerator to marinate for 6 hours, (or overnight), turning the meat from time to time.
Remove from the marinade and pat dry with absorbent paper. Chop the bacon and fry in a flameproof casserole. Add the meat and brown on all sides. Pour over the marinade, together with 250 ml (scant ½ pint) water, cover and simmer over a moderate heat for 1½–2 hours.
Remove the meat to a serving dish. Strain the cooking liquor into a pan and thicken with the blended cornflour. Check the seasoning, stir in the cream and either spoon the sauce over the meat, or serve it separately.
Serves 4–6

Braised Veal Shoulder

METRIC/IMPERIAL
1·5-kg/3-lb piece veal shoulder
2 tablespoons oil
1 teaspoon salt
½ teaspoon pepper
1 onion
few sprigs parsley
1 bay leaf
450 ml/¾ pint stock
2 teaspoons cornflour

Shoulder of veal is also known as the oyster of veal, when the fore knuckle has been removed. When boned and rolled it makes a good dish for a family meal.
Ask the butcher to bone the veal and tie it in a neat shape.
Heat the oil in a frying pan and fry the veal until browned on all sides. Transfer to a casserole dish. Add the seasoning, sliced onion, herbs and stock. Cover and cook in a moderate oven (180° C, 350° F, Gas Mark 4) for about 1½ hours.
Transfer the veal to a serving dish and keep warm. Strain the cooking liquor into a pan and thicken it with the blended cornflour. Check the seasoning and serve with the veal.
Serves 6

Roast Beef – American Style

METRIC/IMPERIAL
1 teaspoon salt
½ teaspoon white pepper
2 teaspoons Worcestershire sauce
4 tablespoons oil
0·75 kg/1½ lb piece beef topside
2 tablespoons brandy
½ teaspoon cayenne pepper
1 carrot
2 sticks celery
1 onion
50 g/2 oz butter
pinch ground nutmeg
3 tablespoons soured cream

Mix the salt, pepper, Worcestershire sauce and oil together. Place the meat in a dish and poor over the oil mixture with the brandy and cayenne pepper. Cover and marinate for 20 minutes. Lift the meat from the marinade. Place in a roasting tin and cook in a hot oven (220° C, 425° F, Gas Mark 7) for 20 minutes. Meanwhile, peel and chop the carrot, chop the celery and onion. Place the vegetables with the meat, dot with butter and sprinkle with nutmeg. Cook for a further 30 minutes.
Place the meat on a serving dish and keep warm. Add the marinade to the roasting tin and bring to the boil, scraping up the sediment. Either press the sauce through a sieve or blend in the liquidiser. Reheat and mix in the cream.
Serves 4

Braised Leg of Lamb

METRIC/IMPERIAL
1 teaspoon salt
1 teaspoon white pepper
1 teaspoon sugar
1 clove garlic
1·5-kg/3-lb leg of lamb
6 tablespoons oil
250 ml/scant ½ pint dry white wine
1 bay leaf
1 teaspoon dried rosemary
1 onion, sliced
100 g/4 oz canned haricot beans
50 g/2 oz streaky bacon

Rub the salt, pepper, sugar and crushed garlic into the meat. Place in a bowl and pour over the oil and white wine. Add the bay leaf and rosemary and leave to marinate for 20 minutes. Remove the lamb from the marinade, pat dry with absorbent paper and place in a roasting tin. Cook in a moderately hot oven (200° C, 400° F, Gas Mark 6) for 40 minutes.
Mix the onion, beans and chopped bacon with the marinade and spoon around the lamb. Continue cooking for a further 35–40 minutes. Serve the lamb on the bed of braised beans and vegetables.
To add the finishing touch, cover the bone with a paper frill.
Serves 4–6

Roast Loin of Veal

METRIC/IMPERIAL
2-kg/4½-lb loin of veal
pinch salt
pinch pepper
100 g/4 oz butter
500 ml/generous ¾ pint hot
 stock
pinch dried basil
2 teaspoons cornflour
6 tablespoons dry white wine
1 tablespoon lemon juice

Ask the butcher to bone the veal and roll it with the kidney. Tie with string. Rub the veal with salt and pepper and place in a roasting tin. Pour over the melted butter and cook in a hot oven (220° C, 425° F, Gas Mark 7) for 15 minutes. Pour in half the hot stock and cook for a further 1 hour. Lower the heat to moderate (180° C, 350° F, Gas Mark 4), pour in the rest of the stock and cook for a further 1–1½ hours, basting the meat with the cooking liquid.
Place the veal on a serving dish and keep warm. Pour the cooking liquor into a pan and add the basil. Mix the cornflour with the wine and lemon juice. Pour into the pan and stirring, bring to the boil. Check the seasoning and serve with the veal. Serve with celery, peas and duchesse potatoes.
Serves 8

Cook's Tip
Do baste veal during cooking, otherwise the meat will become dry.

Hare with Red Cabbage

METRIC/IMPERIAL
4 hare joints
1 teaspoon salt
½ teaspoon white pepper
500 ml/generous ¾ pint red wine
50 g/2 oz butter
50 g/2 oz streaky bacon
1 onion, chopped
1 bay leaf
4 juniper berries
1 cooking apple
1 small red cabbage
pinch ground cloves
1–2 teaspoons cornflour

Place the pieces of hare in a bowl and add the salt, pepper and wine. Marinate in the refrigerator for at least 4 hours.

Remove the hare from the marinade, and pat dry with absorbent paper. Heat the butter in a frying pan and fry the hare until browned. Place in a flameproof casserole with the chopped bacon, onion, the marinade, bay leaf and juniper berries. Cover; simmer for 2 hours. Peel, core and chop the apple; shred the cabbage. Cook the apple and cabbage in a small amount of salted water. Drain, sprinkle with ground cloves and keep hot. Lift out the pieces of hare and keep warm. Boil the cooking liquor for about 5 minutes, then thicken with blended cornflour. Check the seasoning and spoon over the hare. Serve the cabbage separately.
Serves 4

Roast Wild Boar

METRIC/IMPERIAL
1–1·5-kg/2¼–3-lb loin wild boar
1 teaspoon salt
2 teaspoons paprika pepper
100 g/4 oz streaky bacon
10 cloves
250 ml/scant ½ pint oil
1 tablespoon flour
250 ml/scant ½ pint apple juice
250 ml/scant ½ pint stock
4 tablespoons cranberry sauce
1 teaspoon black pepper

Wild boar is not easily available in this country, but they are now being bred. Venison may be used instead.

Trim the meat and rub in the salt and paprika. Wrap the bacon slices around the joint and stick with cloves. Place in a roasting tin with the oil and roast in a moderately hot oven (200° C, 400° F, Gas Mark 6) for 1–1½ hours. Remove the meat to a serving dish. Remove the excess fat from the tin and stir in the flour. Cook for 1–2 minutes stirring. Gradually stir in the apple juice and stock. Bring to the boil, stirring, and cook for 1–2 minutes. Stir in the cranberry sauce and seasoning. Serve with the boar. Potato croquettes are a good accompanying vegetable to this dish.
Serves 6

Braised Venison Steaks

METRIC/IMPERIAL
½ teaspoon garlic salt
1 teaspoon salt
1 teaspoon black pepper
1 teaspoon made mustard
6 tablespoons red wine
2 teaspoons sugar
6 tablespoons oil
4 venison steaks
1 red pepper
2 onions
1 bulb fennel
1 carton soured cream
3 teaspoons paprika pepper
1 small can sauerkraut

Mix together the garlic salt, salt, pepper, mustard, wine and sugar with 2 tablespoons of the oil and use to marinate the steaks for about 30 minutes.
Slice the onions and fennel; seed and slice the pepper. Heat the rest of the oil in a flameproof casserole and brown the drained steaks. Remove. Stir in the onions, fennel, peppers and sauerkraut and sauté for 3–4 minutes. Replace the venison. Add the cream and the marinade, lower the heat and simmer for 30 minutes. Serve from the casserole dish.
Serves 4

Cook's Tip
Venison, like other game meats, must be hung for at least a week before cooking, to tenderise the flesh.

Venison Rolls

METRIC/IMPERIAL
8 thin slices venison fillet
2 tablespoons port
½ teaspoon salt
¼ teaspoon coarsely ground
    black pepper
8 slices salami
1 tablespoon oil
4 tablespoons redcurrant jelly
2 teaspoons made mustard
2 teaspoons paprika pepper

Flatten the venison slices and marinate in the port, salt and pepper for 15 minutes.
Place a slice of salami on each piece of venison, roll up and secure with a wooden cocktail stick.
Place the venison rolls in the oiled grill pan, brush with oil and cook under a moderate grill for 8 minutes, turning to brown the rolls on all sides.
Meanwhile, heat the redcurrant jelly with the mustard, paprika, and marinade.
Allow to simmer for 2–3 minutes. Remove the cocktail sticks from the venison rolls and arrange the meat on a bed of cooked rice and peas. Spoon over the sauce.
Serves 4

Cook's Tip
Well-hung venison may be frozen for up to 12 months. Defrost before using.

Roast Saddle of Hare

METRIC/IMPERIAL
1 saddle of hare
50 g/2 oz streaky bacon
1 teaspoon salt
2 teaspoons paprika pepper
50 g/2 oz pork dripping or 2 tablespoons oil
1 onion, sliced
½ teaspoon sugar
2 tablespoons tomato purée
4 tablespoons redcurrant jelly
4 juniper berries
250 ml/scant ½ pint stock
3–4 tablespoons cream

Lard the saddle with strips of bacon. Rub the salt and paprika all over the saddle. Heat the dripping in a roasting tin and brown the saddle on all sides. Add the onion slices and roast in a moderate oven (180° C, 350° F, Gas Mark 4) for 45–50 minutes, until tender. Remove the saddle and keep warm.
Stir the sugar, tomato purée, redcurrant jelly and juniper berries into the roasting tin. Bring to the boil, scraping up the sediment. Add the stock and simmer for 2–3 minutes. Strain, check the seasoning and just before serving, stir in the cream. Serve with the saddle.
Serves 4

Venison Stroganoff

METRIC/IMPERIAL
0·75 kg/¾ lb lean venison meat
2 onions
100 g/4 oz mushrooms
50 g/2 oz pork dripping or 2 tablespoons oil
4 tablespoons brandy
4 tablespoons cream
juice of ½ lemon
1 pimiento, sliced
½ teaspoon salt
1 teaspoon pepper
4 tablespoons chopped gherkin
1 teaspoon sugar
2 tablespoons chopped parsley

Remove any gristle from the meat and cut into thin strips. Peel and slice the onions; quarter the mushrooms.
Heat the dripping in a frying pan and fry the meat until the pieces are evenly browned all over. Add the onions, brandy, cream and lemon juice. Lower the heat and cook for a further 3–4 minutes, stirring the ingredients all the time.
Mix in the pimiento, mushrooms, seasoning, gherkins and sugar and allow to heat through.
Spoon into a serving dish and serve sprinkled with chopped parsley. Serve with rice.
Serves 4

Roast Haunch of Venison

METRIC/IMPERIAL
50 g/2 oz streaky bacon
1 carrot
2 onions
100 g/4 oz celeriac
0·75-kg/1¾-lb piece haunch of venison
6 tablespoons oil
½ teaspoon salt
1 teaspoon paprika pepper
250 ml/scant ½ pint cream
2 teaspoons lemon juice
2 tablespoons orange juice
2 tablespoons redcurrant jelly
grated rind of 1 orange

Dice the bacon; slice the carrot and the onions. Peel, chop the celeriac. Lightly brown the meat in a flameproof casserole in the oil on all sides, with the bacon, carrots, onions and celeriac. Cover and cook in a moderately hot oven (200° C, 400° F, Gas Mark 6) for 45 minutes–1 hour. Arrange the venison on a serving dish.
Add the salt, paprika, lemon and orange juices, redcurrant jelly and orange rind to the casserole. Bring to the boil, scraping up the sediment. Strain into a saucepan, check the seasoning and stir in the cream. Reheat, but do not allow to boil, then pour around the venison. Serve with pasta.
Serves 4

Potted Hare

METRIC/IMPERIAL
0·75 kg/1½ lb hare meat
2 onions
1 carrot
1 leek
50 g/2 oz almonds or peanuts
2 bread rolls
250 ml/scant ½ pint dry white wine
100 g/4 oz fat bacon
4 tablespoons oil
100 g/4 oz sausagemeat
1 teaspoon salt
1 teaspoon black pepper
1 bay leaf

Cut the hare meat into cubes, removing all the gristle. Cut the onions into quarters, grate the carrot and slice the leek. Coarsely chop the almonds or peanuts. Soak the bread rolls in the wine; dice the bacon.
Heat the oil in a flameproof casserole and fry the meat for about 5 minutes, until brown. Add the vegetables and fry together for a further 5 minutes. Stir in the diced bacon and softened bread. Remove from the heat and stir in the oil, sausagemeat, salt and pepper. Press the mixture into a greased ovenproof dish, smooth the surface. Add the bay leaf, cover and cook in a moderate oven (180° C, 350° F, Gas Mark 4) for 35–40 minutes. Serve hot or cold.
Serves 4

Game

Grilled Venison Steaks

METRIC/IMPERIAL
4 tablespoons oil
½ teaspoon dried sage
½ teaspoon black pepper
½ teaspoon paprika pepper
1 teaspoon salt
4 thin venison steaks
100 g/4 oz butter
2 tablespoons chopped
   parsley
juice of ½ lemon
4 canned pear halves
4 tablespoons cranberry
   sauce
4 walnut halves

Mix the oil, sage, pepper, paprika and salt together. Flatten the steaks and brush on both sides with the oil mixture; leave to marinate for 10–15 minutes.
Soften the butter and mix with the chopped parsley and lemon juice. Form into a square and chill in the refrigerator.
Place the venison steaks in the grill pan and cook under a moderate grill for 5 minutes on each side. Place on a serving dish. Serve garnished with a portion of herb butter and a pear half filled with cranberry sauce. Top with a walnut half. Serve with duchesse potatoes.
Serves 4

Roast Venison Fillet

METRIC/IMPERIAL
0·75-kg/1¾-lb piece venison
   fillet
50 g/2 oz fat bacon
½ teaspoon salt
¼ teaspoon black pepper
4 tablespoons oil
2 tablespoons brandy
2 tablespoons chopped
   parsley
½ bay leaf
1 tablespoon breadcrumbs
few drops Tabasco sauce
Garnish
sautéed mushrooms

Trim the venison. Cut the bacon into narrow strips and use to lard the meat. Place the meat in a bowl, sprinkle with salt and pepper and pour over the oil and the brandy. Leave to marinate for 30 minutes. Remove the meat from the marinade, pat dry and brown in a flameproof casserole in the heated oil. Cover and cook in a moderately hot oven (200° C, 400° F, Gas Mark 6) for 45 minutes–1 hour. Remove the meat and place on a serving dish. Stir 250 ml (scant ½ pint) water into the roasting tin with the marinade, parsley, bay leaf, breadcrumbs and Tabasco sauce. Bring to the boil and simmer for 5 minutes. Remove the bay leaf, pour into a sauce boat and serve with the venison. Serve garnished with sautéed mushrooms.
Serves 4

Hare Casserole

METRIC/IMPERIAL
6 hare joints
2 shallots
4 peppercorns
150 ml/¼ pint vinegar
4 bay leaves
50 g/2 oz butter
2 onions, chopped
600 ml/1 pint brown ale
juice of 1 lemon
few sage leaves
1 teaspoon made mustard
2 teaspoons sugar
1 teaspoon salt
½ teaspoon black pepper
1 teaspoon tomato purée
2 teaspoons cornflour

Remove the bones from the hare and cut the meat into pieces. Place in a bowl with the halved shallots, the peppercorns, vinegar and bay leaves and marinate in the refrigerator for 6–8 hours, or overnight. Remove the hare from the marinade and pat dry with absorbent paper. Heat the butter in a flameproof casserole and brown the hare on all sides. Stir in the onions and sauté for a further 2–3 minutes. Strain in the marinade; add the brown ale, lemon juice, sage, mustard, sugar, seasonings and tomato purée. Bring to the boil, lower the heat, cover and simmer for 1¾–2 hours. Thicken the casserole with the blended cornflour and check the seasoning. Serve from the casserole.
Serves 6

Apple-Stuffed Venison Rolls

METRIC/IMPERIAL
4 venison steaks
½ teaspoon salt
¼ teaspoon black pepper
1 carrot
1 onion
2 cooking apples
2 tablespoons oil
300 ml/½ pint red wine
4 tablespoons apple purée
Garnish
apple slices
25 g/1 oz butter

Beat the venison steaks until they are very thin. Mix the salt and pepper and use to dust both sides of the venison steaks.
Grate the carrot; peel and slice the onions. Peel and core the apples and cut into slices. Divide the grated carrot, onion and apple slices between the venison and form into rolls and secure with wooden cocktail sticks.
Heat the oil in a flameproof casserole and sauté the rolls until browned on all sides. Add the wine and apple purée. Cover and simmer for 20 minutes. Lift out the venison, remove the cocktail sticks and place the meat on a serving dish; keep warm. Boil the cooking liquor until reduced by a third. Pour over the venison rolls and serve garnished with the apple slices sautéed in the butter. Accompany with creamed potatoes or pasta.
Serves 4

Duck with Orange Sauce

METRIC/IMPERIAL
1 carrot
1 onion
4 tablespoons oil
1 (2·25-kg/5-lb) oven-ready duck
2 oranges
4 tablespoons orange liqueur
½ teaspoon salt
1 teaspoon paprika pepper
¼ teaspoon white pepper
150 ml/¼ pint stock
2 teaspoons cornflour
Garnish
parsley

Slice the carrot; peel and quarter the onion. Heat the oil in a roasting tin. Add the carrots and onions and place the duck on top. Roast in a moderately hot oven (200° C, 400° F, Gas Mark 6) for about 1½ hours, turning the duck over halfway through the time. Cut the orange peel into fine strips and squeeze the juice.
Remove the duck to a serving dish. Skim all but 1 tablespoon of the fat from the tin. Rub the onions and carrots through a sieve and return to the roasting tin. Add the orange juice and peel, the liqueur, salt, paprika, pepper and stock and mix together. Bring to the boil, scraping up the sediment. Thicken with the blended cornflour and serve in a sauce boat. Garnish the duck with parsley.
Serves 4

Braised Turkey

METRIC/IMPERIAL
2 frozen turkey portions
½ teaspoon salt
50 g/2 oz streaky bacon
2 onions
2 tablespoons chopped marjoram or 1 teaspoon dried marjoram
4 tablespoons port
1 tablespoon breadcrumbs
2 tablespoons nibbed almonds, browned

Defrost the turkey portions and sprinkle with salt.
Dice the bacon. Peel and thinly slice the onions. Place the bacon, marjoram and onion slices in an ovenproof dish. Place the turkey portions on top, pour over the port, together with 6 tablespoons water. Sprinkle over the breadcrumbs, cover and cook in a moderately hot oven (200° C, 400° F, Gas Mark 6) for about 1 hour. Remove the lid for the last 10 minutes of cooking time to brown the turkey. Arrange on a serving dish with the cooking liquor and vegetables. Sprinkle the turkey portions with the browned almonds.
Serves 2

Variation
Small, whole potatoes and apple quarters may be cooked with the turkey. Add the potatoes for the last 30 minutes of cooking time and the apples for the last 15 minutes.

Turkey Fricassée

METRIC/IMPERIAL
0·75 kg/1½ lb cooked turkey
  meat
1 onion
2 tablespoons oil
50 g/2 oz flour
600 ml/1 pint turkey stock
50 g/2 oz canned mushrooms
1 clove garlic
225 g/8 oz minced pork
½ teaspoon salt
½ teaspoon pepper
juice of 1 lemon
1 can asparagus tips
4 tablespoons cream
2 egg yolks

Chop the turkey meat; slice the onion.
Heat the oil in a pan and sauté the onion until softened. Mix in the flour and cook for 1–2 minutes, without allowing it to brown. Gradually add the stock, stirring until the mixture boils.
Stir in the sliced mushrooms, crushed garlic and turkey.
Form the pork into small balls and add to the pan. Add the seasonings and lemon juice and simmer for 5 minutes. Stir in the chopped asparagus and heat through.
Beat the egg yolks with the cream and gradually blend into the turkey mixture. Allow to heat through, but do not boil. Check the seasoning and spoon into a heated serving dish.
Serve with rice and peas.
Serves 4–6

Roast Duck – French Style

METRIC/IMPERIAL
1 (2·75-kg/6-lb) oven-ready
  duck
1 teaspoon salt
½ teaspoon dried marjoram
12 stuffed olives
2 anchovy fillets
1 apple
4 slices white bread
2 eggs
4 tablespoons Madeira
4 tablespoons sultanas
1 small can artichoke hearts

Rub the duck inside with salt and marjoram. Coarsely chop the olives and anchovy fillets. Peel and core the apple and cut into slices. Soak the white bread in water, squeeze dry and mix with the olives, anchovies, apple slices and eggs. Stuff the neck end of the duck with this mixture and secure the opening with a wooden skewer.
Place in a roasting tin and roast in a moderately hot oven (200° C, 400° F, Gas Mark 6) for 1¾ hours.
Transfer the duck to a serving dish.
Remove the fat from the roasting tin and stir in the Madeira and sultanas.
Bring to the boil scraping up the sediment. Heat the artichoke hearts, drain the liquid into the Madeira sauce.
Serve the duck garnished with artichoke hearts. Serve the Madeira sauce separately.
Serves 4–6

131

Poultry

Chicken Breasts – Chinese Style

METRIC/IMPERIAL
0·5 kg/1 lb chicken breasts
½ teaspoon salt
1 tablespoon soy sauce
1 carrot
2 slices canned pineapple
1 teaspoon cornflour
4 tablespoons oil
2 leeks, thinly sliced
2 tablespoons dry sherry
½ teaspoon sugar

Rub salt on the chicken breasts and sprinkle over the soy sauce. Grate the carrot finely; cut the pineapple slices into small pieces and toss in the cornflour.
Cut the chicken into thin strips. Heat the oil in a frying pan and fry the chicken for 3 minutes. Add the carrot and leek slices and fry for a further 2 minutes, then add the pineapple pieces. Cover and cook over a moderate heat for 12 minutes.
Stir in the sherry and sugar. Serve with rice.
Serves 4

Cook's Tip
If using frozen chicken breasts, allow them to defrost before cooking. The secret of success with this dish is to cut all the ingredients into fine strips.

Herb-Stuffed Poussins

METRIC/IMPERIAL
2 poussins
½ teaspoon salt
few chives
parsley sprigs
marjoram sprigs
rosemary sprigs
1 teaspoon paprika pepper
1 tablespoon flour
2 tablespoons oil

Poussins are small chickens each weighing up to 0·5 kg (1¼ lb).
Rub the insides of the poussins with salt. Make two bunches of mixed herbs and tie with thread. Place a bunch in the neck of each chicken and secure the openings with skewers.
Mix together the paprika, flour and oil to make a smooth paste. Spread over the chickens. Cook under a moderate grill, or on a spit, for about 40 minutes, turning from time to time. Cut each poussin in half and serve on a bed of rice. Accompany with a mixed salad.
Serves 4

Variation
If possible use fresh herbs for this recipe, but if they are not available use a pinch of each of the herbs, dried, and sprinkle over the poussins before spreading with the paprika mixture.

Exotic Duck

METRIC/IMPERIAL
1 (2-kg/4½-lb) oven-ready
  duck
½ teaspoon salt
¼ teaspoon pepper
2 large cooking apples
100 g/4 oz fresh figs
1 teaspoon curry powder
25 g/1 oz butter
3 tablespoons oil
Garnish
parsley

Rub the inside of the duck
with the salt and pepper.
Peel, core and slice the
apples; dice the figs. Mix
together the apples, figs, and
curry powder with the
butter and use to stuff the
neck end of the duck. Sew
the openings with thread, or
secure with skewers.
Heat the oil in a roasting
tin and brown the duck on
all sides. Roast the duck,
breast-side up, in a
moderately hot oven
(200° C, 400° F, Gas Mark
6) for 30 minutes. Turn
over, pour in 250 ml (scant
½ pint) hot water and roast
for a further 45 minutes–1
hour, basting occasionally
with the cooking liquid.
Serve the duck on a bed of
braised red cabbage and
garnish with parsley. If
liked; add a garnish of a
scooped-out apple filled
with apple sauce and topped
with a cherry.
Serves 3–4

Poultry

Delmonico Chicken Parcels

METRIC/IMPERIAL
4 chicken portions
1 teaspoon salt
1 teaspoon paprika pepper
2 tablespoons oil
100 g/4 oz button mushrooms
1 can artichoke hearts
2 red peppers
150 ml/¼ pint double cream

Sprinkle the chicken portions with salt and paprika.
Take four pieces of foil each large enough to wrap a chicken portion. Brush each piece of foil with oil and place a chicken portion on each. Slice the mushrooms; drain and slice the artichoke hearts. Wash and seed the peppers. Scatter the prepared vegetables over each chicken portion. Turn the sides of the foil up all the way round and pour some of the cream over each chicken portion. Form the foil into parcels, place on a baking tray and cook in a hot oven (220° C, 425° F, Gas Mark 7) for 30 minutes. Open the foil and cook for a further 10 minutes to brown the chicken.
Serves 4

Variation
The peppers may be replaced by 2 tomatoes, peeled and chopped.

Duck – Peking Style

METRIC/IMPERIAL
1 (2-kg/4-lb) oven-ready duck
3 tablespoons sugar
3 tablespoons soy sauce
225 g/8 oz flour
1 tablespoon oil

Dry the duck with absorbent paper. Dissolve the sugar in a little water and boil for 2–3 minutes. Brush all over the skin of the duck; hang in a cool place overnight.
Place the duck on a wire tray in a roasting tin. Pour over the soy sauce and sufficient water just to cover the bottom of the tin. Roast in a moderately hot oven (200° C, 400° F, Gas Mark 6) for about 1 hour, basting the duck from time to time. Increase the heat to hot (230° C, 450° F, Gas Mark 8) and cook for a further 15 minutes.
Sieve the flour, and mixing all the time, stir in 300 ml (½ pint) boiling water. Turn the dough on to a floured surface and knead for 10 minutes. Roll out thinly and cut into 5-cm (2-inch) rounds. Brush half the rounds with oil and place the remaining rounds on top. Roll each pair out thinly and cook in a lightly oiled frying pan for about 1 minute.
Strip the skin from the duck and cut meat into squares. Serve with the pancakes.
Serves 4

Chicken Cakes

METRIC/IMPERIAL
450 g/1 lb cooked chicken
3 eggs
50 g/2 oz breadcrumbs
½ teaspoon salt
½ teaspoon white pepper
3 tablespoons double cream
1 teaspoon paprika pepper
pinch ground nutmeg
3 tablespoons flour
25 g/1 oz butter
4 tablespoons oil

Mince or chop the chicken finely.
Place in a bowl and mix with the eggs, breadcrumbs, salt, pepper, cream, paprika, nutmeg and flour and mix well. Melt the butter and stir into the chicken mixture. Divide the mixture into four.
Heat the oil in a frying pan, add one-quarter of the meat mixture, flatten it and cook on each side for 2–3 minutes, until browned. Remove and keep warm while cooking the other three portions.
Serve with a chicory salad and rice.
Serves 4

Cook's Tip
This recipe is a particularly good way of using up leftover cooked poultry or game.

Partridge with Sauerkraut and Pears

METRIC/IMPERIAL
2 oven-ready partridges
½ teaspoon salt
½ teaspoon celery salt
1 teaspoon paprika pepper
¼ teaspoon white pepper
2 stale bread rolls
2 onions, chopped
25 g/1 oz liver sausage
4 tablespoons oil
100 g/4 oz butter
1 bay leaf
450 g/1 lb sauerkraut
1 teaspoon sugar
4 ripe pears
25 g/1 oz bacon, diced

Rub the insides of the partridges with salt, celery salt, paprika and white pepper. Cut the bread rolls into four, pour over hot water to soften them, then squeeze dry. Beat the softened bread and mix with the diced onions and the liver sausage. Use to stuff the partridges.
Heat the oil in a flameproof casserole and quickly brown the partridges all over. Add the butter and bay leaf, cover and simmer for 30 minutes. Heat the sauerkraut separately with 4 tablespoons water for 10 minutes. Add the sugar, peeled, cored and chopped pears and diced bacon and cook for a further 10 minutes. Arrange the sauerkraut on a serving dish with the partridges on top.
Serves 4

Viennese Chicken

METRIC/IMPERIAL
4 chicken portions
2 teaspoons salt
4 tablespoons flour
2 eggs
100 g/4 oz breadcrumbs
oil for deep frying
Garnish
lemon wedges
parsley sprigs

If using frozen chickens, allow them to defrost completely. Rub the chicken portions with salt and coat in the flour. Beat the eggs with a fork and coat the chicken pieces all over and then roll in the breadcrumbs, pressing them on firmly. Heat the oil – if a cube of bread browns immediately, then the oil has reached the correct temperature. Fry the chicken portions until they are golden brown and cooked through. Remove and drain on absorbent paper.
Serve garnished with lemon wedges and parsley sprigs. Serve with a green salad.
Serves 4

Cook's Tip
When serving foods which have been coated in crumbs and deep fried, the garnish of parsley should also be fried in the oil for 2–3 seconds. Drain on absorbent paper.

Chicken Risotto

METRIC/IMPERIAL
1 boiling fowl
1 leek
2 carrots
2 teaspoons salt
1 bay leaf
2 onions
6 tablespoons oil
225 g/8 oz long-grain rice
150 ml/¼ pint double cream
40 g/1½ oz butter
1 tablespoon flour
1 red pepper, chopped
50 g/2 oz peas

Place the chicken, prepared leek and carrots in a pan. Cover with 2 litres (3½ pints) water and add the salt and bay leaf. Bring to the boil, cover and simmer for 1½ hours.
Peel and finely dice the onions and fry in the oil until they become transparent. Add the rice, and fry, stirring for 5 minutes. Add 1 litre (1¾ pints) of the chicken stock. Cover and simmer for 20 minutes, until the liquid is absorbed. Stir in the peppers and peas. Strain the rest of the chicken stock and bring it back to the boil. Remove from the heat and stir in the cream. Work the flour into the butter to form a paste and whisk small amounts into the sauce. Return to the heat; whisk until thick and glossy. Arrange the risotto with chicken portions on top and spoon over the sauce.
Serves 4

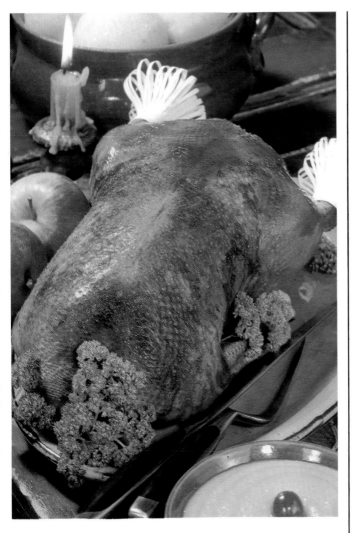

Goose with Apple Stuffing

METRIC/IMPERIAL
6 dessert apples
1 onion
1 clove garlic, crushed
50 g/2 oz breadcrumbs
pinch dried sage
3 tablespoons port
1 (4–5-kg/about 10-lb)
  oven-ready goose
salt and pepper
Garnish
parsley sprigs

Peel, core and chop the apples; peel and chop the onion. Mix together the apples, onion, garlic, breadcrumbs and sage. Bind together with the port. Stuff the goose with apple stuffing. Prick the skin all over with a skewer and sprinkle with salt and pepper. Place the goose on a rack in a roasting tin. Roast in a moderately hot oven (200° C, 400° F, Gas Mark 6) allowing 15 minutes to the 0·5 kg (1 lb) and 15 minutes over.

After 1 hour, spoon the fat out of the tin, add 150 ml (¼ pint) water and continue roasting the goose.

Place the goose on a large platter and garnish with parsley sprigs. Serve with spicy apple sauce (see page 77).
Serves 8

Casseroled Turkey with Fruit

METRIC/IMPERIAL
4 turkey portions
½ teaspoon salt
pinch curry powder
¼ teaspoon white pepper
2 teaspoons paprika pepper
1 leek
50 g/2 oz butter
½ tablespoon flour
150 ml/¼ pint oil
50 g/2 oz each canned sliced
  peaches, pineapples and
  stoned cherries
1 orange, peeled and
chopped

If using frozen turkey portions, allow to defrost completely. Sprinkle the turkey portions with the seasonings; slice the leek. Heat the butter in a pan and sauté the prepared leeks until they become transparent, then sprinkle with the flour. Stir in 5 tablespoons of cold water and leave on a low heat. Heat the oil in a flameproof casserole and brown the turkey portions on all sides. Add the leeks, cover and cook in a moderate oven (180° C, 350° F, Gas Mark 4) for 35–40 minutes. Add the fruits and return to the oven for a further 10 minutes. Serve from the casserole dish, with rice.
Serves 4

137

Stuffed Red Peppers

METRIC/IMPERIAL
0·5 kg/1 lb red peppers
100 g/4 oz button mushrooms
50 g/2 oz streaky bacon
2 onions
3 eggs
pinch salt
4 tablespoons chopped
    parsley
6 tablespoons oil
50 g/2 oz butter
½ teaspoon black pepper
6 tablespoons soured cream
1 teaspoon sugar

Cut off the tops of the
peppers and scoop out the
core and seeds. Blanch in
boiling salted water for 5
minutes. Leave upside down
to drain.

Chop the mushrooms
coarsely; dice the bacon;
peel and dice the onions.
Place the bacon in a pan,
heat until the fat runs,
then add the mushrooms
and onions and sauté for 5
minutes. Lightly beat the
eggs with a pinch of salt and
the parsley and stir into the
vegetables. Cook on a low
heat until the eggs are
lightly set. Remove from
the heat. Use to fill the
blanched peppers. Place in a
roasting tin with the oil.
Cover with foil and cook in
a hot oven (220° C, 425° F.
Gas Mark 7) for 25 minutes.
Melt the butter and mix
with the black pepper,
soured cream and sugar.
Spoon over the peppers and
cook for a further 5 minutes.
Serves 4

Savoy Cabbage with Yogurt

METRIC/IMPERIAL
1 savoy cabbage
3 onions
1 lemon
1 teaspoon salt
1 bay leaf
2 cloves
1 teaspoon sugar
50 g/2 oz butter
1 carton natural yogurt

Cut the cabbage in half and
cut out the stalk and the
coarse outer leaves; cut the
cabbage halves into strips.
Peel and slice the onions
and lemon.
Place the prepared cabbage,
onions and lemon in a pan
with 2 litres (3½ pints)
water. Add the salt, bay
leaf, cloves and sugar.
Bring to the boil, cover and
simmer for 30 minutes.
Melt the butter, stir in the
yogurt and allow to heat
through, but do not boil.
Drain the cabbage mixture
and place in a serving dish.
Pour over the yogurt sauce.
Serve with grilled or fried
pork chops.
Serves 4

Cook's Tip
When buying savoy
cabbage, pick one
with crisp outer
leaves. Reject pale
green savoys as they
are almost certain to
be stale.

138

Buttered Carrot Sticks

METRIC/IMPERIAL
1 kg/2 lb carrots
1 teaspoon salt
2 onions
6 tablespoons oil
4 tablespoons chopped parsley
75 g/3 oz butter

Scrape the carrots and cut in four lengthways, then cut each quarter in 5-cm (2-inch) long strips. Sprinkle with salt; peel and slice the onions. Heat the oil in a pan and fry the onions until they become transparent, then add the carrots together with 6 tablespoons water. Cover with a lid and cook over a moderate heat for 30–35 minutes, until the carrots are just tender. Using a slotted draining spoon, place in a serving dish and dot with the butter. Sprinkle over the parsley and serve with meatballs or beef casseroles.
Serves 4

Cook's Tip
Although carrots are available all the year round, it's a good idea to freeze young carrots. Remove the tops, wash and scrape but leave whole. Blanch for 5 minutes, drain, cool and pack in polythene bags.

Cucumber with Dill

METRIC/IMPERIAL
0·75 kg/1½ lb cucumber
1 teaspoon salt
juice of ½ lemon
1 carton natural yogurt
½ teaspoon sugar
40 g/1½ oz butter
4 tablespoons chopped dill
1 teaspoon cornflour

Cucumber is more usually served in salads, but it also makes a very good hot vegetable dish.
Peel and halve the cucumbers; remove the seeds and rinse the halves thoroughly. Cut the cucumber halves into bite-sized pieces. Place in a pan with the salt, lemon juice, yogurt, sugar and 25 g (1 oz) of the butter; cover and simmer for 10 minutes. Stir in the dill. Make a paste with the cornflour and the remaining butter; whisk into the cucumber and cook, stirring, until thickened. Check the seasoning and serve with sautéed veal escalopes.
Serves 4

Variation
Tarragon or celery seeds may be used in place of the dill. If fresh herbs are not available, use 1 teaspoon of the dried herb.

Vegetable Dishes

Fennel au Gratin

METRIC/IMPERIAL
4 bulbs fennel
50 g/2 oz bacon
500 ml/generous ¾ pint milk
½ teaspoon salt
40 g/1½ oz butter
2 tablespoons flour
4 tablespoons grated cheese

Fennel has a distinct aniseed flavour. Buy bulbs which have well-rounded roots and avoid ones deep green in colour.
Trim and slice the fennel; dice the bacon. Heat the milk in a pan with the salt and the bacon; add the fennel and simmer for 20 minutes. Remove the fennel and bacon with a slotted draining spoon and place in a greased ovenproof dish. Add 250 ml (scant ½ pint) water to the cooking liquor. Work 25 g (1 oz) of the butter into the flour to form a paste. Whisk small amounts of the beurre manié (the flour and butter paste) into the cooking liquor. Stir over a moderate heat until thickened and glossy.
Pour over the fennel and bacon. Sprinkle the cheese over the surface, dot with the remaining butter and place in a hot oven (220° C, 425° F, Gas Mark 7) for 10 minutes, until the cheese has melted and the surface is lightly browned.
Serve with veal escalopes.
Serves 4

Bread Dumplings and Mushrooms

METRIC/IMPERIAL
10 stale white bread rolls
1 teaspoon salt
350 ml/generous ½ pint lukewarm milk
0·75 kg/1½ lb mushrooms
2 onions
100 g/4 oz butter
4 tablespoons chopped parsley
1 teaspoon pepper
3 eggs
6 tablespoons double cream
Garnish
chopped parsley

Slice the bread rolls very thinly and sprinkle with the salt. Pour over the lukewarm milk and leave to soak for 15 minutes.
Slice the mushrooms; peel and finely dice the onions. Heat 50 g (2 oz) of the butter in a pan and sauté the diced onions until softened. Mix the onions, ½ teaspoon of the pepper, the parsley and eggs into the softened bread.
Bring a large pan of salted water to the boil. With wet hands, form the bread mixture into dumplings, the size of an apple; simmer then for 15 minutes.
Meanwhile, heat the rest of the butter and sauté the mushrooms for 10 minutes. Stir in the cream and pepper. Garnish with chopped parsley and serve with the dumplings.
Serves 4

French Beans with Gammon

METRIC/IMPERIAL
2 gammon rashers
0·5 kg/1 lb French beans
8 tomatoes
sprig savory
25 g/1 oz butter
4 tablespoons single cream
½ teaspoon black pepper
1 tablespoon chopped
    parsley

Rind the gammon and slit the fat at intervals to prevent the rashers curling during cooking. Cook under a moderate grill for 4 minutes on each side. Top and tail the beans and cook in boiling salted water until just tender. Drain. Peel and quarter the tomatoes. Cut each gammon rasher in half and place in a flameproof casserole with the beans, tomatoes, savory, butter, single cream and pepper. Allow to cook over a moderate heat for about 5 minutes. Remove the savory and stir in the chopped parsley.
Serves 4

Variation
In place of the gammon, 225 g (8 oz) streaky bacon could be used. Chop the bacon and fry in its own fat until crisp. Stir into the beans with the tomatoes and other ingredients.

Aubergine and Tomato Bake

METRIC/IMPERIAL
0·75 kg/1½ lb aubergines
3 teaspoons salt
3 tablespoons flour
150 ml/¼ pint oil
2 onions, chopped
1 (226-g/8-oz) can tomatoes
3 tablespoons tomato purée
1 teaspoon dried basil
½ teaspoon dried oregano
1 teaspoon sugar
¼ teaspoon black pepper
225 g/8 oz Mozzarella
    cheese, sliced
3 tablespoons grated
    Parmesan cheese

Slice the aubergines into 1-cm (½-inch) slices; sprinkle with 2 teaspoons of the salt and leave aside. Rinse the aubergine slices and pat dry with absorbent paper; toss in the flour. Heat the oil in a frying pan, and fry the slices until brown on each side. Drain. Add the onions, tomatoes, remaining salt, the tomato purée, basil, oregano, sugar and pepper to the oil remaining in the pan and cook for 10 minutes. Cool slightly; blend or sieve. Place half the tomato mixture in a greased dish. Add a layer of the aubergine slices and a layer of cheese slices. Top with the remaining tomato mixture and sprinkle over the cheese. Cook in a moderately hot oven (200° C, 400° F, Gas Mark 6) for 20 minutes.
Serves 4

Vegetable Dishes

Salsify
au Gratin

METRIC/IMPERIAL
1 kg/2 lb salsify
100 g/4 oz butter
juice of ½ lemon
2 tablespoons flour
600 ml/1 pint milk
2 egg yolks
salt and pepper
100 g/4 oz cooked tongue
4 tablespoons grated cheese
2 tablespoons white
   breadcrumbs

Salsify is a root vegetable available from the end of October to May.
Scrub the salsify in cold water and top and tail. Peel and immediately place in cold water with a few drops of lemon juice added.
Drain; cook in boiling salted water for 35 minutes. Heat 50 g (2 oz) of the butter in a pan. Stir in the flour and cook for 1–2 minutes, without browning. Gradually add the milk and stirring, bring to the boil. Simmer for 1–2 minutes, stirring. Remove from the heat and beat in the egg yolks. Season to taste.
Cut the tongue into strips. Mix the drained salsify and tongue with the sauce. Pour into a greased ovenproof dish. Sprinkle over the cheese and breadcrumbs and dot with butter. Cook in a moderately hot oven (200° C, 400° F, Gas Mark 6) for 10 minutes.
Serve with grilled or fried pork or veal chops.
Serves 4

Tomato-Stuffed
Celeriac

METRIC/IMPERIAL
1 kg/2 lb small celeriac
juice of 1 lemon
3 tomatoes
50 g/2 oz cooked tongue
1 onion
½ teaspoon salt
½ teaspoon white pepper
2 tablespoons tomato
   ketchup
6 tablespoons oil
500 ml/generous ¾ pint stock
Garnish .
chopped parsley

Celeriac is the edible root of a variety of celery, available from October to March.
Wash and peel the celeriac. Hollow out the centres and dice the scooped-out flesh.
Place the celeriac in cold water with a few drops of lemon juice added.
Nick the skins of the tomatoes, plunge into boiling water for 2–3 minutes, then peel and chop. Finely dice the tongue. Peel and dice the onion.
Place the tomatoes, tongue, onions, chopped celeriac, seasoning and tomato ketchup in a bowl and mix.
Drain the hollowed-out celeriacs and fill the centres with the tomato mixture. Heat the oil in a flameproof casserole and sauté the celeriacs for 10 minutes. Add the stock, cover and simmer for 20 minutes.
Remove and serve garnished with chopped parsley.
Serves 4

Vegetable Dishes

Stuffed Artichokes

METRIC/IMPERIAL
4 globe artichokes
2 tablespoons wine vinegar
½ teaspoon made mustard
½ teaspoon pepper
2 eggs
100 g/4 oz ham
100 g/4 oz canned mussels
2 tomatoes
4 tablespoons double cream
2 tablespoons mayonnaise
Garnish
red pepper strips

Remove the stalks and cook the artichokes in boiling salted water for 50 minutes. Take the artichokes out of the water, drain, and pull out the inner leaves and the choke so that the firm base of the artichoke can be seen.
Stir the wine vinegar into the mustard and pepper; pour into the artichokes and leave for 30 minutes. Hard-boil the eggs and cut into quarters; cut the ham into strips; drain the mussels and cut in half. Peel and chop the tomatoes. Whip the cream lightly and mix with the mayonnaise. Pour in the vinegar mixture from the artichokes and add the ham strips. Fill the artichokes with the tomatoes, mussels and eggs. Spoon over the mayonnaise mixture and serve garnished with red pepper strips. Accompany with thin slices of freshly made toast.
Serves 4

143

Baked Stuffed Tomatoes

METRIC/IMPERIAL
8 large tomatoes
½ teaspoon celery salt
pinch garlic salt
2 slices white bread
50 g/2 oz cheese, grated
2 tablespoons chopped
    parsley or chives
4 tablespoons chopped ham
25 g/1 oz butter
few drops Worcestershire
    sauce
1 teaspoon cornflour
6 tablespoons soured cream
juice of 1 lemon
1 teaspoon sugar

Cut the tops off the tomatoes and scoop out the centres. Sprinkle the insides with a mixture of celery and garlic salts. Turn upside down and leave to drain.

Soak the bread in hot water, squeeze dry and place in a bowl. Mix in the grated cheese, parsley or chives and ham. Fill the tomato shells with the stuffing and replace the tops. Place in an ovenproof dish.

Melt the butter in a pan, add the Worcestershire sauce, the cornflour blended with the cream, the lemon juice and sugar and about 4 tablespoons of water. Heat, but do not boil, then pour around the tomatoes. Cook in a moderately hot oven (200° C, 400° F, Gas Mark 6) for 15 minutes.

Serve with rice, peas and buttered new potatoes.
Serves 4

Chicory and Ham Parcels

METRIC/IMPERIAL
8 heads chicory
2 tablespoons oil
100 g/4 oz lean bacon
8 slices ham
½ teaspoon salt
¼ teaspoon white pepper
50 g/2 oz butter
4 tablespoons double cream
Garnish
parsley sprigs

Wash the chicory heads and remove any damaged outer leaves. Brush four pieces of foil with oil. Dice the bacon and distribute evenly over the slices of ham. Put one head of chicory on each slice of ham, sprinkle with salt and pepper and roll up.

Put two chicory and ham rolls on each piece of foil and turn up the edges of the foil. Dot with butter and spoon over the cream. Close the foil firmly, place the parcels on a baking tray and cook in a moderately hot oven (200° C, 400° F, Gas Mark 6) for 30 minutes. Remove the foil and arrange the chicory rolls on a serving dish. Garnish with parsley sprigs.
Serves 4

Cook's Tip
When buying chicory, choose firmly packed heads. Reject any which are yellow and have curling leaves.

Brussels Sprouts with Sausagemeat Balls

METRIC/IMPERIAL
0·75 kg/1½ lb fresh or frozen
  Brussels sprouts
100 g/4 oz streaky bacon
pinch salt
½ teaspoon grated nutmeg
100 g/4 oz canned
  mushrooms
100 g/4 oz pork
  sausagemeat

Trim the fresh sprouts,
make a cross in the base of
each and blanch in boiling
salted water for 3 minutes;
drain. (With frozen sprouts,
allow them to defrost.)

Dice the bacon, place in a
pan, and heat until the fat
runs. Add the sprouts and
sauté for 3–4 minutes with a
pinch of salt and the
nutmeg. Pour in 450 ml
(¾ pint) water, cover and
cook for 15 minutes.
Drain and halve the
mushrooms. Form the
sausagemeat into small balls
and add to the sprouts,
together with the
mushrooms. Cook for a
further 5 minutes. Check the
seasoning and transfer to a
serving dish.
Serves 4

Cauliflower with Herbs

METRIC/IMPERIAL
1 large cauliflower
1 teaspoon salt
25 g/1 oz butter
25 g/1 oz flour
4 tablespoons double cream
4 tablespoons chopped
  parsley
2 tablespoons chopped basil
1 tablespoon each chopped
  borage and lemon balm
Garnish
parsley sprig

Cut off the bottom of the
cauliflower stalk, and
remove the outer leaves.
Cover with cold water and
leave for 1 hour.
Bring 1 litre (1¾ pints) of
water and the salt to the

boil. Add the whole
cauliflower and cook for 15
minutes. Drain and reserve
250 ml (scant ½ pint) of the
cooking liquid. Keep the
cauliflower warm in a
serving dish.
Melt the butter in a
saucepan and stir in the
flour. Cook for 1–2 minutes
without allowing the flour
to brown. Gradually stir in
the reserved cooking liquid
and bring to the boil
stirring. Cook for 1–2
minutes. Remove from the
heat and stir in the cream
and herbs. Pour over the
cauliflower and serve
garnished with a parsley
sprig.
Serves 4

Vegetable Dishes

Spinach with Scrambled Eggs

METRIC/IMPERIAL
1 kg/2 lb fresh spinach
1 tablespoon oil
4 tablespoons chopped
    parsley
salt and pepper
4 eggs
25 g/1 oz butter

Pick over the spinach very carefully, wash in several changes of water. Leave to drain in a colander.
Heat the oil in a pan, add the spinach and cook for 10 minutes. Drain thoroughly, squeezing out all the liquid. Stir in half the parsley and season with salt. Keep warm.
Beat the eggs in a bowl with the remaining parsley and season with salt and pepper. Heat the butter in a pan and, stirring, cook the eggs until lightly scrambled. Arrange the spinach in a serving dish and spoon the scrambled egg in the centre. Serve at once with freshly made toast.
Serves 4

Cook's Tip
Spinach needs careful handling as the tender dark green leaves bruise easily. Choose crisp leaves and reject limp ones which will be stale.

Leeks in a Cream and Raisin Sauce

METRIC/IMPERIAL
8 leeks
1 teaspoon salt
8 peppercorns
2 coriander seeds
2 parsley sprigs
2 shallots, sliced
Sauce
300 ml/$\frac{1}{2}$ pint single cream
2 egg yolks
2 tablespoons raisins
$\frac{1}{4}$ teaspoon pepper

Trim, wash and slice the leeks in half, lengthways. Place in a pan, cover with water and add the salt, peppercorns, coriander, parsley and shallots.
Bring to the boil and simmer for 15 minutes. Drain the leeks well, place on a serving dish and keep warm.
To make the sauce, place the cream and egg yolks in a bowl and place over a pan of hot water. Cook, stirring frequently, until thickened. Stir in the raisins and pepper and spoon over the leeks.
Serves 4

Variation
300 ml ($\frac{1}{2}$ pint) white sauce could be used in place of the cream. To make the white sauce, use 150 ml ($\frac{1}{4}$ pint) of the liquor from cooking the leeks.

Baked Stuffed Onions

METRIC/IMPERIAL
4 large onions
100 g/4 oz minced beef
100 g/4 oz lambs' liver,
    finely chopped
2 eggs
1 teaspoon salt
1 tablespoon breadcrumbs
1 tablespoon chopped
    tarragon
½ teaspoon garlic salt
6 tablespoons oil
1 teaspoon paprika pepper
Garnish
parsley sprigs

Peel the onions and scoop out the centres with a sharp-pointed knife; chop the scooped-out onion coarsely and mix with the beef and liver. Add the eggs, salt, breadcrumbs, tarragon and garlic salt. Use this mixture to fill the onion shells, piling it up in the centre. Place in a roasting tin and pour in the oil. Cover with foil and cook in a moderately hot oven (200° C, 400° F, Gas Mark 6) for 35-40 minutes. Transfer to a serving dish and serve garnished with parsley sprigs.
Serves 4

Variation
Other meat fillings may be used to stuff the onions – try 225 g (8 oz) minced pork (or pork and veal mixed) and use fresh sage in place of the tarragon.

Walnut-Stuffed Cabbage Rolls

METRIC/IMPERIAL
175 g/6 oz cooked tongue
50 g/2 oz walnuts
675 g/1½ lb cooked minced
    pork
½ teaspoon celery salt
½ teaspoon white pepper
½ teaspoon dried thyme
50 g/2 oz liver sausage
2 tablespoons breadcrumbs
1 egg
1 medium savoy cabbage
75 g/3 oz vegetable fat
1 carton soured cream
2 tablespoons tomato purée

Finely dice the tongue; chop the walnuts. Mix the pork with the tongue, walnuts, celery salt, pepper, thyme, liver sausage and breadcrumbs. Bind with the lightly beaten egg. Cook the cabbage, whole, in boiling salted water for 30 minutes. Drain, cool slightly and pull the leaves apart. Arrange the leaves in pairs, with the pairs overlapping each other. Put 2–3 tablespoons of the meat mixture on each pair, form into a roll and secure. Heat the fat in a frying pan and sauté the rolls until browned. Add sufficient water or stock to cover the rolls and simmer for 25–30 minutes. Transfer to a serving dish and keep warm. To make the sauce, heat the soured cream with the tomato purée and spoon over the cabbage rolls.
Serves 4

147

Parisian Mushroom Salad

METRIC/IMPERIAL
225 g/8 oz button mushrooms
100 g/4 oz ham
2 tablespoons mayonnaise
2 tablespoons wine vinegar
½ teaspoon sugar
Garnish
hard-boiled egg quarters
pinch cayenne pepper

It is not necessary to wash cultivated mushrooms. Trim the base of the stalks and wipe them with a damp cloth.
Trim and slice the mushrooms; chop the ham. Mix the mayonnaise with the vinegar and the sugar to make a smooth sauce. Place the prepared mushrooms and ham in a serving bowl and toss in the mayonnaise mixture. Serve garnished with hard-boiled egg quarters sprinkled with cayenne pepper.
Serves 4–6

Variation
If preferred the mushrooms and ham may be tossed in 4–6 tablespoons French dressing just before serving. To make this dish more substantial, chopped cooked poultry may also be added to the salad.

Leek and Ham Salad

METRIC/IMPERIAL
1 egg
1 tomato
1 lettuce
225 g/8 oz cooked leeks
100 g/4 oz ham
1 punnet cress
1 teaspoon salt
½ teaspoon white pepper
½ teaspoon garlic salt
2 tablespoons wine vinegar
4 tablespoons oil

Hard-boil the egg for 10 minutes; cool, shell and chop finely. Nick the skin of the tomato, plunge into boiling water for 2–3 minutes, then peel off the skin and cut the tomato into strips.
Wash, dry and shred the lettuce leaves. Slice the cooked leeks; cut the ham into strips. Wash and drain the cress. Mix all the prepared salad ingredients together and place in a serving dish.
Mix together the seasonings, vinegar and oil to make a dressing. Sprinkle over the salad just before serving.
Serves 4

Cook's Tip
When preparing the lettuce, tear it into shreds. Do not cut with a knife as this will cause the edges to turn brown.

Cucumber and Dill Salad

METRIC/IMPERIAL
100 g/4 oz frozen shrimps
½ cucumber
4-6 gherkins
100 g/4 oz courgettes
2 tablespoons coarsely chopped dill
225 g/8 oz strawberries
1 carton soured cream

This salad is particularly refreshing on a hot day. It makes a good accompaniment to cold salmon. Defrost the shrimps. Peel and thinly slice the cucumber; slice the gherkins and courgettes. Mix together the prepared cucumber, gherkins and courgettes and place in a serving bowl. Add the chopped dill and shrimps. Hull and halve the strawberries and add to the salad. Just before serving, spoon over the soured cream.
Serves 4

Variation
The shrimps may be replaced by 100 g (4 oz) frozen crab meat or prawns. Allow them to defrost fully before using.
Raspberries may be used in place of the strawberries.

Roast Beef Salad

METRIC/IMPERIAL
4 thick slices cooked roast beef
3 tablespoons mayonnaise
2 tablespoons piccalilli
4 tomatoes
100 g/4 oz frozen French beans
2–3 gherkins
¼ head celeriac
1 lettuce

Cut the roast beef into strips. Mix the mayonnaise with the liquid from the piccalilli. Nick the skins of the tomatoes, plunge into boiling water for 2–3 minutes, then peel and chop. Cook the beans according to the instructions on the packet. Drain and cool. Slice the gherkins, peel and cut the celeriac into strips. Mix all the prepared ingredients together with the mayonnaise and leave in the refrigerator for 10 minutes to marinate.
Wash and dry the lettuce leaves and use to line a salad bowl. Spoon in the beef salad.
Serves 4–6

Variation
This salad is very pleasant with cabbage instead of lettuce. Choose a green variety of cabbage and shred the leaves, removing the coarse stalk.

Poultry and Orange Salad

METRIC/IMPERIAL
450 g/1 lb cooked chicken
50 g/2 oz cream cheese
2 teaspoons grated
  horseradish
150 ml/¼ pint single cream
4 tablespoons chopped
  parsley
2 oranges

Cut the chicken into 5mm
(¼-inch) cubes. Break up the
cheese with a fork and beat
to a smooth sauce with the
horseradish and the cream.
Stir in the chopped parsley.
Halve the oranges. Scoop
out the orange flesh,
discarding the pips and
membranes, and cut into
small pieces; mix with the
chicken. Stir the cream
sauce into the chicken and
orange mixture.
Pile the mixture into the
orange shells.
Serves 4

Variation
Cottage cheese may be used
in place of the cream cheese.
Use 225 g (8 oz) cooked
chicken and 225 g (8 oz)
chopped dessert apple and
walnuts.

Veal Salad

METRIC/IMPERIAL
450 g/1 lb white cabbage
2 onions
4 tablespoons wine vinegar
½ teaspoon salt
¼ teaspoon garlic salt
4 tomatoes
½ cucumber
450 g/1 lb roast veal
6 tablespoons oil

Cut the cabbage into
quarters and cut away the
stalks. Using a sharp knife,
shred finely. Wash and
leave to drain. Peel the
onions and slice thinly. Mix
the prepared cabbage and
onions together.
Mix together the vinegar,
salt and the garlic salt and
use to toss the cabbage
mixture. Chill in the
refrigerator for 10 minutes.
Nick the skins of the
tomatoes, plunge into
boiling water for 2–3
minutes; then peel and
quarter. Slice the cucumber
thinly. Cut the meat into
matchstick-like strips. Place
all the salad ingredients
together in a bowl and mix.
Just before serving, pour
over the oil and toss the
ingredients.
Serves 4

Variation
Leftover roast lamb, beef or
pork may be used in place
of the veal.

Brazilian Bamboo Salad

METRIC/IMPERIAL
7 tablespoons milk
150 ml/¼ pint soured cream
2 teaspoons curry powder
½ teaspoon salt
1 teaspoon sugar
1 (850-g/1-lb 14-oz) can
  bamboo shoots
1 small can peach halves
½ teaspoon white pepper
¼ teaspoon ground mace
pinch ground cloves
pinch ground cinnamon
2 tablespoons chopped mint

Bamboo shoots are used in Chinese cookery. They are available in cans from stores specialising in Chinese foods.
Whisk the milk with the soured cream, curry powder, salt and sugar. Leave for 15 minutes to allow the flavours to combine.
Drain the bamboo shoots and slice thinly. Cut the peach halves into strips and mix the sliced bamboo shoots.
Mix the rest of the spices and the chopped mint into the sauce.
Place the bamboo shoots and peaches in a serving bowl. Pour over the sauce and toss all the ingredients together until evenly coated in the sauce. Allow to chill for 20 minutes before serving.
Serves 4

Aubergine and Orange Salad

METRIC/IMPERIAL
2 aubergines
2 onions
4 tablespoons olive oil
2 eggs
2 oranges
4 tablespoons chopped mint
1 teaspoon dried rosemary
4 tablespoons wine vinegar
2 teaspoons sugar
1 teaspoon salt

Place the aubergines on a baking tray and cook in a moderate oven (180° C, 350° F, Gas Mark 4) for 10 minutes. Remove and peel off the skins. Slice the aubergines and onions. Heat the oil and fry the aubergine and onion slices together until softened. Leave to become cold.
Hard-boil the eggs for 10 minutes, cool, shell and cut into quarters. Peel and slice the oranges. Mix together the mint, rosemary, vinegar, sugar and salt. Mix the orange slices with the aubergines and onion mixture and pour over the dressing. Leave to marinate for 10 minutes.
Serve garnished with the hard-boiled egg quarters.
Serves 4

Variation
1–2 courgettes may also be added to this salad. Slice the courgettes and fry in the oil with the aubergine and onion slices.

Super Salads

Chef's Salad

METRIC/IMPERIAL
100 g/4 oz Emmenthal cheese
100 g/4 oz cooked tongue
350 g/12 oz cooked poultry
1 large onion
2 eggs, hard-boiled
1 small can artichoke hearts
1 can anchovy fillets
$\frac{1}{4}$ cucumber
1 punnet cress
1 lettuce
4 tomatoes
pinch white pepper
1 teaspoon dry mustard
4 tablespoons wine vinegar
150 ml/$\frac{1}{4}$ pint oil

Slice the cheese and tongue into thin strips. Cut the poultry meat into bite-sized pieces. Peel the onion and cut into rings. Slice the hard-boiled eggs.
Drain the artichoke hearts and the anchovies. Form the anchovy fillets into rings. Thinly slice the cucumber; wash and dry the cress and lettuce.
Peel and cut the tomatoes into quarters.
Arrange all the salad ingredients attractively on a large dish.
Mix the pepper with the mustard, vinegar and oil to make a dressing and serve separately.
Serve with French bread and butter.
Serves 4

Variation
In place of the artichoke hearts, drained canned asparagus spears can be used.

French Bean Salad

METRIC/IMPERIAL
100 g/4 oz frozen shrimps
0·5 kg/1 lb French beans
1 egg
2 tomatoes
1 onion
½ teaspoon salt
4 tablespoons wine vinegar
1 tablespoon chopped savory
2 tablespoons chopped
  borage
2 teaspoons French mustard
4 tablespoons oil

Defrost the shrimps. Top
and tail the beans and cook
in boiling salted water,
until just tender. Drain and
cool.
Hard-boil the egg for 10
minutes, cool, shell and
remove the egg yolk. Press
the egg yolk through a
sieve. Nick the skins of the
tomatoes, plunge into
boiling water for 2–3
minutes; peel and cut into
slices. Peel and dice the
onion and mix with the
salt, vinegar, herbs,
mustard and the sieved egg
yolk. Blend in the oil.
Arrange the beans, shrimps
and tomatoes in a bowl and
spoon over the sauce.
Serves 4

Variation
When in season, French
beans are delicious in a
salad. When out of season,
use frozen beans and cook
according to the instructions
on the packet.

Asparagus Salad

METRIC/IMPERIAL
0·5 kg/1 lb fresh or canned
  asparagus
1 tablespoon wine vinegar
½ teaspoon salt
½ teaspoon sugar
2 tablespoons mayonnaise
4 tablespoons chopped
  parsley
2 slices canned pineapple
100 g/4 oz cooked chicken
Garnish
tomato wedges
parsley sprig

If using fresh asparagus,
peel, and cook in boiling
salted water for 15 minutes.
Refresh in cold water, drain
and cut into 5-cm (2-inch)
lengths. Drain and cut the
canned asparagus into 5-cm
(2-inch) lengths.
Mix the vinegar with the
salt, sugar, mayonnaise and
parsley. Cut the pineapple
slices into small pieces, add
the chicken; mix together.
Mix in the asparagus. Pour
over the dressing and toss
all the ingredients. Spoon
into a salad bowl and serve
garnished with tomato
wedges and a parsley sprig.
Serves 4–6

Variation
The mayonnaise may be
replaced by 2 tablespoons
soured cream.

153

Flambéed Dishes

Veal Kidneys Monsieur

METRIC/IMPERIAL
0·5 kg/1 lb veal kidneys
3 teaspoons salt
2 onions
1 tablespoon flour
3 tablespoons oil
juice of ½ lemon
2 teaspoons made mustard
150 ml/¼ pint soured cream
1 teaspoon sugar
3 tablespoons brandy
2 gherkins
2 tablespoons cocktail
   onions (optional)

Immerse the kidneys in
water for about 10 minutes,
then remove the gristle and
slice into 1-cm (½-inch)
thick pieces. Rub about 2
teaspoons of salt into them,
rinse and dry. Peel and
finely dice the onions.
Sprinkle another teaspoon
of salt on the kidneys and
toss them in the flour.
Heat the oil in a frying pan
and fry the kidney slices for
2 minutes, stirring with a
wooden spoon so that they
brown all over.
Lower the heat. Add the
diced onion to the pan. Mix
the lemon juice with the
mustard, cream and sugar.
Trickle the brandy over the
kidneys, carefully set alight,
let the flame almost go out
and then spoon over the
cream mixture.
Coarsely chop the gherkins,
and add with the cocktail
onions, if used, to the pan.
Stir round well and serve
immediately.
Serves 4

Flambéed Pork

METRIC/IMPERIAL
2 onions
0·5 kg/1 lb pork fillet
1 teaspoon salt
1 teaspoon paprika pepper
½ teaspoon black pepper
2 tablespoons flour
1 red pepper
4 tablespoons oil
5 tablespoons Aquavit
50 g/2 oz peas
6 tablespoons soured cream
1 teaspoon sugar

Peel and finely slice the
onions. Remove any gristle
and surplus fat from the
meat and slice thickly. Mix
together the salt, paprika,
pepper and flour and roll
the meat in it. Wash and
seed the pepper and cut into
strips.
Heat the oil in a frying pan,
fry the onion quickly, add
the meat slices and fry on
each side for 3 minutes.
Then pour over the Aquavit,
carefully set alight and let
the flame go out. Add the
peas and pepper strips.
Mix the cream and sugar
together and pour into the
pan. Let everything bubble
for another 5 minutes, then
serve immediately on
warmed plates.
Serve with a green salad.
Serves 4

Spiced Steak Fillets

METRIC/IMPERIAL
4 fillet steaks
½ teaspoon salt
ground black pepper
½ teaspoon paprika pepper
1 onion
2 tablespoons chopped
    preserved ginger
4 tablespoons oil
2 tablespoons mango chutney
3 tablespoons Chartreuse
    liqueur
4 tablespoons single cream
2 tablespoons chopped
    parsley

Beat the steaks very thinly
and rub the salt, pepper and
paprika into them. Peel and
very finely slice the onion.
Chop the ginger.

Heat the oil in a frying pan
and fry the meat for 1
minute on each side. Put
the onion slices, chopped
ginger (with the syrup) and
mango chutney into the pan.
Let the mixture get hot,
turning constantly with a
wooden spoon. Pour over
the liqueur and carefully set
alight. Extinguish the flames
after 30 seconds with the
cream. Finally sprinkle over
the parsley. Serve
immediately on warm
plates, accompanied by
sautéed potatoes.
Serves 4

Variation
Use rump steak or pork
fillet instead of fillet steak.
Fry for 2 minutes on each
side in the heated oil.

Riviera Trout

METRIC/IMPERIAL
2 fresh or frozen trout
1 teaspoon salt
2 tablespoons flour
1 teaspoon rosemary sprigs
    or ½ teaspoon dried
    rosemary
3 tablespoons oil
25 g/1 oz butter
4 tablespoons Ricard or
    Pernod
4 tablespoons single cream
Garnish
lemon slices
rosemary sprigs

Thaw the trout if using
frozen; then clean and wash
thoroughly in cold water.
Drain and roll in the salt
and flour. Rub the rosemary

inside the trout. Heat the
oil in a frying pan with the
butter. Lay the trout in the
pan and fry for 5 minutes,
turning several times. Then
pour over the Ricard and
carefully set alight; let it
almost go out. Extinguish
the dying flames with the
cream and mix with the
juices in the pan.
Serve immediately on
warmed plates with French
fried or creamed potatoes
and a cucumber salad.
Garnish with halved slices
of lemon and sprigs of
rosemary.
Serves 2

Snails on Toast

METRIC/IMPERIAL
24 canned snails
50 g/2 oz butter
½ teaspoon garlic salt
¼ teaspoon white pepper
6 tablespoons brandy
2 slices wholemeal bread
Garnish
parsley sprigs

Drain the snails in a sieve over a basin, reserving the juice.
Heat the snails with the butter, garlic salt and pepper in a frying pan for 2 minutes, without letting them burn. Then pour over the brandy and carefully set alight. Let it almost go out and extinguish the last flames with the juice from the snails.
Toast the bread and cut diagonally, place on two warmed plates. Spoon the snails with the butter sauce on to the bread. Garnish with parsley and serve immediately, accompanied by a tomato salad.
Serves 2

Variation
Canned snails are delicious served in their shells with garlic butter. Cream 100 g (4 oz) butter with 2 crushed cloves garlic, 4 tablespoons chopped parsley and seasoning. Place a snail in each shell, add a little butter and cook in a moderately hot oven (200° C, 400° F, Gas Mark 6) for 10 minutes.

Louisiana Chicken

METRIC/IMPERIAL
1 chicken, cooked
4 tablespoons oil
pinch saffron
½ teaspoon salt
50 g/2 oz canned sweetcorn
50 g/2 oz green peas
1 tomato
4 tablespoons whisky
2 tablespoons brandy
50 g/2 oz butter
6 tablespoons cream

Joint the chicken into wings, legs and breast pieces and remove the largest bones. Heat the oil in a frying pan and reheat the chicken thoroughly. Sprinkle over the saffron and salt. After 2–3 minutes add the drained sweetcorn and the peas; cover and cook for a further 2 minutes. Slice the tomato.
Mix the whisky and brandy, pour over the chicken pieces and carefully set alight; let the flames almost go out.
Add the tomato slices to the pan and stir in the butter. Finally stir in the cream. Serve immediately on warmed plates, accompanied by a green salad.
Serves 4–6

Variation
If liked, use canned sweetcorn to which diced green and red peppers have been added. This will give even more colour to the dish.

Steak au Poivre in Brandy

METRIC/IMPERIAL
24 black peppercorns
2 fillet steaks
½ teaspoon salt
4 tablespoons oil
few drops Tabasco sauce
4 tablespoons brandy
25 g/1 oz butter

Crush the peppercorns with the blade of a heavy knife or with a pestle. Salt the steaks. Sprinkle the crushed peppercorns on both sides of the steaks and press well in with a knife. Heat the oil in a frying pan and fry on each side for 1–2 minutes, or longer according to taste.

Pour the Tabasco sauce and brandy over the steaks, carefully set alight and let the flames go out. Add the butter and allow to melt in the pan juices. Serve immediately on warmed plates, with French fried potatoes and a mixed salad.
Serves 2

Cook's Tip
When you are flaming food it is better to use high percentage spirits as they will burn better. Whatever spirit you use should in any case have an alcohol content of 38%.

Breast of Chicken Flambé

METRIC/IMPERIAL
4 fresh or frozen chicken
   breasts
50 g/2 oz butter
100 g/4 oz sliced ham
¼ teaspoon garlic salt
1 teaspoon white pepper
4 tablespoons oil
225 g/8 oz canned fruit
   cocktail, drained
6 tablespoons brandy

Thaw the chicken breasts if frozen. Place the chicken between 2 sheets of damp greaseproof paper and beat the meat flat.
Divide the butter and ham into 4 equal portions and season with the garlic salt and pepper. Place a portion on to each chicken slice. Roll up and fasten the chicken breasts with fine string, thread or wooden cocktail sticks. Heat the oil in a shallow ovenproof casserole, fry the chicken breasts for 3 minutes all over and then lower the heat and continue cooking for a further 10 minutes, turning from time to time. Add the fruit cocktail, pour over the brandy, set alight very carefully with a match and serve while still flaming. Serve with buttered rice.
Serves 4

Rump Steaks with Bananas

METRIC/IMPERIAL
1 onion
1 banana
2 rump steaks
3 tablespoons oil
1 teaspoon made mustard
½ teaspoon curry powder
2 tablespoons port
3 tablespoons vodka
½ teaspoon salt
150 ml/¼ pint pouring white
  sauce
1 tablespoon Worcestershire
  sauce
4 tablespoons single cream
25 g/1 oz butter

Peel and slice the onion and banana. Beat the rump steaks very thin. Heat the oil in the frying pan and lightly brown the onion for 2 minutes; then push to one side of the frying pan. Put in the steaks and fry on each side for 2–3 minutes, or longer, according to taste. Push to one side. Stir the mustard and curry powder into the oil in the pan and add the banana. Pour on the port and vodka, carefully set alight and allow to almost go out. Add the salt, white sauce, Worcestershire sauce and cream and stir into the pan juices. Finally melt the butter in the sauce and spoon over the steak and onion. Serve immediately on warmed plates. Accompany with roast potatoes and celery salad, if liked.
Serves 2

Scotch Chicken

METRIC/IMPERIAL
1 small chicken, roasted
2 onions
8 slices salami
6 gherkins
50 g/2 oz pickled beetroot
2 tomatoes
100 g/4 oz frozen peas
4 tablespoons oil
3 tablespoons Scotch whisky
2 tablespoons chopped
  parsley
1 teaspoon salt
½ teaspoon sugar
1 teaspoon paprika pepper

Divide the chicken into fairly large pieces and remove the larger bones. Peel and finely slice the onions. Cut the salami slices in half. Cut the gherkins into matchsticks and coarsely chop the beetroot.
Nick the skins of the tomatoes, plunge into boiling water for 2–3 minutes, peel and quarter. Thaw the peas.
Heat the oil in a frying pan and brown the chicken pieces quickly on all sides. Add the onion and salami and cook for 2 minutes. Pour over the whisky, carefully set alight and allow to almost go out. Add the gherkins, tomatoes, beetroot, peas and parsley and season with the salt, sugar and paprika. Heat through then serve immediately, with roast potatoes and a green salad.
Serves 4

Orange
Pancake

METRIC/IMPERIAL
4 tablespoons flour
1 egg
1 teaspoon sugar
pinch salt
50 g/2 oz butter
2 oranges
12 sugar lumps
5 tablespoons Grand Marnier
    liqueur
4 tablespoons brandy

Beat the flour with enough
cold water to make a thick
batter; then add the egg,
sugar and salt and stir until
smooth. Heat half the
butter in a shallow pan.
Pour in the batter; after 5
minutes turn the pancake
over, cook for 2 more
minutes then slide on to a
board and cut into small
pieces or 2·5-cm (1-inch)
squares.
Rub the orange peel with
the sugar lumps; then grate
the rind and squeeze out
the juice from the oranges.
Melt the remaining butter
in the pan with the orange
rind, juice and the sugar
lumps. Add the pancake
pieces and stir round. Mix
the liqueur and the brandy
together and pour over,
carefully set alight and
allow to go out. Serve
immediately on warmed
plates, with vanilla ice cream.
Serves 2

Jubilee
Cherries

METRIC/IMPERIAL
1 (425-g/15-oz) can stoned
    cherries
50 g/2 oz butter
1 tablespoon Campari
4 tablespoons sugar
5 tablespoons rum
4 tablespoons single cream
50 g/2 oz macaroons, crushed

Drain the cherries,
reserving 4 tablespoons of
the juice. Melt the butter in
a frying pan, but do not let
it get hot. Stir in the
Campari and sugar and mix
well. Add the cherries and
heat for 4–5 minutes,
moving around in the pan.
Now add the rum to the
pan juices and set carefully
alight. After 30 seconds
extinguish the flames with
the cream and the reserved
cherry juice. Cook for a
further 30 seconds. Put the
crushed macaroons into
individual dishes, spoon
over the cherries and sauce
and serve immediately.
Hand macaroons separately.
Serves 2

Variation
You can make a delicious
dessert if you substitute
blackberries for the cherries.
Use a blackberry liqueur or
brandy to flambé.
Note When flaming dishes
at the table, do make sure
that the flambé set stands
firmly on mats to protect
the table and that the pan
sits firmly on the spirit
burner.

Zabaglione with Grapes

METRIC/IMPERIAL
100 g/4 oz black grapes
100 g/4 oz white grapes
500 ml/generous ¾ pint
   Moselle or medium dry
   white wine
100 g/4 oz sugar
grated rind of 1 lemon
2 teaspoons lemon juice
5 egg yolks
2 teaspoons cornflour

Wash the grapes, halve and remove the pips. Half-fill a large pan with water and heat. Place all the ingredients except the grapes in a basin and mix well together. Place the basin over the pan of hot water and whisk until the mixture becomes frothy. Take care not to let the water boil, or the mixture will curdle. When the mixture begins to get creamy and frothy, remove immediately from the heat and pour into 4 glasses while still hot.
Place the grapes on top of each glass and allow to sink into the zabaglione. Serve with frosted grapes.
Serves 4

Cook's Tip
Frost grapes by dipping them into lightly whisked egg white and then toss in castor sugar. Allow to dry on greaseproof paper.

Ice Cream Melba

METRIC/IMPERIAL
1 (411-g/14½-oz) can peach
   halves or 4 fresh peaches
150 g/5 oz icing sugar
8 tablespoons brandy
150 ml/¼ pint double cream
few drops vanilla essence
4 individual bricks vanilla
   ice cream
8 tablespoons raspberry jam,
   sieved

Drain the peach halves. If using fresh peaches plunge them into boiling water for 2 minutes, remove and peel off the skin with a small knife. Cut in half and remove the stones.
Put the peaches in a bowl, sprinkle with the icing sugar and brandy and leave for 30 minutes, to marinate. Whip the cream with the vanilla essence until stiff. Put the ice cream bricks into 4 individual glass dishes. Place the peach halves on top. Mix the brandy marinade with the raspberry jam and pour over. Decorate with piped whipped cream and serve with sponge finger biscuits.
Serves 4

Variation
Instead of raspberry jam you could use fresh or frozen raspberries, puréed with a little sugar.

Melon Filled with Fruit Salad

(in foreground of picture)

METRIC/IMPERIAL
juice of 1 lemon
2 tablespoons clear honey
1 large honeydew melon
1 (312-g/11-oz) can
*   mandarin oranges*
1 apple
1 banana
225 g/8 oz white grapes
50 g/2 oz glacé cherries
300 ml/½ pint double cream
few drops vanilla essence

Mix the lemon juice with the honey. Slice the top third off the melon, remove the pips and scoop out the flesh with a small spoon or melon baller, to form little balls. Drain the mandarin oranges and stir 2 tablespoons of the juice into the lemon and honey mixture. Peel, core and slice the apple. Slice the banana and halve and pip the washed grapes. Mix all the fruit together with the honey juice. Whip the cream with the vanilla essence semi-stiffly and add to the fruit salad. Arrange in the scooped-out melon.
Serves 4

Variations
Mixed Fruit Salad *(centre)*
Mix several different fruits which have been diced or sliced the same size. Sweeten and add lemon, orange or apple juice.

Raspberry Cups *(top right)*
Stir slightly sweetened raspberries into lightly whipped cream and natural yogurt, and arrange in tall glasses.

Strawberry Curd *(bottom right)*
Halve and sweeten fresh strawberries. Mix together with cottage cheese.

East Frisian Pears

METRIC/IMPERIAL
250 g/9 oz round-grain rice
½ teaspoon salt
Scant 1 litre/1½ pints milk
2 tablespoons sugar
grated rind of 1 lemon
3 eggs
few drops vanilla essence
fine white breadcrumbs
oil for deep frying
angelica strips

Wash the rice in cold running water until the water is clear. Then drain and bring to the boil with the salt, milk, sugar and lemon rind. Cook for 20 minutes.
Mix the cooked rice with 1 egg and the vanilla essence and allow to become cold. With wet hands mould into pear shapes. Whisk the remaining eggs. Dip the pears in the egg, then roll in the breadcrumbs. Heat the oil to 180° C (350° F) and fry the pears until a golden brown colour. Drain well on absorbent paper.
Place strips of angelica in the pears for stalks.
Serve with canned cherries, frosted grapes and cream.
Serves 4

Cook's Tip
Before shaping, spread the mixture in a shallow dish and allow to chill in the refrigerator.

Charlotte Cream

METRIC/IMPERIAL
200 g/7 oz icing sugar, sieved
6 egg yolks
25 g/1 oz gelatine
250 ml/scant ½ pint milk
few drops vanilla essence
600 ml/1 pint double cream

Place 100 g (4 oz) icing sugar and the egg yolks in a basin over a saucepan of hot water. Whisk the mixture until creamy. As soon as it begins to thicken, remove from the heat and continue whisking until really thick. Dissolve the gelatine in 3 tablespoons water over a low heat. Heat the milk in another pan, remove from the heat and add the vanilla essence and the dissolved gelatine. Stir a few spoonfuls of the hot milk into the egg mixture, then pour the egg mixture very carefully into the milk. Allow to cool until on the point of setting. Meanwhile, whip the cream fairly stiffly with the rest of the icing sugar and fold into the cooled mixture. Rinse a 1-litre (2-pint) jelly mould in cold water and pour in the cream mixture. Put in the refrigerator and leave to set. To serve, invert the mould on to a dish, cover with a hot cloth and carefully lift the mould off. Decorate with piped cream and crystallised fruit.
Serves 4–6

French Sabayon

METRIC/IMPERIAL
6 eggs
5 tablespoons icing sugar
5 tablespoons Marsala
½ lemon
2 sugar lumps
50 g/2 oz ground hazelnuts

Break the eggs, separate the yolks from the whites. Put the yolks in a basin, sieve the icing sugar and add to the egg yolks with the Marsala. Rub the lemon peel with the sugar lumps and add to the egg yolk mixture. Place the basin over a saucepan of hot water and whisk until frothy. Squeeze the juice from the lemon and stir in.

Whisk the egg whites stiffly and fold into the egg mixture. Finally fold in the ground hazelnuts and pour into individual glasses. Sprinkle chocolate flakes on top, and dredge with a little sieved icing sugar.
Serve immediately with crisp dessert biscuits.
Serves 4–6

Cook's Tip
A Sabayon sauce of egg yolks, sugar and wine may be thickened with a little arrowroot and served separately as a delicious accompaniment to fruit puddings.

Cranberry Cream Trifle

METRIC/IMPERIAL
0·75 kg/1½ lb fresh or frozen
*   cranberries*
225 g/8 oz sugar
juice of 1 lemon
1 cinnamon stick
10 slices brown bread, crusts
*   removed*
600 ml/1 pint double cream
few drops vanilla essence
1 tablespoon chopped
*   pistachio nuts*

Pick over the cranberries, wash in cold water and cook for 20 minutes with 200 g (7 oz) sugar, the lemon juice and the cinnamon stick. Some of the liquid should evaporate. Cool and remove the cinnamon stick.

Make the brown bread into fine breadcrumbs. Arrange a layer of these over the base of a glass bowl. Whip the cream with the vanilla essence and the remaining sugar until fairly stiff. Put a layer of the cooled cranberries with their juice on top of the layer of breadcrumbs, then spread over a layer of the whipped cream. Repeat these layers, finishing with a layer of cream. Chill in the refrigerator for 2 hours. Sprinkle the chopped pistachio nuts on top.
Serves 4–6

Floating Meringue

METRIC/IMPERIAL
6 eggs
250 ml/scant ½ pint milk
25 g/1 oz butter
grated rinds of 1 orange and
    1 lemon
150 g/5 oz sugar
6 tablespoons flour
4 tablespoons icing sugar

Separate the egg yolks from the whites. Warm the milk in a generous 1-litre (2–2½-pint) ovenproof dish, add the butter and grated orange and lemon rinds. Heat through in the oven. Whisk the egg whites stiffly, add half the sugar and whisk again until stiff. Then carefully fold in the rest of the sugar, the egg yolks and the flour. Place large spoonfuls of this mixture in the warm milk, remove from the heat and dust with icing sugar.
Bake in the centre of a hot oven (230° C, 450° F, Gas Mark 8) for 5–8 minutes, then reduce the temperature to 150° C, 300° F, Gas Mark 2, for a further 15–20 minutes. Serve at once.
Serves 4–6

Cook's Tip
This dish will not stand any draught when it comes out of the oven. It should be served immediately before the topping sinks.

Apple Fritters

METRIC/IMPERIAL
4 cooking apples
juice of 1 lemon
50 g/2 oz sugar
few drops vanilla essence
150 ml/¼ pint brandy
pinch each ground
    cardamom, cinnamon and
    cloves
8 tablespoons flour
2 eggs
½ teaspoon salt
4 tablespoons currants
oil for deep frying
1 teaspoon cornflour

Peel and core the apples and cut into thick rings. Place in a flat dish and sprinkle with the lemon juice, 2 tablespoons of the sugar, the vanilla essence, brandy and spices. Leave for 1 hour to marinate.
Mix 6 tablespoons of the flour with 300 ml (½ pint) water until smooth. Then add the eggs, salt, 1 teaspoon of sugar and the currants. Heat the oil to 180° C (350° F). Pick each apple ring from its marinade with a fork, drain, toss in the remaining flour, then dip in the batter. Fry in the oil until golden. Drain on absorbent paper. Sieve the marinade and heat in a saucepan. Mix the cornflour with a little water. Use to thicken the marinade and bring to the boil. Cool and serve as a sauce. Serve the apple fritters with vanilla ice cream.
Serves 4

Austrian Apricot Dumplings

METRIC/IMPERIAL
0·5 kg/1 lb small apricots
sugar lumps
150 g/5 oz butter
150 g/5 oz flour
2 eggs
½ teaspoon salt
75 g/3 oz breadcrumbs
3 tablespoons icing sugar

Halve the apricots and remove the stones. Place a sugar lump in each cavity. In a saucepan bring to the boil 350 ml (generous ½ pint) water with 25 g (1 oz) of the butter. Sieve the flour and put all at once into the boiling water. Beat well with a wooden spoon until the lump of dough comes away from the base of the pan and the surface is shiny. Remove from the heat and beat in the eggs. Shape the still warm dough into rolls and slice into 2.5-cm (1-inch) thick slices. Flatten a little and mould each one round an apricot. Leave to dry for 5 minutes. Bring 2 litres (3½ pints) of water to the boil with the salt. Drop in the dumplings and cook over a medium heat for 8–10 minutes. Brown the breadcrumbs in the rest of the butter. Lift the dumplings out of the water with a ladle, drain well, toss in the bread-crumbs and dust with the icing sugar.
Serves 4

Caramel Pudding

METRIC/IMPERIAL
4 eggs
200 g/7 oz sugar
1 teaspoon vanilla essence
400 ml/scant ¾ pint double
*   cream*
1 tablespoon icing sugar
Decoration
chocolate curls

Lightly beat the eggs with 75 g (3 oz) sugar. Add the vanilla essence and 250 ml (scant ½ pint) cream and stir.
Melt the remaining sugar in a saucepan and cook until it turns a pale caramel colour. Pour the caramel into a 1-litre (1¾-pint) pudding basin and pour over the egg mixture. Cover tightly with greaseproof paper and foil and place the pudding basin in a saucepan of water. Steam gently for 1¼ hours. The water should bubble quietly. Cool the pudding and tip out on to a serving plate.
Stiffly whip the remaining cream with the icing sugar. Decorate the caramel pudding with piped cream and chocolate curls.
Serves 4
Note To make chocolate curls, melt 100 g (4 oz) plain chocolate in a bowl over a pan of hot water. Spread on to a sheet of waxed paper. When cooled and set, scrape the chocolate up into curls with the blade of a knife.

Poires Belle Hélène

METRIC/IMPERIAL
4 ripe dessert pears
250 ml/scant ½ pint
    medium dry white wine
100 g/4 oz sugar
few drops vanilla essence
½ stick cinnamon
100 g/4 oz plain chocolate
150 ml/¼ pint double cream
1 block vanilla ice cream
Decoration
few glacé cherries

Peel and halve the pears. Remove the cores and the stalks. Lay the pear halves in an ovenproof dish and add the wine, sugar, vanilla essence and cinnamon stick and simmer over a medium heat for 10 minutes. Remove from the heat and allow to cool in the liquid. When cold, remove the pears and drain. Meanwhile, put 4 glass bowls in the refrigerator to chill. Break the chocolate into small pieces and melt in a saucepan, add the cream and stir well. Divide the vanilla ice cream into 4 thick slices and place in the chilled dishes. Arrange 2 pear halves on top of each and pour over the hot chocolate sauce. Decorate with glacé cherries and serve immediately.
Serves 4

Creamy Rice Mould

METRIC/IMPERIAL
200 g/7 oz round-grain rice
½ teaspoon salt
15 g/½ oz gelatine
300 ml/½ pint milk
6 tablespoons sugar
few drops vanilla essence
3 glasses Maraschino
    liqueur or cherry brandy
300 ml/½ pint cream
25 g/1 oz pistachio nuts,
    chopped

Wash the rice under cold running water until the water remains clear. Then cook in a saucepan with 1·5 litres (2½ pints) water and the salt for 20 minutes. Dissolve the gelatine in 3 tablespoons water. Warm the milk and add the dissolved gelatine, the sugar and vanilla essence.
Drain the rice and stir into the milk mixture and add the liqueur. Allow to cool slightly. Whip the cream stiffly and fold into the rice. Pour into a rinsed mould and chill in the refrigerator. Turn out on to a serving dish and sprinkle with chopped pistachio nuts. Serve with sieved raspberry jam or raspberry purée made with fresh raspberries.
Serves 4

Variation
Fruit may also be added to the cooked, drained rice. An excellent combination is chopped cherries and nuts, or sultanas, seedless raisins and nuts.

Rum Savarin

METRIC/IMPERIAL
350 g/12 oz flour
20 g/¾ oz fresh yeast
250 ml/scant ½ pint lukewarm
 milk
4 eggs
150 g/5 oz sugar
few drops vanilla essence
½ teaspoon salt
150 g/5 oz butter, softened
2 tablespoons rum
4 tablespoons white wine
1 (425-g/15-oz) can cherries,
 drained
150 ml/¼ pint double cream

Butter and flour a plain (23-cm/9-inch) savarin mould.
Sieve the flour into a bowl, make a well in the centre and add the yeast mixed with the warm milk. Leave for 15 minutes.
Whisk the eggs with 40 g (1½ oz) sugar, stir in the vanilla essence, salt and the softened butter. Stir into the yeast and flour mixture to form a dough. Leave to rise for a further 10 minutes. Pour the dough into the savarin mould, until half full. Leave the dough in a warm place for 30–60 minutes, until it has doubled in volume. Bake in a hot oven (220° C, 425° F, Gas Mark 7) for 40 minutes. Turn out and cool on a wire tray.
Place the rum, white wine, 150 ml (¼ pint) water and the remaining sugar in a saucepan and bring to the boil. Pour carefully over the savarin until all the syrup has been absorbed. Arrange the cherries in the middle of the savarin. Whip the cream until stiff and pipe small rosettes round the savarin.
Serves 6

Chinese Cabbage Soup

METRIC/IMPERIAL
350 g/12 oz lean pork (fillet or from the leg)
1 litre/1¾ pints water
1½ teaspoons salt
2 teaspoons cornflour
2 tablespoons soy sauce
2 teaspoons sugar
1 teaspoon white pepper
2 tablespoons oil
225 g/8 oz Chinese cabbage

Put the meat, water and salt in a saucepan and bring to the boil. Simmer for 1 hour, or until the meat is cooked and tender. Drain the meat, reserving the cooking liquid. Cut the meat into thin slices and mix with the cornflour, soy sauce, sugar, pepper and oil. Leave for 30 minutes.
Wash the cabbage and cut into thin strips. Bring the pork cooking liquid back to the boil and add the cabbage strips. Simmer for 15 minutes, then stir in the meat slices with the soy sauce mixture. Continue to simmer for 10 minutes.
Serve hot.
Serves 4

Potato and Meat Soup

METRIC/IMPERIAL
0·5 kg/1 lb boned brisket of beef
2 litres/3½ pints water
1 teaspoon salt
1 teaspoon celery salt
0·75 kg/1½ lb potatoes
50 g/2 oz butter
4 tablespoons finely chopped chervil
150 ml/¼ pint single cream

Trim off any fat, then put the meat in a saucepan with the water, salt and celery salt. Bring to the boil. Simmer for 45 minutes–1 hour, until the meat is cooked and tender. Meanwhile, peel and finely dice the potatoes. Melt the butter in a frying pan. Add the potatoes and fry lightly for 10 minutes. Remove from the heat.
Remove the meat from the pan, reserving the cooking liquid, and dice finely. Return the diced meat to the pan and stir in the fried potatoes. Bring back to the boil and simmer for 20 minutes, until the potatoes are tender.
Add the chervil and cream and heat without boiling. Serve hot.
Serves 6–8

Variation

225 g (8 oz) of the potatoes may be replaced by 2 carrots and 1 onion. Chop the vegetables and cook them with the potatoes.

168

Meatball Soup

METRIC/IMPERIAL
2 onions
250 ml/scant ½ pint white wine
1 litre/1¾ pints stock
450 g/1 lb sauerkraut
½ teaspoon sugar
225 g/8 oz lean minced beef
pinch dried mixed herbs
pinch salt
pinch black pepper
1 teaspoon tomato purée
2 tablespoons chopped parsley
½ teaspoon black pepper
150 ml/5 fl oz natural yogurt

Peel and thinly slice the onions. Put the wine and stock in a saucepan and bring to the boil. Add the sauerkraut, onion and sugar and simmer for 40 minutes. Mix the minced beef with the herbs, salt, pepper and tomato purée. With wet hands form the mixture into small balls. Add to the pan and cook for 5 minutes, or until the meatballs are firm when pressed.
Pour the soup into individual bowls. Sprinkle with parsley and pepper and put a spoonful of yogurt in the centre of each.
Serves 4

Variation
Soured cream can be used instead of yogurt.

Provençale Fish Soup

METRIC/IMPERIAL
0·5 kg/1 lb mussels
1 kg/2 lb mixed fish (shellfish, halibut, turbot, sole, plaice)
4 onions
4 tablespoons oil
2 litres/3½ pints fish or chicken stock
4 tomatoes, peeled
4 rashers back bacon
2 large potatoes
½ cucumber
100 g/4 oz crab meat
100 g/4 oz spiral noodles
1 tablespoon chopped parsley

Scrub the mussels, removing beards. Discard any which are open or do not shut when tapped. Soak for 1 hour in cold water, then drain. Remove all shell or skin and bones from the fish. Cut the flesh into small pieces. Peel and slice the onions. Heat the oil in a large saucepan, and fry the onion for 5 minutes, then add the fish and mussels. Cook for 5 minutes. Remove the mussel flesh from the shells and return the flesh to the pan with the stock. Bring to the boil and simmer for 15 minutes. Quarter the tomatoes. Rind and dice the bacon. Peel and finely chop the potatoes and cucumber. Add the crab meat, tomatoes, bacon, noodles and potatoes to the pan and simmer for a further 20 minutes. Stir in the cucumber and parsley.
Serves 6–8

Beef Soup

METRIC/IMPERIAL
350 g/12 oz shin of beef or
chuck steak
2·5 litres/4½ pints water
1 teaspoon salt
1 bouquet garni
2 carrots
2 red peppers
150 g/5 oz ribbon noodles
½ teaspoon celery salt
2 teaspoons chopped
parsley

Remove any fat from the
meat and dice. Put into a
saucepan with the water,
salt and bouquet garni
(3 bay leaves, 3 sprigs
parsley, 1 sprig thyme, tied
together) and bring to the
boil. Simmer gently for
2 hours, until the meat is
tender.
Meanwhile, peel the carrots
and cut into sticks. Remove
the pith, seeds and core
from the peppers and cut
into strips. Add the carrots,
peppers, noodles and celery
salt to the pan and continue
to simmer for about 20
minutes, until the vegetables
are tender. Remove the
bouquet garni. Pour into a
heated soup tureen,
sprinkle over the parsley
and serve.
Serves 6–8

Variation
Add 225 g (8 oz) canned,
drained butter beans and
use 150 g (5 oz) runner
beans instead of the
noodles.

Leek Soup

METRIC/IMPERIAL
4 leeks
2 onions
50 g/2 oz butter
1 litre/1¾ pints chicken stock
½ teaspoon sugar
50 g/2 oz ham
1½ teaspoons flour
2 tablespoons water
50 g/2 oz Wensleydale
cheese
300 ml/½ pint single cream
Garnish
4 tablespoons grated
Parmesan cheese

Wash the leeks, and cut into
strips 2·5 cm (1 inch) wide.
Peel and slice the onions.
Melt the butter in a saucepan and add the leeks and
onions. Fry for 5 minutes.
Stir in the stock and bring
to the boil. Simmer for 5
minutes, then add the sugar.
Stir well and leave to
simmer for 15 minutes.
Meanwhile, cut the ham
into thin strips.
Blend the flour with the
water, and stir into the soup.
Continue to simmer,
stirring, until the soup
thickens. Crumble the
cheese and stir in with the
ham and cream. Heat
gently without allowing to
boil. Pour the soup into
individual bowls and
sprinkle over the Parmesan
cheese.
Serves 4

Minestrone

METRIC/IMPERIAL

2 potatoes
2 carrots
2 onions
½ stick celery
1 leek
0·5 kg/1 lb white cabbage
1 clove garlic
2 rashers streaky bacon
50 g/2 oz fresh or frozen
    peas
50 g/2 oz green beans
2 litres/3½ pints beef stock
1 teaspoon salt
½ teaspoon white pepper
4 tablespoons chopped
    parsley
2 tablespoons chopped celery
    leaves
100 g/4 oz cooked long-grain
    rice

Garnish

grated Parmesan cheese

Peel the potatoes and
carrots and cut into strips.
Peel and slice the onions.
Cut the celery into strips.
Wash and slice the leek.
Core and chop the cabbage.
Crush the garlic. Rind and
chop the bacon.
Put the bacon in a saucepan
and fry until the fat runs.
Add the onion and garlic
and fry for 5 minutes,
adding a tablespoon of oil
if necessary. Stir in the
vegetables and stock and
bring to the boil. Simmer
for about 20 minutes, until
the vegetables are just
tender. Add the salt, pepper,
parsley, celery leaves and
rice and simmer for a
further 5 minutes.
Serve garnished with the
Parmesan cheese.
Serves 6–8

Swiss Cheese Soup

METRIC/IMPERIAL

1 onion
4 rashers streaky bacon
1 litre/1¾ pints chicken stock
225 g/8 oz Emmenthal cheese
225 g/8 oz fresh white
    breadcrumbs
300 ml/½ pint dry white wine
2 tablespoons each chopped
    chives, parsley and
    chervil
salt

Peel the onion and slice very
thinly. Fry the bacon until
the fat runs. Add the onion
and fry together until the
bacon is crisp and the onion
golden brown. Remove
from the heat and keep
warm. Meanwhile, heat the
chicken stock to boiling.
Grate the cheese and put in
a warmed soup tureen with
the breadcrumbs. Pour over
the boiling stock and leave
to soak for 3 minutes,
stirring occasionally. The
breadcrumbs should
disintegrate and the cheese
melt. Stir in the wine, herbs
and salt to taste. Garnish
with the bacon and onion
and serve immediately.
Serves 4

Variation

Smoked meat or cooked
ham may also be added to
the garnish. It should be
cut into small strips and
sautéed together with the
bacon and onion.

171

Cream of Tomato Soup

(in foreground of picture)

METRIC/IMPERIAL
2 thick slices white bread
1 tablespoon butter
1 clove garlic, crushed
1 (794-g/1 lb 12-oz) can
  cream of tomato soup
1 tablespoon chopped parsley

Remove the crusts from the
bread and cube. Melt the
butter and fry the garlic and
bread cubes until golden
brown. Heat the soup and
garnish with the croûtons
and parsley.
Serves 4

Variations
Cream of Asparagus Soup
(extreme right)
Drain a 425-g (15-oz) can of
artichoke hearts. Melt 15 g
($\frac{1}{2}$ oz) butter and fry the
artichoke hearts for 2–3
minutes. Add to heated
asparagus soup, with 1
tablespoon single cream per
portion.

Cream of Chicken Soup
(bottom left)
Heat 225 g (8 oz) frozen
peas in cream of chicken
soup for 5 minutes. Whip
4 tablespoons double cream
with 1–2 teaspoons curry
powder until stiff and use
to top each portion of soup.

Cream of Onion Soup
(top left)
Peel and slice 1 onion.
Deseed and slice a green
pepper into rings. Fry in
butter until tender. Heat
diced corned beef with
cream of onion soup and
garnish with the fried onion
and pepper.

Pea Soup *(top centre)*
Heat 100 g (4 oz) frozen
peas with canned cream of
pea soup. Add small cocktail
sausages and sprinkle with
parsley.

Creamy Asparagus Soup

METRIC/IMPERIAL
0·5 kg/1 lb fresh asparagus
25 g/1 oz butter
2 tablespoons single cream
4 tablespoons soured cream
   or natural yogurt
4 egg yolks

Peel the asparagus and trim off the woody ends. Break into small pieces, about 2·5 cm (1 inch) long. Cook in boiling salted water until just tender. Reserve the tips, and blend the remaining asparagus to a purée with generous 1 litre (2 pints) of the cooking liquid and the butter in a liquidiser. Return the puréed soup to the empty saucepan and stir in the cream and soured cream. Heat gently for 5 minutes.

Whisk the egg yolks in a basin and gradually add 2 spoonfuls of the hot soup. Stir the egg mixture into the remaining soup and heat. Do not allow to boil. Add the reserved asparagus tips and serve.
Serves 4

Cook's Tip
Canned asparagus can be used, in which case it should be blended with the liquid from the can and then thinned down with chicken stock to the required consistency.

German Fish Soup

METRIC/IMPERIAL
225 g/8 oz halibut fillets or
   boned salmon steaks
225 g/8 oz herring or cod's
   roe
4–6 onions
½ leek
1 teaspoon salt
750 ml/1¼ pints water
2 sticks celery
6 tablespoons chopped
   parsley
1 teaspoon grated fresh
   horseradish
2 tablespoons finely chopped
   gherkins
2 tablespoons soured cream
25 g/1 oz butter or margarine
dry white wine
finely chopped dill

Skin the fish fillets or steaks and the roe. Chop the roe. Peel and thinly slice the onions. Wash and slice the leek. Put the fish, roe, salt, onion, leek and water in a saucepan and bring to the boil. Simmer for 20 minutes. Dice the celery and add to the pan with the parsley, horseradish, gherkins, soured cream and butter or margarine. Cook gently for a further 10 minutes. Add a dash of white wine and sprinkle with the dill.
Serves 4

Variation
If fresh horseradish is not available substitute 1 teaspoon horseradish sauce.

Pork Fillets with Yogurt Sauce

METRIC/IMPERIAL
1 kg/2 lb pork fillets (in two pieces)
100 g/4 oz Gruyère or Emmenthal cheese
½ teaspoon salt
1 teaspoon paprika pepper
50 g/2 oz flour
50 g/2 oz butter
½ small onion
150 ml/¼ pint chicken stock
150 ml/5 fl oz natural yogurt
Garnish
parsley sprigs

Remove any excess fat from the pork fillets. Slit each fillet to make a pocket. Cut the cheese into matchsticks and put half into each fillet pocket. Close with a skewer or trussing needle and string. Mix together the salt, paprika and flour. Coat the fillets in this mixture. Melt the butter in a flame-proof pan. Add the fillets and brown on all sides. Peel and grate the onion and add to the pan with the stock. Stir to blend and bring to the boil. Stir in the yogurt. Cover and cook gently for 45 minutes–1 hour, until the pork is tender. Garnish with parsley sprigs and serve with Brussels sprouts.
Serves 4

Hungarian Meatballs

METRIC/IMPERIAL
100 g/4 oz streaky bacon
3 onions, chopped
2 tablespoons flour
0·5 kg/1 lb minced pork
100 g/4 oz minced beef
3 tablespoons chopped parsley
2 eggs
3 tablespoons breadcrumbs
1 teaspoon salt
½ teaspoon black pepper
2–3 teaspoons paprika pepper
4 tablespoons oil
300 ml/½ pint beef stock
4 tablespoons double cream

Rind and dice the bacon. Put half in a frying pan and heat until the fat runs. Add two-thirds of the onion and fry until golden brown. Sprinkle with half the flour and stir well. Tip into a bowl. Mix in the minced meats, parsley, eggs, bread-crumbs, salt, pepper and 2 teaspoons paprika. Form the mixture into small balls. Heat the oil and brown the meatballs. Reduce the heat and cook for 10 minutes. Heat the remaining bacon until the fat runs. Add the rest of the onion and fry until soft. Sprinkle with the remaining flour and paprika and stir well. Stir in the stock and bring to the boil. Simmer until thickened, stir in the cream and meatballs. Cook gently for 10 minutes and serve with buttered noodles.
Serves 4

Gammon with Sauerkraut

METRIC/IMPERIAL
2 onions
1 (1·5-kg/3-lb) gammon
  joint, soaked overnight
1 carrot, peeled
3 tablespoons honey
2 cooking apples
2 tablespoons dripping
350 g/12 oz sauerkraut
½ teaspoon salt
300 ml/½ pint stock
150 ml/¼ pint red wine
4 tablespoons soured cream
1 teaspoon cornflour

Peel 1 onion. Put in a saucepan with the gammon and carrot. Cover with fresh water, bring to the boil and simmer for 1½ hours.

Drain the gammon, remove the rind and most of the fat. Brush with honey and roast in a moderately hot oven (200° C, 400° F, Gas Mark 6) for 20 minutes. Dice the second onion. Peel the apples and chop. Melt the dripping and fry the drained sauerkraut and onion for 5 minutes. Stir in the apple, salt and stock and bring to the boil. Cover and simmer for 20 minutes. Drain the sauerkraut, reserving the liquid, and keep warm.
Add the wine to the cooking liquid, boil until reduced to about 150 ml (¼ pint) and stir in the cream and cornflour. Simmer until thickened, season and serve separately.
Serves 4

Pork Rolls in Tomato and Wine Sauce

METRIC/IMPERIAL
1 red or green pepper
100 g/4 oz tomatoes
4 slices pork fillet, each
  weighing 100 g/4 oz
1 teaspoon salt
½ teaspoon ground caraway
  seeds
2 onions, finely chopped
25 g/1 oz butter
150 ml/¼ pint dry white wine
4 tablespoons natural yogurt
1 teaspoon cornflour
75 g/3 oz cheese, grated

Cut the pepper into strips. Peel and chop the tomatoes. Beat the pork slices until quite thin. Sprinkle with salt, caraway, pepper strips and some of the onion. Roll up and secure with wooden cocktail sticks. Melt the butter and brown the pork rolls. Add the remaining onion, the tomatoes and the wine, and cook gently for 40 minutes, turning occasionally. Transfer the pork rolls to an ovenproof serving dish. Mix together the yogurt and cornflour and stir into the frying pan. When thickened, pour over the rolls. Sprinkle the cheese on top and bake in a moderately hot oven (200° C, 400° F, Gas Mark 6) for 10 minutes. Serve with boiled potatoes sprinkled with caraway seeds.
Serves 4

Bacon-Wrapped Liver with Raisin Sauce

METRIC/IMPERIAL
0·75 kg/1½ lb pigs' liver, in
  two pieces
1½ teaspoons salt
2 teaspoons paprika pepper
2 teaspoons Worcestershire
  sauce
1 teaspoon white pepper
100 g/4 oz streaky bacon
100 g/4 oz seedless raisins
25 g/1 oz butter
1½ tablespoons flour
150 ml/¼ pint dry red wine
150 ml/¼ pint stock
1 teaspoon sugar
4 tablespoons double cream

Rub the liver with the salt,
paprika, Worcestershire
sauce and pepper. Leave for
20 minutes.
Wrap the bacon around the
liver, covering the liver
completely. Place in an
oiled roasting tin and cook
in a moderately hot oven
(190° C, 375° F, Gas Mark
5) for 25–30 minutes.
Meanwhile, soak the raisins
in warm water for 15
minutes. Drain well. Melt
the butter in a pan, stir in
the flour and cook for 1
minute. Gradually stir in
the wine and stock and
bring to the boil. Simmer,
stirring, until the sauce
thickens. Add the raisins,
sugar and seasoning to
taste and cook gently for 5
minutes. Remove from the
heat and stir in the cream.
Serve separately.
Serves 4

Blanquette of Veal with Peppered Rice

METRIC/IMPERIAL
1 kg/2 lb lean boned
  shoulder of veal
1 leek, finely chopped
1 large carrot, diced
2 onions, diced
1 teaspoon salt
225 g/8 oz long-grain rice
2 green peppers
5 tablespoons oil
1 teaspoon paprika pepper
½ teaspoon white pepper
50 g/2 oz butter
2 tablespoons flour
100 g/4 oz frozen peas

Cut the meat into chunks,
removing any fat. Put the
meat, leek, carrot, onion
and salt in a saucepan. Add
600 ml (1 pint) water and
bring to the boil. Reduce the
heat and simmer for 1 hour.
Cook the rice. Meanwhile,
finely chop the peppers.
Heat the oil and quickly fry
the chopped peppers,
cooked rice, paprika and
pepper until the peppers are
just tender. Keep warm.
Drain the meat, reserving
the cooking liquid but
discarding the vegetables.
Blend the butter and flour
to form a paste and add in
small pieces to the cooking
liquid. Simmer, stirring,
until the liquid thickens.
Add the peas and meat and
simmer until the peas are
cooked and the meat
reheated. Serve with the
rice.
Serves 4

Sweetbreads with Asparagus

METRIC/IMPERIAL
0·5 kg/1 lb calves'
  sweetbreads
2 pork sausages
100 g/4 oz mushrooms
100 g/4 oz canned asparagus
25 g/1 oz butter
1½ tablespoons flour
300 ml/½ pint milk
1 teaspoon salt
½ teaspoon white pepper
Garnish
parsley

Soak the sweetbreads in water for 2 hours, then drain. Blanch in boiling water for 5 minutes, and drain. Remove the skin and ducts and cut the meat into thick slices. Skin the sausages and form the sausagemeat into small balls. Drop into boiling water and cook for 5 minutes. Drain well. Clean and halve the mushrooms. Drain the asparagus. Melt the butter in a saucepan. Stir in the flour and cook for 1 minute. Gradually add the milk and bring to the boil, stirring all the time. Simmer, stirring, until the sauce thickens. Add the salt, pepper, sweetbread slices, sausagemeat balls, mushrooms and pieces of asparagus. Simmer for 5 minutes. Spoon into a serving dish and garnish with parsley. Serve with a tomato and onion salad.
Serves 4

Braised Knuckle of Veal

METRIC/IMPERIAL
2 large onions
4 tablespoons oil
1 teaspoon salt
1 teaspoon black pepper
pinch marjoram
2 teaspoons paprika pepper
1 (1–1·5-kg/2–3-lb) boned
  and rolled knuckle of veal
300 ml/½ pint stock or water
2 tablespoons tomato purée
1½ tablespoons flour

Peel and chop the onions. Heat the oil in a flameproof casserole. Add the onion and fry for 5 minutes. Stir in the salt, pepper, marjoram and paprika. Lay the veal on the onion and pour in half the stock or water. Cover and braise in a moderate oven (180° C, 350° F, Gas Mark 4) for 1¼–1½ hours, or until the veal is tender.
Mix together the tomato purée, flour and remaining stock or water in a saucepan. Transfer the veal to a carving board. Cut into slices and arrange on a bed of freshly cooked mixed vegetables. Keep warm. Sieve the onion mixture in the casserole and add to the saucepan. Bring to the boil and simmer until the sauce thickens, stirring all the time. Pour into a warmed sauceboat and serve with the meat. Accompany with lightly sautéed boiled potatoes.
Serves 4

Braised Pork Shoulder

METRIC/IMPERIAL
1 (1-kg/2-lb) boned and
rolled shoulder of pork
1 teaspoon salt
1 teaspoon white pepper
2 onions
2 carrots
¼ celeriac or 2 sticks celery
2 tablespoons vegetable oil
300 ml/½ pint stock

Score the skin of the pork to
mark out squares. Rub the
meat with the salt and
pepper. Peel and halve the
onions. Peel and chop the
carrots. Chop the celeriac
or celery.
Heat the oil in a roasting
tin. Put in the meat and
vegetables and roast in a
hot oven (220° C, 425° F,
Gas Mark 7) for 1½ hours.
After 20 minutes, pour half
the stock into the roasting
tin. Add the remaining
stock after a further 20
minutes.
At the end of the roasting
time increase the oven
temperature to very hot
(240° C, 475° F, Gas Mark
9) and roast for a further
8 minutes. Transfer the
meat to a serving platter
and slice. Keep warm. Push
the vegetables and liquid
from the roasting tin
through a sieve and serve as
a sauce. Accompany with
Brussels sprouts and
creamed or boiled potatoes.
Serves 4–5

Roman Lamb Stew

METRIC/IMPERIAL
1 (396-g/14-oz) can tomatoes
1 clove garlic
1 onion
1 kg/2 lb lean lamb
4 tablespoons olive oil
300 ml/½ pint white wine
½ teaspoon dried rosemary
¼ teaspoon dried thyme
1 teaspoon salt
1 teaspoon pepper
450 g/1 lb spaghetti
75 g/3 oz Parmesan cheese,
grated
rosemary sprigs

Drain the tomatoes and
chop roughly. Finely chop
the garlic. Finely chop the
onion. Cut the meat into
2·5-cm (1-inch) chunks.
Heat the oil in a saucepan.
Add the meat and brown on
all sides. Stir in the wine,
onion, tomatoes, garlic,
rosemary, thyme, salt and
pepper. Cover and cook for
about 20 minutes, until the
meat is tender. Stir
occasionally and add more
wine if the mixture becomes
too dry.
Meanwhile, cook the
spaghetti in boiling salted
water for 12–15 minutes,
until just tender. Drain
well, then arrange in a ring
on a warmed serving dish.
Sprinkle the spaghetti with
the cheese and spoon the
lamb stew into the centre.
Garnish with fresh rosemary
sprigs and serve with a
green salad.
Serves 6

Beef Topside with Horseradish Sauce

METRIC/IMPERIAL
1 leek
3 carrots
1 onion
2 whole cloves
1-kg/2-lb piece beef topside
1 teaspoon salt
½ teaspoon celery salt
½ bay leaf
2 litres/3½ pints water
1–2 tablespoons freshly grated horseradish
juice of 1 lemon
1 teaspoon sugar

Wash and chop the leek. Peel the carrots and cut into sticks. Peel the onion and stud with the cloves. Put the meat in a saucepan and add the salt, celery salt, bay leaf, leek, carrots and onion. Pour over the water and bring to the boil. Simmer for 1½–2 hours, until the meat is tender.
Meanwhile, mix the grated horseradish with the lemon juice and sugar.
Cut the meat in thick slices and garnish with vegetables from the the pan. (The cooking liquid makes a good basis for soup.) Serve with the horseradish sauce and a green vegetable such as spinach.
Serves 4

Pork and Green Beans

METRIC/IMPERIAL
1 (1-kg/2-lb) boned shoulder of pork
1 teaspoon salt
½ teaspoon white pepper
pinch cayenne pepper
1 red pepper
6 tomatoes
0·5 kg/1 lb fresh or frozen French beans
1 stock cube
25 g/1 oz butter
1 tablespoon flour

Cut the meat into 2·5-cm (1-inch) chunks. Put in a flameproof casserole and cover with cold water. Add the salt, pepper and cayenne and bring to the boil. Simmer for 20 minutes.

Remove the pith, core and seeds from the pepper and cut into strips. Add to the pot and continue cooking for 15 minutes.
Peel and chop the tomatoes. If using fresh beans, trim and cut into pieces. Add the beans and tomatoes to the casserole with the stock cube, cover and cook for a further 25 minutes. If using frozen beans, add just before the end of the cooking time.
Mix the butter and flour together to form a paste. Add in small pieces to the casserole. Simmer, stirring, until the liquid thickens. Serve with potatoes.
Serves 4

179

Oxtail Stew

METRIC/IMPERIAL

1·5 kg/3 lb oxtail, cut into pieces 5 cm/2 inches long
1 clove garlic
1 teaspoon salt
½ bay leaf
10 juniper berries
juice of 1 lemon
2 teaspoons sugar
1 teaspoon dried rosemary
1 teaspoon dried marjoram
2 tablespoons brandy
50 g/2 oz flour
4–6 tablespoons dripping or oil
300 ml/½ pint red wine
300 ml/½ pint stock or warm water
2 tablespoons tomato purée
1 tablespoon paprika pepper

Lay the pieces of oxtail in a shallow dish. Crush the garlic. Mix the salt, garlic, bay leaf, juniper berries, lemon juice, sugar, herbs and brandy, and pour over the meat. Cover and leave to marinate for 1 hour. Remove the oxtail pieces, dry with absorbent paper and coat with the flour. Heat the dripping or oil in a flameproof casserole. Add the oxtail pieces and brown quickly.

Mix the wine, stock or water, tomato purée and paprika with the marinade and pour into the casserole. Bring to the boil, stirring, then cover and simmer for 3–4 hours, until the oxtail is tender. Serve with noodles and a green salad.
Serves 4

Stuffed Pork Rolls

METRIC/IMPERIAL

75 g/3 oz pork dripping
2 onions, sliced
100 g/4 oz sauerkraut
1 teaspoon salt
2 teaspoons sugar
150 ml/¼ pint water
1 large green pepper
3 rashers streaky bacon
4 slices pork fillet
6 tablespoons flour
2 teaspoons paprika pepper
1 teaspoon white pepper
150 ml/¼ pint buttermilk
150 ml/¼ pint beef stock

Heat half the dripping in a frying pan and fry the onion until golden brown. Add the drained sauerkraut, salt, sugar and water.

Simmer for 30 minutes. Meanwhile, remove the pith, core and seeds from the pepper and cut into strips. Rind and chop the bacon. Heat in another pan until the fat runs. Add the strips of pepper and fry for 5 minutes.

Flatten the pork slices. Top each with the sauerkraut and pepper mixtures. Roll up and secure with wooden cocktail sticks. Mix together the flour, paprika and pepper. Coat the meat rolls with this. Heat the remaining dripping in the frying pan. Add the meat rolls and brown on all sides. Pour in the buttermilk and stock, mixing in any juices from the pan. Cover and cook for about 40 minutes, until tender.
Serves 4

Piquant Heart Casserole

METRIC/IMPERIAL
0·75 kg/1½ lb lambs' hearts
1 onion
2 litres/3½ pints water
½ teaspoon salt
3 allspice berries
3 black peppercorns
1 bay leaf
0·5 kg/1 lb cucumber
1 teaspoon Worcestershire
   sauce
2 teaspoons sugar
1 tablespoon lemon juice
2 tablespoons flour
2 tablespoons finely chopped
   dill

Remove the gristle and tubes from the hearts. Peel the onion and slice thinly. Put the water, salt, allspice berries, peppercorns, bay leaf, hearts and onion in a large saucepan and bring to the boil. Cover and simmer for 3 hours. Meanwhile, peel the cucumber and halve lengthways. Remove the seeds with a spoon and cut the halves into finger-width slices.
Remove the hearts from the pan and cut into chunks. Strain the cooking liquid and return 500 ml (generous ¾ pint) to the pan. Bring back to the boil and add the cucumber. Cover and cook gently for 15 minutes.
Stir in the heart chunks, Worcestershire sauce, sugar and lemon juice. Blend the flour in 3 tablespoons of the hot liquid and add to the pan. Simmer, stirring, until thickened, then cook gently for a further 5 minutes. Sprinkle over the dill and serve with boiled rice.
Serves 4

Savoury Scotch Eggs

METRIC/IMPERIAL
2 slices white bread
4 tablespoons water
2 onions, finely chopped
0·5 kg/1 lb minced beef
1 teaspoon salt
1 teaspoon paprika pepper
½ teaspoon white pepper
4 eggs
50 g/2 oz butter

Sprinkle the bread with the water and leave to soak. Squeeze out and crumble into small pieces. Mix with the onion, meat, salt, paprika and pepper. Hard-boil the eggs, then plunge into cold water. When they are cool, shell them and pat dry with absorbent paper. Divide the meat mixture between each egg, pressing it on firmly and rounding into a ball. Melt the butter in a frying pan. Add the balls and fry, turning carefully, for 10–15 minutes, until well browned and cooked through. Serve hot with buttered noodles, carrots and peas.
Serves 4

Variation
Lay half the meat mixture over the base of an ovenproof dish, press in the hard-boiled eggs and top with the remaining meat mixture. Press on firmly and smooth the top. Bake in a moderately hot oven (190° C, 375° F, Gas Mark 5) for 25–30 minutes, until the meat is cooked through.

Madrid Style Kidneys

METRIC/IMPERIAL
2 onions
1 red pepper
1 clove garlic
4 tablespoons olive oil
½ bay leaf
2 tablespoons flour
150 ml/¼ pint stock
0·75 kg/1½ lb calves' kidneys
1 teaspoon salt
1 teaspoon black pepper
225 g/8 oz frozen peas
4 tablespoons dry sherry

Peel and finely chop the onions. Remove the pith, core and seeds from the pepper and cut into strips. Crush the garlic. Heat 2 tablespoons of oil in a saucepan. Add the onion, pepper, garlic and bay leaf and fry for 5 minutes. Sprinkle over the flour, stir well, then stir in the stock. Simmer for 5 minutes. Meanwhile, remove the fat from the kidneys, halve and remove the core and ducts, then slice. Heat the remaining oil in a frying pan. Add the kidneys and fry until lightly browned. Add the salt, pepper, peas and sherry. Pour over the onion sauce and stir well. Simmer gently for a further 2 minutes. Serve hot with saffron rice.
Serves 4

Hamburgers with Capers

METRIC/IMPERIAL
1 large onion
0·75 kg/1½ lb lean minced beef
2 tablespoons capers
1 teaspoon salt
½ teaspoon celery salt
½ teaspoon garlic salt
½ teaspoon Tabasco sauce
2 eggs
50 g/2 oz butter
2 tablespoons chopped chives
2 teaspoons made mustard
Garnish
parsley sprigs
onion rings

Peel and finely chop the onion. Mix together the beef, onion, capers, salt, celery and garlic salts, Tabasco sauce and eggs. With wet hands, divide the meat into four portions and form each into a patty. Melt the butter in a frying pan. Add the patties and brown quickly on each side. Then reduce the heat and cook for a further 3–4 minutes on each side. Drain on absorbent paper, and transfer the hamburgers to a warmed serving dish. Keep hot.
Remove any excess fat from the pan, add the chives and stir in the mustard. Cook for 1–2 minutes, then pour over the hamburgers and garnish with the parsley sprigs and onion rings. Serve with a tomato salad.
Serves 4

Pork Chops with Celeriac

METRIC/IMPERIAL
4 thick pork chops
1 teaspoon salt
¼ teaspoon white pepper
2 teaspoons dry mustard
4 tablespoons flour
50 g/2 oz pork dripping
¼ celeriac
1 leek
25 g/1 oz butter
4 tablespoons grated cheese

Rub the chops on both sides with the salt, pepper and mustard, then coat with the flour. Heat the dripping in a frying pan, and add the chops. Brown on each side, then reduce the heat and cook for a further 4–5 minutes on each side.

Meanwhile, peel the celeriac, and cut into thin strips or grate. Wash and chop the leek. Melt the butter in a pan and add the celeriac and leek. Fry for about 5 minutes, until the vegetables are just tender.
Place the chops on a warmed serving plate. Top each with a spoonful of the celeriac and leek mixture and a tablespoon of cheese.
Serves 4

Cook's Tip
Use the rest of the celeriac to make a delicious salad; simply peel, grate and mix with mayonnaise and seasoning to taste.

Kidneys in Wine Sauce

METRIC/IMPERIAL
350 g/12 oz calves' kidneys
2 slices white bread
4 tablespoons water
100 g/4 oz minced beef
1 teaspoon salt
1 teaspoon paprika pepper
75 g/3 oz butter
2 onions, finely chopped
3 tablespoons flour
150 ml/¼ pint stock
150 ml/¼ pint red wine
salt and black pepper
chopped parsley

Halve the kidneys, cut out the cores and ducts. Wash and dry, then slice thickly. Soak the bread in the water then squeeze out and crumble into small pieces. Mix together the beef, bread, salt and paprika. Form the mixture into small balls. Melt 50 g (2 oz) butter in a saucepan. Add the meatballs and onion. Fry until the meatballs are lightly browned, then remove. Stir the flour into the pan fat and cook for 1 minute. Gradually stir in the stock and wine, bring to the boil and simmer, stirring, until thickened. Season to taste. Return the meatballs and simmer for 10 minutes. Melt the remaining butter and fry the kidney slices, turning, for 8 minutes. Stir into the meatball mixture and cook for 2 minutes. Sprinkle with parsley.
Serves 4

Pork with Pepper Ragoût

METRIC/IMPERIAL
2 green peppers
2 red peppers
2 sticks celery
2 rashers streaky bacon
50 g/2 oz butter
4 onions, finely chopped
1 clove garlic, crushed
2 tablespoons chopped
  parsley
1 medium aubergine
0·75 kg/1½ lb lean pork
2 teaspoons paprika pepper
1 teaspoon salt
½ teaspoon pepper
4 tablespoons oil

Remove pith, core and seeds from the peppers, then cut into thin strips. Cut the celery into thin strips. Rind and chop the bacon. Melt the butter in a saucepan and add the onion, pepper, garlic, celery, parsley and bacon. Cook gently until the bacon has rendered its fat. Meanwhile, chop the aubergine. Cut the pork into thin strips. Add the aubergine, paprika, salt and pepper to the pan and cook for about 20 minutes, until the vegetables are quite soft. Add a little stock or water if the mixture gets too dry. Heat the oil in a frying pan. Add the pork strips and fry until they are well browned and tender. Arrange the vegetable mixture on a warmed serving dish and pile the pork in the centre.
Serves 4

Hamburgers with Onions

METRIC/IMPERIAL
0·5 kg/1 lb minced beef
2 teaspoons grated fresh
  horseradish
3 tablespoons chopped
  parsley
150 g/5 oz pork sausagemeat
1 teaspoon celery salt
4 tablespoons fresh breadcrumbs
1 egg
1 tablespoon grated celery
1 tablespoon grated carrot
1 tablespoon grated onion
25 g/1 oz butter
2 tablespoons oil
2 onions

Mix together the meat,
horseradish, parsley,
sausagemeat, celery salt,
breadcrumbs, egg and
grated vegetables. With wet
hands, divide into four
portions and shape each
into a patty.
Melt the butter with the oil
in a frying pan. Add the
patties and brown quickly
on each side. Then reduce
the heat and cook for a
further 3–4 minutes on each
side.
Meanwhile, peel and slice
the onions. Add to the pan
and continue to fry for a
further 5–6 minutes, until
the onions are golden
brown and the hamburgers
are cooked through.
Top each hamburger with
the fried onion, and serve
with a mixed salad.
Serves 4

Deep-Fried Veal

METRIC/IMPERIAL
1 kg/2 lb veal escalopes
1 egg
4 tablespoons flour
1 teaspoon salt
1 teaspoon pepper
50 g/2 oz dry breadcrumbs
oil for deep frying
Garnish
1 lemon, sliced
parsley sprigs

Cut the meat into small
pieces. Beat the egg. Mix
the flour with the salt and
pepper. Coat the meat
firstly in the flour, then in
the egg and finally in the
breadcrumbs, so that the
pieces are well covered.
Heat the oil in a deep-frying
pan until it is 180° C
(350° F). Fry the meat for
6 minutes, or until golden
brown and crispy. Drain on
absorbent paper. Arrange
on a warmed serving plate
and garnish with slices of
lemon.
Deep fry individual sprigs
of parsley in the oil for 30
seconds and use to garnish
the veal. Serve with potato
and tomato salads.
Serves 4

Steak and Onions

METRIC/IMPERIAL
4 sirloin or rump steaks
2 teaspoons salt
1 teaspoon white pepper
50 g/2 oz flour
25 g/1 oz butter
2 tablespoons oil
225 g/8 oz onions
150 ml/¼ pint beef stock
parsley sprig

Season the steaks with the salt and pepper and coat lightly in the flour.
Melt the butter with the oil in a frying pan. Add the steaks and brown quickly on each side. Peel the onions and slice thinly. Add to the pan and fry the steaks for a further 2–3 minutes on each side, or longer according to taste. Transfer the steaks to a warmed serving dish, overlapping them slightly, and keep warm.
Continue frying the onions until they are golden brown, then arrange over the meat. Add the stock to the pan, stir well and bring to the boil. Simmer, stirring frequently, for 3 minutes, then pour this sauce over the meat. Garnish with the parsley sprig.
Serves 4

Variation
To make a piquant sauce for the steak, fry some sliced peppers and mush-rooms with the onion. Add 1 tablespoon tomato purée, the stock, seasoning and a good dash of red wine.

Hamburgers with Herb Butter

METRIC/IMPERIAL
2 slices white bread
4 tablespoons water
0·75 kg/1½ lb minced beef
1 teaspoon salt
1 teaspoon white pepper
2 teaspoons paprika pepper
1 egg yolk
75 g/3 oz butter
1 tablespoon chopped parsley
1 tablespoon chopped dill
1 tablespoon lemon juice
½ teaspoon celery salt
Garnish
tomato wedges
dill sprigs

Sprinkle the bread with the water and leave to soak, then squeeze out the water and crumble the bread into small pieces. Mix together the beef, bread, salt, pepper, paprika and egg yolk. With wet hands, divide the dough into 8 portions and shape each into a patty.
Cream the butter with the parsley, dill, lemon juice and celery salt. Make a hollow in each patty and fill with a knob of this herb butter. Bring the meat mixture up over the herb butter to cover it.
Grill the hamburger patties for 3–4 minutes on each side or until they are well browned and cooked through. Garnish with tomato wedges and dill and serve with a potato and sweet red pepper salad.
Serves 4

Baked Ham Rolls

METRIC/IMPERIAL

2 thick slices white bread
2 eggs, beaten
½ teaspoon grated nutmeg
½ teaspoon paprika pepper
1 tablespoon oil
2 tablespoons fresh breadcrumbs
2 tablespoons chopped
  parsley
2 tablespoons chopped
  chives
½ teaspoon salt
¼ teaspoon pepper
4 slices ham

Remove the crusts from the bread, toast and place in a mixing bowl. Cover with the beaten eggs and leave to soak for 2–3 minutes. Whisk in the nutmeg, paprika, oil, breadcrumbs, parsley, chives, salt and pepper. Spread out the slices of ham and cover thickly with the bread mixture. Roll up and, if necessary, secure with wooden cocktail sticks or skewers. Place in a greased ovenproof dish, cover and bake in a moderate oven (180° C, 350° F, Gas Mark 4) for 20 minutes. Serve hot, with a mixed salad.
Serves 4

Variation
For a more substantial dish, make up 450 ml (¾ pint) basic white sauce, stir in 100 g (4 oz) grated cheese, season to taste and pour over the ham rolls. Sprinkle with cheese and bake as above.

Stuffed Pork Chops

METRIC/IMPERIAL

1 clove garlic
4 thick boneless pork chops
½ teaspoon salt
4 small slices ham
4 thin slices Gruyère or
  Cheddar cheese
1 teaspoon dried rosemary
1½ tablespoons flour
2 eggs
4 tablespoons grated cheese
1 teaspoon paprika pepper
50 g/2 oz butter

Finely chop the garlic. Cut a deep pocket in each chop and rub with salt and garlic. Fill each pocket with a slice of ham and cheese and a little rosemary.
Mix together the flour, eggs, grated cheese and paprika to form a paste. Coat the chops in this paste.
Melt the butter in a frying pan. Add the chops and fry gently for about 6 minutes on each side, until crisp and golden brown. Do not cook too quickly or the outside will be brown before the meat is cooked through. Serve hot, with boiled potatoes and asparagus.
Serves 4

Variation
For a change, try filling the pork chops with any of your favourite stuffing mixes; sage and onion, rice and mushroom or apple and raisin. Then coat in the paste and proceed as above.

Liver Risotto

METRIC/IMPERIAL
2 onions
0.5 kg/1 lb calves' or lambs'
    liver
1 large cooking apple
225 g/8 oz long-grain rice
3 tablespoons flour
4 tablespoons oil
1 teaspoon salt
1 teaspoon sugar
2 tablespoons raisins

Peel and finely chop the onions. Finely chop the liver. Peel and core the apple, then chop. Cook the rice according to the instructions on the packet. Meanwhile, toss the liver in the flour. Heat the oil in a pan and add the onions, salt and liver. Fry, turning constantly, for 3 minutes. Add the apple and fry for a further 3 minutes. Stir in the sugar, rice and raisins and cook for a further 3 minutes. Serve hot.
Serves 4

Cook's Tip
To tenderise lambs' liver, soak it in milk for an hour prior to cooking. Drain and pat dry with absorbent paper.

Chicken Soup with Rice

METRIC/IMPERIAL
1 (1¼–1½-kg/2½–3-lb)
    boiling fowl
1 teaspoon salt
1 bouquet garni
2 litres/3½ pints water
150 g/5 oz long-grain rice
100 g/4 oz frozen peas
½ teaspoon pepper
1 (396-g/14-oz) can peeled
    tomatoes

Put the chicken in a saucepan and add the salt, bouquet garni and water. Bring to the boil, half cover and simmer for 2 hours. Remove the chicken from the pan and strain the cooking liquid. Return the cooking liquid to the saucepan and add the rice. Bring to the boil, cover and simmer for 15–20 minutes, until the rice is tender. Meanwhile, when the chicken is cool enough to handle, remove the meat and chop finely. Add to the pan with the peas and pepper and simmer, uncovered, for a further 10 minutes.
Drain the tomatoes and add to the soup. Heat quickly, without stirring, and serve immediately.
Serves 4–6

Fish Stew

METRIC/IMPERIAL

0·75 kg/1½ lb mixed white
  fish (cod, eel, halibut, etc.)
1 teaspoon salt
½ teaspoon white pepper
juice of ½ lemon
4 tablespoons chopped
  parsley
2 tablespoons oil
50 g/2 oz butter
2 leeks, sliced
2 onions, finely chopped
2 tablespoons plain flour
300 ml/½ pint fish stock or
  water
300 ml/½ pint milk
100 g/4 oz mushrooms,
  sliced
1 red pepper, chopped
2 egg yolks
150 ml/¼ pint single cream

Skin and bone the fish and
cut into 2·5-cm (1-inch)
pieces. Mix the salt, pepper,
lemon juice, parsley and oil
and pour over the fish.
Marinate for 2 hours.
Melt the butter in a saucepan and fry the leeks and
onions for 2 minutes.
Sprinkle over the flour.
Cook, stirring, for 3–4
minutes. Gradually stir in
the stock and milk, bring to
the boil, and simmer,
stirring, until thickened.
Add the mushrooms, red
pepper, fish and marinade.
Simmer for 7–8 minutes,
until the fish is cooked.
Cool slightly. Whisk the
egg yolks and cream and
stir carefully into the stew.
Heat through without
boiling.
Serves 4

Spanish Meat and Bean Stew

METRIC/IMPERIAL

225 g/8 oz dried red kidney
  beans
100 g/4 oz streaky bacon, in
  the piece
1 teaspoon salt
2 litres/3½ pints water
1 bay leaf
1 onion
1 clove garlic
1 red pepper
1 green pepper
100 g/4 oz ham
225 g/8 oz cooked beef
100 g/4 oz pressed tongue
100 g/4 oz garlic sausage
½ teaspoon black pepper

Soak the beans in water
overnight, then drain. Rind
the bacon. Put in a saucepan
with the beans, salt, water
and bay leaf and bring to
the boil. Simmer for 1 hour,
or until the beans are
softened.
Meanwhile, peel and finely
chop the onion. Finely chop
the garlic. Remove pith,
core and seeds from the
peppers and cut into strips.
Dice the ham, beef and
tongue. Slice the garlic
sausage.
Remove the bacon from the
pan and dice. Return to the
pan with the onion, garlic,
ham, beef and tongue.
Simmer for 15 minutes,
then stir in the pepper
strips and sausage slices.
Season with the black
pepper and simmer for a
further 15 minutes.
Serves 6

Bean and Vegetable Stew

METRIC/IMPERIAL
*225 g/8 oz dried white
    haricot beans*
*0·5 kg/1 lb streaky bacon, in
    the piece*
500 ml/generous ¾ pint water
225 g/8 oz carrots
0·5 kg/1 lb potatoes
0·75 kg/1½ lb French beans
225 g/8 oz pears
225 g/8 oz dessert apples
1 tablespoon flour
1 teaspoon salt

Soak the beans in water
overnight. Drain and put in
a saucepan. Cover with
fresh water, bring to the
boil and simmer for 20
minutes or until the beans
are tender.

Meanwhile, rind the bacon
and put in another saucepan
with the water. Bring to the
boil and simmer for 20
minutes.
Peel and slice the carrots
and potatoes. Trim the
French beans. Remove the
bacon from the pan and
dice. Return to the pan with
the carrots, potatoes and
French beans. Drain the
haricot beans and add to the
bacon mixture. Simmer for
15 minutes.
Peel and core the pears and
apples, then slice. Add to
the pan and simmer for a
further 5 minutes. Blend the
flour in 2 tablespoons of the
hot stew, then stir into the
pan with the salt. Simmer
until slightly thickened and
serve.
Serves 4

Vegetable Soup

METRIC/IMPERIAL
2 kohlrabi
2 carrots
1 small cauliflower
10 Brussels sprouts
225 g/8 oz French beans
½ head celery
2 leeks
3 potatoes
1 onion
50 g/2 oz butter
*1 tablespoon chopped
    parsley*
1·5 litres/2¾ pints beef stock
1 teaspoon salt
½ teaspoon pepper

Peel and chop the kohlrabi.
Peel the carrots and cut into
sticks. Break the cauliflower
into florets. Trim the

sprouts and French beans.
Slice the celery. Wash and
chop the leeks. Peel and
dice the potatoes. Peel and
slice the onion.
Melt the butter in a saucepan. Add the onion and
parsley and cook for 5
minutes. Stir in the celery,
carrots and kohlrabi and
cook for a further 2–3
minutes. Stir in the stock
and bring to the boil. Add
the remaining vegetables
with the salt and pepper and
simmer for 20 minutes,
until the vegetables are
tender.
Serves 4

Savoury Peppers

METRIC/IMPERIAL
4 green or red peppers
225 g/8 oz continental
  sausage
100 g/4 oz ham
75 g/3 oz butter
2 gherkins, chopped
2 onions, sliced
2 tablespoons tomato purée
2 tablespoons flour
300 ml/½ pint beef stock
2 teaspoons Worcestershire
  sauce
4 tablespoons cottage cheese
1 teaspoon sugar
rind and juice of 1 lemon

Cut the tops off the peppers. Deseed and blanch in boiling salted water for 5 minutes. Drain and cool.

Chop the sausage and ham. Melt 50 g (2 oz) butter in a pan and fry the meats, gherkin, onion and tomato purée for 5 minutes.
Melt the remaining butter. Stir in the flour and cook for 1 minute. Stir in the stock, bring to the boil and simmer, stirring, until thickened. Add the Worcestershire sauce. Stir a third of this sauce into the sausage mixture, simmer for 5 minutes, then fill the peppers and replace tops. Whisk the remaining sauce with the sieved cottage cheese, sugar, grated lemon rind and juice. Pour into a dish and stand the peppers in it. Cover and bake in a hot oven (220° C, 425° F, Gas Mark 7) for 20 minutes.
Serves 4

Portofino Pepper Pot

METRIC/IMPERIAL
0·75 kg/1½ lb lean pork
  (from the leg)
4 teaspoons paprika pepper
1 teaspoon salt
1 red pepper
1 green pepper
½ cucumber
2 bulbs fennel
4 tablespoons oil
4 onions, sliced
2 tablespoons tomato purée
1 stock cube
300 ml/½ pint buttermilk

Cut the meat into strips and rub with the paprika and salt. Remove the pith, core and seeds from the peppers and cut into strips. Peel and dice the cucumber.

Trim and slice the fennel. Heat the oil in a flameproof casserole. Add the pork and onion and fry for 5 minutes. Add the peppers, cucumber and fennel, and stir well. Continue to cook for 2–3 minutes.
Mix together the tomato purée, the stock cube and buttermilk, then pour into the casserole. Simmer for a further 10 minutes. Serve hot.
Serves 4

Variation
Omit the cucumber and fennel and add instead 225 g (8 oz) sliced mushrooms. Substitute 150 ml (¼ pint) soured cream for the buttermilk.

Cassoulet

METRIC/IMPERIAL
0·5 kg/1 lb haricot beans
4 onions
1 leek, finely chopped
225 g/8 oz streaky bacon, in
    the piece
2 chicken drumsticks
2 litres/3½ pints chicken
    stock
½ teaspoon garlic salt
1 teaspoon black pepper
1 teaspoon dried thyme
1 bouquet garni
350 g/12 oz tomatoes
100 g/4 oz garlic sausage
2 tablespoons oil
3 sticks celery, chopped
150 ml/¼ pint dry white wine

Soak the beans in water
overnight, then drain. Peel
and finely chop 3 onions.
Rind the bacon. Put the
leek, chopped onion, bacon,
chicken, stock, seasonings
and herbs in a saucepan.
Bring to the boil and
simmer for 1¼ hours.
Meanwhile, peel and chop
the tomatoes and the
remaining onion. Slice the
garlic sausage.
Remove the bacon and
chicken from the pan. Dice
the meats and strain the
stock.
Heat the oil in a pan and
fry the tomatoes, remaining
onion and the celery for 3
minutes. Stir in the wine
and haricot beans. Layer
the bean mixture, bacon,
chicken and sausage in a
casserole. Pour over the
stock, cover and bake in a
hot oven (220° C, 425° F,
Gas Mark 7) for 1¼ hours.
Serves 4

Hunter's Stew

METRIC/IMPERIAL
0·5 kg/1 lb cooked game
50 g/2 oz streaky bacon
225 g/8 oz onions
350 g/12 oz small button
    mushrooms
350 g/12 oz potatoes
225 g/8 oz carrots
25 g/1 oz margarine
½ teaspoon salt
pinch pepper
300 ml/½ pint stock

Cut the meat into chunks.
Rind and dice the bacon.
Peel and finely chop the
onions. Clean the
mushrooms. Peel and slice
the potatoes and carrots.
Melt the margarine in a
flameproof casserole. Add
the bacon and fry until it
renders its fat. Add the
meat and onion and fry for
5 minutes, then stir in the
salt, pepper, mushrooms,
potatoes and carrots. Pour
over the stock and bring to
the boil. Cover and simmer
for 1 hour. Serve hot, in the
casserole.
Serves 4

Cook's Tip
Small button
mushrooms lose a lot
of their flavour if
peeled. Simply wipe
them with a clean
damp cloth or
absorbent kitchen
paper and use as
required.

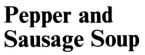

Pepper and Sausage Soup

METRIC/IMPERIAL
4 onions
2 leeks
4 red peppers
6 medium potatoes
4 tomatoes
4 sausages
50 g/2 oz pork dripping
50 g/2 oz butter
2 litres/3½ pints stock
1 teaspoon salt
¼ teaspoon black pepper
pinch rosemary
150 ml/¼ pint single cream

Peel and slice the onions. Wash the leeks and cut in strips. Remove the core, pith and seeds from the peppers and cut into rings. Peel and dice the potatoes. Peel the tomatoes, then halve, remove the seeds and chop.
Grill the sausages until they are well browned all over. Cut into slices.
Melt the dripping in a flameproof casserole and add the onion. Fry until golden brown, then stir in the leeks, peppers, potatoes, butter, tomatoes and sausages. Pour in the stock and bring to the boil. Add the salt, pepper and rosemary and simmer for 20 minutes.
Stir in the cream and heat gently without boiling. Serve hot.
Serves 4

Pork and Veal Risotto

METRIC/IMPERIAL
75 g/3 oz butter
225 g/8 oz long-grain rice
1 teaspoon salt
½ teaspoon celery salt
600 ml/1 pint stock
100 g/4 oz ham
2 onions
100 g/4 oz lean pork (from the leg)
100 g/4 oz lean veal
1 carrot
2 tomatoes
Garnish
2 tablespoons chopped parsley

Melt 25 g (1 oz) of the butter in a saucepan. Add the rice, salt and celery salt and stir to mix well. Fry for 2–3 minutes, then add the stock. Bring to the boil, cover and cook for 15–20 minutes, until the rice is tender and all the stock has been absorbed.
Meanwhile, dice the ham. Peel and thinly slice the onions. Cut the pork and veal into chunks. Grate the carrot. Peel and quarter the tomatoes.
Melt the remaining butter in a saucepan. Add the pork and veal chunks and brown on all sides. Stir in the onion and carrot and fry for 5 minutes, then add the ham, tomatoes and the cooked rice. Continue cooking for 15–20 minutes, until the meat is tender. Sprinkle with parsley before serving with a mixed salad.
Serves 4

Layered Liver Casserole

METRIC/IMPERIAL
225 g/8 oz frozen peas
3 slices white bread
6 tablespoons water
0·5 kg/1 lb lambs' liver
2 tablespoons oil
2 onions, finely chopped
25 g/1 oz butter
3 eggs
1 teaspoon salt
½ teaspoon white pepper
2 tablespoons grated cheese
2 rashers streaky bacon
0·5 kg/1 lb carrots, diced
3 tablespoons chopped
  parsley

Defrost the peas. Sprinkle the bread with the water and leave to soak, then squeeze out and crumble the bread into small pieces. Finely chop the liver. Heat the oil in a saucepan. Add the onion and fry gently for 5 minutes. Add the liver and fry for a further 2–3 minutes. Add the butter and, when it has melted, remove from the heat. Stir in the bread, eggs, salt, pepper and cheese. Rind and dice the bacon. Put the carrots in a baking dish with the parsley, bacon and peas. Cover with the liver mixture. Place the dish in a bain marie and bake in a moderate oven (180° C, 350° F, Gas Mark 4) for 45–55 minutes. The casserole is cooked when a skewer inserted in the centre comes out clean.
Serves 4–5

Italian Fish Bake

METRIC/IMPERIAL
175 g/6 oz potatoes, sliced
1 large carrot, sliced
1 small cauliflower
100 g/4 oz frozen French
  beans
2 (198-g/7-oz) cans tuna,
  drained and flaked
2 tomatoes, skinned and
  sliced
1 beetroot, sliced
5 anchovy fillets
1 onion, chopped
1 clove garlic, crushed
1 tablespoon capers, chopped
4 eggs, separated
25 g/1 oz fresh breadcrumbs
50 g/2 oz ground hazelnuts
50 g/2 oz cheese, grated
1 tablespoon chopped parsley
salt and pepper

Cook the potato and carrot in boiling salted water for 15–20 minutes. Divide the cauliflower into sprigs and add with the beans for the last 10 minutes. Drain. Lightly grease a 2-litre (3½-pint) ovenproof dish. Layer the cooked vegetables, tuna, tomato and beetroot alternately in the casserole. Chop the anchovy fillets and mix with the onion, garlic, capers and egg yolks to a smooth consistency. Stir in the breadcrumbs, hazelnuts and cheese, then fold in the parsley and stiffly beaten egg whites. Season to taste. Spread the topping over the vegetables and bake in a moderately hot oven (200° C, 400° F, Gas Mark 6) for 20–25 minutes.
Serves 4

Potato Hot Pot

METRIC/IMPERIAL
0·5 kg/1 lb potatoes
4 eggs
450 g/1 lb pork sausages
4 tablespoons soured cream
¼ teaspoon salt
pinch pepper
pinch dried thyme
pinch dried oregano
15 g/½ oz butter
½ punnet mustard and cress
½ teaspoon lemon juice
1 teaspoon oil
pinch sugar
pinch salt

Peel the potatoes and place in a saucepan. Cover with water, bring to the boil and simmer for 15–20 minutes, until tender. Drain and slice. Hard-boil the eggs. Shell and slice. Grill the sausages until well browned on all sides, then slice. Mix together the soured cream, salt, pepper, thyme and oregano.
Layer the potato, egg and sausage slices in a well greased baking tin, finishing with a layer of potatoes. (Reserve a few sausage and egg slices for the garnish.) Pour over the soured cream mixture and dot with the butter, cut into small pieces. Bake in a moderately hot oven (200° C, 400° F, Gas Mark 6) for 30 minutes. Meanwhile, cut the cress, rinse in cold water, and dry well. Mix the lemon juice, oil, sugar and salt with the cress.
Garnish the hot pot with the reserved slices of egg and sausage and the cress salad.
Serves 3–4

Cabbage and Meat Layered Casserole

METRIC/IMPERIAL
1 small white cabbage
1 stale bread roll
3 tablespoons water
0·5 kg/1 lb minced meat
pinch grated nutmeg
½ teaspoon celery salt
2 teaspoons paprika pepper
1 teaspoon salt
1 red pepper, sliced
25 g/1 oz butter
2 tablespoons flour
150 ml/¼ pint beef stock
4 tablespoons single cream
4 tablespoons grated cheese

Core the cabbage and separate the leaves. Cook these in boiling salted water for 15 minutes. Drain. Soften the roll in the water, then squeeze out and break into small pieces. Mix the meat with the bread, nutmeg and seasonings. Arrange half the cabbage leaves in a greased oven-proof dish. Top with half the meat mixture and half the sliced pepper, then repeat these layers.
Melt the butter. Stir in the flour and cook for 1 minute. Stir in the stock, bring to the boil and simmer, stirring, until thickened. Remove from the heat and stir in the cream. Pour over the meat mixture and sprinkle on the cheese. Bake in a moderately hot oven (200° C, 400° F, Gas Mark 6) for 35 minutes.
Serves 4–5

Turkish Chicken

METRIC/IMPERIAL
2 oranges
4 tomatoes
4 tablespoons sultanas
4 slices white bread
25 g/1 oz butter
150 ml/¼ pint milk
1 teaspoon salt
½ teaspoon white pepper
2 eggs
1 onion, grated
2 tablespoons oil
4 chicken portions
2 tablespoons finely chopped almonds

Peel and slice the oranges. Peel the tomatoes. Soak the sultanas in warm water to cover. Toast the bread and butter it. Cut into small pieces and spread over the base of an ovenproof dish. Mix together the milk, salt, pepper, eggs and grated onion. Pour into the baking dish.
Heat the oil in a frying pan and cook the chicken portions for 10 minutes, turning frequently, until lightly browned. Drain the chicken and arrange with the tomatoes on the bread, then cover with the orange slices. Drain the sultanas and sprinkle over the oranges with the almonds. Cover with foil and bake in a moderately hot oven (190° C, 375° F, Gas Mark 5) for 45 minutes–1 hour, until the chicken is tender. Serve hot.
Serves 4

Smoked Fish Bake

METRIC/IMPERIAL
6 large kippers, cooked
2 smoked mackerel
225 g/8 oz ham
1 kg/2 lb potatoes
15 g/½ oz butter
600 ml/1 pint milk
1 teaspoon salt
6 eggs
150 ml/¼ pint single cream
4 tomatoes
4 tablespoons grated cheese

Skin the fish and remove the large bones. Mash the fish with a fork. Chop the ham finely. Peel and boil the potatoes, then mash with the butter, 4 tablespoons milk and the salt. Hard-boil 3 eggs, shell and chop.

Heat the remaining milk in a saucepan and stir in the mashed fish. Remove from the heat and stir in the remaining eggs, the cream and ham.
Spread a thick layer of the mashed potato, about 2·5 cm (1 inch) deep, over the bottom of a greased ovenproof dish. Cover with half the fish mixture, then some of the chopped egg. Repeat the layers and finish with a layer of mashed potato. Slice the tomatoes and arrange in two overlapping rows down the centre. Sprinkle with the grated cheese. Bake in a moderately hot oven (200° C, 400° F, Gas Mark 6) for 20–25 minutes.
Serves 8

Amsterdam Cod Bake

METRIC/IMPERIAL
1 kg/2 lb thick cod fillets
1 teaspoon salt
50 g/2 oz flour
2 teaspoons paprika pepper
½ teaspoon white pepper
100 g/4 oz streaky bacon
   rashers
4 onions
50 g/2 oz button mushrooms
1 leek
100 g/4 oz Edam cheese
2 tablespoons oil
600 ml/1 pint milk
4 eggs
pinch grated nutmeg

Remove any bones from the fish, then cut into chunks. Mix together half the salt, the flour, paprika

and pepper. Coat the fish chunks with this mixture. Rind and dice the bacon. Peel and slice the onions. Quarter the mushrooms. Slice the leek. Grate the cheese.
Put the diced bacon in a frying pan and heat until the fat runs. Add the oil, heat, then add the fish chunks and onion and brown the fish on all sides. Remove from the heat. Transfer the bacon, fish and onion to a greased oven-proof dish. Sprinkle over the mushrooms and leek.
Mix together the cheese, milk, eggs, nutmeg and remaining salt. Pour over the fish. Bake in a moderate oven (180° C, 350° F, Gas Mark 4) for 20–25 minutes.
Serves 4

Pepper and Pork Hot Pot

METRIC/IMPERIAL
1 green pepper
1 red pepper
2 slices white bread
4 tablespoons warm water
0.5 kg/1 lb minced pork
1 teaspoon salt
1 teaspoon black pepper
2 teaspoons paprika pepper
10 medium potatoes
450 ml/¾ pint beef stock
150 ml/¼ pint soured cream
4 tablespoons grated cheese

Halve the peppers and remove the cores, pith and seeds. Blanch in boiling salted water for 5 minutes. Drain. Sprinkle the bread with the water and leave to soak, then squeeze out the water and crumble the bread into small pieces. Mix together the bread, pork, salt, pepper and paprika.
Peel and thinly slice the potatoes. Put half the slices in the bottom of a greased ovenproof dish. Cover with two of the pepper halves. Spoon over the meat mixture, then cover with the remaining pepper halves. Arrange the rest of the potato slices on top. Mix together the stock and soured cream and pour over the potatoes. Sprinkle on the cheese. Cover lightly with foil and bake in a moderate oven (180° C, 350° F, Gas Mark 4) for 45 minutes–1 hour, until the potatoes are tender.
Serves 4

Veal and Vegetable Pie

METRIC/IMPERIAL
0.75 kg/1½ lb boned
    shoulder of veal
50 g/2 oz pork dripping
4 onions, chopped
1 teaspoon salt
½ teaspoon white pepper
¼ head celery with leaves
2 eggs, hard-boiled
50 g/2 oz mushrooms
2 tablespoons flour
150 ml/¼ pint stock
2 carrots, sliced
300-g/11-oz packet frozen
    puff pastry, defrosted
1 egg yolk, beaten, to glaze

Cut the veal into 1-cm (½-inch) pieces. Heat the dripping and fry the onion for 5 minutes. Stir in the meat, salt and pepper and cook for 10 minutes. Meanwhile, cut the celery into strips and chop the celery leaves. Slice the eggs. Quarter the mushrooms. Sprinkle the flour over the meat, stir well, then stir in the stock. Bring to the boil and simmer, stirring, until thickened. Mix in the carrots, celery, celery leaves and mushrooms. Transfer to an ovenproof dish. Cover with the egg slices.
Roll out the pastry to cover the dish. Press the edges to seal and decorate with the pastry trimmings. Brush with the egg yolk and bake in a hot oven (220° C, 425° F, Gas Mark 7) for 40 minutes. Serve hot or cold.
Serves 4–6

Ham and Vegetable Casserole

METRIC/IMPERIAL
225 g/8 oz asparagus
225 g/8 oz carrots
225 g/8 oz Brussels sprouts
225 g/8 oz ham, sliced
40 g/1½ oz butter
2 tablespoons flour
225 g/8 oz peas, cooked
6 tablespoons chopped
  parsley
100 g/4 oz prosciutto

Peel and trim the asparagus and cut into pieces. Peel and thinly slice the carrots. Cook the asparagus and carrots in boiling salted water for 8–10 minutes, until tender. Trim the sprouts and cook in boiling salted water for 8–10 minutes. Drain the vegetables, reserving 300 ml (½ pint) of the asparagus cooking liquid.
Cover the base of a greased ovenproof dish with the ham. Spread over half the vegetables. Melt the butter in a saucepan. Stir in the flour and cook for 1 minute. Stir in the reserved cooking liquid and bring to the boil. Simmer, stirring, until thickened. Stir in the remaining vegetables, the peas and parsley. Pour into the baking dish and top with the prosciutto. Bake in a moderate oven (160° C, 325° F, Gas Mark 3) for 15 minutes.
Serves 4

Spring Soufflé

METRIC/IMPERIAL
100 g/4 oz shelled fresh peas
4 tomatoes
100 g/4 oz plain flour
250 ml/8 fl oz water
1 tablespoon chopped
  parsley
3 tablespoons chopped
  chives
1 teaspoon salt
freshly ground pepper
25 g/1 oz Parmesan cheese,
  grated
6 eggs

Cook the peas in boiling salted water for 10–15 minutes until tender. Drain. Scald the tomatoes in boiling water for 2–3 minutes then peel, remove the seeds and chop the flesh.
Blend the flour with the water, whisk to remove lumps then stir in the parsley, chives, salt, pepper and cheese. Separate the egg yolks from the whites. Beat the yolks into the flour mixture, then stir in the peas and tomato flesh. Whisk the egg whites until stiff and fold quickly but thoroughly into the pea mixture. Spoon into a greased 1·5-litre (3½-pint) soufflé dish and bake in a moderate oven (160° C, 325° F, Gas Mark 3) for 45–50 minutes. Serve immediately.
Serves 4

Sauerkraut Baked with Ham

METRIC/IMPERIAL
1 kg/2 lb sauerkraut
0·75 kg/1½ lb potatoes
150 ml/¼ pint milk
1 teaspoon salt
½ teaspoon pepper
pinch grated nutmeg
0·5 kg/1 lb cooked gammon
225 g/8 oz Cheddar cheese
225 g/8 oz green grapes
4 tablespoons oil
2 onions, sliced
50 g/2 oz bacon, diced
50 g/2 oz browned bread-
    crumbs
25 g/1 oz butter

Drain the sauerkraut, then cook in boiling water for 20 minutes. Drain and cool. Peel the potatoes and cook in boiling salted water for 15–20 minutes, until tender. Drain and mash with the milk, salt, pepper and nutmeg. Dice the gammon and cheese. Halve and seed the grapes.
Heat the oil and fry the onion and bacon for 5 minutes. Stir in the sauer-kraut.
Spoon the potato mixture into a greased ovenproof dish and spread out. Top with the sauerkraut mixture, gammon, cheese and grapes. Sprinkle over the bread-crumbs and dot with butter. Bake in a moderately hot oven (200° C, 400° F, Gas Mark 6) for 20 minutes.
Serves 4

Old-Fashioned Cobbler's Pot

METRIC/IMPERIAL
2 soused herrings
100 g/4 oz streaky bacon
4 onions
1·25 kg/2½ lb potatoes
2 teaspoons salt
1 teaspoon black pepper
350 g/12 oz roast pork,
    sliced
150 ml/¼ pint soured cream
300 ml/½ pint milk
3 eggs
100 g/4 oz Cheddar cheese,
    grated

Cut the herrings into strips. Rind and chop the bacon. Peel and thinly slice the onions and potatoes. Put the bacon in a frying pan and heat until the fat runs. Add the onion and fry for 5 minutes, then add the potato slices and fry until lightly browned. Sprinkle over the salt and pepper. Put a layer of this potato mixture in a greased oven-proof dish. Cut the pork into small pieces and mix with the herring. Spoon on to the potato mixture, then spread over the remaining potato mixture. Smooth the top.
Mix together the soured cream, milk and eggs and pour into the dish. Sprinkle over the cheese. Bake in a moderately hot oven (200° C, 400° F, Gas Mark 6) for 40 minutes. Serve hot.
Serves 4

Aubergine and Rice Moussaka

METRIC/IMPERIAL
2 aubergines, thinly sliced
600 ml/1 pint chicken stock
225 g/8 oz round-grain rice
0·5 kg/1 lb minced pork
1 teaspoon salt
2 teaspoons paprika pepper
1 teaspoon white pepper
4 tomatoes, sliced
4 eggs
4 tablespoons dry bread-
  crumbs
4 tablespoons grated cheese
25 g/1 oz butter
parsley

Put the aubergine slices in a colander, sprinkle with salt and leave for 20 minutes. Rinse and dry. Bring the stock to the boil and add the rice. Cover and simmer for 15–20 minutes, until tender. Mix together the pork, salt, paprika and pepper.
Mix together half the cooked rice and the meat mixture. Put half this mixture in a greased oven-proof dish. Lay on the aubergine and tomato slices, then spread over the remaining rice meat mixture. Whisk the eggs, then pour into the dish. Top with the rest of the cooked rice. Sprinkle over the bread-crumbs and cheese. Dot the butter over the top. Bake in a moderate oven (180° C, 350° F, Gas Mark 4) for 40 minutes. Serve garnished with parsley.
Serves 4

Spaghetti Carbonara

METRIC/IMPERIAL
225 g/8 oz spaghetti
100 g/4 oz streaky bacon
1 green pepper
4 tablespoons grated
  Parmesan cheese
4 tablespoons chopped
  parsley
300 ml/½ pint single cream
50 g/2 oz butter
225 g/8 oz lean ham, sliced
2 teaspoons dried mixed
  herbs

Cook the spaghetti in boiling salted water for 12–15 minutes, until just tender to the bite.
Meanwhile, rind and chop the bacon. Remove the core, pith and seeds from the pepper and chop finely.
Put the bacon in a saucepan and heat until it renders its fat and becomes crisp. Stir in the cheese, parsley, cream and green pepper. Cook very gently for 5 minutes. Drain the spaghetti and toss with the butter until well coated. Put the spaghetti in a greased ovenproof dish. Roll up the ham slices and lay on the spaghetti, then cover with the bacon sauce. Sprinkle over the herbs. Bake in a hot oven (220° C, 425° F, Gas Mark 7) for 10 minutes. Serve hot.
Serves 2–4

Egg Pizza

METRIC/IMPERIAL
*0·5 kg/1 lb bread dough made
  with 0·5 kg/1 lb flour etc.
  (see page 285)*
beaten egg for glazing
2 tablespoons grated cheese
4 eggs
*1 (56-g/2-oz) can anchovy
  fillets*
4 tomatoes, thinly sliced
2 tablespoons olive oil
pinch curry powder
4 slices cheese

Divide the dough into four
portions. Roll out each
portion on a floured surface
to a round about 20 cm
(8 inches) in diameter. Place
on greased baking sheets.
Push up the edges of the
dough rounds to make a
raised border. Brush with
beaten egg and sprinkle with
the grated cheese. Leave in a
warm place for 15 minutes,
then bake in a hot oven
(220°C, 425° F, Gas
Mark 7) for 12–15 minutes,
until lightly browned.
Hard-boil the eggs, then
shell and slice. Drain the
anchovy fillets and arrange
on the pizza bases. Cover
with the egg and tomato
slices, then sprinkle over
the oil and curry powder.
Cut the cheese into strips
and arrange in a lattice-
work on top of each pizza.
Bake in the preheated oven
for 5 minutes. Serve hot.
Serves 4

Baked Ham and Pea Omelette

METRIC/IMPERIAL
450 g/1 lb frozen peas
8 eggs
½ teaspoon salt
½ teaspoon celery salt
6 tablespoons single cream
pinch grated nutmeg
1 teaspoon paprika pepper
100 g/4 oz lean ham, sliced

Defrost the peas. Whisk
together the eggs, salt,
celery salt, cream, nutmeg
and paprika. Finely chop
the ham and add to the egg
mixture with the peas.
Pour the mixture into a
greased ovenproof dish.
Cover with foil and bake in
a moderate oven (160° C,
325° F, Gas Mark 3) for
30 minutes. Remove the
foil for the last 5 minutes to
allow the top to brown.
Serve hot.
Serves 2–4

Variation
Try this with grated cheese
and flaked canned salmon.
Omit the peas, ham and
paprika and cook as above.

Ham and Egg Rolls

METRIC/IMPERIAL
4 slices ham
½ teaspoon paprika pepper
8 eggs
6 tablespoons water
1 teaspoon salt
pinch grated nutmeg
2 tablespoons chopped parsley
2 tablespoons chopped chervil
50 g/2 oz butter

Spread out the ham slices on a board and sprinkle with the paprika.
Whisk the eggs with the water, salt, nutmeg and herbs until well mixed. Melt the butter in a large pan. Add the egg mixture and cook gently, turning and stirring frequently, until the eggs are lightly scrambled. They should still be moist, so do not overcook. Remove from the heat and divide the scrambled egg between the ham slices. Roll up the ham and, if necessary, secure the rolls with wooden cocktail sticks. Serve warm or cold with a mixed salad.
Serves 2–4

Variation
Snip 2 tablespoons chives into the eggs, in place of the chervil.

Savoury Baked Eggs

METRIC/IMPERIAL
0·5 kg/1 lb potatoes
300 ml/½ pint milk
1 teaspoon salt
½ teaspoon paprika pepper
¼ teaspoon Tabasco sauce
pinch grated nutmeg
10 eggs
50 g/2 oz butter
2 onions, finely chopped
0·5 kg/1 lb minced pork
2 tablespoons flour
½ cucumber, thinly sliced
3 tomatoes, halved
2 tablespoons chopped parsley
¼ teaspoon white pepper

Peel the potatoes and cook in boiling salted water for 15–20 minutes, until tender. Drain and mash with 4 tablespoons of the milk, half the salt, the paprika, Tabasco and nutmeg. Hard-boil 8 of the eggs. Shell and halve.
Melt the butter in a pan and fry the onion and pork until lightly browned. Sprinkle over the flour, stir well and fry for 3 minutes.
Spread the mashed potato in a greased ovenproof dish. Cover with the pork mixture, then top with the cucumber slices and tomato and egg halves. Whisk the remaining eggs, milk and salt with the parsley and pepper, and pour over the dish. Bake in a moderate oven (160° C, 325° F, Gas Mark 3) for 40 minutes.
Serves 4

Egg Dishes

Spicy Soufflé Omelette

METRIC/IMPERIAL
5 stuffed green olives
5 anchovy fillets
2 tablespoons milk
50 g/2 oz plain flour
½ teaspoon baking powder
300 ml/½ pint water
3 eggs
1 teaspoon salt
2 teaspoons paprika pepper
½ teaspoon dried rosemary
25 g/1 oz butter

Slice the olives. Soak the anchovy fillets in the milk for 5 minutes, then drain. Sieve the flour and baking powder into a mixing bowl and whisk in the water. Separate the egg yolks from the whites. Whisk the yolks into the flour mixture with the salt, paprika and rosemary. Whisk the egg whites until stiff, then fold into the mixture.

Melt the butter in a large omelette pan and spoon in the egg mixture. Cook, lifting the edges of the omelette to let the liquid egg mixture run on to the pan. Sprinkle over the olive slices and anchovy fillets when the omelette is half cooked.

Fold over the cooked omelette and slide out of the pan. Cut in half and serve.
Serves 2

Spinach Pancakes

METRIC/IMPERIAL
100 g/4 oz frozen spinach
100 g/4 oz Cheddar cheese
100 g/4 oz flour
½ teaspoon salt
1 egg
300 ml/½ pint milk
3 tablespoons oil

Cook the spinach according to the instructions on the packet, then drain thoroughly. Chop finely. Grate the cheese and add half to the spinach. Stir well and keep warm.

Sieve the flour into a mixing bowl. Add the salt, egg and half the milk. Whisk together until well blended, then whisk in the remaining milk and 1 tablespoon of the oil.

Heat a little of the remaining oil in a pancake pan. Pour in about one-quarter of the batter and tip to cover the pan. Cook for about 1 minute, then turn and cook the other side for about 30 seconds. Slide the pancake out of the pan. Keep hot while you cook the remaining pancakes in the same way.

Spread the spinach mixture over the pancakes and roll them up. Place in a greased ovenproof dish, sprinkle with the remaining cheese and brown quickly under a hot grill. Serve hot.
Serves 2–4

Asparagus Omelette with Prawns

METRIC/IMPERIAL
*1 (312-g/11-oz) can
  asparagus
100 g/4 oz shelled prawns
40 g/1½ oz butter
6 eggs
2 tablespoons water
½ teaspoon salt
½ teaspoon pepper*
Garnish
parsley sprigs

Drain the asparagus and put in a saucepan with the prawns. Add 15 g (½ oz) butter and 2 tablespoons of the asparagus can juice. Whisk the eggs with the water, salt and pepper until well mixed.
Melt half the remaining butter in an omelette pan. Pour in half the egg mixture and cook, lifting the edge of the omelette to let the egg mixture run on to the pan. While the omelette is cooking place the asparagus and prawns over a low heat and warm through gently. Slide the cooked omelette out of the pan. Keep hot while you cook the second omelette in the same way, using the remaining butter. Top the omelettes with the hot asparagus, fold over and scatter with the prawns. Secure with a wooden cocktail stick if necessary. Garnish with parsley and serve warm with a green salad.
Serves 2

Variation
Make a cheese sauce using 300 ml (½ pint) basic white sauce and 75 g (3 oz) grated Cheddar cheese. Fold in the prawns and pour over the asparagus omelette.

Egg Dishes

Scrambled Eggs and Salmon

METRIC/IMPERIAL
8 large eggs
½ teaspoon salt
½ teaspoon white pepper
6 tablespoons water
2 tablespoons chopped chives
225 g/8 oz smoked salmon
50 g/2 oz butter

Whisk the eggs with the salt, pepper and water until well mixed. Add the chives and stir. Cut the salmon into thin strips.
Melt the butter in a frying pan. Pour in the egg mixture and cook gently, turning and stirring frequently, until the eggs are lightly scrambled. They should still be moist, so do not overcook.

Spoon the eggs on to a warmed dish and garnish with the smoked salmon. Alternatively, the salmon may be added to the eggs when they are half-cooked, and then heated through with the eggs.
Serves 2–4

Variation
Instead of smoked salmon, try 225 g (8 oz) mushrooms, sliced and cooked in butter. Pile on top of the scrambled eggs or fold in.

Fried Eggs with Salami

METRIC/IMPERIAL
2 large slices cheese
25 g/1 oz butter
12 slices salami
8 eggs
Garnish
paprika pepper
tomato quarters
parsley sprigs

Cut the slices of cheese into quarters. Melt half the butter in a frying pan. Place the salami slices in the pan and fry on each side to heat through. Transfer the salami to a warmed serving dish and keep hot.
Add the remaining butter to the pan and, when it has melted, break in the eggs

one at a time. Fry for 1 minute then turn over and fry for 30 seconds. Top each egg with a square of cheese and cover the pan. Cook for a further 30 seconds, or until the cheese is just beginning to melt. Place the eggs on the salami slices. Sprinkle the top of each with a pinch of paprika, then garnish with the tomato quarters and parsley sprigs. Serve hot with crusty bread.
Serves 2–4

Variation
You can substitute slices of garlic sausage or Mortadella for the salami.

Stuffed Omelettes

METRIC/IMPERIAL
1 green pepper
100 g/4 oz mushrooms
50 g/2 oz butter
225 g/8 oz minced beef
½ teaspoon white pepper
8 eggs
1 tablespoon chopped parsley
½ teaspoon salt
6 tablespoons water
½ teaspoon Tabasco sauce

Remove the core, pith and seeds from the pepper and chop finely. Clean and chop the mushrooms. Melt half the butter in a frying pan. Add the green pepper, mushrooms, minced beef and half the white pepper. Fry for 6–8 minutes, until the meat is lightly browned and the pepper just tender. Remove from the heat and keep warm.
Whisk together the eggs, parsley, salt, water, Tabasco and remaining white pepper. Melt half the remaining butter in an omelette pan. Pour in half the egg mixture and cook, lifting the edges of the omelette to let the egg mixture run on to the pan. When the omelette is cooked, slide on to a warmed serving plate. Cook the second omelette in the same way, using the rest of the butter.
Spoon the meat mixture on to the first omelette and top with the second omelette. Serve hot.
Serves 2

Tasty Egg Slices

METRIC/IMPERIAL
1 onion
50 g/2 oz ham
50 g/2 oz butter
1 tablespoon chopped parsley
dash soy sauce
4 eggs
4 slices toast

Peel and finely chop the onion. Finely chop the ham. Melt half the butter in a saucepan. Add the onion and fry for 5 minutes. Stir in the ham, parsley and soy sauce and cook for a further 3 minutes. Remove from the heat and leave to cool. Separate the egg yolks from the whites and stir the yolks into the ham mixture.
Whisk the whites until stiff, then fold into the ham mixture.
Spread the toast with the rest of the butter, then top with the egg and ham mixture and smooth over. Put on a greased baking tray and bake in a moderately hot oven (200°C, 400° F, Gas Mark 6) for about 10 minutes, until set and lightly browned. Cut each slice into quarters and serve hot.
Serves 2–4

Summer Eggs

METRIC/IMPERIAL
8 eggs
225 g/8 oz cottage cheese
150 ml/5 fl oz natural
　yogurt
150 ml/¼ pint single cream
juice of 1 small lemon
½ teaspoon salt
½ teaspoon white pepper
4 tablespoons chopped
　mixed herbs
4 large tomatoes

Hard-boil the eggs, then shell. Sieve the cottage cheese until smooth, then mix in the yogurt and cream. Add the lemon juice, salt, pepper and herbs and stir well.
Pour the herb mixture into a deep serving dish. Halve the eggs and place, cut sides up, in the dish. Peel and halve the tomatoes, then remove the seeds. Slice the flesh into strips and use to garnish the eggs. Serve chilled.
Serves 4

Variation
Substitute cream for cottage cheese for a richer dish.

Cook's Tip
Hold the hard-boiled eggs under cold running water for 1 minute before shelling. This prevents any grey rings forming.

Catalan Beans and Eggs

METRIC/IMPERIAL
0·5 kg/1 lb dried white
　haricot beans
100 g/4 oz ham
2 tomatoes
1 large onion
1 red pepper
1 green pepper
3 tablespoons olive oil
¼ teaspoon cayenne pepper
1 teaspoon salt
4 eggs

Soak the beans in water overnight, then drain. Put in a saucepan and cover with fresh water. Bring to the boil and simmer for 30–45 minutes or until the beans are tender. Drain well.
Dice the ham. Peel and chop the tomatoes and onion. Remove the core, pith and seeds from the peppers and chop.
Heat the oil in a saucepan. Add the onion and peppers and fry for 5 minutes. Stir in the ham, tomatoes, cayenne and salt and cook for a further 5 minutes.
Mix in the beans and continue cooking for about 5 minutes, until all the ingredients are heated through.
Turn the bean mixture into an ovenproof serving dish. Make four hollows and break an egg into each. Bake in a hot oven (220° C, 425° F, Gas Mark 7) for 6–8 minutes or until the eggs are cooked. Serve hot.
Serves 4

Spinach Rolls

METRIC/IMPERIAL
100 g/4 oz plus 1 tablespoon
  plain flour
1 teaspoon salt
1 egg
300 ml/½ pint milk
150 ml/¼ pint single cream
3 tablespoons oil
2 cooking apples, peeled
350 g/12 oz frozen spinach
2 teaspoons brown sugar
pinch grated nutmeg
15 g/½ oz butter
50 g/2 oz cheese, grated

Sieve 100 g (4 oz) flour into a bowl. Whisk in half the salt, the egg and half the milk, then the cream and 1 tablespoon oil. Heat a little oil in a pancake pan. Pour in one-eighth of the batter. Cook for 1 minute, then turn over and cook for 30 seconds. Cook the remaining pancakes in the same way. Chop the apples, then cook gently to a purée. Cook the spinach, drain and chop. Mix in the apple, sugar, nutmeg and remaining salt. Spread over the pancakes, roll up and place in a greased oven-proof dish. Melt the butter, stir in the remaining flour and cook for 1 minute. Add the remaining milk and bring to the boil, stirring until thickened. Add the cheese, pour over the pancakes and bake in a moderate oven (180° C, 350° F, Gas Mark 4) for 15–20 minutes.
Serves 4

Spanish Scrambled Eggs

METRIC/IMPERIAL
100 g/4 oz frozen petits pois
100 g/4 oz ham, sliced
2 onions
40 g/1½ oz butter
4 eggs
3 tablespoons water
½ teaspoon celery salt
¼ teaspoon white pepper
100 g/4 oz cheese, grated
Garnish
2 tablespoons chopped
  parsley

Defrost the peas. Cut the ham into narrow strips. Peel and finely chop the onions.
Melt the butter in a frying pan. Add the onion and fry for 5 minutes. Stir in the ham and peas and cook for a further 3 minutes.
Whisk together the eggs, water, celery salt and pepper. Stir in the cheese and pour this mixture into the pan. Cook gently, turning and stirring frequently, until the eggs are lightly scrambled. They should still be moist, so do not overcook. Sprinkle on the parsley and serve.
Serves 2

Cook's Tip
For extra creaminess, stir 15 g (½ oz) butter and 1 tablespoon cream into the eggs immediately before serving.

209

Spiced Cheese Cakes

METRIC/IMPERIAL
225 g/8 oz cottage cheese
150 ml/¼ pint milk
4 tablespoons chopped
*   mixed herbs (parsley,*
*   chives, tarragon, chervil)*
150 g/5 oz semolina
4 tablespoons fresh
*   breadcrumbs*
1 teaspoon salt
1 teaspoon Worcestershire
*   sauce*
½ teaspoon pepper
½ teaspoon Tabasco sauce
150 g/5 oz ham
beaten egg
dry breadcrumbs
50 g/2 oz butter
2 tablespoons oil

Sieve the cottage cheese until smooth, then mix with the milk, herbs, semolina, breadcrumbs, salt, Worcestershire sauce, pepper and Tabasco sauce. Finely chop the ham and fold into the cheese mixture. The mixture should be thick, so if necessary add more fresh breadcrumbs. Divide the mixture into 8 portions and form each into a patty-shape. Coat with the beaten egg, then with the breadcrumbs. Heat the butter and oil in a frying pan and fry the cakes for 3–4 minutes on each side, until well browned. Drain on absorbent paper and serve hot with a cucumber salad.
Serves 4

Liver with Apples

METRIC/IMPERIAL
4 dessert apples
50 g/2 oz butter
1 teaspoon paprika pepper
0·5 kg/1 lb calves' liver
2 tablespoons flour
½ teaspoon salt
4 slices cheese

Peel and core the apples, then cut into thick slices. Melt half the butter in a frying pan. Add the apple slices and brown lightly. Do not overcook or the apples will break up. Remove from the pan and arrange on a warmed heat-proof serving dish. Sprinkle with ½ teaspoon paprika. Keep warm.

Cut the liver into slices. Mix together the flour, salt and remaining paprika and use to coat the liver slices. Add the remaining butter to the frying pan and, when it has melted, add the liver slices. Cook quickly for 2–3 minutes on each side, until well browned. Do not over-cook or the liver will be tough.
Place the liver on top of the apple slices and lay over the cheese slices. Bake in a hot oven (220° C, 425° F, Gas Mark 7) for 3–5 minutes, until the cheese is beginning to melt. Serve hot.
Serves 4

Celery with Soufflé Topping

METRIC/IMPERIAL
2 heads celery
2 tablespoons oil
1 teaspoon made mustard
1 teaspoon salt
½ teaspoon white pepper
2 tablespoons warm water
225 g/8 oz cottage cheese
3 tablespoons double cream
1 red pepper
1 green pepper
1 onion, chopped
6 green olives, sliced
2 tablespoons chopped
  mixed herbs
3 eggs, separated

Trim and wash the celery, then cook in boiling salted water for 15–20 minutes, until tender. Drain well and slice. Mix together the oil, mustard, salt, pepper and water and stir in the sliced celery. Leave to marinate and keep warm.

Sieve the cottage cheese and mix with the cream. Remove the cores, pith and seeds from the peppers and chop finely. Stir the onion, peppers, olives, herbs and egg yolks into the cottage cheese mixture. Whisk the egg whites until stiff and fold in.

Drain the celery and place in an ovenproof dish. Spoon over the cottage cheese mixture and bake in a hot oven (220° C, 425° F, Gas Mark 7) for 10 minutes, until golden on top. Serve hot.
Serves 4

Cottage Cheese and Ham Rolls

METRIC/IMPERIAL
1 cauliflower
4 tablespoons oil
2 tablespoons vinegar
1 teaspoon made mustard
¾ teaspoon salt
pinch sugar
¾ teaspoon white pepper
225 g/8 oz cottage cheese
pinch garlic powder
pinch celery salt
4 tablespoons chopped
  mixed herbs
milk
4 slices prosciutto

Break the cauliflower into florets and cook in boiling salted water for 10–15 minutes or until tender. Drain well. Mix together the oil, vinegar, mustard, ½ teaspoon salt, the sugar and ½ teaspoon pepper. Pour over the warm cauliflower then leave to cool and marinate for 20 minutes.

Meanwhile, mix together the cottage cheese, garlic powder, celery salt, herbs and remaining salt and pepper. Add a little milk if the mixture is very stiff. It should be creamy.

Spread the cottage cheese mixture over the ham slices and roll up. Arrange the marinated cauliflower in a serving dish and lay the filled ham rolls on top. Serve chilled.
Serves 2–4

Pan-Fried Potato Scones

METRIC/IMPERIAL
1 kg/2 lb potatoes
75 g/3 oz butter
4–6 tablespoons milk
½ teaspoon salt
1 teaspoon pepper
pinch grated nutmeg
225 g/8 oz cheese, grated
6 tomatoes
4 tablespoons chopped chives
½ teaspoon celery salt

Peel the potatoes and put in a saucepan. Cover with water and bring to the boil. Simmer for 15–20 minutes or until the potatoes are tender. Drain well, then mash with 15 g (½ oz) of the butter, the milk, salt, pepper and nutmeg. (Add only enough milk to make a smooth mixture: it should be quite stiff.) Stir in the cheese. Slice the tomatoes. Melt a quarter of the remaining butter in a frying pan. Add a quarter of the potato mixture and spread it out in the pan. Cook for 3–4 minutes, then turn the scone over. Top with slices of tomato and sprinkle with chives and celery salt. Cook for a further 3–4 minutes, then slide out of the pan on to a warmed serving dish. Keep hot while you cook and garnish the remaining three scones in the same way, using the remaining butter. Serve hot.
Serves 4

Cheesy Bread

METRIC/IMPERIAL
½ long French loaf
50 g/2 oz butter
pinch pepper
pinch garlic salt
4 slices cheese
Garnish
parsley sprigs

Make incisions in the bread, cutting to but not through the bottom, 4–5 cm (1½–2 inches) apart. Cream the butter with the pepper and garlic salt. Cut the cheese slices in half diagonally to make triangles.
Spread a little seasoned butter on both sides of the bread inside each incision.

Place a triangle of cheese in each incision, leaving the point to fold over the top. Place the loaf on a baking tray and bake in a moderately hot oven (200° C, 400° F, Gas Mark 6) for 5–10 minutes or until the cheese has melted. Serve garnished with parsley.
Serves 2

Variation
If you enjoy the taste of garlic you could substitute 1 clove of garlic, finely crushed with a little salt, for the garlic salt. 1–2 tablespoons of chopped parsley, creamed into the garlic butter, makes this even more delicious.

Ham and Cheese Sandwiches

METRIC/IMPERIAL
*4 slices Edam or Gouda
  cheese*
4 slices ham
1 tart dessert apple
2 tablespoons flour
2 eggs
½ teaspoon salt
½ teaspoon paprika pepper
2 tablespoons grated cheese
1 tablespoon tomato purée
50 g/2 oz butter
Garnish
parsley sprigs
tomato quarters

Cut the slices of cheese to
the same size as the ham
slices. Peel and core the

apple, then slice thinly in
rounds. Arrange the apple
slices between the four
pairs of cheese and ham
slices. Mix the flour with
the eggs, salt, paprika,
grated cheese and tomato
purée. The mixture should
be slightly runny.
Coat the ham and cheese
sandwiches with the egg
mixture. Melt the butter in
a frying pan and add the
sandwiches. Fry for 4–5
minutes on each side, until
well browned. Garnish with
parsley sprigs and tomato
quarters. Serve hot with a
green salad.
Serves 2–4

Quick Cheese Savouries

METRIC/IMPERIAL
4 slices bread
25 g/1 oz butter
2 teaspoons made mustard
2 slices ham
350 g/12 oz minced beef
4 tablespoons grated cheese
*2 tablespoons chopped
  parsley*
½ teaspoon salt
½ teaspoon pepper
2 slices cheese
*4 tablespoons tomato
  ketchup*
Garnish
parsley sprigs

Toast the bread, then butter
one side of each slice.
Spread with the mustard.
Dice the ham and mix with

the beef, grated cheese,
parsley, salt and pepper.
Pile this mixture on to the
toast and smooth the tops.
Cut the cheese slices into
thin strips and arrange in a
lattice-work over the tops.
Dot the ketchup in between
the cheese strips. Place on
a baking tray and bake in a
moderately hot oven
(200° C, 400° F, Gas Mark
6) for 20 minutes. Garnish
with parsley and serve hot
or cold.
Serves 2–4

Tasty Salads

Beef Cornets

METRIC/IMPERIAL
1 (198-g/7-oz) can sweetcorn
4 tomatoes
1 red pepper
1 green pepper
4 tablespoons mayonnaise
2 teaspoons cider vinegar
$\frac{1}{2}$ teaspoon salt
$\frac{1}{4}$ teaspoon white pepper
1 tablespoon chopped onion
8–12 slices roast beef
few lettuce leaves
lemon juice
$\frac{1}{2}$ punnet mustard and cress

Drain the sweetcorn. Peel and chop the tomatoes. Remove the cores, pith and seeds from the peppers and cut into thin strips. Mix together the mayonnaise, vinegar, salt and pepper. Fold in the sweetcorn, tomatoes, pepper strips and onion. Chill for 20 minutes. Roll the beef slices into cornets and fill with the sweetcorn mixture. Place the lettuce leaves on four or six serving plates and sprinkle with a little lemon juice. Place the beef cornets on top and garnish with the mustard and cress.
Serves 4–6

Variation
For quick Beef Cornets, fill each with 1 tablespoon ready-made coleslaw or Spanish salad.

Spicy Texas Beans

METRIC/IMPERIAL
0·5 kg/1 lb wax or green
    runner beans
1 apple
1 large onion
6 rashers streaky bacon
3 tablespoons oil
4 tablespoons tomato
    ketchup
pinch marjoram
$\frac{1}{4}$ teaspoon cayenne pepper
$\frac{1}{4}$ teaspoon curry powder
pinch paprika pepper
1 teaspoon salt
Garnish
3 tablespoons chopped
    parsley
1 tomato, sliced

Trim the beans, then cut into pieces about 2·5 cm (1 inch) long. Cook in boiling salted water for 10–15 minutes, until tender. Drain and leave to cool. Peel and core the apple, then chop finely. Stir the apple into the drained beans and place in a serving bowl. Peel and finely chop the onion. Rind the bacon rashers and fry until crisp and well browned. Lay on top of the bean mixture. Heat the oil in a saucepan. Add the onion and fry for 5 minutes. Stir in the ketchup, marjoram, cayenne, curry powder, paprika and salt and bring to a simmer. Remove from the heat and allow to cool, then pour over the beans. Garnish with the chopped parsley and tomato slices.
Serves 4–6

Orange and Olive Salad

METRIC/IMPERIAL
1 small round lettuce
1 Chinese cabbage
juice of 1 orange
salt and white pepper
pinch sugar
1 orange
10 black olives, stoned
1 tablespoon olive oil

Separate the lettuce and cabbage into leaves. Wash thoroughly and pat dry with a tea towel. Put in a salad bowl.
Mix the orange juice with the salt, pepper and sugar. Pour over the lettuce and cabbage and toss to coat. Peel the orange. Slice thinly, then halve the slices. Arrange the orange pieces and olives in the bowl and sprinkle over the olive oil. Serve immediately.
Serves 4

Fresh Mixed Salad
Prepare a selection of sliced salad vegetables, such as cucumber, tomato, radish and onion, on a bed of crisp lettuce leaves and mustard and cress. Serve with a dressing of oil and vinegar, mixed with salt, pepper and sugar to taste.

Vegetable Salad

METRIC/IMPERIAL
1 large leek
2 large carrots
1 red pepper
½ head celery
2 tomatoes
¼ white cabbage
½ clove garlic
4 tablespoons wine vinegar
1 teaspoon salt
4 tablespoons water
4 tablespoons oil
2 eggs

Wash and thinly slice the leek. Peel and chop the carrots. Remove the core, pith and seeds from the pepper and cut into thin strips. Trim and thinly slice the celery. Peel and quarter the tomatoes. Wash the cabbage, then shred finely.
Put the leek, carrots, red pepper, celery, tomatoes and cabbage in a bowl and mix well together.
Crush the garlic clove and put in a saucepan with the vinegar, salt, water and oil. Bring to a simmer, then remove from the heat and pour over the vegetables. Toss well together so the vegetables are coated with the dressing. Allow to cool, then chill well.
Hard-boil the eggs. Cool, then shell and slice. Garnish the salad with the egg slices.
Serves 4

Cauliflower and Egg Salad

METRIC/IMPERIAL
1 cauliflower
2 tablespoons mayonnaise
1 teaspoon made mustard
150 ml/5 fl oz natural yogurt
1 teaspoon paprika pepper
½ teaspoon salt
½ teaspoon pepper
pinch sugar
1 tomato
½ lettuce
4 eggs

Break the cauliflower into florets and cook in boiling salted water for 15 minutes or until tender. Drain and place in cold water to refresh.
Mix together the mayonnaise, mustard, yogurt, paprika, salt, pepper and sugar. Peel the tomato, then halve and remove the seeds. Cut the flesh into small pieces. Separate the lettuce into leaves and wash thoroughly under cold running water. Shake the leaves well to remove excess water, then pat dry with a tea towel. Cut the lettuce into shreds. Hard-boil the eggs. Cool, then shell and quarter.
Drain the cauliflower and put in a salad bowl with the tomato pieces, shredded lettuce and egg quarters. Pour over the yogurt dressing and serve.
Serves 4

Caprice Tomato Salad

METRIC/IMPERIAL
4 large tomatoes
1 round lettuce
3 sticks celery
1 (198-g/7-oz) can tuna
50 g/2 oz Gruyère cheese
10 green olives, stoned
10 black olives, stoned
1 tablespoon chopped basil
3 tablespoons wine vinegar
6 tablespoons olive oil
½ teaspoon salt
½ teaspoon pepper

Peel and slice the tomatoes. Separate the lettuce into leaves and wash under cold running water. Shake to remove excess water, then pat dry with a tea towel. Trim and chop the celery.

Drain and flake the tuna. Cut the cheese into very thin strips.
Put the tomatoes, lettuce, celery, tuna and olives in a salad bowl and toss well together. Mix together the basil, vinegar, oil, salt and pepper and pour over the salad. Toss to coat the vegetables with the dressing, then scatter over the cheese. Serve immediately.
Serves 4

Bean and Pickled Herring Salad

METRIC/IMPERIAL
4 soused herrings
300 ml/½ pint milk
0·5 kg/1 lb runner beans
150 ml/5 fl oz natural yogurt
2 tablespoons tomato ketchup
1 tomato
2 onions
3 tablespoons chopped parsley
pinch salt
pinch garlic salt

Soak the herrings in the milk for 2 hours. Meanwhile, trim the beans and cut into pieces, then cook in boiling salted water for

10–15 minutes, until tender. Drain and leave to cool. Drain the herrings and cut into strips. Mix with the beans.
Mix together the yogurt and and ketchup. Peel and finely chop the tomato. Peel the onions and slice into thin rings. Cover the onion rings with boiling water, then drain. Add the tomato and onion rings to the yogurt mixture with the parsley, salt and garlic salt and stir well. Serve this yogurt sauce with the beans and herrings.
Serves 4

Curried Rice and Meat Salad

METRIC/IMPERIAL
600 ml/1 pint stock
225 g/8 oz long-grain rice
100 g/4 oz roast meat (pork, veal, beef)
100 g/4 oz cooked chicken
2 tablespoons mayonnaise
2 tablespoons wine vinegar
2 tablespoons chopped mango chutney
1 teaspoon paprika pepper
2 tablespoons concentrated curry paste, dissolved in 2 tablespoons hot water
2 eggs, hard-boiled

Bring the stock to the boil and add the rice. Cover and simmer for 15–20 minutes or until the rice is tender and has absorbed all the stock.

Meanwhile, finely chop the roast meat and chicken. Mix the meat and chicken with the cooked rice and set aside to cool.
Mix together the mayonnaise, vinegar, chutney, paprika and dissolved curry paste. Shell the eggs and rub the egg yolks through a sieve. Finely chop the egg whites. Add both to the sauce and mix well.
Set aside 3–4 tablespoons of the rice mixture and 1 tablespoon of the sauce. Mix the remaining rice with the rest of the curry sauce. Combine thoroughly and spoon into a serving bowl. Top with the reserved rice mixture and the spoonful of sauce. Serve chilled.
Serves 4–6

Mixed Herring Salad

METRIC/IMPERIAL
2 large soused herrings
150 ml/$\frac{1}{4}$ pint milk
1 gherkin
3 sticks celery
2 tart dessert apples
1 small onion
2 tablespoons wine vinegar
4 tablespoons oil
1 teaspoon salt
$\frac{1}{2}$ teaspoon paprika pepper
1 teaspoon made mustard
2 tablespoons single cream
1 round lettuce

Soak the herrings in the milk for 2 hours, then drain and cut into thin strips. Cut the gherkin into thin strips. Trim the celery, then cut into thin strips. Peel and

core the apples and cut into thin strips, Peel and finely chop the onion.
Mix together the vinegar, oil, salt, paprika, mustard and cream. Add the herrings, gherkin, celery, apples and onion and toss together well. Chill for 20 minutes.
Meanwhile, separate the lettuce into leaves and wash under cold running water. Shake off excess water, then pat dry with a tea towel.
Use the lettuce leaves to line four glass dishes. Spoon in the salad and serve.
Serves 4

Piquant
Fish Salad

METRIC/IMPERIAL
2 onions
0·75 kg/1½ lb cod fillets
1½ teaspoons salt
2 large pickled cucumbers
4 tomatoes
2 tablespoons capers
6 tablespoons cottage cheese
4 tablespoons single cream
5 tablespoons white wine
   vinegar
1 teaspoon sugar
½ teaspoon white pepper

Peel and halve the onions.
Put in a dry saucepan and
fry until browned. Remove
from the heat and add the
fish and 1 teaspoon salt.
Pour over enough water
to cover and bring to the
boil. Simmer for about 20
minutes, until the fish is
cooked. Drain the onions
and fish. Slice the onions
and flake the fish. Set
aside to cool.
Thinly slice the pickled
cucumbers. Peel and quarter
the tomatoes. Mix together
the fish, onion, cucumber,
tomatoes and drained
capers and place in a serving
bowl. Chill for 30 minutes.
Push the cottage cheese
through a sieve until
smooth. Add the cream,
vinegar, sugar, pepper and
remaining salt and stir well.
Pour this dressing over the
salad and serve.
Serves 4

Radish
Salad

METRIC/IMPERIAL
0·5 kg/1 lb radishes
1 tablespoon salt
2 tablespoons wine vinegar
3 tablespoons oil
2 tablespoons chopped
   parsley
2 tablespoons capers
225 g/8 oz Edam cheese

Clean the radishes, then
slice very thinly. Put in a
bowl and sprinkle with the
salt. Cover and leave for 10
minutes, then pour off all
the liquid from the bowl.
Rinse and pat dry with
absorbent paper.
Mix together the vinegar,
oil, parsley and capers.
Add the radishes and toss
well together. Cut the cheese
into thin strips and stir into
the salad. Chill for 20
minutes before serving
with Melba toast.
Serves 4

> **Cook's Tip**
> To make Melba toast,
> put thin slices of
> white bread on a
> lightly oiled baking
> tray. Bake in a
> moderate oven
> (180° C, 350° F, Gas
> Mark 4) for 5 minutes
> or until crisp.
> Alternatively, toast
> thicker slices under
> the grill, slice in half
> to make thin slices
> and toast the un-
> toasted sides.

Tasty Salads

Salad Julienne

METRIC/IMPERIAL
1 round lettuce
1 green pepper
3 tomatoes
100 g/4 oz Emmenthal
   cheese
225 g/8 oz luncheon meat or
   ham
2 tablespoons chopped
   mixed herbs
3 tablespoons oil
5 tablespoons apple juice
$\frac{1}{2}$ teaspoon salt
$\frac{1}{4}$ teaspoon pepper
generous pinch sugar

Separate the lettuce into
leaves and wash thoroughly
under cold running water.
Shake off excess water, then
pat dry with a tea towel.
Tear the leaves into small
pieces. Remove the core,
pith and seeds from the
pepper and chop. Cut the
tomatoes into eighths. Cut
the cheese and luncheon
meat or ham into julienne
strips.
Put the lettuce, green
pepper, tomatoes, cheese
and meat into a bowl. Mix
together the herbs, oil,
apple juice, salt, pepper and
sugar and pour over the
salad. Toss together well,
then spoon into four
individual glass dishes.
Serve immediately.
Serves 4

Sauerkraut Salad

METRIC/IMPERIAL
350 g/12 oz sauerkraut
225 g/8 oz tart dessert apples
100 g/4 oz gherkins
1 small onion
4 tablespoons chopped mixed
herbs (dill, parsley, basil,
borage)
1 teaspoon salt
25 g/1 oz sugar
2 tablespoons lemon juice
6 tablespoons oil

Drain the sauerkraut and rinse well in hot water. Drain again, pressing out all the water. Peel, core and dice the apples. Dice the gherkins. Peel and finely chop the onion. Mix together the sauerkraut, apples, gherkins, onion and herbs. Add the salt, sugar and lemon juice and toss together well.
Heat the oil in a pan and pour carefully over the salad, so that it mixes. Toss again and leave to cool. Serve chilled.
Serves 4

Variation
This salad is also delicious made with white cabbage instead of sauerkraut. Cut away the coarse outer leaves, remove the core and shred finely.

Riviera Onion Salad

METRIC/IMPERIAL
4 onions
1 red pepper
1 green pepper
4 tomatoes
2 eggs
8 green olives, stoned
3 tablespoons wine vinegar
3 tablespoons oil
4 tablespoons hot water
½ teaspoon salt
¼ teaspoon garlic salt
2 teaspoons made mustard

Peel and thinly slice the onions. Remove the cores, pith and seeds from the peppers and cut into thin strips. Blanch the onion slices and pepper strips in boiling water for 3 minutes.

Drain well and leave to cool.
Peel and slice the tomatoes. Hard-boil the eggs. Cool, then shell and quarter. Halve the olives.
Arrange the onions and peppers in a bowl. Add the tomato slices and olive halves, and lay the egg quarters on top.
Mix together the vinegar, oil, hot water, salt, garlic salt and mustard. Pour over the salad and chill for 20 minutes before serving.
Serves 4

Roquefort Dressing

METRIC/IMPERIAL
50 g/2 oz Roquefort or any
  other blue-veined cheese
grated rind and juice of
  2 lemons
2 teaspoons sugar
5 tablespoons single cream
3 tablespoons oil
5 tablespoons milk
5 tablespoons vinegar
3 tablespoons port or
  Madeira wine
5 tablespoons hot water
½ teaspoon cayenne pepper

Push the cheese through a
sieve until smooth, then
mix with the remaining
ingredients to form a
creamy dressing.
This dressing may be served
with vegetable salads as well
as chicken, game and pasta
salads.
Note Danish blue cheese is
ideal for this dressing.
Makes 300 ml (½ pint)
dressing

Variation
A thicker Roquefort
Dressing may be made by
mashing 50 g (2 oz) blue-
veined cheese with 300 ml
(½ pint) mayonnaise. Add
salt, pepper and lemon
juice to taste.

Italian Dressing

METRIC/IMPERIAL
175 ml/6 fl oz wine vinegar
150 ml/¼ pint red wine
1 clove garlic
1 teaspoon salt
2 teaspoons capers
1 tablespoon mustard seed
2 green or red peppers
2 teaspoons made mustard
1 teaspoon black pepper
1 teaspoon dried rosemary
1 teaspoon dried oregano
6 tablespoons oil

Mix the vinegar and red
wine together, and leave for
1 hour. Finely chop the
garlic, then pound in a
mortar with a pestle. Add
the salt, capers and mustard
seed and pound to a paste.

Remove the cores, pith and
seeds from the peppers and
cut into very thin slivers.
Put the vinegar mixture and
garlic paste in a saucepan.
Bring to the boil, stirring,
then add the mustard,
pepper, pepper slivers,
rosemary and oregano.
Remove from the heat,
stir in the oil and allow to
cool.
This dressing is delicious
with vegetable salads, such
as asparagus, cauliflower,
mushroom, pepper and
artichoke, as well as with
fish and cooked meat
salads.
Makes 450 ml (¾ pint)
dressing

Sauces and Dressings

Thousand Island Dressing

METRIC/IMPERIAL
150 ml/¼ pint mayonnaise
2 tablespoons tomato
    ketchup
4 tablespoons hot water
1 teaspoon paprika pepper
150 ml/¼ pint soured
    cream
2 tablespoons vinegar
2 teaspoons sugar
1 tablespoon grated fresh
    horseradish

Whisk together the mayonnaise, ketchup and hot water until frothy. Gradually whisk in the paprika, soured cream, vinegar, sugar and horseradish.
The dressing should be light and airy and used at once. If it is left to stand before serving, it should be whisked again. Serve with chicory, endive, asparagus and beetroot salads, as well as with those containing lobster, herring, chicken or turkey, anchovy, cooked veal or eggs.
Makes 450 ml (¾ pint) dressing

Variation
If you like, add finely chopped canned pimiento, capers and hard-boiled eggs.

Vinaigrette Sauce

METRIC/IMPERIAL
2 eggs
1 egg yolk
2 teaspoons made mustard
½ teaspoon white pepper
½ teaspoon salt
½ teaspoon celery salt
pinch garlic powder
150 ml/¼ pint hot water
1 onion
2 teaspoons capers
3 tablespoons red wine
3 tablespoons wine vinegar
6 tablespoons oil

Hard-boil the eggs. Cool, then shell. Separate the yolks from the whites. Mash the yolks with the uncooked egg yolk until creamy. Stir in the mustard, pepper, salt, celery salt and garlic powder. Gradually stir in the hot water and continue stirring until smooth.
Peel and finely chop the onion. Add to the sauce with the capers, wine, vinegar and oil. Whisk well or liquidise and leave to cool.
Finely chop the hard-boiled egg whites and add to the sauce just before serving.
Try vinaigrette sauce with salads such as potato, mixed vegetable, celery, asparagus, artichoke, shrimp, herring, sausage and roast beef.
Makes 450 ml (¾ pint) sauce

Spicy Tomato Dressing

METRIC/IMPERIAL
5 tablespoons tarragon
  vinegar
1 teaspoon made English
  mustard
½ teaspoon salt
½ teaspoon garlic salt
5 tablespoons olive oil
1½ tablespoons tomato
  ketchup
½ teaspoon Tabasco sauce
3 tablespoons mango chutney

Put all the ingredients in a
liquidiser and blend until
smooth. Taste and add
more Tabasco sauce if you
prefer a hotter, spicier
dressing. Chill for 20
minutes.
Serve with meat salads, such
as beef, sausage, game and
ham, and potato, Chinese
cabbage, herring and pasta
salads.
Makes 250 ml (scant ½ pint)
dressing

Cook's Tip
If you do not possess
a liquidiser, substitute
a smooth chutney
such as peach or
apricot for the
mango, place all the
ingredients in a large
screwtop jar and
shake until blended.

Ravigote Sauce

METRIC/IMPERIAL
4 egg yolks
1 teaspoon made mustard
1 teaspoon grated fresh
  horseradish
½ teaspoon salt
½ teaspoon celery salt
½ teaspoon garlic salt
pinch cayenne pepper
2 teaspoons paprika pepper
5 tablespoons apple juice
5 tablespoons wine vinegar
1 teaspoon sugar
150 ml/¼ pint olive oil
2 tablespoons capers
2 tablespoons chopped
  chervil
2 tablespoons chopped
  chives
¼ teaspoon anchovy
  essence

Mix the egg yolks with the
mustard, horseradish, salt,
celery salt, garlic salt,
cayenne, paprika, apple
juice, vinegar and sugar.
Using a whisk or wooden
spoon, gradually beat in the
oil. When all the oil has
been incorporated, stir in
the capers, herbs and
anchovy essence.
Serve this sauce with
herring, prawn, mixed
vegetable, celery, asparagus,
sausage and egg salads.
Makes 300 ml (½ pint)
sauce

Sauces and Dressings

Russian Sauce

METRIC/IMPERIAL
2 egg yolks
juice of 1 lemon
½ teaspoon salt
½ teaspoon dry mustard
150 ml/¼ pint olive oil
1½ teaspoons paprika pepper
pinch cayenne pepper
1 teaspoon sugar
½ red pepper
½ green pepper
1 egg, hard-boiled
2 gherkins
2–3 tablespoons chopped cooked beetroot

Mix the egg yolks with the lemon juice, salt and mustard. Add the oil, drop by drop, stirring all the time. When half the oil has been added, the remainder may be stirred in more quickly. When all the oil is incorporated, stir in the paprika, cayenne and sugar.
Remove the cores, seeds and pith from the peppers and chop finely. Shell and finely chop the hard-boiled egg. Finely chop the gherkins. Add the peppers, egg, gherkins and beetroot to the sauce and stir well. Chill before serving with herring, smoked fish, sausage, cooked meat, chicken and rice salads and fried liver.
Makes 150 ml (¼ pint) sauce

Escoffier Sauce

METRIC/IMPERIAL
150 ml/¼ pint mayonnaise
2 tablespoons hot water
grated rind of ½ lemon
juice of 1 lemon
juice of 1 orange
2 teaspoons sugar
4 drops Tabasco sauce
2 teaspoons paprika pepper
2 tablespoons chopped chives

Whisk the mayonnaise with the hot water, lemon rind and juice, orange juice, sugar, Tabasco and paprika. Add the chives to the sauce and stir well. Serve chilled with salads, such as pepper, cooked meat, sausage, fish and pasta.

Makes 300 ml (½ pint) sauce
Note This sauce may be stored in a covered container in the refrigerator for 3–4 days.

Cook's Tip
This goes especially well with a cold meat and fruit salad. Try chicken with peaches or ham with pineapple, served with the sauce and accompanied by a rice salad.

Caesar Salad Sauce

METRIC/IMPERIAL
5 tablespoons oil
4 tablespoons wine vinegar
2 tablespoons red wine
generous pinch garlic salt
1 teaspoon sugar
$\frac{1}{4}$ teaspoon black pepper
1 teaspoon made mustard
1 clove garlic
2 slices bread
1 rasher streaky bacon

Mix the oil with the vinegar, wine, garlic salt, sugar, pepper and mustard until smooth. Thinly slice the garlic. Cut the bread into cubes.
Rind and finely dice the bacon. Put in a frying pan and heat until the fat runs.
Add the garlic and bread cubes and fry for 5–7 minutes or until the bread cubes are lightly browned on all sides. Remove from the heat and drain the mixture on absorbent paper.
Mix the salad with the dressing and garnish with the bacon and bread cubes. Suitable salads are lettuce and pepper (Caesar Salad), onion, fennel, fish, potato and beef.
Makes 150 ml ($\frac{1}{4}$ pint) sauce

Horseradish Cream Sauce

METRIC/IMPERIAL
3 tablespoons double cream
150 ml/$\frac{1}{4}$ pint mayonnaise
grated rind of 1 lemon
3 tablespoons grated fresh
   horseradish
pinch cayenne pepper
3 tablespoons wine vinegar
2 teaspoons sugar
2–3 drops anchovy essence
$\frac{1}{4}$ punnet mustard and cress
   (optional)
2 tablespoons chopped
   parsley

Whip the cream until it is stiff. Stir in the mayonnaise, lemon rind, horseradish, cayenne, vinegar, sugar and anchovy essence.
Wash the mustard and cress, then chop finely. Mix into the sauce with the parsley. Serve this sauce chilled with any of these salads: vegetable, potato, mushroom, tomato and cucumber, fish, hard-boiled egg and spring onion, and cold cooked meat.
Makes 300 ml ($\frac{1}{2}$ pint) sauce

Cook's Tip
This is an excellent sauce to use for a fondue party or as a dip for a selection of sliced raw vegetables.

Sweet and Sour Dressing

METRIC/IMPERIAL
2 onions
3 tablespoons brown sugar
300 ml/½ pint unsweetened
    pineapple juice
3 drops Tabasco sauce
½ teaspoon freshly ground
    black pepper
2–3 tablespoons pineapple
    jam
150 ml/¼ pint vinegar

Peel and finely chop the onions. Put the sugar and pineapple juice in a saucepan and heat, stirring to dissolve the sugar. Add the onion and bring to the boil. Simmer until the onion is tender.
Stir in the Tabasco, pepper, jam and vinegar. Continue simmering for 10–15 minutes to reduce the sauce and thicken. Allow to cool, then chill and serve with salads such as chicken or turkey, pasta, celery, chicory, fruit, cooked meat and avocado.
Makes 300 ml (½ pint) dressing

Variation
For a slightly different flavour, without destroying the balance of sweet and sour, substitute apricot nectar for the pineapple juice and apricot jam for the pineapple jam.

Herb Cream Dressing

METRIC/IMPERIAL
2 tablespoons chopped
    chervil
2 tablespoons chopped
    tarragon
1 tablespoon chopped
    parsley
½ teaspoon salt
½ teaspoon celery salt
1 egg
2 tablespoons cottage cheese
4 tablespoons oil
1 teaspoon made mustard
6 tablespoons vinegar
2 tablespoons mayonnaise
4 tablespoons single cream

Put the chervil, tarragon, parsley, salt and celery salt in a mortar and pound with a pestle until well mixed to a paste. Hard-boil the egg. Cool, then shell and separate the white from the yolk. Add the yolk to the herb paste and mix well. Rub the cottage cheese through a sieve until smooth. Beat into it the oil, mustard, vinegar, mayonnaise, cream and herb mixture. Finely chop the egg white and stir into the dressing. Chill well.
Pour this dressing over cold cooked meat and sausages, hard-boiled eggs and cold vegetables such as cauliflower, asparagus, tomatoes and artichokes.
Makes 300 ml (½ pint) sauce

Variation
Stir in 1–2 tablespoons of tomato ketchup.

Potato Salad Dressing

METRIC/IMPERIAL
2 onions
300 ml/½ pint water
2–3 teaspoons made mustard
6 tablespoons cider vinegar
1¼ teaspoons sugar
1 teaspoon salt
1 teaspoon celery salt
½ teaspoon black pepper
6 tablespoons oil
1 tablespoon chopped parsley

Peel and finely chop the onions. Bring the water to the boil in a saucepan. Add the onion, mustard, vinegar, sugar, salt, celery salt and pepper. Simmer for 1 minute, then remove from the heat. Stir in the oil and parsley.

Dress some cooked sliced potatoes while they and the dressing are still warm, then allow to cool. Serve at room temperature. This dressing can also be used for celery, tomato, French bean, beetroot, sausage and fish salads.
Makes 450 ml (¾ pint) dressing

Cook's Tip
Tiny new potatoes are ideal for a potato salad. Cook in their jackets for maximum flavour, and toss in the dressing while still warm.

Cocktail Sauce

METRIC/IMPERIAL
150 ml/¼ pint double cream
3 tablespoons milk
3 tablespoons mayonnaise
3 tablespoons tomato
  ketchup
½ teaspoon Tabasco sauce
1 tablespoon icing sugar
1½ tablespoons vinegar
pinch cinnamon
pinch garlic salt
½ teaspoon hot curry powder
3 tablespoons oil

Whip the cream until thick but not stiff. Add the milk, mayonnaise and ketchup and continue whisking for 2 minutes. Stir in the Tabasco sauce, icing sugar, vinegar, cinnamon, garlic salt and curry powder. The sauce should be light pink in colour. Finally add the oil and serve at once.
This sauce will enhance many hors d'oeuvres, such as shellfish cocktail, mushroom salad and oysters.
Makes 450 ml (¾ pint) sauce

Variations
This sauce may also be flavoured with Worcestershire sauce instead of the Tabasco, and sharpened with lemon juice instead of the vinegar.

Indian Curry Sauce

METRIC/IMPERIAL
1 large cooking apple
1 onion
6 tablespoons buttermilk
3 tablespoons milk
3 tablespoons mild curry powder
1 tablespoon sugar
2 tablespoons white wine
3 tablespoons oil
1½ tablespoons vinegar
1½ tablespoons mayonnaise
1½ tablespoons hot water
2 tablespoons chopped chives

Peel and core the apple, then slice. Peel and finely chop the onion. Put the apple, onion, buttermilk, milk, curry powder, sugar and white wine in a saucepan. Bring to the boil and simmer for 15 minutes. By this time, the apple should be a purée. Remove from the heat.
Whisk in the oil, vinegar, mayonnaise, then the hot water. Allow to cool, then add the chives.
This sauce can be served with fish salads, chicken or turkey salad, shellfish hors d'oeuvres, and pasta salad.
Makes 300 ml (½ pint) sauce

Soured Cream Mayonnaise Dressing

METRIC/IMPERIAL
150 ml/¼ pint mayonnaise
150 ml/¼ pint hot water
150 ml/¼ pint soured cream
3 tablespoons wine vinegar or lemon juice
1 tablespoon castor sugar
2 teaspoons paprika pepper

Whisk the mayonnaise with the hot water, then whisk in the soured cream until the mixture becomes creamy. Add the vinegar or lemon juice, sugar and paprika and continue whisking for a further 2 minutes.
Serve chilled with lettuce and chicory salad, fish salad, egg salad, smoked salmon and mushroom salad.
Makes 450 ml (¾ pint) dressing

Cook's Tip
To introduce a flavour of herbs, try using a herb-flavoured vinegar instead of the wine vinegar. Mint and tarragon have an aromatic flavour, but almost any herb such as sage, marjoram, basil, thyme, can be used.

Sauerkraut and Sausage Hot Pot

METRIC/IMPERIAL
50 g/2 oz streaky bacon
400 g/14 oz sauerkraut
1 sugar cube
1 onion, thinly sliced
225 g/8 oz continental
  sausage, sliced
150 ml/¼ pint soured cream
2 teaspoons paprika pepper
1 teaspoon cornflour
1 teaspoon salt

Rind and dice the bacon. Drain the sauerkraut. Put the sauerkraut in a saucepan, cover with water and bring to the boil. Simmer for 20 minutes, then drain well.

Put the bacon in another saucepan and heat until the fat runs. Add the sugar cube and, when it has dissolved, add the onion. Fry for 6–8 minutes, until the onion turns golden brown. Stir in the sauer-kraut and sausage slices and cook for 5 minutes.

Mix together the soured cream, paprika, cornflour and salt. Add to the sauce-pan and bring to the boil, stirring well. Simmer until slightly thickened, then serve hot with Spicy Texas Beans (see page 214).
Serves 2

Tomato-Flavoured Liver

METRIC/IMPERIAL
0·5 kg/1 lb tomatoes
0·5 kg/1 lb calves' or lambs'
  liver
1 small onion
0·75 kg/1½ lb potatoes
milk
50 g/2 oz butter
salt and black pepper
2 tablespoons flour
1 tablespoon paprika pepper
3 tablespoons natural yogurt

Peel and slice the tomatoes. Cut the liver into bite-sized pieces. Peel and finely chop the onion. Cook the potatoes in boiling salted water for 15–20 minutes. Drain, then mash with a little milk, butter and

seasoning to taste, to make a smooth thick purée. Keep hot.

Coat the liver pieces with the flour. Melt the remaining butter in a frying pan. Add the onion and fry for 5 minutes. Add the liver pieces and brown quickly on all sides. Stir in the tomato slices, paprika, and salt and pepper to taste. Cover and cook for 5–7 minutes. Meanwhile, spoon or pipe the potato around the edge of a warmed serving dish. Stir the yogurt into the liver mixture and heat through for 1 minute, then pile in the centre of the potato ring. Serve immediately, accompanied by peas.
Serves 3–4

Shredded Potato Savoury

METRIC/IMPERIAL
4 large potatoes
½ teaspoon salt
½ teaspoon white pepper
1 teaspoon flour
50 g/2 oz streaky bacon
50 g/2 oz black pudding
2 egg whites
50 g/2 oz sliced cheese

Peel the potatoes and cook in boiling salted water for 8–10 minutes. Drain well and grate. Mix with the salt, pepper and flour. Rind and dice the bacon. Slice the black pudding. Whisk the egg whites until they are stiff but not dry and fold into the potato mixture. Put the bacon in a frying pan and heat until the fat runs. Remove. Place the potato mixture in the pan and spread out over the bottom. Arrange the black pudding slices and bacon on top.
Cook for 15–20 minutes. Place the cheese on top, cover the pan and cook for a further 2–3 minutes, until the cheese has melted. Serve hot with a sauerkraut and caraway salad.
Serves 2

Chicken and Sausage Ragoût

METRIC/IMPERIAL
0·5 kg/1 lb chicken breasts
1 pickled cucumber
50 g/2 oz butter
2 teaspoons paprika pepper
½ teaspoon salt
½ teaspoon white pepper
150 ml/¼ pint stock
150 ml/¼ pint white wine
225 g/8 oz continental sausage, sliced
4 tablespoons single cream

Cut the chicken into bite-sized pieces. Slice the pickled cucumber. Melt the butter in a saucepan and add the pieces of chicken, paprika, salt, pepper, stock and wine. Bring to the boil and simmer for 25–30 minutes, until the chicken is tender.
Add the sausage slices, cucumber and cream and heat through gently for 5 minutes. Serve hot.
Serves 3–4

Cook's Tip
The flavour of this dish can be varied according to the type of sausage used. Choose from sausage made with herbs or garlic or with the minimum of seasonings.

Tortellini with Chicken Livers

METRIC/IMPERIAL
350 g/12 oz chicken livers
½ onion
350 g/12 oz tomatoes
0·5 kg/1 lb tortellini
3 tablespoons olive oil
½ teaspoon salt
½ teaspoon white pepper
½ teaspoon celery salt
25 g/1 oz butter
6 tablespoons grated
   Parmesan cheese

Remove any membrane or gristle from the livers and cut the meat into bite-sized pieces. Peel and finely chop the onion. Peel and chop the tomatoes.

Cook the tortellini in boiling salted water for 12–15 minutes, until just tender to the bite. Meanwhile, heat the oil in a frying pan. Add the onion and liver and fry for 3 minutes. Stir in the salt, pepper, celery salt and tomatoes and continue cooking for 4–5 minutes. Drain the tortellini and add the butter. Toss well to coat the pasta with the butter, then arrange on four warmed serving plates. Top each with a serving of the liver sauce and sprinkle over the Parmesan cheese.
Serves 4

Meat Pizzas

METRIC/IMPERIAL
1 stale bread roll
3 tablespoons warm water
2 onions
0·5 kg/1 lb minced beef
1 egg
salt and pepper
¼ teaspoon cayenne pepper
1–2 tablespoons chilli sauce
3 tablespoons oil
2 eggs, hard-boiled
2 tomatoes
12 stuffed green olives
4 slices cheese
8 anchovy fillets

Soften the roll in the warm water, then squeeze out the water and crumble the roll into small pieces. Peel and finely chop the onions. Mix

together the bread, onion, beef, egg, salt and pepper, cayenne and chilli sauce. Divide into four portions and form each into a patty. Fry the patties in the oil for 3–4 minutes on each side, until crisp. Transfer to a baking tray.
Shell and slice the eggs. Slice the tomatoes and olives. Cut the cheese into thin strips. Top each meat patty with egg, tomato and olive slices, anchovy fillets and finally strips of cheese. Bake in a moderately hot oven (200° C, 400° F, Gas Mark 6) for 5–7 minutes, until the cheese begins to melt. Serve hot.
Serves 4

Spaghettini with Garlic

METRIC/IMPERIAL
0·5 kg/1 lb spaghettini
  (thin spaghetti)
3 cloves garlic
4 tablespoons olive oil
1 teaspoon salt
2 tablespoons chopped
  parsley
1 teaspoon black pepper

Cook the spaghettini in boiling salted water for 10–12 minutes, until just tender to the bite. Meanwhile, finely chop the garlic.
When the spaghettini is cooked, drain well. Put in a warmed serving dish and keep hot. Heat the oil in a pan and add the garlic.

Fry until golden brown. Stir in the salt, then pour over the spaghettini. Toss well so all the strands are coated, then sprinkle over the parsley and pepper. Serve immediately.
Serves 4

Cook's Tip
The long strands of spaghettini should not be broken up when added to the pan. Hold the spaghettini at one end and lower the strands into the boiling water. As they soften and curl round in the water, carefully push the rest of the strands down.

Caper Steaks

METRIC/IMPERIAL
2 frying steaks (175 g/6 oz
  each)
25 g/1 oz butter
4 tablespoons soured cream
2 tablespoons made mustard
2 tablespoons chopped capers
2 teaspoons finely chopped
  mixed herbs
½ teaspoon salt
½ teaspoon black pepper
Garnish
parsley sprigs

Pound the meat with a mallet to tenderise it. Melt the butter in a frying pan. Add the steaks and brown quickly on both sides. Remove from the pan. Add the soured cream,

mustard, capers, herbs and salt and pepper to the fat in the pan. Stir well and bring this sauce to the boil. Replace the steaks in the pan and spoon the sauce over. Cook for 5–7 minutes longer (for rare steaks) or until the meat is cooked as you like it.
Transfer the steaks to a warmed serving dish and cover with the sauce. Garnish with the parsley and serve hot with mixed vegetables and boiled potatoes.
Serves 2

Open Veal Escalope Sandwiches

METRIC/IMPERIAL
25 g/1 oz butter
4 slices white bread
1 round lettuce
4 small veal escalopes
  (100 g/4 oz each)
2 tablespoons flour
3 tablespoons oil
4 tomatoes
½ teaspoon celery salt
½ teaspoon garlic salt

Butter the slices of bread. Separate the lettuce into leaves, wash thoroughly, pat dry with a tea towel and shred. Pound the veal escalopes with a mallet to flatten and tenderise them.

Coat with the flour.
Fry the escalopes in the oil for 2–3 minutes on each side or until lightly browned. Remove from the pan and keep warm.
Halve the tomatoes and place in the pan, cut sides down. Fry for 3 minutes, then turn over and sprinkle with the celery and garlic salts. Remove from the heat.
Place the bread on four individual dishes. Put an escalope on each slice, then add a layer of shredded lettuce. Top with two tomato halves and serve.
Serves 4

Tongue with Bacon Sauce

0·5 kg/1 lb potatoes
25 g/1 oz butter
1 teaspoon salt
1 teaspoon pepper
2–3 tablespoons milk
1 small onion
50 g/2 oz streaky bacon
2 tablespoons flour
175 ml/6 fl oz stock
4 slices tongue
2 tablespoons tomato purée

Peel the potatoes and cook in boiling salted water for 15–20 minutes, until tender. Drain and mash with half the butter, half the salt and pepper and enough milk to make a smooth thick purée. Keep warm.

Peel and finely chop the onion. Rind and dice the bacon. Put the bacon in a pan and fry until the fat runs. Add the onion with the remaining butter and fry for 5 minutes. Sprinkle over the flour, then stir well. Gradually stir in the stock, bring to the boil and simmer, stirring all the time, until thick and smooth. Add the tongue slices and tomato purée with the remaining salt and pepper and simmer gently for 5 minutes.
Arrange the puréed potato in a ring on a warmed serving dish. Spoon the tongue and sauce into the centre and serve hot, accompanied by a tomato salad.
Serves 2

Sausage Stroganoff

METRIC/IMPERIAL
*225 g/8 oz continental
    sausage, such as Brat-
    wurst*
1 small gherkin
1 small onion
50 g/2 oz button mushrooms
*50 g/2 oz pickled sliced
    beetroot*
2 tablespoons oil
2 tablespoons double cream
2 tablespoons brandy
2–3 drops anchovy essence
*1 teaspoon freshly ground
    black pepper*
2 tablespoons soured cream

Cut the sausage into thin
strips. Cut the gherkin
into strips. Peel and finely
chop the onion. Clean and
quarter the mushrooms.
Chop the beetroot.
Heat the oil in a saucepan.
Add the onion, sausage and
gherkin and cook for 5
minutes. Stir in the mushrooms and beetroot, then
add the cream, brandy,
anchovy essence and
pepper. Heat through
gently for 2–3 minutes,
stirring well. Top with
soured cream and serve
hot with brown bread.
Serves 2

Variation
If preferred, serve the
stroganoff as a cold dish
accompanied by a crisp
green salad or cucumber
salad.

Pepper and Onion Minced Meat

METRIC/IMPERIAL
½ red pepper
1 onion
75 g/3 oz streaky bacon
175 g/6 oz minced beef
175 g/6 oz minced pork
1 teaspoon black pepper
1 teaspoon celery salt
2 tablespoons brandy

Remove the core, pith and
seeds from the pepper and
dice. Peel and thinly slice
the onion. Rind the bacon
and cut into thin strips.
Put the bacon in a frying
pan and heat until the fat
runs. Add the onion and
fry for 5 minutes, then
stir in the remaining
ingredients. Cook for a
further 8–10 minutes,
stirring frequently, until
the meat is well browned.
Serve hot with a potato
salad.
Serves 2

Cook's Tip
As a substitute for the
potato salad, serve
with hot jacket
potatoes split open
and topped with a
swirl of soured
cream and crisp-
fried crumbled
bacon.

235

Vienna Steaks

METRIC/IMPERIAL
½ green pepper
2 thick slices lean roast beef
    (each about 150 g/5 oz)
1 teaspoon salt
½ teaspoon black pepper
1 tablespoon flour
2 tablespoons dripping
1 medium onion, sliced
½ teaspoon caraway seeds
2 teaspoons paprika pepper
1 tablespoon tomato purée
1 teaspoon dried marjoram
300 ml/½ pint hot water
1 large potato, cooked and
    sliced
1 pickled cucumber, sliced

Remove the core, pith and seeds from the pepper and cut into thin strips. Cut each slice of meat into four. Mix the salt, pepper and flour and use to coat the meat. Heat the dripping in a frying pan. Fry the meat for 2 minutes on each side or until well browned. Remove. Add the onion to the pan and fry until lightly browned. Stir in the pepper strips, caraway seeds, paprika, tomato purée, marjoram and water. Bring to the boil and simmer for 5 minutes. Add the potato slices and meat to the sauce and continue cooking for 5 minutes. Garnish with the pickled cucumber and serve hot with a sauerkraut or coleslaw salad.
Serves 2

Quick Supper Rice

METRIC/IMPERIAL
1 onion
100 g/4 oz ham
100 g/4 oz luncheon meat or
    other cooked meat
100 g/4 oz cheese
2 tablespoons oil
1 teaspoon salt
1 teaspoon paprika pepper
1 teaspoon pepper
100 g/4 oz cooked long-
    grain rice
3 tablespoons chopped
    chives

Peel and finely chop the onion. Dice the ham, luncheon meat and cheese. Heat the oil in a frying pan and add the onion. Fry for 5 minutes. Stir in the salt, paprika and pepper, then add the diced ham and luncheon meat. Fry for 1 minute. Add the rice and mix thoroughly. Continue to cook for 4–5 minutes to reheat the rice. Add a spoonful or two of water if the mixture is too dry. Stir in the cheese and cook for a further 1–2 minutes, until the cheese begins to melt. Sprinkle over the chives and serve hot, with French beans.
Serves 2

Food in a Hurry

Banana Beef Sandwiches

METRIC/IMPERIAL
3 large tomatoes
1 banana
lemon juice
1 medium onion
50 g/2 oz butter
225 g/8 oz minced beef, or half beef and half pork
1 tablespoon flour
1 teaspoon salt
½ teaspoon pepper
4 bread rolls

Peel and halve 2 of the tomatoes. Slice the third tomato into four. Peel and slice the banana. Sprinkle the slices with lemon juice to prevent them discolouring. Peel and finely chop the onion. Melt the butter in a frying pan. Add the onion and fry for 5 minutes. Add the minced meat and peeled tomato halves and fry until the meat is well browned, stirring to break up the tomatoes. Sprinkle over the flour, salt and pepper and stir well. Cook for a further 1 minute.

Slice the tops off the bread rolls. Scoop out some of the soft centre and fill with the meat mixture. Garnish with the tomato and banana slices and serve hot with a tomato cocktail.
Serves 2

Goulash in a Hurry

METRIC/IMPERIAL
225 g/8 oz cooked silverside or brisket of beef
225 g/8 oz haslet
2 pickled cucumbers
25 g/1 oz butter
2 onions, chopped
25 g/1 oz flour
600 ml/1 pint stock
1 teaspoon each salt, pepper and paprika pepper
pinch sugar
1 tablespoon tomato purée
225 g/8 oz minced pork
beaten egg to bind
2 tomatoes, quartered

Cut the beef and haslet into cubes. Chop the pickled cucumbers.

Melt the butter in a saucepan. Add the onion and cook for 5 minutes. Stir in half the flour and cook for 1 minute, then gradually stir in the stock. Bring to the boil, stirring, and simmer until thickened. Add the salt, pepper, paprika, sugar and tomato purée and continue to simmer for 5 minutes.

Meanwhile, mix the remaining flour into the pork and bind with a little beaten egg. Form into small balls. Drop into the sauce and simmer for 8–10 minutes, until firm. Add the meat cubes, pickled cucumber and tomato quarters and cook for 10 minutes to heat through. Serve hot with creamed potatoes.
Serves 4

Bavarian Apple Strudel

METRIC/IMPERIAL
275 g/10 oz plain flour
½ teaspoon salt
1 tablespoon oil
1 egg
175 ml/6 fl oz lukewarm
   water
8–10 cooking apples
lemon juice
50 g/2 oz butter, melted
300 ml/½ pint soured cream
2 tablespoons raisins
100 g/4 oz sugar
about 150 ml/¼ pint milk
icing sugar

Sieve the flour and salt into a bowl. Stir in the mixed oil, egg and water. Knead to a dough and continue kneading for about 10 minutes. Cover, leave in a warm place for 30 minutes. Peel and core the apples. Slice thinly and sprinkle with lemon juice.
Roll out the dough on a floured cloth then stretch it until very thin. Brush with the melted butter then with the soured cream. Top with the apple slices, raisins and sugar. Roll up the strudel, using the cloth to lift it.
Cut into portions to fit one or two greased baking trays. Brush with milk and bake in a hot oven (230° C, 450° F, Gas Mark 8) for 40–45 minutes, until golden brown. Brush with milk three or four times during baking. Dredge with icing sugar and serve warm or cool.
Serves 6–8

Emperor's Omelette

METRIC/IMPERIAL
75 g/3 oz raisins
8 eggs
50 g/2 oz sugar
300 ml/½ pint milk
225 g/8 oz flour
½ teaspoon salt
75 g/3 oz butter
75 g/3 oz icing sugar

Cover the raisins with boiling water, then drain. Separate the egg yolks from the whites. Mix the yolks with the sugar, milk, flour and salt and whisk until smooth. Whisk the egg whites until stiff and fold into the mixture. Add the raisins, but do not stir in. Leave for 10 minutes.
Melt a quarter of the butter in a frying pan. Pour in a quarter of the mixture and cook gently for 2 minutes. Turn the omelette over, adding a little more butter to the pan, and cook for a further 2 minutes. Using two forks, separate the omelette into small pieces and allow to cook for another 30 seconds.
Turn the omelette pieces on to a warmed plate or dish and dust with icing sugar. Keep warm while you cook the remaining omelettes in the same way, using the remaining butter. Serve warm with cream.
Serves 4

Jam Omelettes

METRIC/IMPERIAL
3 eggs
1 teaspoon salt
5 tablespoons water
3 tablespoons raspberry jam
3 tablespoons brandy
50 g/2 oz walnuts, chopped
2 tablespoons sultanas
50 g/2 oz butter
75 g/3 oz icing sugar

Whisk the eggs in a mixing bowl. Add the salt and water and whisk until well mixed. Put the jam, brandy, walnuts and sultanas in a saucepan and warm gently over low heat. Meanwhile, melt a quarter of the butter in an omelette pan. Add a quarter of the egg mixture and cook, lifting the edges of the omelette to allow the liquid egg mixture to run on to the pan. When the omelette is set, slide it on to a warmed plate. Keep warm while you cook the three remaining omelettes in the same way.
Spread the omelettes with the jam mixture. Roll them up and serve hot, sprinkled with icing sugar.
Serves 4

Variation
Try black cherry jam with cherry brandy. Serve hot with thick cream.

Rice Pudding

METRIC/IMPERIAL
600 ml/1 pint water
225 g/8 oz round-grain rice
½ teaspoon salt
100 g/4 oz sultanas
450 ml/¾ pint milk
50 g/2 oz sugar
1 teaspoon grated lemon rind
4 egg yolks
300 ml/½ pint single cream
50 g/2 oz butter

Bring the water to the boil and add the rice and salt. Simmer for 10 minutes. Meanwhile, cover the sultanas with boiling water and leave for 5 minutes. Drain the rice and sultanas. Add the sultanas to the rice with the milk, sugar and lemon rind. Pour into a greased baking dish. Mix together the egg yolks and cream and pour over the rice mixture. Cut the butter into small pieces and dot over the top.
Bake in a moderate oven (180° C, 350° F, Gas Mark 4) for 30 minutes or until the rice is tender and the mixture is creamy. A golden brown crust should have formed on top.
Serves 4

Cook's Tip
Serve with poached fruit, rhubarb, gooseberries or apricots.

Cherry Pudding

METRIC/IMPERIAL
100 g/4 oz castor sugar
500 ml/generous ¾ pint milk
12 slices bread, crusts
  removed
1 (425-g/15-oz) can stoned
  black cherries, drained
4 eggs, separated
juice and grated rind of
  1 lemon
few drops vanilla essence
250 ml/scant ½ pint double
  cream
3 tablespoons icing sugar

Dissolve a quarter of the castor sugar in half the milk. Dip the bread slices in the milk mixture so they are saturated, but not soggy and falling apart. Grease a baking dish and sprinkle with another quarter of the sugar. Arrange half the bread slices in the dish and lay over the cherries, reserving a few for decoration. Cover with the remaining bread.
Mix the egg yolks with the remaining milk, lemon juice and rind, vanilla essence, remaining castor sugar and the cream. Whisk the egg whites until stiff, then fold into the yolk mixture. Spoon over the baking dish. Bake in a moderate oven (180° C, 350° F, Gas Mark 4) for 30–35 minutes. Do not let the top become too brown. Sprinkle with the icing sugar and decorate with the reserved cherries.
Serves 4–6

Pear Sponge Pudding

METRIC/IMPERIAL
1 (410-g/14½-oz) can pears
1 cinnamon stick
100 g/4 oz butter
100 g/4 oz sugar
4 eggs
250 g/9 oz plain flour
50 g/2 oz cornflour
1 teaspoon baking powder
pinch salt
grated rind of 1 lemon
a little milk
icing sugar

Drain the pears, reserving the juice. Put the juice in a saucepan with the cinnamon stick. Bring to the boil and simmer for 10 minutes. Remove the cinnamon stick and leave the juice to cool.

Cream the butter with the sugar until light and fluffy. Beat in the eggs, adding a tablespoon of flour with each. Sieve the remaining flour with the cornflour, baking powder and salt and fold in. Stir in the lemon rind and enough milk to give the batter a consistency that will just drop from the spoon.
Put the pears in a greased baking dish. Spoon over the batter and smooth the top. Bake in a moderate oven (180° C, 350° F, Gas Mark 4) for 40 minutes or until the top is lightly browned. Sprinkle with icing sugar and serve warm with the cinnamon-flavoured juice.
Serves 4–5

Frankfurt Pudding

METRIC/IMPERIAL
1 kg/2 lb cooking apples
juice of 1 lemon
90 g/3½ oz sugar
1 teaspoon cinnamon
10–12 slices stale bread
*600 ml/1 pint apple wine or
    juice*
2 tablespoons raisins
icing sugar

Peel and core the apples and cut into slices. Sprinkle with lemon juice to prevent discoloration, then sprinkle with the sugar and cinnamon.
Toast the bread slices in a moderate oven (180° C, 350° F, Gas Mark 4) for 10–12 minutes, until they are lightly browned and very dry. Rub through a coarse strainer or grind in a liquidiser. Add enough apple wine to the crumbs to moisten them thoroughly. Put half the bread mixture in a greased baking dish. Spoon over the apple slices and sprinkle with the raisins. Cover with the remaining bread mixture. Bake in a moderately hot oven (190° C, 375° F, Gas Mark 5) for 45 minutes. Sprinkle with icing sugar and serve warm with cream.
Serves 4

Spanish Apple Slices

METRIC/IMPERIAL
225 g/8 oz plain flour
100 g/4 oz butter
75 g/3 oz sugar
1 egg
few drops vanilla essence
1 kg/2 lb cooking apples
*1 tablespoon dried pepper-
    mint leaves*
2 teaspoons cinnamon
pinch ground cardamom
75 g/3 oz sultanas
1 egg yolk, beaten

Sieve the flour on to a working surface and make a well in the centre. Add the butter in small pieces with the sugar, egg and vanilla essence. Mix well together with one hand to form a soft pastry dough. Chill for 20 minutes.
Peel, core and thinly slice the apples. Mix with the peppermint, cinnamon, cardamom and sultanas. Set aside one-third of the pastry. Roll out the remainder on a floured surface and use to line a well-greased 20-cm (8-inch) square baking tin. Fill with the apple mixture. Roll out the remaining pastry to cover. Press the edges together to seal and prick all over. Brush with the egg yolk.
Bake in a hot oven (220° C, 425° F, Gas Mark 7) for 45 minutes, until golden. Cool slightly, then remove carefully from the tin. Serve warm.
Serves 4–6

Cherry and Cottage Cheese Cake

METRIC/IMPERIAL
3 eggs
75 g/3 oz butter
100 g/4 oz sugar
100 g/4 oz semolina
400 g/14 oz cottage cheese
1 teaspoon baking powder
1 tablespoon rum
grated rind of 1 lemon
1 (425-g/15-oz) can stoned
  cherries
450 ml/¾ pint double cream

Separate the egg yolks from the whites. Cream the butter with the sugar until light and fluffy. Beat in the egg yolks and then the semolina. Push the cottage cheese through a sieve until smooth and add to the creamed mixture with the baking powder, rum and lemon rind.

Drain the cherries, reserving the can juice. Stir the cherries into the cottage cheese mixture. Whisk the egg whites until stiff, then fold into the mixture. Spoon into a greased baking dish and bake in a moderately hot oven (200° C, 400° F, Gas Mark 6) for 40 minutes. Beat the cream with 3–4 tablespoons of the reserved cherry juice until stiff. Allow the cherry cake to cool very slightly before serving, topped with the cream.
Serves 6

Cheese Rolls with Cherry Compote

METRIC/IMPERIAL
4 soft bread rolls
6 tablespoons milk, warmed
225 g/8 oz cottage cheese
100 g/4 oz currants
1 tablespoon sugar
few drops vanilla essence
pinch salt
1 (450-g/1-lb) can stoned
  cherries
1 tablespoon cornflour
1 tablespoon water
¼ pint cherry brandy

Slice the tops off the rolls to make lids and scoop out the insides. Turn over in the warmed milk so they become saturated not soggy. Sieve the cottage cheese until smooth, then mix with the currants, sugar, vanilla essence and salt. Fill the rolls with this mixture and replace the lids. Put on a baking tray and bake in a moderately hot oven (200° C, 400° F, Gas Mark 6) for 10–15 minutes, until golden brown. Meanwhile, drain the juice from the cherries and warm it. Dissolve the cornflour in the water and add to the cherry juice. Bring to the boil and simmer until clear and thickened. Stir in the cherries and cherry brandy and heat through for 5 minutes.
Serve the cheese rolls and cherry compote hot or cold.
Serves 4

Pancakes with Nut Sauce

METRIC/IMPERIAL
100 g/4 oz plain flour
pinch salt
1 teaspoon castor sugar
1 egg
300 ml/½ pint milk
2 tablespoons oil
175 g/6 oz ground hazelnuts
300 ml/½ pint double cream
75 g/3 oz icing sugar

Sieve the flour, salt and sugar into a bowl. Make a well and add the egg and half the milk. Beat until smooth, then gradually beat in the remaining milk and 1 teaspoon oil. Set aside. Mix together half the hazelnuts, 4 tablespoons cream and half the icing sugar. This filling should be thick.

Heat a little of the remaining oil in a 25-cm (10-inch) pancake pan. Spoon in a quarter of the batter and tip to cover the pan. Cook for 1 minute, then turn over and cook for about 30 seconds. Slide out of the pan and keep hot while you cook the remaining three pancakes in the same way.

Spread the pancakes with the hazelnut filling and roll up. Arrange on a warmed serving dish. Gently heat the remaining hazelnuts, cream and icing sugar in a sauce-pan, and pour over the pancakes.
Serves 2–4

Steam-Baked Apples

METRIC/IMPERIAL
4 large apples
4 tablespoons raisins
50 g/2 oz sugar
40 g/1½ oz butter
1 tablespoon ground almonds or walnuts
1½ tablespoons brandy
1½ tablespoons cherry brandy
4 slices bread
4 eggs
450 ml/¾ pint milk
1 orange, sliced

Slice the tops off the apples to form lids. Scoop out the cores, making a hole about 2·5 cm (1 inch) wide. Finely chop the raisins, then mix with the sugar, butter, nuts and brandies. Fill the apples with this and chill for 10 minutes. Meanwhile, soak a clay cooking pot (schlemmertopf or chicken brick) in water for 10 minutes. Remove and pat dry the inside of the bottom section. Arrange the bread slices over the base and pour on the whisked eggs and milk. Place the stuffed apples on top. Lay an orange slice on each apple. Top with the apple lids. Put the lid on the pot and place in a cold oven. Turn the oven to very hot (240° C, 475° F, Gas Mark 9) and bake for 40 minutes. Serve hot.
Serves 4

Special Fruit Desserts

Surprise Grapefruit

METRIC/IMPERIAL
350 g/12 oz blackberries
    (fresh, frozen or canned)
4 small grapefruit
75 g/3 oz icing sugar
2 tablespoons blackberry
    liqueur or brandy
150 ml/¼ pint double cream
65 g/2½ oz castor sugar
1 egg white
1½ tablespoons chopped
    hazelnuts

If using frozen blackberries, defrost them. Drain canned berries. Cut a slice from the top of each grapefruit and scoop out the flesh. Remove the core, pith and seeds. Chop the flesh and mix with the blackberries. Stir in the icing sugar and liqueur or brandy. Fill the grapefruit with the mixture. Chill for 20 minutes.
Meanwhile, beat the cream with half the castor sugar until it is thick. Whisk the egg white until stiff, then fold into the cream. Pile on top of the stuffed grapefruit.
Melt the remaining sugar in a saucepan. Add the hazelnuts and stir well. Sprinkle over the cream topping. Allow to cool slightly before serving.
Serves 4,

Cook's Tip
A stiffly whisked egg white folded into whipped cream will make the cream go further. Sweeten to taste with castor sugar and vanilla essence.

Strawberries in Wine

METRIC/IMPERIAL
0·5 kg/1 lb fresh strawberries
75 g/3 oz icing sugar
juice of 1 large lemon
6 tablespoons Marsala
300 ml/½ pint single cream

Wash the strawberries
carefully and hull, then pat
dry with absorbent paper.
Cut into halves or quarters,
depending on size. Arrange
in four individual glass
dishes and sprinkle with the
icing sugar and lemon juice.
Leave for 20 minutes.
Pour over the Marsala and
chill for 30 minutes before
serving, topped with the
cream.
Serves 4

Variation
Honeydew Melons in Wine
Halve two small honeydew
melons and scoop out the
seeds. Peel the melons and
cut the flesh into cubes or
balls. Put the melon into
four glass serving dishes.
Mix together 6 tablespoons
Marsala and 2 tablespoons
clear honey and pour over
the melon. Chill for 30
minutes, then serve with
whipped cream flavoured
with a pinch of ground
ginger.

Puff-Topped Apples

METRIC/IMPERIAL
2 apples
1½ tablespoons currants
1½ tablespoons clear honey
1½ tablespoons chopped
  walnuts
50 g/2 oz butter
2 eggs
1 teaspoon cornflour
1½ tablespoons icing sugar
1 tablespoon chopped
  candied orange peel

Peel the apples. Halve
horizontally and remove the
cores. Mix together the
currants, honey, walnuts
and half the butter. Fill the
hollows in the apples with
this mixture.
Separate the egg yolks from
the whites. Whisk the yolks
with the cornflour and icing
sugar. Whisk the whites
until stiff, then fold into the
yolk mixture. Sprinkle the
candied orange peel over the
apple halves, then cover
each with the egg mixture,
piling it up.
Melt the remaining butter
in a frying pan. Put the
apple halves in the pan,
apple sides down, and fry
for 3 minutes, then cover
the pan and cook for a
further 2 minutes. Serve hot.
Serves 2–4

Variation
Fill each apple half
with a generous spoonful
of mincemeat instead of
the honey mixture.

Cherry and Pear Salad

METRIC/IMPERIAL
1 (425-g/15-oz) can stoned
black cherries or 0·5 kg/
1 lb fresh cherries
2 juicy pears
juice of 1 lemon
65 g/2½ oz castor sugar
2 tablespoons brandy
2 tablespoons cherry liqueur
(optional)
4 large or 16 small
macaroons

If using fresh cherries, stone them. Drain the canned cherries, reserving the can juice. (This may be used to replace the 2 tablespoons of cherry liqueur.) Peel and quarter the pears, then remove the cores. Slice the pears and mix with the cherries. Stir in the lemon juice, castor sugar, brandy and cherry liqueur or can juice. Break the macaroons into small pieces and add to the fruit mixture. Toss together well and spoon into four individual glass dishes. Serve chilled.
Serves 4

Cook's Tip
Grate the rind of a lemon before squeezing the juice. Keep in the fridge and use to flavour cakes and puddings.

Peach Flames

METRIC/IMPERIAL
1 (410-g/14½-oz) can peach
slices or 4 large fresh
peaches
4 large plain digestive
biscuits
3 tablespoons brandy
2 egg whites
100 g/4 oz icing sugar

Drain the canned peaches. If using fresh peaches, scald them in boiling water, then remove the skins. Halve and stone, then cut into slices. Put a biscuit in each of four greased individual baking dishes. Sprinkle the biscuits with the brandy and cover with the peach slices. Whisk the egg whites until very stiff then fold in the icing sugar. Pipe the meringue on to the peaches to form a peak. Bake in a hot oven (230° C, 450° F, Gas Mark 8) for 2–3 minutes, until the meringue is lightly browned and firm. Serve hot or warm.
Serves 4

Variation
Use canned peach halves or peeled, stoned fresh peach halves. Arrange the peach halves in a baking dish, cut sides uppermost, and fill the hollows in the peaches with chocolate ice cream or cranberry sauce. (Mix a little brandy with the cranberry sauce, if you like.) Top with the meringue and bake as above.

Apple Salad

METRIC/IMPERIAL
2 tablespoons raisins
2 tablespoons currants
4 tablespoons clear honey
juice of 1 lemon
2 tablespoons castor sugar
2 large dessert apples
1 large pear
8 apricots

Cover the raisins and currants with boiling water and leave for 5 minutes. Warm the honey in a saucepan until it is very liquid. Drain the raisins and currants and add to the honey with the lemon juice and sugar. Remove from the heat.
Peel and quarter the apples and pear. Remove the cores and cut the fruit into thin slices. Halve the apricots, remove the cores and cut into quarters.
Add the fruit to the honey mixture and stir well. Spoon into a serving dish. Cool, then chill for 30 minutes before serving.
Serves 4

Variation
Other fruits may be used with the apples, such as bananas or mandarin oranges. If fresh apricots are not available, use dried ones and soak them in cold water for 4 hours before making the salad.

Peach Meringue

METRIC/IMPERIAL
4 large fresh peaches or 8 canned peach halves
4 slices white bread
4 eggs
300 ml/½ pint milk
50 g/2 oz castor sugar
1 teaspoon cornflour

Scald the fresh peaches with boiling water, then remove the skin. Halve and stone. Drain the canned peach halves. Arrange the bread slices on the bottom of a greased baking dish. Separate the egg yolks from the whites. Scald the milk, then strain into a bowl. Add 2 tablespoons of the sugar. Allow to cool slightly, then whisk in the egg yolks. Pour over the bread slices. Bake in a cool oven (150° C, 300° F, Gas Mark 2) for 25 minutes.
Meanwhile, whisk the egg whites until stiff, then fold in the remaining sugar and the cornflour.
Put the peach halves, cut side down, on top of the baked egg custard mixture, spoon over the meringue and bake for a further 8–10 minutes, until the meringue is golden brown. Serve warm.
Serves 4

Vanilla Soufflé

METRIC/IMPERIAL
*2 tablespoons finely crushed
 digestive biscuits*
4 eggs
50 g/2 oz sugar
½ teaspoon cornflour
½ teaspoon vanilla essence

Press the biscuit crumbs on
to the bottom and sides of a
greased baking dish.
Separate the egg yolks from
the whites. Whisk the yolks
with the sugar in a heat-
proof bowl placed over a
pan of simmering water.
Continue whisking until the
mixture is pale and thick
and will make a ribbon
trail on itself when the
whisk is lifted. (If you use
an electric mixer, there is
no need to whisk over heat.)
Fold in the cornflour and
vanilla essence.
Whisk the egg whites until
stiff and fold into the egg
yolk mixture. Spoon into
the baking dish and smooth
the top. Bake in a cool oven
(150° C, 300° F, Gas
Mark 2) for 30 minutes or
until golden brown.
Serve immediately, with
fruit salad.
Serves 2

Variation
Lemon Soufflé
Whisk the egg yolks with
the sugar and the juice of 1
lemon, as described above.
Follow the recipe, substitut-
ing 1 teaspoon grated
lemon rind for the vanilla
essence.

Fruit Muesli

METRIC/IMPERIAL
2 dessert apples
1 ripe pear
1 banana
1 orange
juice of 1 lemon
1–2 tablespoons castor sugar
4 tablespoons muesli
4 tablespoons milk or water

Peel, core and slice the
apples and pear. Peel and
slice the banana. Peel the
orange, removing all the
white pith, and chop. Put
the fruit in a bowl and add
the lemon juice and sugar.
Toss well so the fruit is
covered with the lemon
juice.
Mix the muesli with the
milk or water. Add to the
fruit and stir well. Leave for
10 minutes before serving.
Serves 4

Variation
Substitute clear honey for
the sugar. Add 2 table-
spoons chopped nuts.

Cook's Tip
Put the orange in
a small bowl, cover
with boiling water
and leave for 2
minutes. It is then
easy to peel.

248

Special Fruit Desserts

Stuffed Oranges

METRIC/IMPERIAL
450 g/1 lb strawberries
4 oranges
225 g/8 oz cottage cheese
a little milk
grated rind of ½ orange
50 g/2 oz sugar
2 tablespoons orange liqueur

Wash the strawberries carefully and hull. Pat dry with absorbent paper and cut into quarters. Cut the tops off the oranges to form a lid and scoop out the flesh. Remove all the pith and seeds and chop the flesh.
Push the cottage cheese through a sieve until smooth. If it is very thick, add a little milk. Stir in the orange rind, sugar and orange liqueur. Fold in the strawberries and orange flesh. Fill the oranges with the cottage cheese mixture and replace the lids. Chill before serving.
Serves 4

Variation
Grapefruit may be stuffed in the same way.

Cook's Tip
If you have a liqui-diser, use this to blend the cottage cheese, adding a little milk, instead of sieving it.

Strawberry Jellies

METRIC/IMPERIAL
225 g/8 oz strawberries
1 packet strawberry jelly
1 packet blackcurrant jelly
150 ml/¼ pint double cream
1 tablespoon castor sugar
1 tablespoon finely chopped pistachio nuts

Wash the strawberries carefully and hull. Pat dry with absorbent paper and cut in half.
Prepare the jellies separately, according to the directions on the packets. Cool slightly, then pour a quarter of the strawberry jelly into each of four individual glass dishes. Chill in the refrigerator until set, then top with the strawberries. Fill the dishes with the still-liquid blackcurrant jelly and chill until set.
Whip the cream with the castor sugar until stiff. Pipe on to the jellies and sprinkle with the pistachio nuts.
Serves 4

Variation
Use other fruit – cherries, raspberries, peaches, pears – with complementing jelly flavours.

249

Rum Pudding

METRIC/IMPERIAL
2 teaspoons gelatine
2 tablespoons water
4 eggs, separated
75 g/3 oz castor sugar
grated rind and juice of 1
    lemon
3 tablespoons sweet white
    wine
3 tablespoons rum
4 small macaroons
stewed fruit (cherries,
    pineapple, peaches)

Sprinkle the gelatine over
the water and leave until
spongy. Place the bowl in a
pan of simmering water and
heat until the gelatine
dissolves completely.
Whisk the egg yolks, sugar,
lemon rind and juice in a
heatproof bowl over a pan
of simmering water.
Continue whisking until the
mixture is thick and pale
and will make a ribbon
trail on itself when the
whisk is lifted. (If using an
electric mixer, no heat is
needed.) Remove from the
heat.
Strain the dissolved
gelatine into the egg yolk
mixture and stir well. Add
the wine and rum. Fold in
the stiffly whisked egg
whites. Spoon into four
individual glass dishes and
chill until set.
Decorate with the
macaroons and pieces of
fruit and serve.
Serves 4

Chilled Plum Pudding

METRIC/IMPERIAL
0·5 kg/1 lb ripe plums
250 ml/8 fl oz water
1½ tablespoons gelatine
100 g/4 oz sugar
rind and juice of 2 lemons
3 tablespoons brandy
pinch cinnamon
½ teaspoon vanilla essence
175 g/6 oz almonds, chopped
150 ml/¼ pint double cream
2 tablespoons finely chopped
    pistachio nuts

Halve the plums, remove
stones and poach in a
saucepan with 6 tablespoons
of the water for 10–15
minutes, until very soft.
Sprinkle the gelatine over
3 tablespoons of the water
and leave until spongy.
Purée the fruit in a
liquidiser. Return to the
saucepan and add the sugar,
lemon rind and juice. Taste
and add more sugar if
preferred.
Dissolve the gelatine over
a pan of simmering water.
Strain into the plum purée
and stir well. Add the
brandy, cinnamon, vanilla
essence and remaining
water. Mix well and pour
into a dampened ring
mould. Smooth the top and
chill until set.
Turn out the pudding on a
serving plate. Press on the
chopped almonds. Whip the
cream until stiff, pipe in
rosettes around the base
and sprinkle with the
pistachios.
Serves 4–6

Smyrna Fig Dessert

METRIC/IMPERIAL
1½ tablespoons gelatine
3 tablespoons water
450 ml/¾ pint sweet white
  wine
50 g/2 oz sugar
juice of 2 lemons
3 tablespoons brandy
300 ml/½ pint double cream
0·5 kg/1 lb ripe figs
chocolate caraque

Sprinkle the gelatine over the water and leave until spongy, then place the bowl in a saucepan of simmering water and heat until dissolved.
Heat the wine in a saucepan with the sugar, lemon juice and brandy until the sugar

has completely dissolved. Remove from the heat. Strain the gelatine into the wine mixture and stir well. Leave to cool.
Whip the cream until stiff. Peel and chop the figs. Stir the cream into the wine mixture, reserving a little cream for the garnish. Fold in the chopped figs.
Spoon the fig dessert into four individual glass dishes. Chill until set then pipe a rosette of cream on top of each serving. Decorate with chocolate caraque.
Serves 4

Lemon and Wine Jelly

METRIC/IMPERIAL
2 ripe lemons
225 g/8 oz sugar
25 g/1 oz butter
1½ tablespoons gelatine
300 ml/½ pint water
250 ml/8 fl oz medium-dry
  white wine
150 ml/¼ pint whipping
  cream

Thinly pare the rind from one lemon. Peel both lemons, removing all the white pith. Slice the flesh thinly and remove any pips. Spread the slices on a baking tray covered with aluminium foil. Sprinkle over 200 g (7 oz) sugar and dot with the butter. Bake in

a moderate oven (180° C, 350° F, Gas Mark 4) for 40 minutes or until candied. Leave to cool then arrange in four glass dishes, reserving any cooking juices.
Sprinkle the gelatine over 3 tablespoons of the water and leave until spongy. Pour the reserved juices into a saucepan. Add the remaining water, the wine, lemon rind and remaining sugar. Bring to the boil, stirring to dissolve the sugar. Discard the lemon rind. Add the softened gelatine and stir until completely dissolved. Cool, then pour into the glass dishes. Chill until set, then decorate with a spoonful of whipped cream.
Serves 4

Coffee Creams, Budapest-Style

METRIC/IMPERIAL
600 ml/1 pint double cream
75 g/3 oz icing sugar
½ teaspoon vanilla essence
1½ teaspoons instant coffee
  powder
3 tablespoons hot water
2 eggs
225 g/8 oz ripe cherries

Whip the cream, icing sugar and vanilla essence together until the mixture is stiff. Dissolve the coffee in the water. Leave to cool then beat into the cream. Separate the egg yolks from the whites. Add the yolks to the cream, and beat in well. Whisk the egg whites until stiff and fold into the cream.

Divide the cherries between 4 individual glasses, reserving about 12 for the garnish. Spoon in the cream and chill for 30 minutes. Garnish with the reserved cherries just before serving.
Serves 4

Variation
Try dissolved cocoa powder, apricot brandy or orange liqueur instead of the instant coffee.

Cook's Tip
If using canned cherries, drain and dry on absorbent paper.

Meringue Trifle

METRIC/IMPERIAL
1 kg/2 lb mixed fruit
  (gooseberries, raspberries,
  blackberries, apricots)
175 g/6 oz castor sugar
225 g/8 oz sweet biscuits
3 tablespoons maraschino or
  cherry brandy
250 ml/8 fl oz milk
6 tablespoons single cream
1½ tablespoons custard
  powder
4 egg whites

Wash the fruit. Remove stalks, stones and skin, then chop or slice as necessary. Put in a large, ovenproof dish and sprinkle with 4 tablespoons of the sugar. Lay the biscuits over the fruit and sprinkle with the liqueur to moisten.
Heat almost all the milk in a saucepan with the cream and 4 tablespoons of the remaining sugar. Mix the reserved milk with the custard powder, then pour on the hot milk. Stir well and return to the saucepan. Bring to the boil, stirring all the time, and simmer until thick. Cool, then pour over the biscuits and fruit.
Whisk the egg whites until frothy. Gradually add the remaining sugar, whisking until stiff. Pile over the trifle and bake in a moderate oven (180° C, 350° F, Gas Mark 4) for 8–10 minutes, until the meringue is set. Serve at room temperature or chilled.
Serves 4–6

Italian Zabaglione

METRIC/IMPERIAL
6 egg yolks
3 tablespoons castor sugar
2 tablespoons Marsala
maraschino cherries

Put the egg yolks in a heat-proof bowl placed over a pan of simmering water, or in the top of a double sauce-pan. Whisk the yolks until they are pale and creamy. Add the sugar and Marsala and continue whisking until the mixture is very light and frothy. Do all this as quickly as possible and do not let the bowl become too hot or the eggs will cook and stick to the bowl.
Remove from the heat.

Spoon into four individual glasses and garnish with the cherries. Serve immediately, with sponge finger biscuits.
Serves 4

Variation
To 'stretch' this dessert, fold 2–3 stiffly whisked egg whites into the finished zabaglione.

Cook's Tip
Egg whites stored in a covered container in the refrigerator will keep successfully for several days. Use to make dessert meringue toppings.

Melting Orange Toasts

METRIC/IMPERIAL
2 oranges
5 tablespoons apricot jam
1–2 tablespoons brandy
4 slices bread
50 g/2 oz butter
1 teaspoon drinking
   chocolate powder
   (optional)
2 egg whites
4 tablespoons icing sugar

Peel the oranges, slice and remove any pips. Mix the apricot jam with the brandy. Cut the crusts off the bread and, if liked, cut each slice into four small squares. Melt the butter in a frying pan and fry the bread golden brown on both sides.

Drain on absorbent paper, then sprinkle with the chocolate powder, if used. Arrange the slices on a flameproof dish.
Halve the orange slices and place on the bread slices. Spread with the jam mixture. Whisk the egg whites until frothy. Gradually add the sugar, whisking until stiff. Pile on to the orange slices. Bake in a hot oven (230° C, 450° F, Gas Mark 8) for 2–3 minutes, until the meringue is lightly browned. Serve warm or cold.
Serves 4

Variation
This recipe can be prepared using slices of apple, pear, peach or banana. Fruits that discolour should be first sprinkled with lemon juice.

Blackberry Toasts

METRIC/IMPERIAL
300 ml/½ pint double cream, or
   300 ml/10 fl oz natural
   yogurt
350 g/12 oz blackberries
3 tablespoons sugar
50 g/2 oz butter
4 slices bread
75 g/3 oz plain chocolate
2 tablespoons warm water
3 tablespoons egg liqueur
   (advocaat)

If using cream, whip until stiff. Fold the berries and half the sugar into the cream or yogurt.
Melt the butter in a frying pan and dissolve the remaining sugar in it. Add the bread slices and fry on one side. Transfer to four plates, fried sides up. Spread with the berry mixture.
Melt the chocolate in a heatproof bowl placed over a pan of simmering water, or in the top of a double saucepan. Stir in the water until smooth and remove from the heat.
Top each serving with a spoonful of egg liqueur and then pour over the chocolate sauce. Serve immediately.
Serves 4

Variation
Use bilberries, raspberries or strawberries instead.

Old Viennese Chestnut Dessert

METRIC/IMPERIAL
1 kg/2 lb fresh sweet
   chestnuts
100 g/4 oz sugar
6 tablespoons water
300 ml/½ pint double cream
50 g/2 oz icing sugar
½ teaspoon vanilla essence
glacé cherries

With a sharp knife, make a slit in the hard skin of each chestnut. Lay the chestnuts on a baking tray and bake in a hot oven (220° C, 425° F, Gas Mark 7) for 30 minutes. Remove the shells and skin from the chestnuts. Put the sugar and water in a saucepan and bring to the boil, stirring to dissolve the sugar. Simmer until a syrup is formed. Add the chestnuts and cook for 10 minutes. Remove from the heat and leave to cool for 15 minutes. Grate the chestnuts and pile in the centre of a serving dish. Whip the cream with the icing sugar and vanilla essence until stiff, then pipe in rosettes around the grated chestnuts. Cut the cherries into small pieces and place on the cream rosettes.
Serves 4

Variation
Beat the whipped cream into a small can of sweetened chestnut purée.

Currant and Semolina Desserts

METRIC/IMPERIAL
1 litre/1¾ pints milk
3 tablespoons sugar
grated rind of ½ lemon
½ teaspoon vanilla essence
250 g/9 oz semolina
50 g/2 oz ground almonds
75 g/3 oz currants
2 eggs
1 (213-g/7½-oz) can peach
  slices
1 (213-g/7½-oz) can cherries

Bring the milk to the boil in a saucepan. Add the sugar, grated lemon rind, vanilla essence and semolina and simmer, stirring constantly, for 10 minutes or until the mixture is thick. Remove from the heat and stir in the ground almonds and currants.
Add the eggs and mix well. Pour the semolina mixture into four dampened soup bowls. Smooth the tops and chill for 2–3 hours or until firm.
Drain the peaches and cherries, reserving the juice. Turn the semolina desserts out on to four plates. Spoon over a little of the reserved juice and decorate with the peach slices and cherries.
Serves 4

Variation
Omit the currants and add instead chopped walnuts, pineapple pieces and glacé cherries.

Blushing Girls

METRIC/IMPERIAL
25 g/1 oz gelatine
6 tablespoons water
4 sugar cubes
2 lemons
100 g/4 oz sugar
1 litre/1¾ pints buttermilk
red food colouring
150 ml/¼ pint double cream

Sprinkle the gelatine over half the water and leave until spongy. Then place the bowl in a saucepan of simmering water and heat until the gelatine has dissolved. Remove from the heat.
Rub the sugar cubes over the skin of one lemon to extract the zest. Put the sugar cubes in a saucepan with the remaining water and the sugar. Heat gently, stirring to dissolve the sugar. Add the juice from the one lemon. Remove from the heat. Strain in the gelatine and stir well, then add the buttermilk. Mix in enough red food colouring to give a good rich colour. Pour into individual bowls and chill until set. Pipe small 'nests' of whipped cream on top of each serving. Pare the rind from the remaining lemon into curls and use as garnish.
Serves 4–6

Variation
To make 'Geisha', use oranges instead of lemons and omit the red food colouring.

Zermatt Iced Coffee

METRIC/IMPERIAL
1 litre/35·2 fl oz vanilla ice
   cream
3 tablespoons ground
   hazelnuts
1 litre/1¾ pints strong,
   lukewarm coffee
3 tablespoons orange liqueur

Soften the vanilla ice cream and mix in the hazelnuts. Spoon the mixture into tall glasses or large coffee mugs. Pour the coffee over the ice cream and then sprinkle with the liqueur.
Serves 4–6

Variation
Boulevard Iced Coffee
Cut 225 g/8 oz vanilla ice cream into cubes and divide between four glasses. Fill the glasses with an equal mixture of strong lukewarm coffee and lukewarm drinking chocolate. Top each serving with a table-spoon of brandy and decorate with whipped cream. If you like, sprinkle the top with drinking chocolate powder or grated chocolate.

Cook's Tip
Soften ice cream by transferring to the main part of the refrigerator about 30 minutes before needed.

Citrus Sorbet

METRIC/IMPERIAL
juice of 4 large oranges
juice of 4 large lemons
300 ml/½ pint sparkling
   white wine
225 g/8 oz icing sugar
4 egg whites
1 tablespoon castor sugar
4 tablespoons raspberry jam

Turn the refrigerator to its coldest setting. Mix together the orange juice, lemon juice, wine and half the icing sugar. Put to one side.
Meanwhile, whisk the egg whites with the remaining icing sugar until thick. Dampen a 1-kg (2-lb) loaf tin and sprinkle with the castor sugar. Stir the whisked egg white into the wine mixture. Pour into the tin and put in the freezing compartment of the refrigerator. Freeze for 10 minutes then turn the sorbet into a bowl and whisk for 1 minute. Return to the tin and freeze for a further 15 minutes. Whisk again, and again after a further 25 minutes. Freeze for 1 hour, whisk well, then freeze until solid.
Remove the sorbet from the freezer and allow to soften slightly, then mix in the raspberry jam. Spoon into four tall glasses and serve. Remember to return the refrigerator to its normal setting.
Serves 4

Jubilee Ice Cream Dessert

METRIC/IMPERIAL
225 g/8 oz mixed candied fruit
2 tablespoons rum
1 tablespoon boiling water
150 ml/¼ pint double cream
500 ml/17·6 fl oz vanilla ice cream
1 tablespoon finely chopped pistachio nuts

Halve the large pieces of candied fruit and leave the smaller ones whole. Mix together the rum and water and pour over the fruit. Leave for 30 minutes. Whip the cream until it is thick. Put two or three spoonfuls of ice cream in each of four individual glass dishes. Divide the fruit between the glasses. Pipe a rosette of cream on each serving and sprinkle with the pistachio nuts. Serve immediately.
Serves 4

Variation
Canned apricot halves or poached fresh apricots may be used instead of the candied fruit. Prepare the servings of ice cream and apricots as above, then sprinkle each with a tablespoon of orange liqueur and garnish with grated or flaked chocolate.

Cook's Tip
Cream for piping should be whipped until thick enough to stand in peaks. Overwhipping will curdle the cream.

Cassis Ice

METRIC/IMPERIAL
600 ml/1 pint blackcurrant
  juice
6 tablespoons water
juice of 1 large lemon
100 g/4 oz icing sugar
600 ml/1 pint double cream
8 wafer biscuits

Turn the refrigerator to its coldest setting. Mix together the blackcurrant juice, water, lemon juice and icing sugar. Whip the cream until it is thick. Reserve about 3 tablespoons of cream and whisk the remainder with the blackcurrant mixture. Pour into a shallow freezer tray or other container that will fit into the freezing compartment of your refrigerator. Freeze for 3 hours or until firm.
Dip the freezer tray into hot water to loosen the ice. Cut it into squares. Arrange the wafer biscuits on a serving dish and top with the cassis ice squares. Spoon over the reserved whipped cream and serve. Remember to return the refrigerator to its normal setting.
Serves 4

Variation
For a special occasion, substitute 2 tablespoons of cassis (blackcurrant liqueur) for 2 tablespoons of the water.

Emma Calvet's Ice Cream Dessert

METRIC/IMPERIAL
350 g/12 oz frozen
  raspberries
100 g/4 oz plain chocolate
150 ml/¼ pint double cream
2 tablespoons cherry brandy
500 ml/17·6 fl oz vanilla ice
  cream
1 (425-g/15-oz) can stoned
  black cherries, drained

Chill four glass dishes. Put the raspberries in a sieve and leave to defrost, then push through the sieve. Gently melt the chocolate with the cream. Stir in the cherry brandy and pour into a sauceboat.

Put a spoonful of ice cream into each glass. Top with the cherries, then the remaining ice cream. Pour over the raspberry sauce and serve with the chocolate sauce.
Serves 4

Variation
Instead of raspberries and cherries, use oranges. Peel 2 oranges and chop the flesh. Mix with 4 table-spoons orange liqueur and 2 tablespoons brown sugar. Put a spoonful of ice-cream in each of four chilled glasses and top with some of the orange mixture. Add the remaining ice cream and then the rest of the orange mixture. Make a chocolate sauce as above, omitting the cherry brandy.

Nougat Ice Cream Cake

METRIC/IMPERIAL
50 g/2 oz ground hazelnuts
16 small wafer biscuits
1 (439-g/15½-oz) can
    pineapple chunks or 225 g/
    8 oz candied pineapple
500 ml/17·6 fl oz vanilla
    ice cream
500 ml/17·6 fl oz chocolate
    ice cream
100 g/4 oz plain chocolate
100 g/4 oz nougat
450 ml/¾ pint whipping
    cream

Sprinkle a greased 450-g
(1-lb) loaf tin with the
ground hazelnuts. Arrange
12 wafer biscuits over the
base and sides.
Drain the canned or chop
the candied pineapple.
Soften the two ice creams.
Break the chocolate into
small pieces. Spoon the
vanilla ice cream into the
tin and smooth over. Mix
three-quarters of the pineapple and all the chocolate
into the chocolate ice cream.
Spread smoothly over the
vanilla ice cream.
Cut the nougat into small
pieces and sprinkle over the
chocolate ice cream. Cover
with the remaining wafer
biscuits. Put into the freezer
compartment of the
refrigerator for 3 hours.
Whip the cream until thick.
Turn out the ice cream cake
on to a serving plate. Pipe
over the whipped cream and
decorate with the remaining
pineapple.
Serves 4–6

Fruit and Ice Cream Pancakes

METRIC/IMPERIAL
50 g/2 oz plain flour
pinch salt
1 teaspoon castor sugar
1 egg
150 ml/¼ pint milk
1½ tablespoons oil
5 tablespoons blackcurrant
    jam
1 tablespoon orange liqueur
1 tablespoon icing sugar
150 ml/¼ pint double cream
500 ml/17·6 fl oz vanilla ice
    cream, cubed
1 (439-g/15½-oz) can fruit
    salad, drained
1 banana, sliced

Sieve the flour, salt and
sugar. Beat in the egg and
half the milk until smooth,
then gradually beat in the
remaining milk and ½ tea-
spoon oil.
Heat a little oil in a 20-cm
(8-inch) pancake pan.
Spoon in a quarter of the
batter and tip to cover.
Cook for 1 minute, then
turn over and cook for
about 30 seconds. Slide
out of the pan. Similarly
cook the remaining
pancakes and cool.
Gently heat the jam, liqueur
and icing sugar, stirring to
dissolve the sugar. Fold in
the whipped cream. Remove
from the heat.
Fold over the pancakes and
fill with the ice cream and
fruit. Spoon over the warm
sauce and serve.
Serves 4

Fish Salad

METRIC/IMPERIAL
2 (225-g/8-oz) white fish
fillets
2 medium onions
1 teaspoon Worcestershire
sauce
1 teaspoon salt
1 teaspoon made mustard
1–2 tablespoons white wine
4 tablespoons water
225 g/8 oz mixed pickled
vegetables (cucumber,
carrot, cauliflower,
onion, etc.)
2 tomatoes
3 tablespoons wine vinegar
5 tablespoons oil

Place the fish fillets in a shallow dish. Peel and finely chop the onions. Mix the onions with the Worcestershire sauce, salt, mustard and wine and pour over the fish. Leave to marinate for 1 hour.

Place the fish in a saucepan and add the water. Bring to the boil, cover and steam for 8–10 minutes, until the fish is cooked and will flake easily. Remove the fish from the pan and take off the skin. Flake the fish and leave to cool.

Finely chop the mixed vegetables. Quarter the tomatoes. Add the vegetables and tomatoes to the fish with the vinegar, oil and fish marinade. Mix well and place in a serving dish. Chill before serving.
Serves 6 (about 795 joules/ 190 calories per serving)

Orange Baskets

METRIC/IMPERIAL
0·5 kg/1 lb carrots
2 small dessert apples
juice of 1 lemon
50 g/2 oz sultanas
4 oranges
4 sticks celery
25 g/1 oz sugar
Garnish
25 g/1 oz pistachio nuts,
chopped

Peel and finely grate the carrots. Peel and core the apples, then slice thinly. Sprinkle with the lemon juice to prevent discoloration. Cover the sultanas with boiling water and drain.

Halve two of the oranges, cutting in a zig-zag pattern for a more decorative effect. Scoop out the flesh, discarding all the white pith and pips, and chop finely. Peel the other two oranges and finely chop the flesh, discarding all the white pith and pips.

Grate or finely chop the celery. Mix together the carrots, apples, sultanas, orange flesh, celery and sugar. Leave for 20 minutes, then fill the orange halves with this salad. Sprinkle over the pistachio nuts and serve.
Serves 4 (about 835 joules/ 200 calories per serving)

Slimming Salads

Fennel Salad

METRIC/IMPERIAL
2 large or 3 medium bulbs
    fennel
1 large onion
1 teaspoon salt
1 teaspoon black pepper
3 tablespoons wine vinegar
3 tablespoons oil
1 slice bread
15 g/½ oz butter or margarine
½ teaspoon garlic salt
100 g/4 oz continental
    sausage, sliced

Trim the fennel and halve
lengthways. Wash and slice
thinly. Peel and finely chop
the onion. Place the fennel
in a shallow dish. Mix
together the onion, salt,
pepper, vinegar and oil and
pour over the fennel. Leave
to marinate for 20 minutes
in the refrigerator.
Trim the crust from the
bread, then cut into small
cubes. Melt the butter or
margarine in a frying pan.
Add the garlic salt and
bread cubes and fry until
golden brown on all sides.
Drain on absorbent paper.
Cut the sausage into thin
strips and mix with the
fennel. Sprinkle over the
bread croûtons and serve.
*Serves 4 (about 1105 joules/
265 calories per serving)*

Cucumber and Shrimp Salad

METRIC/IMPERIAL
225 g/8 oz shelled shrimps
    (fresh or frozen)
1 cucumber
salt
2 tablespoons wine vinegar
½ teaspoon monosodium
    glutamate (optional)
4 tablespoons oil
2 teaspoons soy sauce
½ teaspoon sugar
1–2 tablespoons chopped dill
Garnish
1 egg
3–4 tablespoons canned fruit
    cocktail, drained

If using frozen shrimps,
allow them to defrost. Slice
the cucumber very thinly,
using a mandoline or the
slicer on a cheese grater.
Sprinkle the cucumber
slices with salt and leave for
20 minutes. Rinse and
drain well.
Put the cucumber slices and
shrimps in a bowl. Mix
together the vinegar, monosodium glutamate (if used),
oil, soy sauce, sugar and
dill. Pour over the cucumber
and shrimps and toss well.
Chill for 20 minutes.
Meanwhile, hard-boil the
egg. Cool, then shell and
slice. Garnish the salad with
the egg slices and fruit and
serve.
*Serves 6 (about 730 joules/
175 calories per serving)*

Radish and Beetroot Salad

METRIC/IMPERIAL
1 large white radish
2 medium cooked or pickled
beetroots
2 large onions, sliced
2 teaspoons grated
horseradish
1 teaspoon made mustard
1½ tablespoons wine vinegar
2 tablespoons water
3 tablespoons oil
1 teaspoon salt
pinch garlic salt
pinch Tabasco sauce
6 tablespoons chopped
parsley
4 lettuce leaves

Peel the radish, then grate.

Peel the beetroot, making sure you remove a thick layer of outer skin, and coarsely grate.
Mix together the onions, horseradish, mustard, vinegar and water in a saucepan. Bring to the boil, then remove from the heat. Strain the liquid into a bowl and discard the onions. Add the oil, salt, garlic salt and Tabasco sauce to the liquid and mix well. Taste, and if the sauce is too sour, add a little sugar or spoonful of natural yogurt. Stir in the parsley.
Arrange the radish and beetroot in alternating rows on a serving dish. Garnish with the lettuce leaves and serve with the parsley sauce.
Serves 6 (about 418 joules/ 100 calories per serving)

Majorcan Medley

METRIC/IMPERIAL
2 anchovy fillets
4 tablespoons milk
12 stuffed green olives
225 g/8 oz sweet gherkins
2 slices ham
2 tablespoons capers
2 medium onions
3 tablespoons chopped
parsley
2 teaspoons sugar
1 teaspoon salt
1 tablespoon dry sherry
2 tablespoons oil
6 lettuce leaves

Soak the anchovy fillets in the milk for 1 hour, then drain and chop. Slice the olives and gherkins. Cut the ham into strips. Mix together the anchovies, olives, gherkins, ham and capers.
Finely chop 1 onion. Put with 1 tablespoon parsley, the sugar, salt, sherry and oil in a liquidiser and blend to a purée. Pour into a saucepan and bring to the boil. Boil for 1 minute, then pour over the salad. Mix well. Chop the remaining onion. Arrange the lettuce leaves on a serving dish. Pile on the salad, sprinkle over the chopped onion and remaining parsley and chill well before serving.
Serves 6 (about 500 joules/ 120 calories per serving)

Chicken Madeleine Salad

METRIC/IMPERIAL
350 g/12 oz cooked chicken
100 g/4 oz frozen peas
100 g/4 oz frozen green beans
½ small onion
2 tablespoons wine vinegar
1 teaspoon sugar
½ teaspoon salt
½ teaspoon black pepper
½ teaspoon made mustard
½ teaspoon grated
    horseradish
2 tablespoons oil
lettuce leaves

Chop the chicken. Cook the peas and beans according to the directions on the packet, then drain and cool.

Peel and finely chop the onion. Put in a saucepan with the vinegar, sugar, salt, pepper, mustard, horseradish and oil. Cook gently until the onion is soft, then remove from the heat. Thin this dressing with a little water if necessary. Allow to cool.
Mix the chicken with the vegetables. Add the dressing and toss well. Chill for 30 minutes.
Arrange lettuce leaves on a serving dish. Pile the salad in the centre and serve.
Serves 6 (about 855 joules/ 205 calories per serving)

Brussels Salad

METRIC/IMPERIAL
225 g/8 oz lambs' lettuce or
    fresh young spinach
2 heads chicory
2 ripe pears
2 onions
2 slices canned pineapple
3 tablespoons pineapple
    juice (from the can)
2 teaspoons sugar
pinch cayenne pepper
3 tablespoons wine vinegar
½ teaspoon salt
Garnish
1 egg

Wash the lettuce or spinach leaves and shake to remove excess water, then pat dry with a tea towel. Wash and thinly slice the chicory. Peel

and quarter the pears, remove the cores and slice thinly. Peel and finely chop the onions. Chop the pineapple slices.
Mix together the pineapple juice, sugar, cayenne, vinegar and salt. Hard-boil the egg, then cool, shell and finely chop.
Put the lettuce or spinach, chicory, pears, onion and pineapple in a bowl. Add the dressing and toss well. Garnish with the chopped hard-boiled egg and serve.
Serves 6 (about 335 joules/ 80 calories per serving)

Slimming Salads

Carrot and Apple Salad

METRIC/IMPERIAL
0·5 kg/1 lb carrots
2 medium dessert apples
8 red radishes
3 tablespoons sultanas
4 tablespoons chopped
  parsley
3 tablespoons oil
juice of 2 lemons
150 ml/5 fl oz natural yogurt
½ teaspoon white pepper
1½ teaspoons sugar
½ teaspoon salt

Peel the carrots and cook in boiling salted water to cover for 10 minutes. Drain well and allow to cool, then slice thinly.
Peel and quarter the apples, remove the cores and thinly slice. Wash and thinly slice the radishes. Put the carrots, apples, radishes and sultanas in a bowl.
Mix together the parsley, oil, lemon juice, yogurt, pepper, sugar and salt. Pour over the salad and toss well. Chill for at least 20 minutes before serving.
Serves 4 (about 880 joules/ 210 calories per serving)

Variation
Instead of cooking the carrots, grate them before mixing with the remaining ingredients.

Chicken and Celery Salad

METRIC/IMPERIAL
300 g/11 oz frozen petits pois
½ head green celery
2 sticks white celery
450 g/1 lb cooked chicken
2 gherkins
3 tablespoons wine vinegar
1 teaspoon salt
1 teaspoon white pepper
1–2 tablespoons oil
100 g/4 oz cottage cheese

Cook the peas according to the directions on the packet. Drain and allow to cool. Trim and thinly slice the green celery. Trim the white celery and cut into very thin julienne strips. Chop the chicken. Cut the gherkins into strips.

Mix together the vinegar, salt, pepper and oil. Push the cottage cheese through a sieve until smooth, then stir into the dressing. Blend thoroughly.
Put the peas, celery, chicken and gherkins into a bowl and toss well together. Chill well, then spoon over the dressing.
Serves 4 (about 1465 joules/ 350 calories per serving)

Cook's Tip
To cool peas quickly, hold in a sieve under cold running water.

Cabbage and Fruit Salad

METRIC/IMPERIAL
1 large red cabbage
1 head celery
0.75 kg/1½ lb white cabbage
2 grapefruit
2 dessert apples
2 tablespoons mayonnaise
3 tablespoons soured cream
pinch salt
pinch pepper
Garnish
8 walnut halves

Remove the outer leaves from the red cabbage and cut the stalk close to the leaves. Cut out the middle of the cabbage carefully, so that the outer circle of leaves remains intact, like a bowl. (You can use the inner part of the cabbage for another recipe.) Soak the circle of leaves in cold water for 1 hour, then leave to drain.
Trim the celery and cut into thin strips. Remove the outer leaves from the white cabbage. Quarter it and cut out the core. Shred the cabbage. Blanch the cabbage and celery strips in boiling water for 2 minutes, then drain well and allow to cool.
Peel the grapefruit, removing all the white pith. Separate the segments. Peel and quarter the apples. Remove the cores and slice thinly.
Mix together the mayonnaise, soured cream, salt and pepper. Add the celery and white cabbage strips, most of the grapefruit segments and the apple slices and blend well. Spoon into the red cabbage 'bowl'. Garnish with the remaining grapefruit segments and the walnuts.
Serves 6 (about 545 joules/ 130 calories per serving)

Liver and Apple Rings

METRIC/IMPERIAL
0·5 kg/1 lb dessert apples
1 large onion
25 g/1 oz butter
4 tablespoons oil
0·75 kg/1½ lb calves' or
  lambs' liver, sliced
½ teaspoon salt

Peel and core the apples, then slice into rings. Peel the onion and slice thinly into rings. Melt the butter with the oil in a large frying pan. Add the onion rings and fry until golden brown. Push to one side and add the liver slices. Fry for 2–3 minutes on each side or until just firm. (If your frying pan isn't large enough, it may be necessary to fry the liver in batches.) Remove the liver and onion from the pan and keep warm.
Put the apple rings in the pan and fry quickly until golden brown on each side. Arrange the liver, onion and apple rings on a warmed serving dish and sprinkle with salt. Serve immediately.
Serves 4 (about 1860 joules/ 445 calories per serving)

Cook's Tip
Liver is extremely nutritious yet low in calories, even when fried.

Baked Fish with Cheese

METRIC/IMPERIAL
0·75 kg/1½ lb white fish
  fillets
50 g/2 oz button mushrooms
1 teaspoon salt
1 teaspoon garlic salt
1 teaspoon white pepper
1 teaspoon paprika pepper
1 teaspoon sugar
450 ml/¾ pint buttermilk
1 chicken stock cube
2 tablespoons chopped chives
100 g/4 oz cheese, sliced
  (Emmenthal or Gouda)

Skin the fish and cut into finger-size pieces. Wash and halve the mushrooms. Mix together the salt, garlic salt, pepper, paprika, sugar, buttermilk and stock cube.
Put the fish in a shallow baking dish. Scatter with the mushrooms and pour over the buttermilk mixture. Sprinkle over the chives and cover with the cheese slices. Bake in a moderate oven (180° C, 350° F, Gas Mark 4) for 15–20 minutes, until the fish is cooked. If the cheese topping begins to brown too much, cover with aluminium foil. Serve hot.
Serves 4 (about 1210 joules/ 290 calories per serving)

Sausages with Apple and Raisins

METRIC/IMPERIAL
1 onion
25 g/1 oz butter or margarine
2 large German sausages or 4 large pork sausages
1 cooking apple
2 tablespoons raisins
2 tablespoons clear honey
1 teaspoon paprika pepper
1 teaspoon salt
½ teaspoon white pepper

Peel and thinly slice the onion. Melt the butter or margarine in a frying pan and fry the onion for 5 minutes, then push to one side. Add the sausages to the pan and fry until well browned on all sides. Meanwhile, peel and core the apple and cut into thick slices.
Remove the sausages from the pan and slice. Keep warm. Add the apple slices to the pan and cook until very soft. Strain off excess fat. Stir in the raisins, honey, paprika, salt and pepper. Mix with the onions.
Return the sausage slices to the pan and heat through before serving.
Serves 2 (about 2255 joules/ 540 calories per serving)

Variation
Add 100–175 g (4–6 oz) canned drained sauerkraut to the apple mixture.

Shrimp and Sweetcorn

METRIC/IMPERIAL
100 g/4 oz shelled shrimps (fresh or frozen)
1 (198-g/7-oz) can sweetcorn
450 ml/¾ pint buttermilk
25 g/1 oz butter or margarine
1 tablespoon cottage cheese
2 teaspoons cornflour
50 g/2 oz button mushrooms
50 g/2 oz ham, sliced
½ teaspoon salt
½ teaspoon white pepper
2 drops Tabasco sauce
Garnish
1 tablespoon chopped parsley

If using frozen shrimps, allow to defrost. Drain the sweetcorn and put in a deep frying pan. Add the butter-milk and bring to the boil. Melt the butter or margarine and blend with the cottage cheese and corn-flour. Stir into the butter-milk mixture. Simmer until thickened.
Wash and chop the mush-rooms. Cut the ham into strips. Add the mushrooms, ham, salt, pepper, Tabasco and shrimps to the pan and cook gently for 5 minutes. Sprinkle with parsley and serve with omelettes or pancakes.
Serves 2 (about 1840 joules/ 440 calories per serving)

Variation
Substitute a (212-g/7½-oz) can drained, flaked salmon for the shrimps, and 225 g (8 oz) defrosted frozen peas for the sweetcorn.

Easy Paella

METRIC/IMPERIAL
2 onions
100 g/4 oz mackerel fillets
350 g/12 oz plaice fillets
600 ml/1 pint water
1 teaspoon salt
225 g/8 oz long-grain rice
4 tablespoons oil
2 small tomatoes
100 g/4 oz shelled, cooked mussels
100 g/4 oz shelled shrimps (fresh or frozen)

Peel and slice the onions. Remove the skin from the mackerel and plaice fillets and cut into small pieces. Bring the water to the boil. Add the salt and rice, cover and cook gently for 15–20 minutes, until the rice is tender and has absorbed all the water. Remove from the heat.

Heat the oil in a frying pan. Add the onions and fry until golden brown. Stir in the mackerel and plaice pieces. Cook for 5–6 minutes, until the fish is firm and cooked.

Cut the tomatoes into small pieces and add to the pan with the rice, mussels and shrimps. Cook, stirring, for a further 5 minutes or until all the ingredients are heated through. Add a spoonful or two of water if the mixture becomes too dry. Serve hot.

Serves 4 (about 2090 joules/ 500 calories per serving)

Fish and Vegetable Omelette

METRIC/IMPERIAL
0·5 kg/1 lb cod fillet
½ lemon, sliced
1½ teaspoons salt
1 bay leaf
2 small potatoes, peeled
40 g/1½ oz butter or margarine
1 onion, sliced
1 small gherkin, sliced
2 small tomatoes, quartered
2 eggs
1½ tablespoons chopped dill

Put the cod in a saucepan with the lemon slices, 1 teaspoon salt, the bay leaf and water to cover. Bring to the boil. Simmer for 15 minutes or until the fish is cooked. Meanwhile, cook the potatoes in boiling salted water for 15 minutes, until tender. Drain and slice. Drain the fish. Remove the skin and cut into chunks or flake. Keep warm.

Melt the butter in a frying pan. Fry the onion for 5 minutes. Add the potato, gherkin, tomato and fish and stir well. Whisk the eggs with the remaining salt and the dill and pour into the pan. Cook, lifting the edges of the omelette to let the egg run on to the pan. When the omelette is set, cut into two and slide on to warmed serving plates.

Serves 2 (about 2090 joules/ 500 calories per serving)

Veal with Vegetables

METRIC/IMPERIAL
0·75 kg/1½ lb lean pie veal
1 teaspoon celery salt
1 teaspoon white pepper
50 g/2 oz flour
50 g/2 oz butter or margarine
600 ml/1 pint chicken stock
300 g/11 oz frozen petits pois
300 g/11 oz frozen mixed
   vegetables
1 (326-g/11½-oz) can
   sweetcorn
¼ cucumber

Cut the veal into chunks.
Mix together the celery
salt, pepper and flour and
use to coat the chunks of
veal.
Melt the butter or margarine in a saucepan. Add the
veal and brown on all sides.
Pour in the chicken stock
and bring to the boil,
stirring well. Cover and
simmer for 1½ hours or
until the veal is tender.
Defrost the petits pois and
mixed vegetables. Drain the
sweetcorn. Thinly slice the
cucumber. Add the vege-
tables to the pan, cover and
cook for a further 5 minutes.
Serve hot with boiled
potatoes.
*Serves 4 (about 2300 joules/
550 calories per serving)*

Kidney and Apple Goulash

METRIC/IMPERIAL
8 lambs' kidneys
2 onions
50 g/2 oz butter or margarine
1½ tablespoons flour
1 teaspoon salt
½ teaspoon white pepper
300 ml/½ pint red wine
225 g/8 oz dessert apples
4 tablespoons single cream

Remove any fat and skin
from the kidneys. Halve
and cut out the cores and
ducts. Wash, pat dry with
absorbent paper and cut
into slices. Peel and slice the
onions.
Melt the butter or margarine in a saucepan. Add the
onions and fry for 5
minutes. Add the kidney
slices and brown on each
side. Sprinkle over the flour,
salt and pepper and stir
well, then gradually stir
in the wine. Bring to the
boil and simmer for 10
minutes.
Meanwhile, peel the apples.
Quarter them and remove
the cores, then slice. Add
the apples to the pan and
cook for a further 3
minutes. Stir in the cream
and heat through gently.
Serve hot.
*Serves 4 (about 1465 joules/
350 calories per serving)*

Variation
Omit the cream and top
each portion with a
spoonful of natural yogurt.

Tolstoy Steak

METRIC/IMPERIAL
2 medium potatoes
225 g/8 oz rump steak
2 tomatoes
$\frac{1}{2}$ gherkin
25 g/1 oz butter or margarine
2 tablespoons oil
1 onion, sliced
2 tablespoons flour
150 ml/$\frac{1}{4}$ pint beef stock
1 tablespoon tomato purée
$\frac{1}{2}$ teaspoon black pepper
$\frac{1}{2}$ teaspoon salt
2 tablespoons double cream

Peel the potatoes and cook in boiling salted water for 15–20 minutes, until tender. Drain and slice. Remove any fat from the meat, then cut into small cubes. Peel and quarter the tomatoes. Cut the gherkin into strips. Melt the butter with the oil in a frying pan. Fry the onion for 5 minutes. Add the meat and brown quickly on all sides. Remove the meat from the pan. Sprinkle the flour over the onion and stir well, then gradually stir in the stock. Bring to the boil and simmer, stirring, until thickened. Stir in the tomato purée, pepper and salt. Add the potatoes, tomatoes and gherkin and cook for 5 minutes. Return the meat to the pan, heat through for 2–3 minutes then stir in the cream. Serve hot with a mixed vegetable salad.
Serves 2 (about 2800 joules/ 670 calories per serving)

Westmorland Delight

METRIC/IMPERIAL
1 bread roll
225 g/8 oz minced pork
350 g/12 oz lean minced beef
1 teaspoon celery salt
$\frac{1}{2}$ teaspoon garlic salt
$\frac{1}{2}$ teaspoon black pepper
1$\frac{1}{2}$ tablespoons oil
2 tablespoons flour
150 ml/$\frac{1}{4}$ pint beef stock
2 teaspoons made mustard
3 tablespoons chopped parsley
1 tablespoon chopped chervil
3 tablespoons cocktail onions
2 teaspoons sugar

Soften the bread roll in 3 tablespoons warm water, then squeeze out and crumble into small pieces. Mix with the minced pork, minced beef, celery and garlic salts and pepper. Shape into 8 patties. Heat the oil in a frying pan and brown the patties well on each side. Remove and keep warm. Stir the flour into the fat in the pan and cook, stirring, for 1 minute. Gradually stir in the stock, bring to the boil and simmer, stirring, until thickened. Add the mustard, parsley, chervil, onions and sugar. Return the meat patties and simmer for a further 3–4 minutes, until cooked through.
Serves 4 (about 2300 joules/ 550 calories per serving)

Low Calorie Recipes

Stuffed Baked Cucumbers

METRIC/IMPERIAL
4 eggs
3 tablespoons single cream
½ teaspoon salt
½ teaspoon white pepper
pinch grated nutmeg
1 tablespoon chopped
*   parsley*
1 tablespoon chopped dill
4 ridge cucumbers or large
*   courgettes*
350 g/12 oz ham
2 small onions
1½ tablespoons oil
150 ml/¼ pint hot chicken
*   stock*
Garnish
2 tomatoes
few dill sprigs

Hard-boil the eggs, then cool, shell and halve. Rub the whites through a sieve. Mash the yolks and beat in the cream, salt, pepper, nutmeg, parsley and dill. Stir in the egg whites. Slice off the tops, length-wise, from the cucumbers. Scoop out the seeds with the tip of a teaspoon. Dice the ham. Peel and finely chop the onions. Heat the oil in a saucepan. Add the onions and fry for 5 minutes. Add the ham and brown lightly. Remove from the heat and allow to cool slightly. Stir in the egg mixture. Fill the cucumbers with this mixture and replace the tops. Place the cucumbers in a baking dish and pour in the stock. Cover and bake in a cool oven (150° C, 300° F, Gas Mark 2) for 40 minutes.
Cut the tomatoes into quarters. Arrange the stuffed cucumbers on a serving plate and garnish with the tomato quarters and dill sprigs. Serve hot.
Serves 4 (about 1610 joules/ 385 calories per serving)

Bendor Steak

METRIC/IMPERIAL
0·5 kg/1 lb fillet or rump
   steak
6 tablespoons oil
1 teaspoon white pepper
½ teaspoon cayenne pepper
1 teaspoon dried rosemary
½ teaspoon celery salt
3 tablespoons brandy
2 tablespoons flour
2 tablespoons grated cheese
1 teaspoon paprika pepper
25 g/1 oz butter or
   margarine
Garnish
rosemary sprig

Remove any fat from the
steak and cut into finger-
length strips. Put into a
shallow dish. Mix together
the oil, pepper, cayenne,
rosemary, celery salt and
brandy. Pour over the steak
and leave to marinate for
30 minutes.
Mix together the flour,
cheese and paprika. Remove
the steak strips from the
marinade and coat with the
flour mixture. Grill for 5–6
minutes, turning to brown
all sides. Pile the steak
strips on a warmed serving
dish and keep hot.
Melt the butter in a saucepan and add the marinade.
Stir well and bring to the
boil, then pour into a
sauceboat. Garnish the meat
with the rosemary sprig and
serve with the marinade
sauce.
Serves 4 (about 2255 joules/
540 calories per serving)

Minced Steaks with Stuffed Tomatoes

METRIC/IMPERIAL
½ carrot
2 tablespoons capers
1 onion
0·75 kg/1½ lb lean minced
   steak
2 teaspoons salt
2 teaspoons paprika pepper
1 teaspoon black pepper
1 egg
2 large tomatoes
1 tablespoon oil
3 tablespoons breadcrumbs
2–3 teaspoons grated
   horseradish
parsley sprigs

Peel and grate the carrot.
Chop the capers. Peel and
finely chop the onion. Mix
together the carrot, capers,
onion, steak, salt, paprika
and pepper. Add the egg
and knead together. Form
into two large patties.
Halve the tomatoes and
scoop out the centres. Mix
the tomato flesh with 2
teaspoons oil, the bread-
crumbs and horseradish.
Use to fill the tomatoes.
Heat the remaining oil in a
frying pan. Add the beef
patties and fry for 5–6
minutes on each side, until
well browned. Add the
tomatoes after the patties
have been cooking for 5
minutes. If you prefer, grill
the beef patties and
tomatoes instead of frying.
Garnish with parsley.
Serves 4 (about 1590 joules/
380 calories per serving)

Meat Dishes to Keep You Slim

Pernod-Flavoured Kidneys

METRIC/IMPERIAL
2 dessert apples
4 sticks celery
4 tablespoons chopped
   chervil
1 tablespoon vinegar
2 calves' kidneys
2 teaspoons celery salt
2 teaspoons black pepper
3 teaspoons made mustard
3 tablespoons oil
3 tablespoons Pernod
150 ml/5 fl oz natural yogurt
parsley sprigs

Peel and core the apples, then cut into thin slices. Thinly slice the celery. Mix together the apple, celery, chervil and vinegar. Remove any fat from the kidneys, then skin, halve and cut out the cores and ducts. Wash and pat dry with absorbent paper. Rub the celery salt and pepper into the kidney halves. Mix together the mustard, oil and the liquor. Put the kidney halves in a shallow dish and pour over the mustard mixture. Leave to marinate for 10 minutes. Remove the kidney halves from the marinade and grill for 2–3 minutes on each side. Baste with the marinade if necessary. Heat the yogurt. Spoon over the kidney halves and garnish with parsley. Serve with the apple salad.
Serves 4 (about 1360 joules/ 325 calories per serving)

Steaks with Red Peppers

METRIC/IMPERIAL
300 ml/½ pint water
100 g/4 oz long-grain rice
2 teaspoons salt
2 red peppers
50 g/2 oz walnuts
0·75 kg/1½ lb fillet or rump
   steak
½ teaspoon celery salt
1 teaspoon black pepper
3 tablespoons oil
Garnish
4 parsley sprigs

Bring the water to the boil. Add the rice and 1 teaspoon salt. Cover and simmer for 15–20 minutes, until the rice is tender and has absorbed all the water. Halve the peppers length-ways. Remove the cores, pith and seeds. Finely chop the walnuts and mix with the rice. Fill the pepper halves with this mixture. Cut the meat into four portions and trim off any fat. Rub with the remaining salt, the celery salt and pepper. Heat the oil in a frying pan. Place the pepper halves in the pan, pepper sides down, and fry for 4 minutes. Add the steaks and fry for 2–4 minutes on each side, according to taste.
Place the steaks on the stuffed pepper halves and garnish with the parsley sprigs. Serve hot with a green salad.
Serves 4 (about 2485 joules/ 595 calories per serving)

Liver Budapest-Style

METRIC/IMPERIAL
1 red pepper
1 green pepper
1 egg, hard-boiled
2 tablespoons wine vinegar
4 tablespoons oil
1 tablespoon made mustard
6 tablespoons finely chopped chives
0·75 kg/1½ lb calves' or lambs' liver
1 teaspoon salt
1 teaspoon dried marjoram
1 teaspoon dried rosemary
2 teaspoons paprika pepper
3 onions, sliced
rosemary sprig

Remove the cores, pith and seeds from the peppers, then cut into strips. Cover with boiling water and leave to soak for 10 minutes. Finely chop the egg. Drain the pepper strips. Mix together the vinegar, 1 tablespoon oil, the mustard, chives and chopped egg. Add the pepper strips and leave to marinate for 20 minutes. Meanwhile, cut the liver into pieces. Mix together the salt, marjoram, rosemary and paprika and use to coat the liver.
Heat the remaining oil in a frying pan. Add the liver and sliced onion and fry for 6–7 minutes or until the liver is just firm and the onions are golden brown. Serve hot, garnished with a rosemary sprig, accompanied by the pepper salad. *Serves 4* (about 1715 joules/ 410 calories per serving)

Austrian Chicken

METRIC/IMPERIAL
350 g/12 oz frozen peas
2 poussins (0·5 kg/1 lb each)
1½ teaspoons salt
1½ teaspoons white pepper
2 eggs
50 g/2 oz breadcrumbs
50 g/2 oz ground hazelnuts
2 teaspoons paprika pepper
4 tablespoons oil
150 ml/5 fl oz natural yogurt

Cook the peas according to the directions on the packet, then drain and leave to cool. Cut the chickens in half, using poultry scissors or a very sharp knife. Rub the chicken halves with the salt and pepper. Whisk the eggs. Mix together the bread- crumbs, hazelnuts and paprika. Coat the chicken halves first with the egg and then with the breadcrumb mixture.
Heat the oil in a frying pan. Add the chicken halves and brown well on each side, then cook gently for 45 minutes or until the chicken is tender. Meanwhile, mix together the peas and yogurt. Serve the hot chicken with the pea salad. *Serves 4* (about 2425 joules/ 580 calories per serving)

Variation
This delicious nutty coating can also be used for pork or veal escalopes.

Meat Dishes to Keep You Slim

Peppered Steaks with Tomatoes

METRIC/IMPERIAL
½ teaspoon celery salt
½ teaspoon paprika pepper
4 fillet steaks (about
   75–100 g/3–4 oz each)
4 tablespoons black
   peppercorns
1 kg/2 lb tomatoes
100 g/4 oz cheese
2 tablespoons oil
25 g/1 oz butter or margarine
6 tablespoons beef stock
½ teaspoon salt
2 tablespoons chopped
   parsley

Rub the celery salt and paprika into the steaks. Roughly crush the pepper-corns and press on to both sides of the steaks. Peel and quarter the tomatoes. Discard the seeds and chop the flesh. Grate the cheese. Heat the oil in a frying pan. Add the steaks and fry for 3–4 minutes on each side. Meanwhile, put the tomato flesh, butter, stock, salt and cheese in a saucepan and cook gently for 5 minutes. Transfer to a warmed serving dish with the steaks and sprinkle over the parsley. Serve hot.
Serves 4 (about 1880 joules/ 450 calories per serving)

Gentleman's Steaks

METRIC/IMPERIAL
1 (350-g/12-oz) can wax or
   white French beans
1 apple
1 onion
2 tablespoons vinegar
1 teaspoon sugar
½ teaspoon salt
3 tablespoons cottage cheese
1 tablespoon mayonnaise
1 tablespoon chopped dill
1 tablespoon chopped parsley
1 tablespoon chopped
   tarragon
1 gherkin, finely chopped
4 small, thick slices of lean
   roast beef (100g/4 oz
   each)
2 teaspoons oil
1 teaspoon black pepper
1 egg, hard-boiled

Drain the beans. Quarter the apple. Remove the core and slice crossways. Peel and finely chop the onion. Mix together the beans, apple, onion, vinegar, sugar and salt.
Sieve the cottage cheese until smooth. Beat in the mayonnaise, dill, parsley, tarragon and 2 tablespoons warm water. Mix the gherkin into the sauce with 1–2 tablespoons of the gherkin water.
Brush the meat with the oil. Sprinkle with the pepper, then grill for 3 minutes on each side.
Garnish with slices of the egg and serve with the herb sauce and bean salad.
Serves 4 (about 1610 joules/ 385 calories per serving)

Maltese Chicken Salad

METRIC/IMPERIAL
0·75 kg/1½ lb frozen mixed
   vegetables
0·5 kg/1 lb cooked chicken
2 oranges
4 tablespoons cottage cheese
150 ml/5 fl oz natural yogurt
4 tablespoons mayonnaise
1 teaspoon vinegar
1 teaspoon made mustard
1 teaspoon sugar
½ teaspoon salt
½ teaspoon pepper
2 tablespoons warm water

Cook the vegetables
according to the directions
on the packet, then drain
and leave to cool. Slice the
chicken or cut into chunks.
Peel the oranges, removing
all the white pith, and slice.
Push the cottage cheese
through a sieve until
smooth. Beat in the yogurt,
mayonnaise, vinegar,
mustard, sugar, salt, pepper
and water. Fold the mixed
vegetables into the dressing,
then turn into a serving dish.
Arrange the orange slices
on top and then the chicken.
Chill for 20 minutes before
serving.
*Serves 4 (about 1650 joules/
395 calories per serving)*

Stuffed Cucumber Slices

METRIC/IMPERIAL
1 large cucumber (about
   0·75 kg/1½ lb)
½ teaspoon salt
½ teaspoon celery salt
100 g/4 oz ham
2 small onions
225 g/8 oz cottage cheese
1 teaspoon paprika pepper
4 tablespoons chopped
   parsley

Wash the cucumber, and
halve lengthways. Scoop
out the seeds with the tip
of a teaspoon. Rub the
inside of one half with the
salt and celery salt.
Finely chop or dice the ham.
Peel and finely chop the
onions. Push the cottage
cheese through a sieve until
smooth, then beat in the
paprika and parsley. Stir in
the ham and onions. Pile
this mixture on the un-
seasoned cucumber half.
Replace the other half and
press on firmly.
Chill for 20 minutes. Serve
the cucumber, in slices,
with crispbread and a
green salad.
*Serves 4 (about 650 joules/
155 calories per serving)*

Cook's Tip
Choose straight firm
cucumbers no more
than 5 cm (2 inches)
wide. The skin is
perfectly edible.

Suppers and Snacks

Asparagus and Egg Salad

METRIC/IMPERIAL
0·75 kg/1½ lb asparagus
4 eggs
75 g/3 oz butter or
    margarine, softened
juice of ½ lemon
¾ teaspoon sugar
50 g/2 oz cooked peas
1 red pepper
3 tablespoons flour
½ teaspoon salt

Trim and scrape the asparagus. Tie in a bundle and place in a saucepan of boiling salted water, keeping the tips above water. Simmer for 10–15 minutes until tender. Drain and cool.
Hard-boil 2 eggs. Cool,
shell and finely chop. Mix with 50 g (2 oz) butter, the lemon juice, ½ teaspoon sugar and the peas. Cut the asparagus into pieces. Remove the core, pith and seeds from the pepper, then cut into thin strips. Add with the asparagus to the pea mixture.
Blend the flour with 6 tablespoons water. Whisk in the remaining eggs and sugar and the salt. Melt the remaining butter in a frying pan. Pour in the egg mixture and cook, lifting the edges to let the liquid egg run on to the pan. Finish cooking under the grill to brown the top, then cut into strips. Arrange round a dish and pile in the asparagus salad.
Serves 4 (about 1400 joules/ 335 calories per serving)

Green-Red Slices

METRIC/IMPERIAL
4 slices brown bread
25 g/1 oz butter or margarine
100 g/4 oz cottage cheese
2 tablespoons milk
½ teaspoon paprika pepper
pinch salt
pinch sugar
2 tablespoons chopped
    parsley
2 tablespoons chopped chives
1 tablespoon chopped
    tarragon
1 tablespoon chopped
    chervil
8 large red radishes
4 tomatoes
1 round lettuce

Spread the slices of bread with the butter or margar-
ine. Mix the cottage cheese with the milk, then beat in the paprika, salt, sugar, parsley, chives, tarragon and chervil. Spread this mixture thickly and evenly on the bread.
Wash the radishes, then cut into slices. Quarter the tomatoes. Arrange the radish slices and tomato quarters in two rows on the slices of bread.
Separate the lettuce into leaves and wash well in cold running water. Shake off excess water, then pat dry with a tea towel. Arrange the lettuce leaves on a serving plate and place the bread slices on top.
Serves 4 (about 795 joules/ 190 calories per serving)

Greek Mushrooms

METRIC/IMPERIAL
225 g/8 oz mushrooms
2 teaspoons salt
juice of 2 lemons
2 tablespoons oil
2 teaspoons paprika pepper
250 ml/8 fl oz buttermilk
4 rashers streaky bacon
1 teaspoon sugar
1 teaspoon soy sauce

Wash the mushrooms and trim the stalks almost level with the caps. Place in a bowl and sprinkle over the salt and half the lemon juice. Leave for 10 minutes, then rinse in cold water. Shake off excess water and pat dry with absorbent paper.

Heat the oil in a saucepan. Stir in the paprika, then add the mushrooms. Fry for 3–4 minutes, shaking the pan or stirring occasionally. Add the buttermilk, stir well and simmer for 5 minutes.
Meanwhile, fry or grill the bacon rashers until they are crisp and golden. Drain on absorbent paper and allow to cool.
Stir the sugar, soy sauce and remaining lemon juice into the mushroom mixture. Remove from the heat and cool. Place the bacon slices on top and serve cool or chilled.
Serves 4 (about 605 joules/145 calories per serving)

Madras Chicken Sandwiches

METRIC/IMPERIAL
4 slices brown bread
25 g/1 oz butter or margarine
2 tablespoons mayonnaise
4 lettuce leaves
225 g/8 oz cooked chicken
150 ml/¼ pint double cream
1 teaspoon curry powder
1 dessert apple
1 tablespoon lemon juice

Toast the slices of bread, then spread with the butter or margarine. Cover with the mayonnaise, then place a lettuce leaf on top of each slice.
Cut the chicken into small pieces and arrange on the lettuce. Whip the cream with the curry powder until it is thick. Spoon over the chicken.
Peel and core the apple. Grate and mix with the lemon juice to prevent discoloration, then place on top of the cream.
Serves 4 (about 1755 joules/420 calories per serving)

Variation
Use cooked turkey or veal instead of chicken.

> **Cook's Tip**
> Make a slimmer's mayonnaise by mixing equal quantities of a low calorie salad dressing with natural yogurt.

Veal and Fruit Ragoût

METRIC/IMPERIAL
0·75 kg/1½ lb veal (from the
*   shoulder or breast)*
25 g/1 oz butter or margarine
175 ml/6 fl oz water
2 tablespoons flour
225 g/8 oz green grapes
1 dessert apple
1 ripe pear
½ teaspoon salt
½ teaspoon paprika pepper
2 tablespoons single cream

Remove any fat from the meat and cut into chunks. Melt the butter or margarine in a saucepan. Add the veal chunks and fry until golden brown on all sides. Add all but 3 tablespoons of the water, cover and simmer for 40–45 minutes, until the veal is tender. Mix the flour with the remaining water to form a smooth paste. Stir into the veal and cook for a further 5 minutes.
Peel the grapes, halve and remove the pips. Peel and quarter the apple and pear. Remove the cores and dice. Stir the salt, paprika and cream into the veal mixture, then fold in the fruit. Heat through gently for 2–3 minutes. Serve hot.
Serves 4 (about 1945 joules/
365 calories per serving)

Shrimp and Egg Sandwiches

METRIC/IMPERIAL
0·5 kg/1 lb shelled shrimps
*   (fresh or frozen)*
4 eggs
3 tablespoons oil
1 small onion, chopped
½ teaspoon salt
½ teaspoon paprika pepper
4 slices bread
25 g/1 oz butter or margarine
4 lettuce leaves
2 tomatoes, quartered

If using frozen shrimps, allow to defrost. Hard-boil 2 eggs. Cool, shell and cut into wedges.
Heat the oil in a frying pan. Add the onion, fry for 5 minutes, then push to one side. Add the shrimps and cook for 2–3 minutes to heat through. Remove the shrimps from the pan and keep warm.
Whisk the remaining eggs with the salt and paprika. Pour into the pan and cook quickly but gently, stirring in the onion, until lightly scrambled.
Meanwhile, toast the bread. Spread it with the butter and place a slice on each of four warmed plates. Place a lettuce leaf on each slice, then spoon on the scrambled egg. Top with the shrimps and garnish with the hard-boiled egg wedges and tomato quarters. Serve hot.
Serves 4 (about 1965 joules/
470 calories per serving)

Cottage Cheese with a Difference

METRIC/IMPERIAL
0·5 kg/1 lb cottage cheese
6 tablespoons milk
1 teaspoon salt
1 (225-g/8-oz) can stoned
cherries, drained
1 tablespoon icing sugar
4 tablespoons lemon juice
2 tablespoons chopped
mixed herbs
grated rind of 1 lemon
1 teaspoon sugar
2 oranges
4 tablespoons ground
hazelnuts
1 egg, hard-boiled, chopped
1 tablespoon chopped gherkin
1 tablespoon chopped red
pepper

½ teaspoon celery salt

Beat the cottage cheese, milk and salt until smooth. Divide into four portions. Chop most of the cherries. Mix with the icing sugar, half the lemon juice and one portion cottage cheese. Garnish with whole cherries. Add the mixed herbs, lemon rind and sugar to another portion of cottage cheese. Peel the oranges and cut into chunks. Add to a third portion of cottage cheese with the hazelnuts.
Mix the chopped egg with the gherkin, red pepper, celery salt, remaining lemon juice and final portion of cottage cheese.
Serves 4 (about 1440 joules/ 345 calories per serving)

Plum Wine Soup

METRIC/IMPERIAL
225 g/8 oz small plums
3 tablespoons sugar
450 ml/¾ pint red wine
300 ml/½ pint water
2 whole cloves
pinch ground cinnamon
thinly pared rind of 1 lemon
2 tablespoons sago
1 tablespoon cornflour
8 small macaroons

Halve and stone the plums. Tip into a bowl and sprinkle over 2 tablespoons sugar. Leave for 30 minutes. Put the wine, all but 2 tablespoons of the water, the cloves, cinnamon, remaining sugar and the lemon rind in a saucepan.

Bring to the boil. Stir in the sago and simmer for 10 minutes. Add the plums and cook for a further 5 minutes, until very soft. Remove from the heat. Take out and reserve the lemon rind. Discard the cloves. Purée the soup in a liquidiser and return to the pan. Bring back to the boil. Blend the cornflour with the remaining water and add to the pan. Simmer, stirring, until slightly thickened. Return the lemon rind to the soup. Ladle into four bowls and float two macaroons on each. Serve hot or chilled.
Serves 4 (about 1190 joules/ 285 calories per serving)

Egg and Anchovy Sandwiches

METRIC/IMPERIAL
4 eggs
4 slices brown bread
25 g/1 oz butter or margarine
12 anchovy fillets
4 tablespoons milk
2 stuffed green olives
½ teaspoon paprika pepper

Hard-boil the eggs. Cool, then shell and slice thinly. Spread the bread with the butter or margarine. Arrange the egg slices over the bread.
Soak the anchovy fillets in the milk for 5 minutes, then drain. Rinse with water and pat dry with absorbent paper. Cut the fillets into thin strips and arrange over the eggs, to form a lattice-work. Finely chop the olives and sprinkle over the egg. Add a pinch of paprika to each serving.
Serves 4 (about 730 joules/ 175 calories per serving)

Cook's Tip

To slice hard-boiled eggs successfully, dip the knife blade into a bowl of boiling water between each slice.

Yogurt and Ginger Soup

METRIC/IMPERIAL
600 ml/1 pint milk
1½ tablespoons cornflour
2 egg yolks
300 ml/10 fl oz natural yogurt
3 tablespoons sugar
grated rind and juice of 1 lemon
4 tablespoons slivered preserved ginger
2 tablespoons ginger syrup (from the jar of preserved ginger)
12 small macaroons (optional)

Put all but 3 tablespoons of the milk in a saucepan and bring to the boil. Blend the cornflour with the remaining milk. Pour the hot milk over the corn-flour mixture and stir well, then return all to the saucepan. Bring back to the boil, stirring constantly, and simmer until thickened. Whisk the egg yolks with the yogurt. Add a spoonful of the hot milk mixture, then stir the yogurt mixture into the saucepan. Heat gently, but do not allow to boil.
Stir the sugar, lemon rind and juice, preserved ginger and ginger syrup into the soup. Pour into 4 bowls and float 3 macaroons on each, if liked. Serve warm or chilled.
Serves 4 (about 1420–2050 joules/340–490 calories per serving)

Savoury Pastries

Cheese and Bacon Quiche

METRIC/IMPERIAL
275 g/10 oz plain flour
½ teaspoon salt
150 g/5 oz butter
2–3 tablespoons water
225 g/8 oz streaky bacon or
    ham
4 eggs
250 ml/scant ½ pint single
    cream
pinch pepper
100 g/4 oz cheese, grated

Sift the flour and salt into
a mixing bowl. Rub in the
butter until the mixture
resembles breadcrumbs.
Stir in enough water to bind
together, and form into a
dough. Chill for 20 minutes.
Roll out the pastry and use
to line a greased 25-cm
(10-inch) sandwich tin, or
flan ring placed on a baking
tray.
If using bacon, remove the
rind, then cut it or the ham
into very thin strips. Lay the
strips in the pastry case.
Separate the egg yolks from
the whites. Whisk the yolks
with the cream and
seasoning to taste. Stir in
the cheese. Whisk the egg
whites until stiff, then fold
into the egg yolk mixture.
Spread over the bacon.
Bake in a moderately hot
oven (200° C, 400° F, Gas
Mark 6) for 30–40 minutes,
until the pastry is golden
and the filling set. Ease the
quiche out of the tin and
serve.
Serves 6–8

Game Pies

METRIC/IMPERIAL
368-g/13-oz packet frozen
    puff pastry
100 g/4 oz cooked game
50 g/2 oz streaky bacon
1 leek, trimmed
1 onion, chopped
50 g/2 oz liver sausage
¼ teaspoon salt
½ teaspoon paprika pepper
¼ teaspoon dried thyme
pinch dried marjoram
beaten egg to glaze

Defrost the pastry. Chop
the game; rind and chop the
bacon. Place the bacon in a
frying pan and heat until the
fat runs. Add the game and
fry with the bacon for 5
minutes. Wash and slice the
leek, add to the pan with
the onion and cook for a
further 5 minutes. Cool
slightly, then either blend
in the liquidiser, or mince
finely. Mix in the liver
sausage, seasonings and
herbs to form a smooth
paste.
Roll out the pastry on a
floured surface. Cut into an
even number of circles with
a 6-cm (2½-inch) fluted
cutter. Spoon the meat
filling on to half the circles.
Dampen the edges and press
on the remaining circles.
Place the pies on a baking
tray and brush with the
beaten egg. Bake in a
moderately hot oven
(200° C, 400° F, Gas
Mark 6) for 20–25 minutes.
Serve hot or cold.
Makes 15

282

Savoury Upside-Down Pie

METRIC/IMPERIAL
213-g/7½-oz packet frozen
  puff pastry
0·75 kg/1½ lb minced beef
1 teaspoon salt
½ teaspoon black pepper
1 large onion, chopped
3 egg yolks
100 g/4 oz mushrooms
50 g/2 oz blue cheese
100 g/4 oz streaky bacon
  rashers
1½ tablespoons each chopped
  sorrel and chervil

Defrost the pastry. Mix the
minced beef with the salt,
pepper and onion; bind
with the egg yolks. Wash
and quarter the mushrooms.
Crumble the cheese.
Cover the base of a 20-cm
(8-inch) loose-bottomed
cake tin with the streaky
bacon. Arrange the cheese,
herbs and mushroom
quarters on top. Cover with
the meat mixture, pressing
it down firmly and
smoothing the top.
Roll out the pastry on a
floured surface to a circle
large enough to cover the
filling. Place over the filling
and prick the pastry with a
fork. Bake in a moderately
hot oven (200° C, 400° F,
Gas Mark 6) for 50
minutes–1 hour.
Remove from the oven,
invert the tin over a warm
plate or wire tray and
turn out the pie.
Serves 6–8

Meat Pasty Morsels

METRIC/IMPERIAL
3 red or green peppers
0·5 kg/1 lb minced beef
2 cloves garlic, crushed
½ teaspoon white pepper
¼ teaspoon cayenne pepper
1 teaspoon cardamom seeds
1 teaspoon cinnamon
½ teaspoon salt
juice of 1 lemon
0·5 kg/1 lb onions, chopped
2 tablespoons oil
368-g/13-oz packet frozen
  puff pastry
oil for deep frying

Remove cores, pith and
seeds from the peppers,
then chop finely. Put the
minced beef, chopped
pepper, garlic, spices, salt
and lemon juice in a frying
pan and fry for 5–10
minutes, stirring.
Fry the onions lightly in the
oil, then add to the meat
mixture. Allow to cool.
Defrost the pastry and roll
out to a rectangle about
53 × 33 cm (21 × 13
inches). Trim and cut into
strips 5 cm (2 inches) wide
and 15 cm (6 inches) long.
Place a spoonful of the meat
mixture at one end and
roll up tightly, pressing the
edges together to seal.
Deep fry in oil heated to
190° C, (375° F) for 4–5
minutes, until golden
brown. Drain on absorbent
paper.
Makes 20

Sausage and Meat Flan

METRIC/IMPERIAL
*368-g/13-oz packet frozen
    puff pastry*
1 onion, sliced
3 tablespoons oil
1 clove garlic, crushed
½ teaspoon salt
¼ teaspoon black pepper
100 g/4 oz minced beef
100 g/4 oz minced pork
*2 tablespoons fresh white
    breadcrumbs*
few drops anchovy essence
2 beef or pork sausages
*50 g/2 oz garlic sausage,
    sliced*
2 eggs
1 teaspoon dried marjoram
½ teaspoon dried thyme
3 tablespoons milk

Defrost the pastry. Roll out on a floured surface, and use to line a 23-cm (9-inch) flan ring or tin.
Fry the onion in the oil until soft. Add the garlic, salt and pepper and fry for a further 5 minutes. Mix together the minced beef and pork, the breadcrumbs, anchovy essence and the onion mixture. Spread into the pastry case.
Grill or fry the sausages until well browned, then slice. Arrange the sausage and garlic sausage slices over the minced meat mixture. Whisk the eggs with the herbs and milk and pour over. Bake in a moderately hot oven (200° C, 400° F, Gas Mark 6) for 40 minutes.
Serves 6

Savoury Tartlets

METRIC/IMPERIAL
*450 g/1 lb frozen shortcrust
    pastry*
175 g/6 oz lean minced beef
pinch salt
pinch white pepper
1 egg, beaten
pinch dried mixed herbs
50 g/2 oz mushrooms
50 g/2 oz cheese, diced
50 g/2 oz tongue, diced
*50 g/2 oz garlic sausage,
    diced*
½ cucumber
100 g/4 oz liver sausage
*2 tablespoons chopped
    parsley*

Defrost the pastry. Grease 12 patty tins and dust with flour. Roll out the pastry on a floured surface and use to line the tins.
Mix the minced beef with the salt, pepper, egg and herbs, and fill four of the tins with this mixture.
Chop the mushrooms. Mix with the cheese, tongue and garlic sausage and use to fill four more tins. Grate the cucumber coarsely. Mix with the liver sausage and parsley and use to fill the remaining tins.
Place the filled patty tins on a baking tray and cook in a moderately hot oven (200° C, 400° F, Gas Mark 6) for 20 minutes. Cool on a wire tray, then carefully remove the tartlets from the tins.
Makes 12

Cheese Twists

METRIC/IMPERIAL
0·5 kg/1 lb frozen puff pastry
1 egg
1 tablespoon milk
½ teaspoon ground cloves
25 g/1 oz butter
4 tablespoons fresh brown breadcrumbs
3 tablespoons single cream
50 g/2 oz cheese, grated
2 drops anchovy essence
1 teaspoon ground coriander
½ teaspoon grated nutmeg
3 tablespoons water

Defrost the pastry. Roll out on a floured surface until about 5 mm (¼ inch) thick. Brush with the egg, milk and cloves, beaten together. Melt the butter and stir in the breadcrumbs, cream, cheese, anchovy essence, coriander, nutmeg and water. Spread evenly over the pastry then cut into strips about 2·5 cm (1 inch) wide. Press two strips together, with the pastry and filling alternating. Holding the ends, twist in opposite directions. Repeat with the remaining strips. Place the plaited strips on a floured baking tray and bake in a moderately hot oven (200° C, 400° F, Gas Mark 6) for 25 minutes. Serve warm or cold, cut into 7·5-cm (3-inch) strips.
Makes about 15

Stuffed Bread

METRIC/IMPERIAL
15 g/½ oz fresh yeast or 2 teaspoons dried yeast
2 teaspoons sugar
50 g/2 oz butter
250 ml/8 fl oz milk, warmed
0·5 kg/1 lb plain flour, sieved
1 onion, sliced
4 tablespoons oil
225 g/8 oz white cabbage, chopped and blanched
100 g/4 oz mushrooms
salt and pepper
350 g/12 oz minced beef
3 tablespoons chopped chives
1 egg, beaten

Mix the yeast with 4 tablespoons warm water and the sugar. Leave in a warm place for 15–20 minutes, until frothy. Melt the butter in the milk and pour into the flour with the yeast mixture. Mix to a smooth dough, knead. Leave to rise in a warm place for 1–1½ hours. Fry the onion in the oil until soft then add the cabbage, chopped mushrooms, salt and pepper and fry for 5 minutes. Add the minced beef and cook for 5 minutes. Stir in the chives. Knead the dough again. Roll into a circle about 1 cm (½ inch) thick. Pile the meat filling in the centre. Seal, and place on a greased baking tray, joins underneath. Prove for 40 minutes. Brush with the egg and bake at 180° C, 350° F, Gas Mark 4 for 50 minutes.
Serves 4–6

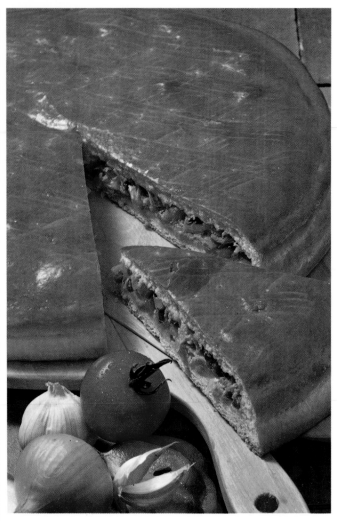

Spanish Chicken Pie

METRIC/IMPERIAL
1 red pepper
1 green pepper
1 large onion
225 g/8 oz tomatoes
50 g/2 oz ham
350 g/12 oz cooked chicken
½ clove garlic, crushed
2 tablespoons oil
1 teaspoon salt
¼ teaspoon pepper
0·5 kg/1 lb bread dough, made with 0·5 kg/1 lb flour etc (see page 285)
1 egg, beaten

Remove cores, pith and seeds from the peppers, then chop finely. Peel and chop the onion and tomatoes. Dice the ham and chicken.
Heat the oil and fry the peppers, onion and garlic gently for 10 minutes. Add the tomatoes, ham and chicken and bring to a simmer. Stir in the salt and pepper. Remove from heat. Divide the dough in half and roll out on a floured surface 2 circles about 30 cm (12 inches) in diameter. Place 1 circle on a greased baking tray. Spread over the chicken mixture to within 1 cm (½ inch) of the edge. Place the second dough circle on top and press the edges together to seal. Score with a knife, brush with the egg and bake in a moderately hot oven (200° C, 400° F, Gas Mark 6) for 45 minutes.
Serves 6–8

Cheese and Grape Puffs

METRIC/IMPERIAL
0·5 kg/1 lb frozen puff pastry
2 eggs
2 tablespoons water
1 teaspoon paprika pepper
¼ teaspoon black pepper
1 teaspoon mixed spice
225 g/8 oz Red Windsor or Cheddar cheese
100 g/4 oz white grapes
100 g/4 oz continental sausage, sliced

Defrost the pastry. Roll out on a floured surface to a rectangle about 3 mm (⅛ inch) thick and cut into 5-cm (2-inch) squares. Mix the eggs with the water, paprika, black pepper and spice, and brush some of this mixture over the pastry squares.
Cube the cheese. Halve the grapes, and pip. Cut the sausage slices into small pieces. Place a cube of cheese, grape and piece of sausage on each pastry square. Bring the corners of the pastry inwards to form an envelope, and press together firmly. Brush with the remaining egg mixture. Place on a greased baking tray and bake in a moderately hot oven (200° C, 400° F, Gas Mark 6) for 15 minutes or until lightly browned. Serve warm.
Makes 35–40

Piquant Cheese Flan

METRIC/IMPERIAL
300 g/11 oz frozen shortcrust
pastry
50 g/2 oz butter
175 g/6 oz onions, finely
chopped
2 tablespoons flour
250 ml/8 fl oz milk
175 g/6 oz Emmenthal or
Gruyère cheese, grated
3 eggs, beaten
4 tablespoons chopped chives
2 tablespoons chopped
parsley
2 teaspoons paprika pepper

Defrost the pastry. Roll
out on a floured surface to a
circle about 5 mm (¼ inch)
thick. Use to line a 25-cm
(10-inch) shallow cake tin or
flan ring placed on a baking
tray. Bake blind in a
moderately hot oven
(200° C, 400° F, Gas
Mark 6) for 10 minutes.
Remove and reduce oven
temperature to 150° C,
300° F, Gas Mark 2.
Meanwhile prepare the
filling. Melt the butter in a
saucepan. Add the onion
and fry for 5 minutes.
Sprinkle over the flour, stir
well, then stir in the milk.
Bring to the boil, stirring,
and simmer until slightly
thickened. Remove from the
heat, and add the cheese,
eggs, chives, parsley and
paprika.
Pour into the pastry case,
and bake on the bottom
shelf for 40 minutes, until
golden brown.
Serves 6–8

Mushroom Pasties

METRIC/IMPERIAL
300 g/11 oz frozen puff
pastry
100 g/4 oz streaky bacon
1 small onion
175 g/6 oz button mushrooms
2 teaspoons tomato purée
½ teaspoon celery salt
½ teaspoon white pepper
25 g/1 oz butter
1 egg, beaten

Defrost the pastry. Rind
and dice the bacon. Peel and
finely chop the onion. Clean
and slice the mushrooms.
Fry the bacon and onion
together until the bacon
has rendered its fat. Add
the mushrooms, tomato
purée, celery salt, pepper
and butter, and fry until the
liquid evaporates. Remove
from the heat.
Roll out the pastry on a
floured surface. Cut into
10-cm (4-inch) circles. Place
a spoonful of filling on one
half of each circle and fold
over the other half to cover,
forming a half-moon shape.
Press the edges together to
seal, using the prongs of a
fork for decorative effect.
Brush with the beaten egg
and place the pasties on a
floured baking tray. Bake in
a moderate oven (180° C,
350° F, Gas Mark 4) for
25 minutes. Serve hot or
cold, garnished with a sprig
of parsley.
Makes 8–10

Autumn Pie

METRIC/IMPERIAL
225 g/8 oz plain flour
¼ teaspoon salt
100 g/4 oz butter
1 egg
100 g/4 oz castor sugar
350 g/12 oz blackberries or
    loganberries
2 teaspoons cornflour
3 tablespoons gooseberry jam
3 egg whites
6 tablespoons icing sugar

Sieve the flour and salt into a bowl. Rub in the butter. Stir in the egg and 2 table-spoons castor sugar. Form into a dough, chill for 20 minutes.
Sprinkle the berries with the remaining castor sugar.

Leave to drain in a sieve over a saucepan. Warm the berry juice. Blend the corn-flour with 1 tablespoon water, stir into the berry juice, bring to the boil, stirring, and simmer until thickened. Add the berries and cool. Roll out the pastry to line a greased 20-cm (8-inch) flan ring. Bake blind at 160° C, 325° F, Gas Mark 3 for 15–20 minutes. Cool. Spread the jam over the pastry base. Spoon in the berry mixture. Whisk the egg whites with the icing sugar until stiff, then pipe over a lattice work. Bake at 180° C, 350° F, Gas Mark 4 for 15 minutes. Cool before serving.
Serves 6–8

Plum Slices

METRIC/IMPERIAL
15 g/½ oz fresh yeast
    or 2 teaspoons dried yeast
50 g/2 oz granulated sugar
150 ml/¼ pint milk, warmed
50 g/2 oz butter, softened
½ teaspoon salt
grated rind of ½ lemon
1 egg
350 g/12 oz plain flour
1 kg/2 lb plums
50 g/2 oz flaked almonds
50 g/2 oz castor sugar

Mix the yeast with 2 teaspoons of the granulated sugar and 2 tablespoons of the milk. Leave in a warm place for 15 minutes, or until frothy.
Melt the butter in the

remaining milk and add to the yeast with the remaining granulated sugar, the salt, lemon rind and egg.
Sieve the flour into a bowl. Pour in the yeast mixture and mix thoroughly. Turn out on a floured surface and roll to fit a greased 23 × 33-cm (9 × 13-inch) baking tray. Leave to rise in a warm place for 1–1½ hours.
Wash the plums. Halve, remove the stones and slice. Arrange the plum slices on the dough and sprinkle with the almonds. Leave in a warm place for 10 minutes. Bake in a moderate oven (180° C, 350° F, Gas Mark 4) for 40 minutes. Sprinkle over the castor sugar and cool before slicing.
Makes 15–20

Puddings, Cakes and Biscuits

Marble Cake

METRIC/IMPERIAL
*2 tablespoons dry bread-
   crumbs
100 g/4 oz butter or
   margarine
150 g/5 oz castor sugar
grated rind of ½ lemon
2 large eggs
150 ml/¼ pint milk
50 g/2 oz cornflour
200 g/7 oz plain flour
1 teaspoon baking powder
25 g/1 oz cocoa powder
1 tablespoon icing sugar*

Grease a 19-cm (7½-inch) fluted savarin tin. Sprinkle in the breadcrumbs and tip the tin to coat the sides. Cream the butter with 100 g (4 oz) of the castor sugar and the lemon rind until light and fluffy. Add the eggs, one at a time, with a little of the milk and beat well. Sieve the cornflour, flour and baking powder into the bowl and fold into the creamed mixture with all but 2 tablespoons of the remaining milk.
Spoon half the mixture into the tin. Add the cocoa powder and remaining castor sugar to the other half and mix well with the remaining milk. Spoon into the tin over the plain mixture, and stir gently with a knife into spirals. Bake in a moderately hot oven (200° C, 400° F, Gas Mark 6) for 60–70 minutes or until a skewer inserted in the cake comes out clean. Turn the cake out on to a wire tray. Leave to cool, then sprinkle with the icing sugar.
Serves 6–8

Viennese Almond Biscuits

METRIC/IMPERIAL
3 egg whites
225 g/8 oz castor sugar
$\frac{1}{2}$ teaspoon vanilla essence
pinch salt
150 g/5 oz ground almonds
175 g/6 oz plain chocolate
15 g/$\frac{1}{2}$ oz unsalted butter

Whisk the egg whites until they hold a stiff peak. Add the castor sugar, vanilla essence, salt and ground almonds and fold in quickly with a metal spoon. Place spoonfuls of the mixture on to baking trays lined with non-stick or rice paper, leaving space between each spoonful. Bake in a moderate oven (160° C, 325° F, Gas Mark 3) for 10 minutes. The biscuits should dry out rather than bake, and be firm to the touch, not soft. Leave to cool, then remove carefully from the non-stick paper. If you have used rice paper, which is edible, just cut around each biscuit with scissors. Melt the chocolate with the butter and stir well. Dip the base of each biscuit in the chocolate, then leave upside-down to dry.
Makes 15–20

Rice Cake

METRIC/IMPERIAL
212 g/7$\frac{1}{2}$ oz frozen puff pastry
100 g/4 oz round-grain rice
600 ml/1 pint milk
300 ml/$\frac{1}{2}$ pint single cream
$\frac{1}{4}$ teaspoon salt
3 tablespoons castor sugar
2 eggs
2 egg yolks
40 g/1$\frac{1}{2}$ oz candied peel, finely chopped
50 g/2 oz red and yellow glacé cherries, chopped
25 g/1 oz almonds, chopped
50 g/2 oz raisins

Defrost the pastry. Put the rice, milk, cream, salt and 2 tablespoons castor sugar in a saucepan and bring to the boil. Cover and simmer for 20–25 minutes, until the rice is tender and has absorbed all the liquid. Cool then beat in the eggs and 1 egg yolk.
Roll out the pastry to line a 23-cm (9-inch) flan ring. Bake blind at 200° C, 400° F, Gas Mark 6 for 10 minutes. Mix the rice with the candied peel and spread half in the pastry case. Mix the remainder with the cherries, almonds and raisins, spoon over and smooth the top. Whisk the remaining egg yolk and castor sugar and pour over the rice mixture. Bake at 200° C, 400° F, Gas Mark 6 for about 25 minutes. Cool then sprinkle with icing sugar.
Serves 6–8

Puddings, Cakes and Biscuits

Fruit Tartlets

METRIC/IMPERIAL
225 g/8 oz plain flour
¼ teaspoon salt
100 g/4 oz butter
1 egg
pinch castor sugar
fruit (see method)
25 g/1 oz butter
25 g/1 oz flour
1 tablespoon castor sugar
1 egg yolk
150 ml/¼ pint milk
¼ teaspoon vanilla essence
4 tablespoons apricot jam

Sieve the flour and salt into a bowl. Rub in the butter then stir in the egg and castor sugar. Form into a dough, adding a little water if necessary. Chill for 20 minutes. Roll out and use to line 12 greased and floured tartlet tins. Bake blind in a moderate oven (160° C, 325° F, Gas Mark 3) for 20 minutes. Cool on a wire tray.

Any fruit can be used for the filling, fresh, cooked or canned.

Melt the butter in a saucepan and stir in the flour and sugar. Beat the egg yolk with the milk and strain into the pan. Cook, stirring, until the mixture comes to the boil, then remove from the heat. Stir for 1 minute, then add the vanilla essence. Cool and spoon into the pastry cases. Top with the drained fruit, then brush with a glaze of the sieved heated apricot jam.
Makes 12

Apple Cake

METRIC/IMPERIAL
300 g/11 oz plain flour
225 g/8 oz sugar
150 g/5 oz butter
2 egg yolks
pinch salt
0·5 kg/1 lb cooking apples
juice of 1 lemon
pinch cinnamon
50 g/2 oz raisins
50 g/2 oz ground almonds
50 g/2 oz ground hazelnuts
2 tablespoons apricot jam
50 g/2 oz icing sugar
2 tablespoons kirsch or
  cherry brandy

Sieve the flour into a bowl. Stir in 150 g (5 oz) of the sugar and rub in the butter. Add the egg yolks and salt and mix quickly to a dough. Chill for 20 minutes.

Roll out half the dough to line a 25-cm (10-inch) flan ring. Bake blind at 200° C, 400° F, Gas Mark 6 for 15 minutes. Peel, core and slice the apples. Mix with the remaining sugar, the lemon juice, cinnamon, raisins and nuts. Moisten with a little water to blend. Spoon into the pastry shell and smooth over.

Roll out the remaining dough to cover the flan. Bake in the preheated oven for 30 minutes. Cool in the tin overnight.

Warm the jam and spread over the cake. Combine the icing sugar and kirsch, spread over the jam and leave to set.
Serves 6–8

291

Uncooked Cheesecake

METRIC/IMPERIAL
175 g/6 oz plain flour
50 g/2 oz cornflour
100 g/4 oz butter
2 egg yolks
150 g/5 oz sugar
1 tablespoon rum
0·5 kg/1 lb cottage cheese
150 ml/¼ pint single cream
grated rind of 1 lemon
2 teaspoons lemon juice
juice of 1 orange
100 g/4 oz raisins
15 g/½ oz gelatine
2 tablespoons apricot jam
toasted flaked almonds

Sieve the flours on to a
working surface. Make a
well and add the butter, cut
into small pieces, the egg
yolks, 2 tablespoons sugar
and the rum. Mix to a dough
and chill for 20 minutes.
Press into the base of a
greased 20-cm (8-inch) loose-
bottomed cake tin. Bake
blind at 200° C, 400° F, Gas
Mark 6 for 25 minutes. Cool
in the tin.
Sieve the cottage cheese and
beat with the cream, lemon
rind and juice, orange juice
and remaining sugar. Stir in
the raisins. Dissolve the
gelatine in 4 tablespoons
water in a bowl over a pan
of simmering water. Strain
into the cheese mixture and
stir well. Spoon into the
cake tin, smooth over.
Warm the jam and spread
over. Chill in the refrigerator
until set. Decorate with the
almonds.
Serves 8–10

Viennese Whirls

METRIC/IMPERIAL
150 g/5 oz butter
100 g/4 oz icing sugar
50 g/2 oz cornflour
4 tablespoons milk
pinch salt
grated rind of ½ lemon
225 g/8 oz plain flour
175 g/6 oz plain chocolate

Cream the butter with the
sieved icing sugar and cornflour until light and fluffy.
Beat in the milk, salt and
lemon rind. Sieve the flour
into the bowl and mix
together thoroughly, adding
more milk if the mixture is
too thick to pipe.
Using a piping bag fitted
with a large star nozzle,
pipe the mixture on to
greased baking trays in
S-shapes or circles. Bake in
a moderate oven (180° C,
350° F, Gas Mark 4) for
10 minutes or until light
brown. Cool the biscuits on
a wire tray.
Melt the chocolate gently
in the top of a double saucepan. Dip the biscuits in the
chocolate so they are half-
coated. Allow to dry on
greaseproof paper.
Makes 40

Variation
Use the melted chocolate
to sandwich together pairs
of the biscuits.

Puddings, Cakes and Biscuits

Banana Cake

METRIC/IMPERIAL
150 g/5 oz butter
150 g/5 oz sugar
juice and grated rind of
*   1 lemon*
2 eggs
200 g/7 oz plain flour
50 g/2 oz cornflour
1 teaspoon baking powder
pinch each salt, ground
*   ginger, cinnamon, cloves*
*   and nutmeg*
4 bananas

Cream the butter and sugar until light and fluffy. Beat in the lemon rind and eggs. Sieve 150 g (5 oz) of the flour, the cornflour, baking powder, salt and spices into the creamed mixture and fold in. If the mixture is too dry to combine, add a little milk. (It should not be too soft.) Use half the mixture to line the base of a greased loose-bottomed 23-cm (9-inch) cake tin. Bake in a moderate oven (180° C, 350° F, Gas Mark 4) for 25 minutes. Cool.
Peel the bananas and cut or dice them. Sprinkle with the lemon juice, then spoon into the tin and spread out. Mix the remaining cake mixture with the remaining flour to form a dough. Roll out a circle to cover the tin. Lay over the filling and press to seal the edges. Bake in the preheated oven for 35 minutes. Sprinkle with icing sugar and leave to cool in the tin.
Serves 6–8

Buttercream Fingers

METRIC/IMPERIAL
15 g/½ oz fresh yeast or
*   2 teaspoons dried yeast*
175 g/6 oz sugar
250 ml/8 fl oz warm milk
0·5 kg/1 lb plain flour
90 g/3½ oz butter
1 egg
½ teaspoon grated lemon rind
100 g/4 oz almonds, chopped
75 g/3 oz unsalted butter
175 g/6 oz icing sugar
½ teaspoon vanilla essence

Mix the yeast with 1 tablespoon sugar and 2 tablespoons warm milk. Leave in a warm place for 15 minutes, until frothy. Sieve the flour into a bowl and pour in the yeast mixture.
Melt 50 g (2 oz) butter in the remaining warm milk and add to the bowl with the egg, 50 g (2 oz) sugar and the lemon rind. Form into a dough, knead. Spread out on a greased baking tray and leave to rise for 1–1½ hours. Melt the remaining butter, and stir in the remaining sugar and the almonds. Mix in 1 tablespoon of milk, cool, then spread over the dough. Bake at 200° C, 400° F, Gas Mark 6 for 40 minutes. Cool and cut into fingers. Split each finger in half through the centre. Cream the butter, icing sugar and vanilla essence until light and fluffy. Use to sandwich together the split fingers.
Makes 25–30

Black Forest Cherry Cake

METRIC/IMPERIAL
100 g/4 oz plain chocolate
100 g/4 oz butter
100 g/4 oz sugar
4 eggs
75 g/3 oz ground almonds
50 g/2 oz plain flour
50 g/2 oz cornflour
2 teaspoons baking powder
450 ml/¾ pint double cream
0·75 kg/1½ lb canned stoned
  cherries, drained
6 tablespoons kirsch
12 red glacé cherries
chocolate caraque

Melt the chocolate in the top of a double saucepan. Cool. Cream the butter and sugar until light and fluffy. Beat in the eggs, almonds and melted chocolate. Sieve the flour, cornflour and baking powder into the creamed mixture and fold in, mixing well. Turn into 3 greased 18-cm (7-inch) sandwich tins. Bake at 180° C, 350° F, Gas Mark 4 for 20–25 minutes, until cooked. Leave to cool. Whip the cream until thick. Dry the cherries on absorbent paper. Remove the cake layers from the tins. Sprinkle each layer with 2 tablespoons of kirsch. Sandwich together with the cherries and cream, leaving enough cream to spread over the top and sides of the cake, and to pipe a border. Decorate with the glacé cherries and pile chocolate caraque in the centre.
Serves 8–10

Cinnamon Stars

METRIC/IMPERIAL
4 small egg whites
225 g/8 oz icing sugar
300 g/11 oz ground almonds
1½ tablespoons ground
  cinnamon
grated rind of ½ lemon
castor sugar

Put the egg whites into a heatproof basin. Whisk until frothy, then add the icing sugar. Place the bowl over a pan of simmering water and continue whisking until the meringue is thick and will hold its shape. Remove the bowl from the pan. Put 3–4 tablespoons of the meringue to one side.

Fold the ground almonds, cinnamon and lemon rind into the remaining meringue. Leave to cool for 1 hour.
Sprinkle a work surface with castor sugar and roll out the meringue until about 5 mm (¼ inch) thick. The mixture will be soft and must be rolled out very carefully. Cut into stars with a biscuit cutter. Place the stars on a greased and floured baking tray. Spread the reserved meringue carefully over the stars and bake in a moderate oven (160° C, 325° F, Gas Mark 3) for 15–20 minutes, until just firm. Transfer the stars carefully to a wire tray and leave to cool.
Makes about 60

Puddings, Cakes and Biscuits

Jam Rings

METRIC/IMPERIAL
4 eggs
225 g/8 oz butter, softened
100 g/4 oz icing sugar
½ teaspoon vanilla essence
pinch salt
300 g/11 oz flour, sieved
100 g/4 oz castor sugar
100 g/4 oz almonds, chopped
1 egg, beaten
3 tablespoons blackcurrant jam

Hard-boil the eggs for 10 minutes. Cool and shell. Halve and tip the yolks into a sieve. (Keep the whites for another recipe.) Sieve the yolks and beat in the butter, 75 g (3 oz) icing sugar, the vanilla essence and salt. Add the flour and mix well. Roll out to a thickness of 1 cm (½ inch). Cut into circles, using a fluted 5-cm (2-inch) biscuit cutter. Cut smaller circles from the centre of each to form rings.
Mix together the castor sugar and almonds. Brush one side of each ring with the beaten egg, then dip into the almond mixture. Lay the rings, almond side up, on a greased baking tray, and bake in a moderate oven (180° C, 350° F, Gas Mark 4) for 10–15 minutes, until browned. Cool on a wire tray.
Warm the jam and sandwich together pairs of biscuits. Sprinkle over the remaining icing sugar.
Makes 25–30

Sachertorte

METRIC/IMPERIAL
7 eggs, separated
200 g/7 oz castor sugar
50 g/2 oz cocoa powder
100 g/4 oz plain flour
100 g/4 oz butter, melted
50 g/2 oz biscuit crumbs
4 tablespoons dry bread-crumbs
5 tablespoons apricot jam
225 g/8 oz plain chocolate
6 tablespoons double cream
350 g/12 oz icing sugar

Whisk the egg yolks with 100 g (4 oz) castor sugar until frothy. Fold in the sieved cocoa and flour. Stir in the butter. Whisk the egg whites until frothy. Add the remaining castor sugar and whisk until stiff. Fold into the egg yolk mixture with the biscuit crumbs. Grease two 23-cm (9-inch) sandwich tins and coat with the breadcrumbs. Spoon in the cake mixture and bake in the centre of a moderately hot oven (200° C, 400° F, Gas Mark 6) for 30 minutes. Reduce heat to 180° C, 350° F, Gas Mark 4, and cook for 15–20 minutes. Cool in the oven, with the door slightly open, for 15 minutes then remove to cool completely. Warm the jam and use to sandwich the layers and spread over the sides of the cake. Melt the chocolate. Cool, then beat in the cream and icing sugar. Spread smoothly over the top and sides of the cake.
Serves 8–10

295

Puddings, Cakes and Biscuits

Strawberry Swiss Roll

METRIC/IMPERIAL
225 g/8 oz strawberries
75 g/3 oz castor sugar
3 large eggs, separated
100 g/4 oz icing sugar
65 g/2½ oz plain flour
40 g/1½ oz cornflour
150 ml/¼ pint double cream

Hull and quarter the strawberries. Sprinkle with 2 tablespoons of the castor sugar and leave for 30 minutes.
Whisk the egg yolks with the remaining castor sugar. Whisk the egg whites until frothy, then add half the icing sugar. Whisk until stiff then fold into the yolk mixture. Sieve the flours and fold in quickly but thoroughly. Spread smoothly in a 23 × 30-cm (9 × 12-inch) Swiss roll tin lined with greaseproof paper. Bake in a moderately hot oven (200° C, 400° F, Gas Mark 6) for 10–15 minutes. Turn out carefully on to clean greaseproof paper, peel off the first paper and roll up with the clean paper inside. Cool. Drain the strawberry juice and whip with the cream until thick. Fold in the remaining icing sugar and the strawberries. Unroll the cake. Spread over the filling and roll up, using the paper to lift the cake. Sprinkle with extra icing sugar and serve.
Serves 4–6

Aniseed Biscuits

METRIC/IMPERIAL
4 eggs
225 g/8 oz icing sugar
pinch salt
300 g/11 oz plain flour
2 teaspoons ground aniseed

Separate the egg yolks from the whites. Cream the egg yolks with the icing sugar and salt until pale and frothy. Whisk the egg whites until very stiff, then fold into the yolk mixture. Sieve the flour and aniseed on to the mixture, and fold in quickly but thoroughly. Grease a baking tray and sprinkle with flour. Fill a piping bag, fitted with a plain nozzle, with the biscuit mixture and pipe in small rounds on the baking tray. Leave to dry out overnight, then bake towards the top of a moderate oven (160° C, 325° F, Gas Mark 3) for 20 minutes. Cool on a wire tray.
Makes 36

Variation
To make Vanilla Biscuits, substitute 1 teaspoon vanilla essence for the ground aniseed.

Puddings, Cakes and Biscuits

Brandy Pretzels

METRIC/IMPERIAL
225 g/8 oz butter
150 g/5 oz icing sugar
1 egg yolk
pinch salt
½ teaspoon vanilla essence
300 g/11 oz plain flour
2–3 tablespoons brandy

Cream the butter with 100 g (4 oz) of the icing sugar until light and fluffy. Beat in the egg yolk, salt and vanilla essence. Sieve the flour into the bowl and mix well. Chill for 2–3 hours. Break off pieces of the dough and roll into 'worms' about 5 mm (¼ inch) thick and 15 cm (6 inches) long. Twist each worm into a pretzel (see photograph) and place on a baking tray. Bake in a moderate oven (160° C, 325° F, Gas Mark 3) for 10 minutes or until golden. Cool on the baking tray.

Mix together the brandy and remaining icing sugar and brush over the pretzels. Leave to set on a wire tray until the glaze becomes shiny.
Makes about 45

Cook's Tip
For quick creaming, use soft margarine instead of butter.

Chocolate Macaroons

METRIC/IMPERIAL
100 g/4 oz plain cooking chocolate
4 egg whites
200 g/7 oz castor sugar
225 g/8 oz ground almonds

Grate the chocolate. Whisk the egg whites until stiff. Add the sugar gradually and continue whisking until the mixture is thick and glossy. Fold in the ground almonds and grated chocolate. Drop spoonfuls of the mixture on to a baking tray lined with non-stick or rice paper, leaving space between each biscuit. Bake in a moderate oven (180° C, 350° F, Gas Mark 4) for 15–20 minutes.

Do not let the macaroons become too dark or they will taste bitter. Cool on the baking tray, then carefully peel the macaroons off the non-stick paper or cut around each biscuit on the edible rice paper.
Makes about 30

Variation
Topped macaroons
Prepare in the same way as above, but use 5 egg whites and 225 g (8 oz) castor sugar. Leave 4–5 tablespoons of the egg white and sugar mixture to one side, and then place a small spoonful on each chocolate macaroon before baking.

297

Strawberry Yogurt Cake

METRIC/IMPERIAL
200 g/7 oz plain flour
50 g/2 oz margarine
175 g/6 oz sugar
1 egg
25 g/1 oz gelatine
3 tablespoons water
0·5 kg/1 lb strawberries
900 ml/1½ pints natural
  yogurt
150 ml/¼ pint double cream
1 small apricot

Sieve the flour on to a working surface. Make a well in the centre and put in the margarine, cut into small pieces, 100 g (4 oz) of the sugar and the egg. Mix quickly together to form a dough. Press into the base of a greased 23-cm (9-inch) loose-bottomed cake tin. Prick all over with a fork and bake blind in a moderately hot oven (200° C, 400° F, Gas Mark 6) for 25 minutes or until cooked. Leave to cool.
Sprinkle the gelatine over the water and leave to soften. Hull the strawberries, then sieve or liquidise three-quarters of them. Mix with the yogurt and the remaining sugar. Dissolve the gelatine in a bowl over simmering water, then strain into the yogurt mixture.
Put aside a few strawberries for decoration and halve the rest. Arrange the halves, cut side down, on the pastry base. Spoon over the yogurt mixture and chill until set.
Remove from the tin. Whip the cream and pipe on top of the cake. Decorate with pieces of strawberry and apricot.
Serves 6–8

Puddings, Cakes and Biscuits

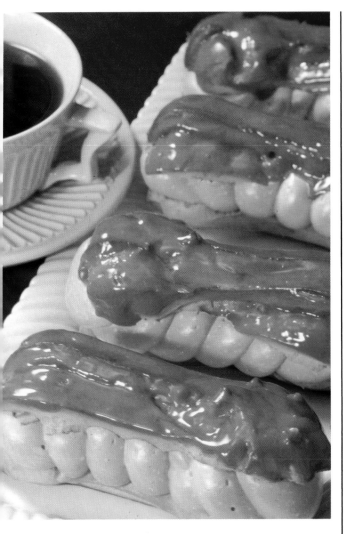

Éclairs with Mocha Cream Filling

METRIC/IMPERIAL
150 ml/¼ pint water
pinch salt
50 g/2 oz butter
65 g/2½ oz plain flour
2 small eggs
grated rind of ½ lemon
300 ml/½ pint double cream
2 teaspoons coffee essence
50 g/2 oz icing sugar
1 teaspoon coffee powder
1–2 tablespoons warm water

Put the water and salt
in a saucepan and bring to
the boil. Add the butter
and, when melted, sieve in
the flour. Remove from the
heat and beat well until the
mixture leaves the sides of
the pan. Cool slightly, then
beat in the eggs and lemon
rind. Fill a piping bag with
the mixture and pipe on to a
floured baking tray in
7·5-cm (3-inch) strips.
Bake in a moderately hot
oven (200° C, 400° F, Gas
Mark 6) for 25 minutes.
Slit the éclairs lengthways
and leave to cool.
Whip the cream with the
coffee essence until thick.
Fill the éclairs with the
cream, piping it for a more
decorative effect.
Combine the icing sugar,
coffee powder and warm
water and use to glaze the
tops of the éclairs. Allow
the glaze to set, then serve.
Makes about 15

Butter Biscuits with Marzipan

METRIC/IMPERIAL
200 g/7 oz butter
75 g/3 oz icing sugar
50 g/2 oz marzipan
grated rind of ½ lemon
250 g/9 oz plain flour
1 egg yolk
castor sugar

Cream the butter and icing
sugar together until light
and fluffy. Beat in the
marzipan and lemon rind,
then sieve the flour on to
the mixture. Knead well
together. Divide the dough
in three and form each piece
into a roll about 4 cm
(1½ inches) thick. Chill for
20 minutes.
Lightly beat the egg yolk
and brush over the rolls of
dough. Roll them in castor
sugar, then cut into slices
5 mm (¼ inch) thick. Place
the slices on greased baking
trays, leaving space between
the slices, and bake at
200° C, 400° F, Gas
Mark 6 for 8–10 minutes,
until lightly browned. Cool
on a wire tray.
Makes about 60

Cook's Tip
The rolls of uncooked
dough, without the
egg yolk and sugar
coating, may be
wrapped in grease-
proof paper and kept in
the refrigerator for up to
a week.

Marzipan Hearts

METRIC/IMPERIAL
0·5 kg/1 lb marzipan
300 g/11 oz icing sugar
2 egg whites
1 egg yolk
candied angelica
glacé cherries

Work the marzipan and 200 g (7 oz) of the icing sugar together. Roll out on a surface dusted with icing sugar until 1 cm (½ inch) thick. Cut out small hearts with a biscuit cutter. With the remaining marzipan mixture, cut thin strips long enough to form the heart shape. Brush the edges of the hearts with egg white, then place the strips on top to form a raised border. Flute with the prongs of a fork, then brush the borders with the beaten egg yolk. Place the hearts on a baking tray and bake in a hot oven (220° C, 425° F, Gas Mark 7) for 3–5 minutes. Mix together the remaining egg whites and icing sugar and brush in the centres of the hearts. Leave to set, then decorate with the candied fruit.
Makes about 20

Variation
Use a selection of biscuit cutters to make different marzipan shapes.

Hazelnut and Almond Fingers

METRIC/IMPERIAL
200 g/7 oz plain flour
1 teaspoon baking powder
1 egg
2 tablespoons milk
175 g/6 oz sugar
100 g/4 oz ground hazelnuts
100 g/4 oz butter or
* margarine*
1 egg yolk
25 g/1 oz ground almonds
25 g/1 oz flaked almonds

Sieve the flour and baking powder into a bowl, and make a well in the centre. Put the egg, milk and half the sugar into the well and mix together. Add the remaining sugar, the hazelnuts and butter or margarine, cut into small pieces, and mix quickly to a dough. Chill for 20 minutes. Form the dough into small fingers. Brush with the beaten egg yolk and roll in the ground and flaked almonds. Put on a greased baking tray and bake in a moderately hot oven (200° C, 400° F, Gas Mark 6) for 12–15 minutes, or until firm and lightly browned.
Makes about 30

Cook's Tip
Keep butter in the refrigerator, and then grate it for easier mixing.

Puddings, Cakes and Biscuits

Vanilla Crescent Biscuits

METRIC/IMPERIAL
275 g/10 oz plain flour
100 g/4 oz ground almonds
150 g/5 oz castor sugar
200 g/7 oz butter
2 egg yolks
1 teaspoon vanilla essence

Sieve the flour on to a working surface. Add the almonds, 75 g (3 oz) of the castor sugar, the butter, cut into small pieces, the egg yolks and vanilla essence. Mix together by hand very quickly, then chill the dough for 2–3 hours. Form the dough into 'worms' about 5 cm (2 inches) long, then

curve into crescent shapes. Place the crescents on a greased baking tray and bake in a moderate oven (180° C, 350° F, Gas Mark 4) for 8–10 minutes or until golden.
Sprinkle the crescents with the remaining sugar while still warm, then cool on a wire tray.
Makes about 60

Cook's Tip
The sugar sprinkled on the biscuits may be flavoured with vanilla. To make vanilla sugar, put castor sugar in a stoppered jar. Add a vanilla pod and leave for 1 week.

Brandy Snap Ring

METRIC/IMPERIAL
350 g/12 oz butter
175 g/6 oz castor sugar
¼ teaspoon salt
3 eggs
1 tablespoon rum
juice and grated rind of
½ lemon
150 g/5 oz plain flour
1 tablespoon baking powder
75 g/3 oz cornflour
350 g/12 oz icing sugar
1 egg yolk
6–8 brandy snaps, crushed
150 ml/¼ pint double cream
8 red glacé cherries

Cream 175 g (6 oz) butter with the castor sugar until light and fluffy. Beat in the salt, eggs, rum, lemon juice

and rind. Fold in the sieved flour, baking powder and cornflour. Pour into a greased 23-cm (9-inch) ring mould and bake in a moderate oven (180° C, 350° F, Gas Mark 4) for 45–60 minutes. Cool slightly in the tin, then turn out on a wire tray to cool completely. Cut into four layers.
Cream the remaining butter with the icing sugar and egg yolk. Use to sandwich together the four layers and to cover the completed cake. Press on the crushed brandy snaps to cover completely. Decorate with the cream, whipped and piped, and halved glacé cherries.
Serves 6–8

Aperitifs

Aperitifs, which are served before a meal, should not be too sweet or strong, but dry. Most aperitifs contain vermouth or wine. They should be served in small, short-stemmed glasses.

Bombarral (*illustrated on the right*)
Put 2 teaspoons vodka, 4 teaspoons port and a few ice cubes in the goblet of the liquidiser and blend for about 10 seconds. Pour into a glass, and put a slice of lemon on the rim of the glass.

Berlenga
Mix 1 glass port with 2 teaspoons gin and some ice cubes; shake well. Pour into a glass and put a slice of lemon on the rim of the glass.

Adonis
Mix 2 teaspoons red Italian vermouth with ice, 4 teaspoons sherry and a dash of Angostura bitters. Pour into a glass.

Sixty-Six (*illustrated on the left*)
Mix 2 teaspoons Campari, 2 teaspoons French vermouth, 2 teaspoons sherry and 2 teaspoons gin with a few ice cubes. Pour into a glass and add a few drops of lemon juice.

Each of the above recipes makes 1 drink

Prince of Wales Drinks

The origin of these drinks is not known, but originally they were served in silver glasses. If you do not have any silver or pewter mugs, serve the drinks in tall glasses, with straws.

Prince of Wales (*illustrated on the right*)
Put 4 ice cubes in a silver or pewter mug, or a tall glass. Pour in 4 tablespoons Curaçao and 2 drops of Angostura bitters. Stir, and top with champagne. Decorate with an orange segment placed on the rim of the glass.

Duke of York (*illustrated on the left*)
Put a few ice cubes in a glass, add the juice of 1 orange and 1 teaspoon of grenadine. Stir, and then top with champagne. Decorate with a thin slice of lemon placed on the rim of the glass.

Eden Rocks
Half-fill a glass with crushed ice. Add 1 teaspoon of raspberry syrup and 4 tablespoons cherry brandy. Stir, and top with champagne. Decorate with an orange wedge placed on the rim of the glass.

Each of the above recipes makes 1 drink

Fruity Daiquiris

These drinks are very refreshing and always contain rum, either light or dark. The light rum has a slightly sweeter flavour. Serve in cocktail glasses.

Daiquiri
Mix ice with 1 teaspoon grenadine, 2 teaspoons lemon juice and 4 teaspoons white rum. Pour into a cocktail glass.

Daiquiri Banana (*illustrated on the left*)
Place 4 teaspoons crushed ice, 2 teaspoons orange juice, 2 teaspoons sugar, 4 tablespoons white rum and 1 peeled banana in the goblet of the liquidiser and blend for 10 seconds. Pour into a glass and serve with a slice of banana placed on the rim.

Martinique Daiquiri
(*illustrated right background*)
Mix 3 ice cubes with 2 tablespoons dark rum, 1 teaspoon grapefruit juice, 1 teaspoon pineapple juice, 1 teaspoon lime juice and 1 teaspoon lemon juice. Shake well and serve.

Havana Club (*illustrated on the right*)
Mix a few ice cubes with 2 teaspoons red Italian vermouth and 4 teaspoons dark rum. Serve in a cocktail glass and decorate with a cherry, if liked.

Each of the above recipes makes 1 drink

Highball Sodas

A highball soda is a sweet drink and is often made with ginger ale and soda. Highball sodas are usually served in whisky tumblers.

Dundee Highball Soda
(*illustrated on the left*)
Mix 1 teaspoon Curaçao with 2 teaspoons lemon juice, 2 teaspoons sugar syrup and 4 tablespoons rum. Add some crushed ice, shake well and pour into a glass. Top up with soda.

Eton Highball Soda
Mix 1 teaspoon rum with 2 teaspoons lemon juice, 2 teaspoons sugar syrup and 2 tablespoons each of cherry brandy and gin. Add some crushed ice, shake well and pour into a glass. Top up with soda.

Crystal Highball Soda
(*illustrated in the background*)
Mix some crushed ice with 2 tablespoons French vermouth and 2 tablespoons orange juice. Pour into a tumbler and top up with soda.

Victory Highball Soda
(*illustrated on the right*)
Mix 2 ice cubes with 2 tablespoons Pernod and 2 tablespoons grenadine. Pour into a glass and top up with soda.

Each of the above recipes makes 1 drink

Piquant Tomato Cocktail

METRIC/IMPERIAL
1 kg/2 lb tomatoes
few parsley sprigs
2 teaspoons paprika pepper
pinch salt
1 small head celery
1 large apple
10 ice cubes
freshly ground black pepper

Peel and quarter the tomatoes; wash and dry the parsley. Place the tomatoes, parsley, paprika and salt in the goblet of the liquidiser and blend until smooth. Pour the mixture into a jug. Chop the celery; peel, core and chop the apple. Blend the apple and celery and mix with the tomato juice. Add the ice cubes. Pour the cocktail into four small glasses and sprinkle with the black pepper.
Makes 4 drinks

Variation
Mix 6 tablespoons cream into the cocktail, and replace the celery with $\frac{1}{2}$ teaspoon celery salt.

Vegetable Cocktail

METRIC/IMPERIAL
0·5 kg/1 lb carrots
1 tomato
1 parsley sprig
100 g/4 oz celery
juice of 1 grapefruit
pinch salt
4 lemon slices

Peel and chop the carrots. Place them in the goblet of the liquidiser together with the peeled and quartered tomato, parsley and chopped celery and blend for 30 seconds. Pour the juice into a jug and add the grapefruit juice and salt, mixing it well. Pour the cocktail into four glasses and place a lemon slice as decoration on the rim of each of the glasses before serving.
Makes 4 drinks

Cook's Tip
Other vegetables may be used in place of the carrots. Orange juice may be used if preferred instead of the grapefruit juice.

Pre-dinner Drinks, Long and Short

Strawberry Squash

METRIC/IMPERIAL
225 g/8 oz strawberries
3 tablespoons castor sugar
2 tablespoons strawberry
    ice cream
500 ml/generous ¾ pint milk
juice of 1 lemon
juice of 1 orange
grated rind of 1 lemon
3 tablespoons icing sugar
4 ice cubes

Halve the strawberries and place in a bowl. Sprinkle over the castor sugar and leave for 30 minutes for juice to be extracted. Blend the strawberries and juice in the liquidiser, add the ice cream, milk, lemon juice, orange juice, grated rind of lemon and icing sugar and blend for a further 30 seconds. Pour into four glasses and add an ice cube to each one.
Makes 4 drinks

Variation
Pineapple Squash
Replace the strawberries with canned or fresh pineapple. Use vanilla ice cream in place of the strawberry. Pour 1–2 tablespoons chocolate syrup on top before serving.

Honey and Fruit Cocktail

METRIC/IMPERIAL
2 dessert apples
3 tablespoons clear honey
500 ml/generous ¾ pint
    apple juice
500 ml/generous ¾ pint
    grape juice
10 hazelnuts, chopped
3 tablespoons double cream

Peel, core and slice the apples. Heat the honey with the apple and grape juices until it has dissolved. Pour the mixture into the goblet of the liquidiser and add the hazelnuts and sliced apples. Blend for 2 minutes and pour into four glasses. Lightly whip the cream and place a spoonful on each drink. Serve at once.
Makes 4 drinks

Variation
The apples may be replaced with 225 g (8 oz) stoned plums, or 2 bananas and the juice of 2 oranges and ½ grapefruit. If liked, pieces of fruit may be added to the drink just before serving.

Cook's Tip
If clear honey is not available, use sugar syrup.

Orange Punch

3 large oranges
2 teaspoons icing sugar
2 bottles dry white wine
1 bottle champagne
about 10–15 ice cubes

Peel the oranges and cut away all the pith. Cut the fruit into thin slices, removing the skin and pips. Place in a punch bowl, then sprinkle with the icing sugar. Pour in the white wine and chill for 20–30 minutes. Just before serving, add the champagne and ice cubes.
Serves 10–12

Variation
The punch may also be prepared using equal quantities of dry red and white wine. Chill the oranges in the white wine and add the red wine just before serving.

Cook's Tip
To reduce cost, substitute a sparkling white wine for the champagne.

Fizzy Drinks

Fizzy drinks are made with soda water. If champagne is used the drink is known as a Royal Fizz. They should be served in tumblers with a straw and drunk immediately, whilst still fizzy.

Gin Fizz (*illustrated on the left*)
Mix 5 ice cubes, juice of 1 lemon, 3 teaspoons of sugar and 1 measure of gin in a liquidiser and blend for 1 minute. Pour into a glass and top up with soda water.

Golden Fizz (*illustrated on the right*)
Mix 1 egg yolk with ice, juice of 1 lemon, 2 teaspoons of sugar and 1 measure of gin. Strain into a glass and top up with soda water.

Orange Fizz (*illustrated in the background*)
Mix the juice of 2 oranges with ice, 2 teaspoons of sugar and 1 measure of gin in a liquidiser and blend. Strain into a glass and top up with soda water.

Apricot Fizz
Mix the juice of $\frac{1}{2}$ lemon and $\frac{1}{2}$ orange with ice and 1 measure of apricot brandy in a liquidiser and blend. Strain into a glass and top up with soda water.

Each of the above recipes makes 1 drink

Pre-dinner Drinks, Long and Short

Quick Family Drinks

These are relatively simple drinks to make and should be served in tumblers. The ingredients are just stirred. It is advisable to make these drinks as required, as they do not keep.

Whisky Fix (*illustrated on the right*)
Fill a glass one-third full with crushed ice cubes. Then add the juice of 1 lemon, half a measure of Orange Curaçao and 1 measure whisky. Stir with a spoon and float a slice of lemon on top. Serve with a straw.

Brandy Fix (*illustrated on the left*)
Prepare as above, but substitute cherry brandy for Curaçao and use brandy instead of whisky.

Gin Fix
Prepare as above, but substitute gin for whisky.

Rum Fix
Prepare as above, but substitute rum for whisky.

Cherry Fix
Prepare as above and substitute 1 measure of cherry brandy for Curaçao and use kirsch instead of whisky.

Each of the above recipes makes 1 drink

Special Cucumber Punch

1 medium cucumber
2 bottles chilled dry white wine
2 glasses maraschino juice
1 bottle champagne

Wash the cucumber, dry and slice thickly. Place in a punch bowl and pour the chilled wine over the cucumber. Allow to stand for 30 minutes. Add the maraschino juice and leave for 5 minutes. Remove the cucumber slices and pour in the chilled champagne. Serve immediately.
Serves 10–12

Variation
The champagne may be replaced by a bottle of sparkling white wine.

Cook's Tip
When making this drink in hot weather, immerse a small jug of ice cubes in the punch. This will cool it down without diluting it.
If liked, extra cucumber may be cut into thin slices and floated on the punch when serving to give added colour.

Famous Gin Cocktails

The various types of gin differ in flavour and aroma. Serve gin cocktails in champagne glasses.

Queen's Cocktail (*illustrated in the foreground*)
Mix 6 ice cubes with 2 teaspoons gin, 2 teaspoons Steinhäger and 2 teaspoons red Italian vermouth. Shake well and strain into a glass over 1 piece of pineapple and a slice of orange.

Lady Brown Cocktail
Mix 3 ice cubes, 2 teaspoons lemon juice, half a measure gin and 2 teaspoons Orange Curaçao. Shake briefly and strain into a glass.

Gin Cocktail (*illustrated in the background*)
Mix 1 teaspoon grenadine with ice and 1 measure of gin. Shake, strain into a glass and serve with a cocktail cherry.

Orange Blossom
Mix a few ice cubes with a splash of grenadine, half a measure of orange juice and half a measure of gin. Shake well and serve.

White Lady
Mix ice cubes with 2 teaspoons each of gin, Orange Curaçao and lemon juice. Shake well and serve in a champagne or cocktail glass.

Each of the above recipes makes 1 drink

Coolers for Hot Days

These are cool, refreshing drinks, served with fruit, and are similar to highballs.

Brandy Cooler (*illustrated in the background*)
Mix a few crushed ice cubes with a teaspoon of sugar, the juice of half a lemon and half a measure of brandy. Shake, pour into a large whisky glass and top up with ginger ale. Serve with a few maraschino cherries and slices of orange.

Gin Cooler
Prepare as above, but substitute gin for brandy.

Eyebright Cooler
Place 3 ice cubes in a large whisky glass with the juice of half a lemon, half a measure of Calvados and half a measure of Médoc; top up with ginger ale. Stir carefully and serve with two cocktail cherries and pieces of pineapple.

Cablegram Cooler
(*illustrated in the foreground*)
Pour the juice of half a lemon, 2 teaspoons of grenadine and half a measure of whisky into a large whisky glass, with 3 ice cubes. Top up with ginger ale and serve with cocktail cherries.

Each of the above recipes makes 1 drink

Pre-dinner Drinks, Long and Short

Melon Punch

1 very ripe melon
2 tablespoons icing sugar
2 bottles Riesling wine
1 bottle champagne or Asti
Spumante
15 ice cubes (optional)

Quarter the melon; remove
the pips and peel and cut
the flesh into small dice.
Put the diced melon in a
punch bowl and sprinkle
with icing sugar. Pour
half a bottle of white wine
over the pieces of melon
and leave covered for 30
minutes. Add the remaining
wine, and just before serving
pour in the champagne.
Add ice cubes if liked.
Serves 10–12

Cook's Tip
When choosing fruit
for punches make
sure it is really ripe
and unblemished, so
that it will give a
sweet aroma to the
punch.
Always add the
champagne just
before serving as it
will lose its sparkle
very quickly.

Coffee Fluff

METRIC/IMPERIAL
12 glacé cherries
6 teaspoons instant coffee powder
6 eggs
4 tablespoons icing sugar
3 tablespoons advocaat

Cut the cherries in half. Mix the coffee with 450 ml (¾ pint) of hot water and cool. Separate the egg yolks from whites. Mix the yolks with 2 tablespoons of icing sugar and stir until creamy. Pour in half the cooled coffee, stir well and then add the remainder. Whisk the egg whites until stiff, then whisk in the remaining icing sugar until stiff. Fold the whites into the coffee, and add half the cherries. Serve in tall glasses and lace with the advoçaat, then top with the remaining cherries. Serve immediately. *Serves 6–8*

Variation
Chocolate Fluff
Use cocoa or chocolate powder instead of coffee, and Tia Maria instead of advocaat.

Spiced Coffee with Prunes

METRIC/IMPERIAL
4 tablespoons whipped cream
2 tablespoons icing sugar
500 ml/generous ¾ pint strong black coffee
1 teaspoon cinnamon
4 cooked prunes
4 tablespoons brandy

Mix the cream with the icing sugar. Heat the coffee and stir in the cinnamon. Place a prune in each of four cups, lace with the brandy and pour over the hot coffee.
Top each cup with a tablespoon of whipped cream.
Serves 4

Variation
Use plums instead of prunes, and allow to infuse in a little brandy for a few hours before using. Choose dessert plums with a sweet and juicy flesh. If under-ripe, keep in a cool place for 1–3 days before using.

Oriental Orange Coffee

METRIC/IMPERIAL
3 oranges
4 sugar lumps
150 ml/¼ pint double
   cream, whipped
100 g/4 oz icing sugar
25 g/1 oz butter
3 tablespoons castor sugar
4 tablespoons Grand
   Marnier
6 tablespoons brandy
1 litre/1¾ pints black coffee

Remove thin strips of peel from one of the oranges and then extract the juice. Rub the second orange with the sugar lumps and cut the third orange into 10 thin slices. Mix the whipped cream with the icing sugar.

Melt the butter in a saucepan and add the castor sugar. Add the sugar lumps and orange juice and allow to dissolve slowly. Remove from heat. Add the Grand Marnier and brandy, ignite and let it burn for half a minute. Pour the orange mixture into coffee cups and add 1 strip of orange peel. Heat the coffee and pour into cups, top with whipped cream and garnish with slices of orange.
Serves 6–8

Austrian Coffee

METRIC/IMPERIAL
4 egg yolks
1 tablespoon clear honey
2 tablespoons brandy or
   cognac
150 ml/¼ pint cream
generous litre/2 pints strong
   black coffee

Heat 4 large coffee cups by filling them with hot water; leave for a couple of minutes, then pour the water away. Whisk the egg yolks with the honey and brandy or cognac, until well mixed. Pour into the heated coffee cups and pour the cream on top. Heat the coffee and fill each cup.
Serves 4

Variation
Prince Melange
Instead of mixing the egg yolks with honey and brandy, use 2 tablespoons of icing sugar and 2 tablespoons of Tia Maria. Pour hot chocolate or cocoa into the cups instead of coffee. Top with whipped cream and grated chocolate.

Manhattan Cocktails

Manhattans are American cocktails which are believed to have originated in Manhattan.

Original Manhattan
(*illustrated on the right*)
Mix 3 ice cubes with a dash of Angostura bitters, half a measure of red Italian vermouth and 1 measure of whisky and shake several times. Strain into a short-stemmed glass and serve with a cocktail cherry.

Manhattan Dry (*illustrated on the left*)
Prepare as above, but use dry red vermouth and serve with a green olive.

Manhattan Latin Style
Mix 3 ice cubes with half a measure of red Italian vermouth and 1 measure of white rum. Serve with a cocktail cherry.

Sweet Manhattan
Mix 3 ice cubes with half a measure of red vermouth, 2 dashes of Orange Curaçao and 1 measure of whisky. Serve with a cocktail cherry.

Each of the above recipes makes 1 drink

Daisy Fruit Cocktails

For these drinks you will need champagne glasses and small spoons for the fruit. Daisy cocktails are very fruity drinks, containing at least two fruits of different colour.

Champagne Daisy
(*illustrated in the foreground*)
Fill a liquidiser one third full with crushed ice, the juice of a quarter of a lemon, 1 teaspoon of grenadine and half a measure of brandy and blend for 30 seconds. Strain into a champagne glass. Then add a dash of chilled champagne, 2 red cherries and 2 pieces of pineapple.

Brandy Daisy
Use 1 measure of brandy instead of half a measure and top with soda water.

Gin Daisy (*illustrated in the background*)
Use gin instead of brandy.

Rum Daisy
Use rum instead of brandy.

Whisky Daisy
Use whisky instead of brandy.

Each of the above recipes makes 1 drink

Cocktails and Punches

Long Drinks Using Tonic and Fruit Juices

Gin and Tonic
Put a few ice cubes in a medium-sized glass, add 1 measure of gin and top with tonic water. Serve with a slice of lemon.

Rabbit's Revenge
(*illustrated in the foreground*)
Put several ice cubes in a medium-sized glass, add 2 dashes of grenadine, 1 teaspoon of pineapple juice and 1 tablespoon of whisky, and top with tonic water. Serve with a slice of orange.

Dett Long
Place a little crushed ice in a medium-sized glass and add 1 measure of cherry brandy. Top with tonic water and serve with a slice of lemon.

Apple Knocker (*illustrated in the background*)
Half-fill a whisky glass with crushed ice. Add 1 measure of vodka, stir, and then top with apple juice.

Barbed Wire
Pour 1 measure of whisky into a medium-sized glass, add a little crushed ice and top up with apple juice.

Each of the above recipes makes 1 drink

International Vodka Cocktails

Vodka has a neutral flavour and can be used widely. Most vodka cocktails are mixed with fruit juices and served in tumblers or champagne glasses.

Towarisch
Mix half a measure of Russian vodka with ice, 1 tablespoon of kummel liqueur and 1 teaspoon lemon juice. Serve in a cocktail glass with a prune.

Olive (*illustrated in the foreground*)
Mix 1 measure Russian vodka with ice and 1 tablespoon sherry. Shake briefly, strain into a cocktail glass and sprinkle with finely grated lemon peel. Serve with a stuffed olive.

Volga Boatman
Mix 1 tablespoon of vodka, a few ice cubes, 1 tablespoon cherry brandy and 1 tablespoon orange juice. Shake well and serve.

Vodkatini (*illustrated in the background*)
Mix 1 measure Russian vodka with a few cubes of ice, 2 teaspoons of French vermouth (Napoleon or Noilly) and 2 dashes of Angostura bitters. Serve with a cocktail cherry.

Each of the above recipes makes 1 drink

Cocktails and Punches

Pick-Me-Up's for Parties

These long cocktails are suitable for serving on festive occasions.

Brandy Pick-Me-Up
(*illustrated in the background*)
Mix 4 crushed ice cubes with 1 measure of brandy or cognac. Shake for 30 seconds and then pour into a cocktail glass. Top up with champagne and serve.

Champagne Pick-Me-Up
Prepare as above, but use half a measure of brandy instead of a whole measure and half a measure of French vermouth. Shake well and serve immediately.

Pink Carter Pick-Me-Up
(*illustrated in the foreground*)
Place 2 ice cubes in a cocktail glass, add 3 dashes of Angostura bitters and half a measure of gin. Top up with champagne and a little grated lemon peel. Serve immediately.

Hanseatic Pick-Me-Up
(*illustrated centre right*)
Mix 2 ice cubes with 1 tablespoon of whisky, 1 tablespoon of brandy and 1 tablespoon of blackberry brandy. Top up with champagne and serve with a slice of orange and lemon.

Each of the above recipes makes 1 drink

Brandy Cocktails

Sweet liqueurs and brandy are typical ingredients used to make these drinks.

Sidecar
Mix several ice cubes with 1 tablespoon of brandy, 1 tablespoon of Curaçao and 2 teaspoons of lemon juice and shake. Serve in a cocktail glass.

Alexander Cocktail
(*illustrated on the left*)
Mix 1 tablespoon brandy with a little crushed ice, 1 tablespoon of crème de cacao and 1 tablespoon of cream. Shake quickly. Serve topped with a spoonful of whipped cream.

Bazooka
Mix 1 tablespoon brandy with a little crushed ice, 2 teaspoons of cherry brandy and 2 teaspoons of gin. Strain into a cocktail glass and serve with a piece of pineapple.

Femina Cocktail
(*illustrated on the right*)
Mix 1 tablespoon of cognac with a little crushed ice, 1 tablespoon of Cointreau and 1 tablespoon of orange juice. Strain into a cocktail glass.

Each of the above recipes makes 1 drink

Bronx and Other Cocktails

There are many other cocktails and aperitifs besides the classic Martinis and Manhattans, including those containing bitter liqueurs and herbal liqueurs.

Bronx

Mix half a measure of orange juice with 3 ice cubes, half a measure of gin and half a measure of red Italian vermouth. Strain into a cocktail glass.

Dry Bronx

As above, but use dry white vermouth instead of red.

Bronx Terrace (*illustrated on the left*)
Mix half a measure of lemon juice with a few ice cubes, half a measure of dry French vermouth and 1 measure of gin. Strain into a glass.

Mezz' e Mezz' (*illustrated centre right*)
Mix half a measure of white Italian vermouth with a few ice cubes, half a measure of fresh or canned grapefruit juice and 2 teaspoons of Campari. Strain into a glass.

Each of the above recipes makes 1 drink

Highball Long Drinks

These very refreshing drinks are similar to sodas. They nearly always contain ginger ale, and are usually served with a slice of orange or lemon. They are very popular drinks for men because of their herbal flavour. They should be served in brandy or whisky glasses.

Bourbon Highball
(*illustrated above*)
Place 2 ice cubes in a glass and add 1 measure of whisky. Top up with ginger ale. Serve with a twist of orange or lemon peel.

Gin Highball
Substitute gin for the whisky.

Angostura Ginger Ale
Place 2 ice cubes in a glass, with 1 teaspoon of Angostura bitters. Top up with ginger ale, and stir.

Gin Buck
Pour 1 measure of gin and the juice of half a lemon into a glass. Add some crushed ice or small ice cubes, and top up with ginger ale.

Each of the above recipes makes 1 drink

Cocktails and Punches

Swedish Glögg

METRIC/IMPERIAL
1 litre/1¾ pints red wine
150 ml/¼ pint aquavit
½ cinnamon stick
5 pieces ginger
½ teaspoon ground cardamom
10 cloves
225 g/8 oz sugar
few raisins

Place all the ingredients in in a large saucepan and heat slowly (but do not allow to boil). Allow to stand for 30 minutes so that the flavours can infuse. Reheat slowly, then strain and ladle into heat-proof glasses.
Serves 6–8

Variation
Dissolve the sugar in 150 ml (¼ pint) water. Omitting the aquavit, add all the ingredients except the wine. Boil together in a pan until reduced by half. Strain, add the wine and reheat.

Cook's Tip
To avoid having to strain the Glögg, tie the spices and raisins in a muslin cloth and allow to float in the wine whilst infusing.

Mandarin Punch

METRIC/IMPERIAL
125 ml/scant ¼ pint orange
 juice
300 ml/½ pint apple juice
125 ml/scant ¼ pint canned
 mandarin juice
500 ml/generous ¾ pint
 white wine
thinly pared rind of ½ lemon
thinly pared rind of ½
 orange
1 tablespoon sugar
4 cloves
1 stick cinnamon
1 (312-g/11-oz) can
 mandarin oranges, drained

Bring the orange, apple and mandarin juices to the boil. Add the white wine, pared lemon and orange rinds, the sugar, cloves and cinnamon stick. Heat over a moderate heat for 5 minutes, but do not allow to boil.
Stir in the mandarins, and reheat. Remove the cloves and cinnamon stick before serving.
Pour into a punch bowl and serve hot.
Serves 6

Variation
This punch can also be served chilled.

Martini Cocktails

These drinks are also known as dry martinis. They are often copied, but are seldom correctly made.

Extremely Dry Martini
(*illustrated above*)
Mix 3 ice cubes with 1 measure of gin, 1 dash of Angostura bitters and a dash of dry French vermouth. Strain into a glass and place a small piece of lemon rind in the glass. When a spot of oil appears on the surface, the lemon aroma has been absorbed. Serve with a green olive speared on a cocktail stick.

Dry Martini
Mix 3 ice cubes with 1 dash of Angostura bitters, 1 measure of gin and half a measure of dry white vermouth. Strain into a glass and serve with a green olive.

Sweet Martini Cocktail
Mix 3 ice cubes with 1 dash of grenadine, half a measure of gin and a measure of white Italian vermouth. Strain into a glass and serve with a Maraschino cherry.

Each of the above recipes makes 1 drink

Frosted Drinks

These are long drinks, served in glasses with frosted rims. The rim of each glass is dipped in lemon juice or egg white, swirled to remove excess moisture and then dipped in castor sugar to give a frosted effect, hence the name of the drinks. If serving a brandy cocktail, grenadine may be substituted for lemon juice when preparing the glass for frosting.

Rum Crusta (*illustrated in the centre*)
Frost the rim of a whisky glass. Mix together 5 ice cubes, the juice of half a lemon, 2 dashes of Angostura bitters and 1 glass of rum. Shake for 30 seconds and strain into the glass.

Brandy Crusta (*illustrated bottom left*)
Use brandy instead of rum.

Whisky Crusta (*illustrated bottom right*)
Use whisky instead of rum.

Gin Crusta (*illustrated top right*)
Use gin instead of rum.

Each of the above recipes makes 1 drink

Original Irish Coffee

METRIC/IMPERIAL
300 ml/½ pint double cream
150 ml/¼ pint Irish whiskey
sugar
1 litre/1¾ pints black coffee

Warm the glasses by filling with hot water whilst making the coffee. Whip the cream until fairly stiff. Pour the whiskey into 6 glasses and add a teaspoon of sugar to each glass. Heat the coffee and pour into the glasses to within 1 cm (½ inch) of the top. Spoon the whipped cream on to the coffee so that it floats.
Serves 6

Variation
Do not whip the cream but pour it over the back of a teaspoon on to the coffee, so that it floats and finds its own level.

Cook's Tip
Some people maintain that Irish coffee can only be made properly with demerara sugar. Try it – it does make a difference. But any sugar in the coffee will help the cream to float.

Fruit Cocktails

These are mixed drinks which can be served between meals. They should be served in small, short liqueur glasses.

Widow's Kiss
Mix a few ice cubes with a measure of Calvados, 3 dashes of yellow Chartreuse and a dash of Angostura bitters. Shake, and strain into a glass.

Black Forest Cocktail
Mix a few ice cubes with 2 tablespoons of damson brandy (sliwowitz), 1 tablespoon of gin and a dash of maraschino. Strain into a glass.

Apri (*illustrated on the right*)
Mix 1 tablespoon of apricot brandy with some ice cubes, 2 teaspoons of yellow plum brandy and 2 teaspoons of orange juice. Shake well and strain into a glass.

Alsatian (*illustrated on the left*)
Mix 1 tablespoon of cherry brandy with a few ice cubes, 1 tablespoon of brandy, 1 teaspoon of cold black coffee and 1 teaspoon of sugar. Shake well and strain into a glass.

Each of the above recipes makes 1 drink

Cocktails and Punches

Sugar Loaf Punch

bottles red wine
cloves
stick cinnamon
ew strips lemon rind
uice of 2 oranges
uice of 1 lemon
sugar loaf
bottle rum

Heat the wine with the loves, cinnamon and lemon ind in a heatproof claret up or a heatproof dish laced over a burner. Add the orange and lemon uice. Using tongs, hold the ugar loaf over the heated ine and sprinkle a little of he rum carefully over the ugar. When the rum has oaked into the sugar,

carefully ignite it. Gradually pour the remaining rum over the sugar; the sugar loaf should burn until it has completely melted into the wine. Pour into heatproof glasses and serve. *Serves 10–12*

Cook's Tip
Jamaican rum, which is heavy-bodied and dark, is more suitable for using in this kind of drink than the lighter Puerto Rican rum.

Liqueurs

These drinks are very much like flips as they contain egg yolks. Their attraction is the use of fruit liqueurs. Always strain and serve in small glasses.

Armagnac
Mix half a measure of peach brandy, 1 egg yolk sprinkled with ground almonds, half a measure of Armagnac brandy and ice.

Brandy (*illustrated left*)
Lightly whisk half a measure of Orange Curaçao, 1 egg yolk, half a measure of brandy and ice.

Whiskey
Mix half a measure of

crème de cacao liqueur, 1 egg yolk, half a measure of Irish whiskey and ice.

Calvados
Mix half a measure of herb liqueur, 1 egg yolk, chopped nuts and half a measure of Calvados.

Chartreuse
Mix half a measure of green Kloster liqueur, lemon peel, 1 egg yolk, half a measure of vodka and a dash of maraschino.

Scotch (*illustrated right*)
Mix half a measure of cherry brandy, 1 egg yolk and half a measure of Scotch whisky.

Each of the above recipes makes 1 drink

319

Herbs and Spices

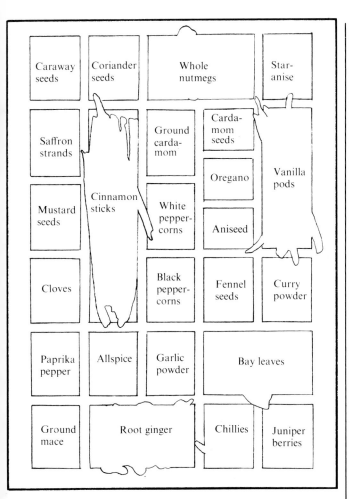

The herbs and spices illustrated left are identified above. A guide to their use in cooking can be found on page 322.

Caraway seeds · Coriander seeds · Whole nutmegs · Star-anise · Saffron strands · Ground cardamom · Carda-mom seeds · Vanilla pods · Cinnamon sticks · Oregano · Mustard seeds · White pepper-corns · Aniseed · Cloves · Black pepper-corns · Fennel seeds · Curry powder · Paprika pepper · Allspice · Garlic powder · Bay leaves · Ground mace · Root ginger · Chillies · Juniper berries

The seasoning of dishes is very much a matter of personal and family preference. As there are so many different seasonings to choose from you can change the flavour of a dish by adding varying herbs and spices. First, however, you have to learn the basics – which flavourings have a special affinity with which foods; you need to become acquainted with as many different herbs and spices as possible so that you can identify the flavours which you prefer. With herbs there is some difference between the fresh and dried varieties. It is not difficult to grow herbs and even if you do not have a garden some herbs can be cultivated success-fully in pots indoors. The flavour of fresh herbs is certainly preferable to that of the dried variety. Most of the recipes in this book use fresh herbs, unless otherwise stated, and you will see that a larger amount of fresh herbs is used. Do not expect to achieve the same flavour in a finished dish from fresh and dried herbs and do remember to be sparing in the amount of dried herbs you use. Dried herbs should be purchased from a store which has a quick turnover as the flavour of old stock will be impaired.

Herbs

Herbs are plants which provide us with flavoured leaves (e.g. mint), flowers (e.g. borage) or stems (e.g. fennel) for use in cooking. Herbs are available fresh or dried.

Spices

Strictly speaking, these are the group of seasonings, many of tropical origin, which come from roots (e.g. horseradish), rootstocks (e.g. ginger), bark (e.g. cinnamon), flowers or parts of flowers (e.g. cloves, saffron), berries (e.g. pepper-corns), pods (e.g. vanilla), fruits (e.g. aniseed) or seeds (e.g. nutmeg). Spices are always dried and often crushed or ground when purchased and used.

Using Herbs and Spices

The amount used does depend on your personal preferences and the dish. As a guide, when using fresh herbs allow ½–1 teaspoon, chopped, per portion. Use half the amount of dried herbs, or simply a pinch. Much smaller amounts of spices are used in dishes. For general purposes, allow a pinch of spice per serving.

- Too little seasoning is always better than too much as it can be rectified before serving. Herbs and spices are used to bring out the flavour of a dish, not to overwhelm it. Avoid using too many spices in the one dish.
- Many spices are sensitive to light, so buy them in non-transparent containers and store them in a cupboard.
- Spices quickly lose their aroma if they are not kept in sealed containers. If you buy your spices loose, decant them into airtight containers for storage.
- Buy herbs and spices in small amounts and use them up as quickly as possible.
- When possible buy spices unground, or in leaf form, so that they can be ground or crushed just before being added to a dish. This imparts a better flavour to the dish.
- Immediately after use, re-seal the containers. Do not store different spices in the same container as they will taint each other.
- When using fresh herbs, rinse them in cold water and pat dry with absorbent paper. Chop them on a board prior to adding them to the dish, or using as a garnish.
- It helps to bring out the aroma of dried herbs if you rub them between your fingertips before use.
- For grinding spices which are in berry form, such as peppercorns, use a mill. Keep separate mills for white and black peppercorns. For nutmeg there is a traditional nutmeg grater.
- For garlic use a garlic crusher, or crush the clove with a little salt and the blade of a knife.
- One of the best implements for crushing all dried spices, and herbs too, is a pestle and mortar. It is certainly worthwhile investing in one.
- The flavour of certain seasonings in cooked dishes does change when frozen. When preparing a dish for the freezer under-season it and at the reheating stage, taste the dish and adjust the seasoning as necessary.
- Most fresh herbs are excellent freezer candidates – the freezing of herbs does not impair their flavour. To freeze herbs, wash and dry and pack in polythene containers or wrap in freezer foil. Seal and label. When frozen, herbs can be crumbled and added to the dish.

A–Z of Herbs and Spices

The following is a list of the more common herbs and spices used in cooking.

Allspice Is available ground or whole. The whole berries are used in pickling, casseroles and soups. Ground allspice is used in baking.
Aniseed Is available ground or whole. It has a liquorice flavour and is used mainly in baking.

Basil Is available fresh or dried. Used in fish, veal, pork and lamb dishes and in salads. Basil goes particularly well in tomato-based dishes such as pizza and bolognaise sauce.
Borage Is available fresh or dried, but not so aromatic when dried. Borage goes well in tomato and mustard sauces, salads (particularly cucumber) and with vegetables.
Bouquet garni Made up with a bay leaf, 2–3 sprigs parsley, and a sprig of thyme all tied in a piece of muslin. Use when cooking soups, stews and casseroles and remove before serving. Also available in sachets.

Capers Are preserved in vinegar and sold in jars. Capers go well with fish, veal, mutton and poultry dishes and sauces.
Caraway Seeds with a distinctive flavour. Goes with meat dishes, vegetables (potatoes, cabbage and sauerkraut in particular), soups and sauces. Caraway seeds are also used in breads and biscuits.
Cardamom Is available ground or whole. The whole seeds are used in pickling and curried dishes; ground cardamom is used mainly in baking.
Cayenne Is the dried spice of the chilli, a member of the capsicum family. Used sparingly in fish, beef and pork dishes.
Chervil The leaves are available fresh or dried, and in powder form. Chervil goes with fish, meat, poultry and vegetable dishes. It is also used in soups, salads and sauces.
Chillies Are from the capsicum family and are very hot. Fresh chillies are used in curries and Mexican cuisine. Chilli powder is also available and should be used sparingly.
Chives Available fresh or dried, chop (or cut with scissors) and add to soups, salads, sauces and egg dishes just before serving. Chives are also used as a garnish.
Cinnamon Available in stick or powder form and used in sweet dishes (milk puddings, stewed fruit), cakes, pastries and biscuits.
Cloves Available whole or ground. Used in meat and vegetable dishes, soups, sauces, stewed fruit, pastries and mulled wine. Remove whole cloves from a dish before serving.
Coriander Available as seeds or in powder form. Goes with meat dishes.
Curry Powder Is a mixture of spices used in Indian cuisine. Curry powder varies in strength according to the spices used. Curry powder can be added to veal, beef, lamb, pork and chicken casseroles; prawn and vegetable dishes.

Dill The leaves are available fresh or dried; the seeds are available dried. Used in fish, beef and lamb dishes; with vegetables, salads, eggs and egg-based sauces.

Fennel Is available dried or fresh. Use dried fennel in marinades for fish, salads and mushrooms. Use the fresh variety in salads and mayonnaise. Fennel has an aniseed flavour and is interchangeable with dill.

Garlic The cloves are used very finely chopped or crushed. Garlic salt and powder is also available. Garlic is used in fish, meat and poultry dishes, salads, sauces, cheese fondues, salad dressings and mayonnaise.

Ginger Available in root or powder form, or preserved in sugar or syrup. Used mainly in cakes and biscuits.

Horseradish Has a strong hot flavour similar to mustard. Use the roots grated, mix with cream and serve as a sauce with beef, sausages and ham. Horseradish sauce is available in jars.

Juniper Available as berries. Used in meat and game dishes and marinades.

Mace Available in blades, or ground. Use in fish and veal dishes, sauces, cakes and pastries.

Marjoram The leaves are available fresh or dried and go with pork, poultry and game stews; also used in soups and sauces.

Mint Better to use the fresh variety. Goes with lamb and veal dishes; stuffings, peas, new potatoes and salads.

Mustard Available ready prepared in various strengths. The whole seeds are used in pickling; ground mustard is used in meat, cheese and poultry dishes, sauces and marinades.

Nutmeg Available whole or ground. It is used with vegetables (potatoes, spinach and cauliflower in particular), in soups, sauces and cheese dishes.

Oregano A herb much used in Italian cuisine. It goes with meat and vegetable dishes, meat and tomato sauces and pizzas.

Paprika Available ground in mild, hot and very hot varieties. Good with fish, meat and vegetable dishes, soups, sauces and salad dressings.

Parsley It is better to use the fresh variety, which is available throughout the year, as dried parsley has very little flavour. Parsley can be used in most savoury dishes and as a garnish, either chopped or as sprigs.

Pepper Available whole or ground. For a better flavour use the whole peppercorns and grind freshly when needed. Pepper is used in all savoury dishes. Use the black variety for dark coloured dishes and white pepper for pale coloured dishes such as poultry or veal fricassées.

Rosemary Available fresh or dried. To extract the flavour from the fresh spiky leaves, crush them in a pestle and mortar. Rosemary goes with pork, lamb, veal and chicken dishes. It is also used as a garnish.

Saffron Has a distinctive flavour and is sold in strands and powdered form. Used in certain classic dishes (e.g. paella), fish, rice and chicken dishes and in curries. It is also used in baking.

Sage Available fresh or dried. The leaves are used in stuffings for pork, goose and duck; in savoury meat dishes and soups.

Savory Available fresh or dried and used in fish, poultry, meat and vegetable dishes. Use sparingly, particularly the dried variety.

Tarragon Available fresh or dried. The fresh leaves are used to flavour vinegar. Also used in egg, fish and poultry dishes, sauces, savoury butters, salads and vegetables.

Thyme Available fresh or dried. Used in fish, meat and poultry dishes, stuffings, sauces and soups.

Vanilla The pods are used in sweet dishes (puddings, soufflés, stewed fruit) and in cakes and pastries. Vanilla essence is also available, but the flavour is less acceptable.

Using a Freezer

If you enjoy cooking and eating well, are a busy career girl, a housewife or a bachelor cook, a freezer can often be one of your best investments. You can prepare and cook food when you are less busy and store it perfectly safely in the freezer until required. You can prepare larger quantities of a favourite dish – it takes very little extra time to make, for example, a casserole to serve 12 people than one to serve six portions – serve half of it and freeze the remainder for future use. If you do this once or twice a week it won't be long before there's a good selection of dishes in the freezer all ready for reheating. A further advantage of owning a freezer is that you can store certain foods which can sometimes be difficult to find, and seasonal foods. This way you are able to enjoy the delicious soft fruits during the winter months.

Providing a few basic rules with regard to packaging and selection are adhered to, food stored in a freezer will remain in perfect condition.

The Importance of Temperature

For the successful home freezing of food you need an appliance which is capable of reducing a specified weight of food daily to $-18°$ C ($0°$ F) within a 24-hour period without affecting the food already frozen and stored. The rapid freezing process protects the food from any deterioration and enables it to retain its nutritional quality, value and flavour.

All freezers are now already marked with a four-star symbol (see below) which means that the appliance is capable of freezing down the specified weight of food. The freezer compartment of a refrigerator marked with the three-star rating (below, left) is not suitable for freezing down food as it cannot achieve a sufficiently low temperature, but it may be used for storing already-frozen food.

When purchasing a combined freezer/refrigerator, each door will have its respective star rating, to avoid confusion. When freezing down food, do refer to the maker's instructions with regard to the amount which can be frozen at any one time; the smaller the portion, the faster it will freeze. When freezing liquids or semi-liquids do remember that you will want to reheat the frozen block, so bear in mind the capacity of your saucepans for reheating. It is often more convenient, and cuts down on the reheating time, to freeze food in, say, two-portion packs rather than in four- or six-portion ones. Obviously this depends on your particular requirements.

The quality, flavour and nutritional value of most foods remain the same after freezing as when fresh, but remember that there is no magic wand inside the freezer to improve the quality of poor food. No amount of freezing is going to turn a scrawny old chicken into a plump young one.

The Right Way to Pack

All foods destined for the freezer must be protected from the cold, dry air inside the freezer cabinet for two main reasons – to prevent dehydration and cross flavours occurring. The packaging materials used must be moisture- and vapour-proof. If using polythene containers they must be able to withstand sub-zero temperatures and make sure that the lids give an airtight seal. To ensure a proper seal, freezer tape may be used. Use heavy-duty or freezer foil or film.

No matter what packaging material is used, the same golden rules always apply – make sure that as little air is left inside the package as possible, that the food is tightly and closely wrapped and that there is an airtight seal. Certain delicate foods, such as soft fruits and decorated gâteaux, should be open frozen before packing. Put them on a suitable plate or tray and place in the freezer until hard, then pack in bags or containers, seal and return to the freezer.

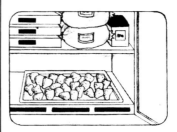 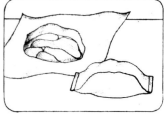

Open freezing strawberries. Soft fruits should be open frozen on a tray until hard, then packed.

Foods for freezing should be wrapped closely and tightly, excluding as much air as possible.

When packing certain foods, remember to allow a headspace for the expansion of the liquid content on freezing. Fruits and vegetables require very little headspace as there are small areas around them to allow for expansion. Liquid and semi-liquid foods – soups, casseroles and sauces – are a different story. If packed in a shallow container giving a larger surface area, allow about a 1-cm ($\frac{1}{2}$-inch) headspace; in a deeper container with less surface area a 1·5-cm ($\frac{3}{4}$-inch) headspace should be left. It's very convenient to freeze stock (and other liquids) in ice cube trays. When frozen, the cubes can be packed

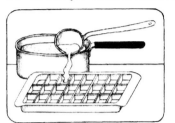

Stock (and other liquids) can be frozen in ice cube trays. When

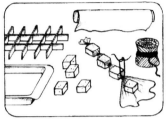

frozen pack individually. Use the frozen cubes for soups, stews, etc.

individually and used as required for soups, stews etc. To keep your freezer in order every package must be marked with its contents, weight (or number of servings) and date of freezing. It's invaluable to keep a record in a notebook of all the packages in the freezer, but don't forget to cross items off the list when you take them from the freezer.

Careful Defrosting

Foods already cooked, to be eaten cold, such as breads, cakes, cold meats etc, must be fully thawed. On removing the package from the freezer, loosen or take off the wrapping and allow the package to thaw in the refrigerator or in a cool place.

Cooked made-up dishes, such as casseroles, may be reheated from frozen. It is usually easier to do this in a suitable container in the oven, as on top of the cooker the food needs to be stirred from time to time, to prevent it from sticking. Pre-blanched vegetables may be cooked from frozen. It is most important to allow uncooked frozen poultry to defrost fully before cooking. In an emergency, joints of meat may be cooked from frozen, but a better result is obtained if the meat is allowed to defrost before cooking. To ensure that a frozen joint is sufficiently cooked in the centre it is advisable to use a meat thermometer. When preparing food for the freezer and

A meat thermometer. When cooking a joint of meat from frozen it is advisable to use a meat thermometer so that you can see when the joint is cooked in the centre.

defrosting it do remember not to leave it sitting in a warm kitchen as this will encourage the growth of bacteria. Cool it quickly before freezing; defrost it in a refrigerator or cool place.

The question of refreezing foods is one which often worries freezer owners. It is mostly a matter of common sense. If you purchase frozen meat and make a casserole it is perfectly safe for it to be refrozen. Soft fruits, strawberries in particular, do not benefit from being refrozen, but this is due to their nature, not from the safety point of view. Obviously, you wouldn't keep some cooked leftover meat in the refrigerator for 2–3 days and then decide to turn it into a cottage pie and freeze it.

What to Freeze

- Fruits in season which can be used for favourite dishes
- Perishable foods that are not always easy to obtain and foods that are advantageous to buy in bulk
- Dishes which can be cooked in larger quantities just as easily as in small quantities, e.g. soups, casseroles, sauces and pâtés
- Any commercially frozen foods
- Vegetables in season – home-grown or bought from the greengrocer's. Prior to freezing, vegetables should be blanched
- Home-baked breads, biscuits, pies, quiches and cakes
- Sandwiches for packed meals
- Fresh herbs

What not to Freeze

- Green salad vegetables
- Boiled or poached eggs
- Egg-based sauces e.g. mayonnaise
- Radishes
- Avocado pears
- Bananas
- Uncooked potatoes

Ten Golden Rules to Freezing

- Select the freshest and best food for freezing
- Package the food correctly and exclude as much air as possible
- Keep utensils and packing materials scrupulously clean
- Prepare, cook, cool, wrap and freeze food quickly
- Label and record all your freezer packages
- Add garlic, cream, yogurt and egg yolks at the reheating stage
- Lightly season dishes for freezing and re-check the seasoning when reheated
- Undercook pasta dishes
- Use your frozen packages in rotation
- Clear out and defrost the freezer at least once a year

A Guide to Entertaining

Today more and more people are entertaining in their own homes due mainly to the ever-increasing costs of eating out. The menu need not be lavish to impress your guests; in fact a simple dish, well cooked and nicely served, can be just as appealing as a more elaborate one. Remember too, that you, as the hostess, want to enjoy the evening with your friends, so avoid worrying about the meal and spending all your time in the kitchen. With a little pre-planning and organisation and bearing the following points in mind you will be able to produce a meal to delight your friends, as well as enjoying their company.

• The ideal menu should offer contrast, colour and flavour. Avoid choosing a starter, main course and dessert all of which contain cream.
• If you are having a casserole as a main course, don't choose dishes of a similar texture for your starter and dessert.
• When planning any menu, bear in mind the foods which are in season and likely to be at their best. It is usually easiest to select the main course and from there choose the other dishes to give the necessary contrast in ingredients, flavour, colour and texture.
• Keep a watchful eye on the budget. You don't have to choose the most expensive cuts of meat to produce a good meal. The less expensive cuts can be turned into delicious dishes.
• Do not choose dishes all of which require last minute attention. It's possible to select a starter and a dessert which can be prepared in advance, leaving you free to concentrate on the main course.
• Bear in mind the facilities you have. Don't invite 20 people to a formal meal unless you have adequate seating space, cutlery, china, glasses, etc.
• It does help to plan your shopping list and order of work. This way you can be sure that nothing is forgotten.
• Wash up and keep the kitchen tidy as you go along. If you have a freezer use it to its fullest advantage when entertaining.
• Start your preparation well in advance to avoid any last minute panic.
• Serve hot food on warm plates.
• Make sure that your cutlery and glasses are shiny.

Buffets

If you plan to invite a large number of people, a buffet meal is usually the best way of coping. Certain extra points have to be borne in mind when planning a buffet:

• Choose food which your guests will be able to eat with a fork.
• Arrange the food on the table in such a way that your guests can help themselves easily.
• Be sure to have sufficient serving utensils, cutlery, crockery and serviettes.
• Make sure there are enough chairs and small tables for your guests to put their plates and glasses.
• When your guests have served themselves, put the contents of half-empty bowls together so that the buffet looks appetising for seconds.
• Avoid having candles on a buffet table as they can be easily knocked over. Instead, have a low arrangement of flowers.
• Keep hot food on a hotplate.

Successful Parties

Parties can be the liveliest and most spontaneous kind of entertainment, providing that the hostess plans the event beforehand. There are many types of parties, but whatever type you plan to give the following guide lines will help yours to be a success:

• Bear in mind the size of the room. Do not invite more people than can be comfortably accommodated in the space you have available.
• Plan to have somewhere for everyone to sit, and provide sufficient small tables and ashtrays.
• Choose your guests carefully. Avoid inviting people known to dislike each other on the same evening. Do not invite either too many men, or too many women.
• Invite your guests well in advance – at least a week – and ask them to let you know whether they can accept.
• Don't keep secret the reason for your party if you are celebrating a birthday, anniversary or other happy event.
• Give your guests a hint about what clothes to wear. No

one likes to arrive formally dressed for an informal party, for example.
• Give your guests a specific time to arrive to avoid your party getting off to a slow start.
• As soon as your guests arrive offer them a drink.
• When catering for large numbers you may need to hire cutlery, china and glasses. Alternatively, for an informal buffet, you could use paper plates.
• Keeping drinks cold can be a problem. If you have a freezer make plenty of ice cubes in advance.
• If you are not inviting your neighbours, it is fair to tell them that you are planning to hold a party.
• If at the end of the party some of your guests may have had a little too much to drink, order a taxi to take them home.

Advice on Drinks and Wines

What drinks and wines you serve does of course depend on your pocket, menu and on the likes and dislikes of your guests. Never serve too many different alcoholic drinks at one time and remember you may have some guests who prefer non-alcoholic drinks, so their needs must be catered for too.

As an aperitif before a meal or to welcome your guests you can offer champagne, sherry, vermouth, Campari, Cinzano, Pernod, whisky, vodka or gin. Aperitifs may be served with soda or tonic water and a twist of lemon. Pernod is served with iced water. With the pre-dinner drinks offer your guests a selection of tit-bits – nuts, crisps, small savoury biscuits etc.

Wines Fine wines deserve more attention than any other drinks and much has been written about them. It is said that good wine pleases three of our senses: the colour pleases the eye, the bouquet pleases the nose and the taste pleases the palate. To achieve these three pleasures wine must be treated with the respect it deserves. Choose the correct glass – it must not be too small as a wine glass should not be more than half-filled in order to allow the bouquet to gather in the glass. The glass should be slightly bulbous in shape, narrowing at the top, so that the bouquet remains in the glass, and finally it should be made of clear, colourless glass so that you can see the true colour of the wine.

Wine only gives off its best aroma if stored and served at the correct temperature. White wines should certainly be served chilled, but not straight from the refrigerator. Red wines are normally served at room temperature.

If you are anxious to serve (and drink) wines at the correct temperature – which does take practice – you can buy a wine thermometer which is placed in a glass of wine to determine the exact temperature. Achieving the correct temperature is a matter of putting the bottle in the correct temperature a few hours before consumption.

Always serve lighter wines before the fuller, heavier ones; chilled wines before warmed ones and dry white wines before red. Give your guests a glass of water to sip and bread to nibble between wines to clear their palates. It's often a good idea to serve the cheese before the sweet so that guests may finish off the main wine. Here are a few hints on what wines to serve:

• A dry white wine with shellfish. With oysters, a Chablis, champagne or Muscadet.
• It is not necessary to serve a wine with soup, but if the soup contains wine you can serve the same wine to accompany it.
• With fish dishes, a white Burgundy; for delicately flavoured dishes serve a Moselle or Loire wine. A white Burgundy is excellent with salmon.
• With lightly seasoned pork and veal dishes a dry white wine is pleasant.
• With lamb and beef dishes, red wines are best – Bordeaux or Burgundy. These wines also go well with ham dishes.
• Full-bodied, dark red wines go well with game dishes.
• With poultry dishes – and in particular chicken dishes – which are delicate in flavour, serve a white Burgundy or a light red wine. With duck and goose serve a Rhine wine or Châteauneuf du Pape.
• If serving a separate wine with the cheese, choose a full-bodied red wine, or port.
• With desserts, serve Madeira, port, Muscatel, Tokay or a Sauternes.

A Guide to Cooking Terms

Here is a list of some cookery terms with which you may be unfamiliar.

Al dente Refers to pasta when sufficiently cooked – firm to the bite.

Au gratin Cooked food, coated with a sauce and sprinkled with grated cheese and breadcrumbs. The dish is browned under the grill before serving.

Bain marie A pan containing hot water; a dish containing the food to be cooked is placed in the water bath so that the food cooks slowly and evenly.

Bake blind To partly bake a pastry case without any filling. This prevents the filling making the pastry soggy.

Barding Covering joints of lean meat, game birds and poultry with pieces of fat bacon to keep the flesh moist during roasting.

Basting Spooning the cooking juices over meat and poultry during roasting.

Beurre manié Equal quantities of flour and butter kneaded together to form a paste. The mixture is whisked into a sauce or casserole, bit by bit at the end of the cooking time, to thicken it.

Canapé A small appetiser with a toast, bread or biscuit base topped with a savoury mixture.

Cocotte Small ovenproof dishes used for baking and serving egg dishes, mousses and soufflés.

Dice To cut food (usually raw vegetables) into small cubes.

Dough A basic mixture which is kneaded or rolled into the required shape.

Dredging Sprinkling food with flour or sugar.

Dressing A cold sauce based on vinegar and oil which is served with salads.

Dripping The fat which drips out of a joint, poultry or game during roasting. This can be stored and re-used.

Dumpling A savoury mixture formed in balls and simmered in liquid. Served with soups and stews.

En croûte Food encased and cooked in a pastry case.

Escalope A thin slice of meat (veal or pork) which is beaten flat, coated in egg and breadcrumbs and fried.

Fines herbes A mixture of finely chopped fresh herbs – parsley, chervil, tarragon and chives.

Flake To separate food into smaller pieces.

Flambé Cooked in a pan to which brandy (or other spirit) is added and set alight.

Garnish To enhance a savoury dish with an edible decoration e.g. parsley.

Gelatine A powder made from animal bones which melts in hot water and is used to set or stiffen dishes.

Giblets The edible internal organs from poultry and game.

Glaze A glossy finish given to food by brushing it with milk, beaten egg, or syrup before baking. A jelly glaze may be spooned over cooked and cooled dishes.

Gugelhupf A yeast cake baked in a fluted mould.

Hulling Removing the stalks from soft fruits.

Infusing Steeping ingredients in hot water or other liquid to extract their flavour.

Joint A prime cut of meat for roasting. To joint, divide into individual pieces.

Kebab Pieces of food threaded on a skewer and grilled.

Larding Threading strips of fat bacon through a lean joint of meat to keep it moist, from within, during cooking.

Marinade A mixture of oil, wine, vinegar and seasoning used to flavour and tenderise pieces of meat, fish etc. prior to cooking.

Marinate To steep food in a marinade.

Meringue A mixture of egg whites and sugar. Either spooned on top of puddings or piped into shapes and baked in a very cool oven.

Moussaka An eastern dish containing minced meat (usually lamb), aubergines, onions and tomatoes, topped with a cheese sauce, savoury custard or natural yogurt.

Mousse A light-textured sweet or savoury dish.

Niçoise A dish containing tomatoes, onions, garlic and olives.

Offal The edible internal organs from an animal.

Paella A traditional Spanish dish containing rice, saffron, chicken and shellfish.

Pasta A food made from flour and water, sometimes with the addition of eggs and spinach, and formed into various shapes.

Pastry A dough made from flour, fat and water – sometimes enriched with egg yolks.

Pâté A savoury meat mixture served cold.

Pipe To form a mixture, placed into a bag fitted with a tube, into various shapes.

Piquant Pleasantly sharp in flavour.

Pith The white layer beneath the skin of citrus fruits.

Pizza A savoury mixture on a yeast or scone base.

Purée Sieved (or blended in the liquidiser) raw or cooked food.

Quiche A savoury flan.

Ragoût A meat and vegetable stew.

Ratatouille A vegetable dish made from aubergines, tomatoes, onions, garlic, peppers and courgettes.

Reduce To concentrate the flavour of a liquid by rapid boiling.

Rice paper An edible paper used to line baking trays for a macaroon mixture.

Sauté To seal food in hot fat, prior to the main cooking.

Savarin A yeast cake baked in a ring mould and soaked in a sugar syrup flavoured with a liqueur.

Score To cut grooves into the surface of food.

Seasoned flour A mixture of flour, salt and pepper which is used to coat food prior to cooking.

Sifting (or sieving) Passing foods through a sieve to remove lumps.

Simmering Cooking food in a liquid which is kept at just below boiling point.

Skewer Metal or wooden utensil used to secure food during cooking.

Sousing Preserving food in brine or vinegar.

Spit A revolving metal skewer on to which meat and poultry is secured and cooked in front of the direct heat.

Strudel Thin pieces of pastry filled with a sweet or savoury filling, formed into rolls and baked.

Stuffing A savoury mixture, based on breadcrumbs, used to fill poultry, meat or fish.

Trussing Tying a bird or joint of meat into a neat shape prior to cooking.

Vanilla sugar Sugar stored in a container with a vanilla pod to give flavour to the sugar. Vanilla sugar is used in baking.

Zest The oily outer skin of citrus fruits, grated and used to flavour food.

Index

335